RUSSIAN RESEARCH CENTER STUDIES, 91

Published under the auspices of the
Davis Center for Russian Studies,
Harvard University

Reinventing Russia

*Russian Nationalism and the
Soviet State, 1953–1991*

Yitzhak M. Brudny

HARVARD UNIVERSITY PRESS

Cambridge, Massachusetts

London, England

Second printing, 2000

First Harvard University Press paperback edition, 2000

Library of Congress Cataloging-in-Publication Data
Brudny, Yitzhak M.
Reinventing Russia : Russian nationalism and the Soviet state, 1953–1991 /
Yitzhak M. Brudny.
p.   cm.—(Russian Research Center studies ; 91)
Includes index.
ISBN 0-674-75408-5 (cloth)
ISBN 0-674-00438-8 (pbk.)
1. Soviet Union—Politics and government—1953–1985.
2. Soviet Union—Politics and government—1985–1991.
3. Nationalism—Soviet Union. I. Title. II. Series.
DK274.B77   1998
947.085—dc21   98-23969

To Catherine

Contents

Acknowledgments

I grew up in the Soviet Union of the 1960s and the Israel of the 1970s and 1980s. In both places I was a witness to the rising tide of nationalism. This book is a result of my years-long fascination with the phenomenon. My original ideas on nationalism in general, and its Russian variant in particular, were articulated in my Princeton University Ph.D. thesis. I am most grateful to my advisers, Stephen F. Cohen, Robert C. Tucker, and Richard S. Wortman, who encouraged me to undertake this project and provided precious advice and support when I most needed it. Special thanks also go to Nancy Bermeo, who taught me comparative politics in my years in Princeton, and to Mildred Kalmus, the department's graduate secretary, who has guided me (together with so many other graduate students) through the Princeton experience with an unbelievable amount of patience and kindness.

My project benefited enormously from interviews that I conducted in Moscow on several occasions, starting in October 1989. I especially thank Lev Anninsky, Ivan Antonovich, Tatiyana Glushkova, Aleksandr Kazintsev, Stanislav Kunayev, Anatoly Lanshchikov, Oleg Mikhailov, Boris Mozhaev, Pyotr Palamarchuk, Pyotr Palievsky, Vsevolod Sakharov, Anatoly Salutsky, Vladimir Tikhonov and Sergei Vikulov for their time and patience. I also acknowledge the invaluable help of the staff of the Central Repository of Contemporary Documentation (TsKhSD), who enabled me to find the Central Committee documents cited in this study.

I am deeply grateful to Michael Walzer of the Institute for Advanced Study at Princeton, and Henry Rosovsky of the Harvard Academy for International and Area Studies, both of whom were most supportive of my project.

Earlier drafts of chapters 2 and 7 were discussed at the Workshops on Soviet Domestic Politics sponsored by the Social Science Research Council. I thank the conference organizers, Thane Gustafson of Georgetown University, Susan and Peter Solomon of the University of Toronto, as well as Jerry F. Hough of Duke University and Ronald Grigor Suny of the University of Chicago, the senior faculty participants in the workshops, for their comments.

I also thank David D. Laitin of the University of Chicago, Juan J. Linz of Yale University, and Peter Rutland of Wesleyan University, who provided invaluable comments on an earlier draft of this book.

I am sincerely grateful to Shlomo Avineri and Gur Ofer of the Hebrew University of Jerusalem for inviting me to spend four months as a visiting scholar which allowed me to complete the final editing of the manuscript without undue distractions.

I express my deep appreciation to Jeff Kehoe of Harvard University Press, whose help was crucial in turning the original manuscript into the present book, and to Amy Olener and Jane Judge Bonassar of Editorial Services of New England, who did a superb job of editing my work.

I especially want to thank Timothy J. Colton and Marshall J. Goldman, both of the Davis Center for Russian Studies, Harvard University, and the Lynde and Harry Bradley Foundation for making the publication of this book possible.

Finally, I thank my wife, Catherine, who spent countless hours helping me with this project. Without her, this book would never have been finished. This work is dedicated to her.

REINVENTING RUSSIA

Russian Nationalists in Soviet Politics

The Nature of the Problem

One of the main features of the democratization processes at work in Eastern Europe and the Union of Soviet Socialist Republics (USSR) in the late 1980s was the emergence of nationalist movements in virtually every country of the region. Some of these movements gained significant power and played a key role in the fate of many of the communist regimes, while others remained too weak to influence the course of events. What led to the emergence of these movements? What was the role of the communist regimes in fostering them, and why did some turn out to be more successful than others? This book examines these questions through a study of the Russian nationalist movement, from its origins within the Russian intellectual elite in the 1950s to its institutionalization into electoral alliances, parliamentary factions, and political movements in the early 1990s. In particular, the book focuses on a set of ideas concerning Russian national identity articulated by Russian nationalist intellectuals during this period and responses to these ideas by the communist regime.

Scholarly opinion is divided on the underlying causes of these movements and their varying degrees of success. There are two main interpretive approaches: the primordial and the instrumentalist.[1] The basic premise of the primordial approach is that group ties based on blood, race, language, residence, religion, and custom are stronger than any other ties—including those based on ideology, class, or professional affiliation—especially in societies with weak democratic civil and political institutions. In such societies, these group ties are also the most natural bases of political mobilization, which explains why nationalism is so prominent in newly independent or democratizing countries.[2]

Primordial explanations of the rise of nationalism in the USSR and Eastern Europe assume that nationalist sentiments among East European nationalities were always strong but were suppressed by the communist regimes. The removal of coercive controls during democratization accounts for the rise of nationalism.

Despite common assumptions among proponents of the primordial approach, there are also some important interpretive variations. The political culture and functionalist explanations. According to Brzezinski, a leading proponent of the political culture explanation, the explosion of nationalism was an inevitable outcome of the political culture of communism and democratization. The political culture of communism perpetuated attitudes of "intolerance, self-righteousness, rejection of social compromise and massive inclination toward self-glorifying oversimplification," while the democratization process "*automatically* [emphasis added] created an opportunity for long-suppressed national grievances to surface."[3]

According to the functionalist explanation, nationalism "predominates when institutions collapse, when existing institutions are not fulfilling people's basic needs, and when satisfactory alternative structures are not available." In other words, the functionalist explanation views the rise of nationalism in Eastern Europe and the former Soviet Union as a defensive response by ethnic communities to threats to their economic and physical well-being which accompany the process of democratization and the transition to a market economy.[4]

One of the main weaknesses of the primordial approach in general, and its application to the former Soviet Union in particular, is its inability to explain why some nationalist movements were much more successful than others in mobilizing their ethnic communities, even when the existing political and socioeconomic conditions were most favorable for such a mobilization. The instrumentalist approach, which focuses on the manipulative and organizational skill of elites, provides an explanation.

The instrumentalist approach rejects the primordial approach's assertion that nationalism is caused by the politicization of the primordial ties during periods of political and economic upheaval. Instead, it points to the fluid and changing nature of national identity and argues that nationalism is an outcome of the elites' manipulation of ethnic identities as a means of gaining or preserving power. Thus, the instrumentalist approach does not view the rise of nationalism as inevitable. As Brass points out, "Political and economic circumstances may cause elites to downplay or discard the symbolic manipulation of cultural forms, values and practices."[5]

The instrumentalist explanation, applied to the rise of nationalism in Eastern Europe and the former Soviet Union, can be subdivided into institutional and rational choice approaches. The institutionalists explain the rise of nationalist movements in the former USSR and Yugoslavia as the unavoidable consequence of the communist regimes' policy of the institutionalization of ethnicity as the most important social marker and the elimination of all competing foci of group solidarity. These policies had two main consequences: the process of nation-building based on ethnic identity and the growth of local political, intellectual, and professional elites who were increasingly wary of the central government. The democratization process, combined with deepening economic crisis, led to the formation of ethnic political movements headed by members of professional and intellectual elites and often supported by local political elites.[6]

Rational choice views nationalism as merely a tool in the hands of elites or ethnic groups in their struggle for power and socioeconomic benefits. The emergence of nationalist movements is viewed as contingent on the calculations of the members of the ethnic group that the benefits (mostly of an economic nature) derived from engaging in nationalist collective action outweigh their costs.[7] Thus, this approach explains the emergence of strong nationalist movements in the former Soviet Union in terms of change in the incentive structures: a decline in coercion significantly lowers the cost of engaging in nationalist politics, which makes the emergence of a successful nationalist movement possible. The success or failure of these movements is explained by the strategies adopted by local political elites, which in turn are based on the calculation of relative career chances in the unified versus the independent state.[8]

This book adopts the basic premise of the instrumentalist approach to explain the Russian nationalist movement. It argues that the rise of the movement was not a consequence of the politicization of the ethnic Russians' primordial sentiments. Instead, it was the combined result of the reinvention of the Russian national identity by a group of intellectuals in search of new political ideals in the aftermath of the Twentieth Party Congress and of a decades-long policy pursued by the Communist Party of the Soviet Union (CPSU), which actively supported this reinvention in order to gain a new basis of political legitimacy. The failure of a mass Russian nationalist movement to emerge during the *perestroika* years of 1985 to 1991 was a direct consequence of the political strategy adopted by the founders of this movement and the remarkable ability of the liberal–democratic movement and its leadership to usurp the most popular Russian nationalist slogans and symbols for their own use.

At the same time, this book adds one important dimension to the instrumentalist approach. The instrumentalists view nationalist ideologies as merely a screen that masks the ethnic elites' drive to gain and preserve power and therefore dismisses them as insignificant in explaining the political fortunes of nationalist movements. As a consequence, the issue of the impact of these ideas on the movement's success or failure remains beyond the scope of the instrumentalist analysis. However, Kohn, Greenfeld, and Haas have shown that political ideas to which nationalist movements adhere do matter.[9] As Haas points out: "Ideas are switches that make a set of actors to travel on one historic track rather than another. . . . Ideas in form of ideologies about origin, function, place, and mission of the nation, furnish the visions of various futures available to actors."[10]

Contemporary Russia is no exception. This book argues that ideology constitutes an important independent variable in explaining the fate of the Russian nationalist movement during the last forty years of Soviet rule. Between the mid-1960s and the mid-1980s, the views of Russian nationalist intellectuals concerning the nature of Russian national identity played a decisive role in the CPSU's policy to promote this group of intellectuals over all others; between the late 1980s and the early 1990s, Russian nationalist views on the introduction of democracy and a market economy, and the future of the Soviet state determined the movement's political strategy and subsequently the degree of support it enjoyed among members of the political elite and society at large.

Nation, Nationalism, and Russian Nationalism

Before presenting the argument in greater detail, it is important to clarify the use of the concepts "nation," "nationalism" and "Russian nationalism" in this work. As Connor rightly points out, "state," "nation," "nation-state," and "nationalism" are often used interchangeably.[11] The concept of the nation used in this book draws on Weber's notion of ethnicity as a form of group solidarity based not on primordial attributes such as blood relations but on invented ones such as "subjective belief in common descent," and on Deutsch, Gellner, and Anderson, who argue that nations are creations of modernity because their existence requires an industrial society on its higher levels of literacy, mass communication, and vernacular high culture.[12] Thus, the nation is a modern political form of group solidarity based on jointly held beliefs that the group's origins, territory, language, history, culture, and political or religious creed make it distinct from any other social group. These beliefs are not immutable. They change over time and often are subject to manipulation.

Nationalism is defined in this work as an ideology that views "the nation as the terminal community to whom ultimate loyalty is owed" and judges legitimacy of a political regime on the basis of its adherence to this principle.[13] Thus, a nationalist ideology differs from other political ideologies in its elevation of the nation above all other forms of group solidarity and above all other principles of regime legitimacy, be it kinship, class, or religion.

All nationalist ideologies have three principle components, which are usually embedded in the conception of the national identity and the analysis of the nation's past, present, and future. First, each nationalist ideology explicitly or implicitly defines who is a member of the nation. The two most prevailing criteria for membership are civic-territorial, which grounds membership in the citizenship of a given state, and ethnic, which grounds membership in common descent, as well as in other primordial aspects of ethnicity.[14]

Second, nationalist ideology defines the nation's "proper" territorial boundaries. The determination of these boundaries can be driven by the principle "one state–one nation" and excludes regions where other nations constitute a majority or the borders can be drawn to accommodate an imperial conception of the nation, thus including regions populated by other nationalities.

Finally, nationalist ideology postulates what political, social, economic, and cultural arrangements are best suited to the nation.[15] A combination of these elements determines the nature of a given nationalist ideology; it can be imperial or nonimperial, democratic or authoritarian, liberal or conservative, radical left or radical right.[16]

Such a conception of nationalism implies a variety of possible relations between the nationalist movement, an organizational framework committed to the realization of policy prescriptions explicitly or implicitly embedded in the nationalist ideology, and the state. Brubaker suggests a useful basic typology of nationalist movements in their relationships to the state. He distinguishes between polity-seeking nationalism, which strives to establish a national state, and nation-shaping nationalism, which seeks to "nationalize" the existing state.[17] Elaborating on this distinction, I argue that polity-seeking nationalism is usually the nationalism of a national minority that is striving to separate itself from the existing state, which is dominated by another nation or national majority. The core ideological principle of this nationalism is one nation–one state. The legitimacy of the existing state is rejected as not representing the true nation.

Nation-shaping nationalism is articulated by representatives of the dominant nation who find the existing political, social, economic, and cultural realities of their own state in contradiction to their ideological principles. Often the prevailing arrangements are denounced as detrimental to the nation and its well-being, with the alternative presented as restoring the nation's vitality. This type of nationalism has a rather complex relationship with the existing state; it accepts the legitimacy of the existing state, although not necessarily its territorial borders or its regime.

The principle of one nation–one state is rarely upheld by nation-shaping nationalism, because its ideology argues for the inclusion of regions populated by other ethnic groups in the nation's territorial boundaries. Nation-shaping movements may pay lip-service to the principle of one nation–one state, however, they usually have no hesitation in legitimizing their rule over the national minorities residing within their territory.[18]

Nation-shaping nationalism must be distinguished from official (or state) nationalism, the ideology of the governing regime. Like any other nationalist ideology, it has its own definitions of membership, territorial boundaries, and proper political, social, economic, and cultural arrangements. Official nationalism also has a policy dimension—a set of policies aimed at the realization of its ideological tenets.[19]

Nation-shaping nationalism may challenge some or all elements of the ideology and policies of official nationalism, and when it does, official nationalism may incorporate some elements of the former into its own ideology in an effort to co-opt its challengers. In any case, the existence of nation-shaping nationalism suggests that the legitimacy of the official nationalism is being challenged.

This distinction of the polity-seeking, nation-shaping, and official types of nationalism is helpful in clarifying the concept of Russian nationalism as used in this book. This concept designates groups of intellectuals, organizations, and, since the late 1980s, political parties that asserted that the Russian nation is that "terminal community, to whom ultimate loyalty is owed" and made claims to speak on its behalf, especially concerning the political, social, economic, and cultural arrangements best suited for the Russian nation.[20]

Soviet nation-building policies deliberately created ambiguity as to whether the USSR was the Russian nation-state or a multinational federation.[21] This ambiguity was reflected in both the ethnic composition of Soviet political, administrative, and military elites, which were predominantly ethnic Russians, and in the weak institutional differentiation between the Russian Soviet Federal Socialist Republic (RSFSR) and the USSR. Thus, until 1990–1991, the RSFSR was the only Soviet republic without its own Communist party, KGB, or Academy of Sciences, making the CPSU, the USSR KGB, and the USSR Academy of Sciences simultaneously Soviet and Russian institutions. The result was that the Russian population in general, and Russian nationalists in particular, viewed the USSR as essentially a Russian nation-state rather than an empire. The problem with the USSR, they insisted, was that it was not Russian enough.[22]

This nation-shaping Russian nationalism can be distinguished from the official nationalism of the Soviet state. Official Soviet nationalism had a strong Russian nationalist component, including such repressive policies as the russification of non-Russian nationalities, but, as Beissinger rightly points out, it was a mere "instrument of rule, not the regime's guiding principle."[23] In the Soviet era, nation-shaping Russian nationalism challenged the official nationalism of the Soviet state because it rejected two of its three primary components: the officially defined object of ultimate loyalty and the proper political, social, economic, and cultural arrangements that would best suit the Russian nation. Thus, nation-shaping Russian nationalism in effect challenged the legitimacy of the Soviet state itself.

On the key issue of the object of ultimate loyalty, nation-shaping Russian nationalism rejected the civic-ideological concept of the Soviet nation promoted by the official Soviet nationalism, which extended membership in the nation to all ethnic groups living on USSR territory, in favor of the ethnically defined notion of the Russian nation, which excluded all those who were not ethnically Russian.[24] Although Russian nationalist groups could seldom agree among themselves on the best political, social, economic, and cultural arrangements for Russia, they harshly criticized and uniformly rejected the official policies of the Soviet state in these spheres.

In the late Soviet period, the differences between nation-shaping Russian nationalism and the official state nationalism became increasingly pronounced as a consequence of Gorbachev's political and economic reforms. The differences became especially profound when Boris Yeltsin assumed power in the Russian Republic in 1990. Official Russian nationalism, as articulated by Yeltsin and his government, differed from the nation-shaping Russian nationalism in its conception of membership in the Russian nation, the territorial boundaries of the Russian state, and its vision of the proper political, social, economic, and cultural arrangements best suited for both the state and the nation. Thus, the Russian nationalist ethnic definition of the Russian nation *(Russkaya natsiya)* stood in sharp contradiction to the civic definition of the Russian nation *(Rossiiskaya natsiya)* adopted by Yeltsin and his government; Russian nationalist demands to extend the borders of the Russian state to coincide with the borders of the former USSR challenged the legitimacy of the dissolution of the USSR and the emergence of the Commonwealth of Independent States. Finally, the Russian nationalist rejection of democracy, a market economy, and cultural openness to the West sharply contradicted the official embrace of all of these principles.

A Typology of Russian Nationalism

The nation-shaping Russian nationalist movement was never very homogeneous. Under Khrushchev and Brezhnev, Russian nationalist intellectuals split ideologically on many key issues. Although this difference of opinion significantly narrowed between 1985 and 1991, important ideological differences nonetheless remained. One of the most often cited efforts to classify Russian nationalists by ideology is Szporluk's twofold typology which distinguishes between "nation builders" and "empire savers."[25] However, this unidimensional typology neglects the fact that Russian nationalists—in fact, most Russians—viewed the Soviet Union as a nation-state rather than an empire and that this issue was only one of many on the Russian political agenda. Moreover, this definition is less applicable to the pre-Gorbachev period, when political discourse focused on an entirely different set of issues.

The typology I used in this book is multidimensional and applicable to the entire period between 1953 and 1991.[26] It distinguishes three types of Russian nationalism—liberal, conservative, and radical—and is based on ideological positions on a set of nine key issues ranging from attitudes to Western political, social, and cultural values in the pre-*perestroika* period to responses to political and economic reforms initiated by Gorbachev (Table 1.1).[27]

In the pre-perestroika period (1953–1985), these labels largely refer to the views of individuals and literary journals. During the *perestroika* period (1985–1991), these categories are also applicable to weekly and daily newspapers, cultural organizations, political movements, and electoral alliances and parliamentary factions in the Soviet and Russian parliaments with similar ideological orientations and political goals (Table 1.2). One should remember, however, that due to the absence of parties, associations, or

Table 1.1 Political and Ideological Orientations of Russian Nationalists, 1953–1991

Ideology	Liberal Nationalists	Conservative Nationalists	Radical Nationalists
Liberalizing political and economic reforms (before 1985)	+	+/−	−
Western politicial, social, and cultural values	+/−	−	−
Antisemitism and xenophobia	−	+	+
Modernity	+/−	−	+/−
Tsarist past	+	+	+/−
Soviet past: The Stalinist period	−	−	+
Soviet present: The post-Stalin period	−	−	−
Gorbachev's political, economic, and cultural reforms	+	−	−
Preservation of the Soviet Union	+/−	+	+
August 1991 coup attempt	−	+	+
Yeltsin's politics	+	−	−

Note: + = positive orientation
− = negative orientation
+/− = ambivalent orientation

Table 1.2 Evolution of the Russian Nationalist Movement, 1953–1991

Type of Russian Nationalism	Soviet Period: Pre-Perestroika Era (1953–1985)	Soviet Period: Perestroika Era (1985–1991)
Liberal nationalism	Liberal wing of the village prose literary movement, *Novy Mir* (1950s–1960s)	Democratic Russia (elements of)
Conservative nationalism	Conservative wing of the village prose literary movement, *Moskva, Nash Sovremmenik, Volga, Sever*	Russia parliamentary faction, Russia Club, Patriotic Bloc (electoral bloc), RFRSR Writers' Union, *Moskva, Nash Sovremmenik, Sibirskie ogni, Literaturnaya Rossi Russky Vestnik*
Radical nationalism	*Molodaya gvardiaya, Nash Sovremmenik, Volga*	Pamyat, Otechestvo, Patriotic Bloc, Council National-Patriotic Movements, Liberal-Democratic Par of USSR (Zhirinovsky) *Molodaya gvardiaya, Na Sovremmenik, Kuban, Voenno-istorichesky zhurnal, Literaturnaya Rossiya, Sovetskaya Rossi Den, Domostroi*

other formal groupings that help to consolidate and institutionalize differences of political opinion, ideological differences among Russian nationalist intellectuals were often blurred. Nonetheless, these differences were real and the classification that highlights them is helpful not only in tracing the ideological and organizational origins of contemporary Russian nationalist organizations and parties but is also very important in understanding the development of Russian politics in general.[28]

From its origins in the early years of the post-Stalin era, liberal nationalism was a constituent but distinct part of the Russian liberal-reformist movement. Liberal nationalists rejected the Russian liberal reformers' excessive preoccupation with individual rights and did not share their view that indiscriminate adoption of Western political, social, cultural, and economic institutions would be the panacea for all the social and moral ills of the Russian nation. At the same time, liberal nationalists insisted that Russian national renewal required radical economic and political reforms, including the decisive repudiation of the Stalinist legacy in Soviet politics.

Contrary to conservative and radical nationalism, liberal nationalism did not idealize the traditional Russian village as the embodiment of Russia's moral values. It was also free of the aggressive anti-intellectualism and xenophobia (on its most anti-Western and anti-Semitic dimensions) that is typical of other types of Russian nationalism. Liberal nationalists embraced Gorbachev's reforms and later supported Yeltsin when he assumed the leadership of the liberal reformist movement. This group constituted an important component of Democratic Russia, the liberal-reformist social movement that played a crucial role in Yeltsin's victory in the 1991 presidential elections and was instrumental in rallying public opposition to the organizers of the August 1991 coup. Finally, they were ambivalent in their attitude toward the preservation of the empire. While strongly opposing the political forces that made preservation of the USSR their top political priority, they did not call for the dismantling of the Soviet Union.

The conservative nationalists underwent perhaps the greatest political evolution in the post-Stalin period. They moved from close cooperation with the liberal nationalists in the 1960s to an alignment with the radical nationalists, as well as with the orthodox communist opponents of radical reforms, in the 1980s and 1990s. At the core of conservative nationalist ideology stood a highly idealized vision of the traditional Russian peasantry and its moral and cultural values. These values were elevated to the status of the main moral pillar of the Russian nation, and their revitalization was proclaimed to be crucial to Russian national survival. In the 1950s and 1960s, the focus of the conservative nationalists was on the hardships experienced by the peasantry and on the Stalinist legacy responsible for these hardships. In the 1970s, as rural living standards improved and Russian society became progressively more urban and more Westernized, their focus shifted to criticism of the moral corruption of society brought about by a modern urban lifestyle and the Westernized urban intelligentsia they held responsible for this corruption.

These positions effectively preordained the conservative nationalists' rejection of the Gorbachev reforms. Between 1987 and 1991, confronting the reality of political and cultural interaction with the West and the emergence of powerful nationalist movements in the non-Russian republics demanding secession from the USSR, conservative nationalists became fierce opponents of *perestroika*. In the process, they allied themselves with radical nationalists, as well as with the antireformist forces within the CPSU, the KGB, and the military, whom they viewed as guarantors of the preservation of the empire and the bulwark against the penetration of Western political, social, and cultural influences.

The essence of radical nationalism was its militant rejection of the Western values that had been penetrating the Soviet Union since the end of the Stalin era. Its representatives elaborated a set of ideas emphasizing the importance of recreating a powerful authoritarian state capable of preventing the penetration of corrupting Western values into Russian society. They believed that the Cold War contained an important cultural and spiritual component that must not be diminished in the pursuit of détente.

The belief in the all-powerful state constituted the core of the radical nationalists' theory of legitimacy. They believed that the right to rule Russia belongs to those who have proved their ability to create and preserve a powerful state capable of rebuffing Western aggression—cultural, ideological, or military. Radical nationalist admiration for Stalin, the leader they saw as embodying this strength and ability, was conspicuously present in their writing in the 1960s and 1970s, and led to the harsh criticism of his successors, whom they regarded as incapable of or unwilling to prevent the undermining of the Russian state through the penetration of Western ideas and values.

The ideological positions developed by radical nationalists during the Brezhnev era help us to understand why they were among the earliest open critics of perestroika and *glasnost*. They argued that the policies of political and economic liberalization were aimed at destroying the Soviet-Russian state and loudly supported every effort to reverse these policies and remove Gorbachev, and later Yeltsin, from power. More important, in the late Gorbachev era, radical nationalist ideas became the ideological foundations of many of the Russian nationalist political organizations, movements, and parliamentary factions, and were adopted by the prominent antireform members of the CPSU establishment.

Phases in the Evolution of Russian Nationalism

In the introductory chapter of her book on the relationship between Romanian intellectuals and the Ceausescu regime, Verdery states:

> Most of this book deals with apparently esoteric matters—arguments among sociologists, literary critics, historians, and philosophers. Its significance, however, goes far beyond these. To begin with, it is precisely the nexus between politics and culture which enables us to understand why the new government that emerged in late December 1989 included not only communist reformers but several poets . . . , literary critics . . . , philosophers and aestheticians . . . , and a teacher of French.[29]

With only a few minor adjustments, this statement is applicable to the political and cultural reality of the USSR in the post-Stalin era. The reason this book examines in such detail similar debates on seemingly esoteric matters is that these were, in fact, debates about Russian national identity and had far-reaching political consequences. Indeed, one of the important features of the politics of communist regimes is politics by culture. In other words, important political debates took the form of discussions on seemingly nonpolitical issues. These debates constitute a form of what Scott termed "hidden transcripts," in which behind the veil of the obligatory citations from the founding fathers of Marxism-Leninism or from general secretaries of the CPSU, which adorned discussions of literary works, scholarly publications, music scores, works of visual arts, and architectural designs, are narratives that challenged official ideology and policies on a wide range of politically sensitive subjects.[30]

These discussions and the hidden transcripts they generated represented a crucial stage in the evolution of the Russian national movement. In *Social Preconditions of National Revival in Europe,* Hroch proposed a three-stage model of the growth of nationalist movements. According to this model, nationalist movements usually began (Phase A, in his terms) with scholars' debating the seemingly apolitical issues of national language, history, and culture. Phase B is the period of "patriotic agitation" during which nationalist societies emerge, and their activists promote nationalist ideas among the population. The development of the nationalist movement culminates during Phase C, when the nationalist movement acquires a truly mass following.[31]

Hroch's chronology, designed to explain the rise of the nationalist movements in Eastern and Northern Europe in the nineteenth century, is applicable, with some modifications, to the evolution of the nationalist movements under the communist regimes of Eastern Europe and the former Soviet Union. The period between 1953 and 1989 in the Soviet Union effectively constituted the combination of Phases A and B, since scholarly and semischolarly debates about Russian history and culture went hand in hand with the propagation of nationalist ideas in mass-circulated journals, movies, and books. Accordingly, I will call it the A-B Phase. During this period, Russian nationalist activities were almost exclusively restricted to the cultural realm and were completely dominated by the cultural intelligentsia. Since the Soviet state did not tolerate independent political organization, the literary journals and publishing houses spread the nationalist message, fulfilling the function equivalent to that of the nationalist societies in the nineteenth century. The Russian A-B Phase could also be called the era of politics by culture. In the years 1986–1989, politics by culture reached its peak, with the cultural intelligentsia playing a highly visible and important role in defining both the terms and the issues of the unfolding political debate, a fact reflected by the meteoric jump in circulation of cultural newspapers and periodicals during this period, as well as by the cultural intelligentsia's heavy representation in the USSR Congress of People's Deputies, the first freely elected Soviet parliament (1989).

The spring 1990 elections to the RSFSR Congress of People's Deputies marked the beginning of Phase C in the evolution of Russian nationalism. A sharp decline began in the importance of politics by culture, duly reflected in a drop in the circulation of cultural newspapers and periodicals, as well as in the political representation of the cultural intelligentsia in Russia's main political institutions. The writers, poets, philosophers, and literary critics were superseded by the leaders of parliamentary factions and the heads of political parties and electoral alliances as the most important representatives of the Russian nationalist movement. Thus, this study deals mostly with the A-B Phase and covers only the beginning of Phase C.

Hroch emphasizes the crucial importance of developments during Phase B for the future of the nationalist movement. In his view, Phase B determines whether Phase C will even occur. The A-B Phase is crucial for the understanding of both the nature of contemporary Russian nationalism and its political fortunes. During this stage, the political and ideological orientation of the Russian nationalist movement, as well as its organizational nature, was decisively shaped and this, in turn, effectively determined its political agenda and strategy during Phase C.

Hroch also stresses the importance of socioeconomic factors, such as industrialization and urbanization, in the development of nationalism during Phase B. This book does not deny the significance of socioeconomic factors. Urbanization and industrialization certainly played a critical role in creating both the Russian nationalist intellectual elite and Russian urban society at large, the main consumer of Russian nationalist political literature. At the same time, I emphasize the importance of political factors— the politics of the Soviet state toward the Russian nationalist intelligentsia during the entire post-Stalin period (the A-B Phase). Indeed, one of the main features of this period was the exceptionally privileged status of the nondissident Russian nationalist intellectuals. From the mid-1960s through the mid-1980s, Russian nationalists controlled some of the USSR's leading literary publications, millions of copies of their books were printed, and their leading figures were awarded cultural prizes, including the most prestigious prize awarded in the USSR, the Lenin Prize. Clearly, during the A-B Phase, the Soviet state helped to spread Russian nationalist ideas and rewarded those who articulated them.

Politics of Inclusion

Why did the Soviet regime cultivate for so long the very people whose ideas represented a direct challenge to its official ideology? The answer to this question requires an exploration of the role of intellectuals in communist regimes, specifically the role of nationalist intellectuals in post-Stalinist communist society. As Verdery points out, intellectuals played a disproportionately important role in communist societies. In the absence of a market economy and capital, the most important power, after political power, wielded by the *nomenklatura*, was not economic power but symbolic power.[32] Intellectuals were regarded as crucial to the communist regime because of their role as creators of national symbols and myths. Indeed, every communist regime throughout its history has attempted to gain the loyalty of the intellectuals through a variety of means, be it terror, coercion, or co-optation.

Once the threat of terror was removed in the post-Stalinist era, all communist regimes faced the dilemma, best described by Hirschman, as the dilemma of "exit," "voice," and "loyalty."[33] Communist policies regarding intellectuals during this period aimed to maximize the "loyalty" and minimize the "exit" by granting partial "voice." In other words, terror was no longer an option in ensuring the loyalty of intellectuals. The regime could use other means of coercion to gain loyalty, but this could and did provoke some intellectuals to exit the system and join the dissident movement, something the regime was anxious to prevent. Although Brezhnev was determined not to liberalize the communist political or economic system, he was equally determined to avoid the mass exit of intellectuals out of the system.

Jowitt argues that communist regimes tried to ensure the political loyalty of key social groups without launching political and economic reform through what he termed "policy of inclusion." In his view, this policy signify "a shift from a socio-political order based almost exclusively on command and violence to one in which the leadership skills of manipulation and persuasion are more significant than in the past." The inclusionary politics involves the creation of "articulated audiences," that is, "politically knowledgeable and oriented" groups "capable of offering the regime support of a more differentiated and sophisticated character. Unlike publics, citizens who voluntarily organize themselves around major political issues, these 'audiences' are restricted in their political behavior to those roles and actions prescribed by the regime itself."[34]

My study suggests that the post-Stalinist Soviet regime clearly intended to transform Russian nationalist intellectuals into a group that closely fits Jowitt's description of an articulated audience. By the mid-1960s, leading members of the Soviet political elite clearly realized that orthodox Marxist-Leninist ideology had lost its power as a mobilizing force, yet they were unwilling to launch radical political and economic reforms, which they regarded as undermining the regime itself. The emerging group of Russian nationalist intellectuals was selected to be an articulated audience because its ideas, although critical of the official ideology and party policies in many areas, were regarded as not threatening the authoritarian nature of the regime itself. In fact, because of their anti-Western nature, these ideas indirectly legitimized the Soviet regime. Soviet leaders believed that by giving Russian nationalist intellectuals privileged access to newspapers, journals, and publishing houses, as well as bestowing on them prestigious state awards, they would acquire a stake in the system which would allow the regime to control and manipulate their activities. Soviet leaders intended to use Russian nationalist intellectuals to provide a new ideological legitimacy for the regime and to justify their determination to avoid political and economic reform.

This policy of inclusionary politics, which began in the mid-1960s and lasted until the death of Brezhnev in late 1982, ultimately failed to transform Russian nationalist intellectuals into a regime-supporting articulated audience. In fact, by the end of the Brezhnev era, Russian nationalists more closely resembled a public than an articulated audience.

The policy of inclusionary politics of the Brezhnev era had far-reaching political consequences for Gorbachev and Yeltsin. Through it, Russian nationalists became a powerful intellectual group whose ideas would serve as the ideological basis for many of the political movements and parties of the late Gorbachev and Yeltsin periods.

The Politics of the Russian Nationalist Movement

Intellectuals articulating Russian nationalist ideas appeared in the Soviet political arena quite soon after Stalin's death. The first group of Russian nationalists to be actively involved in Soviet politics were the so-called village prose writers—intellectuals who wrote fictional and nonfictional accounts of the social realities of the Russian countryside in the post-Stalin era. Their work harshly criticized the Stalinist legacy and called for radical reform of Russian agriculture. I will argue that the village prose of the 1950s provided the basis for liberal and conservative Russian nationalism.

The popularity of both trends of the village prose among Soviet readers grew rapidly in the 1960s. The policy of inclusionary politics was aimed at splitting the anti-Stalinist alliance among the Soviet intelligentsia and transforming village prose writers into an articulated audience. This was the major reason that the works of the these writers continued to be published in the late 1960s while other anti-Stalinist writers increasingly were forced to publish their work in *samizdat*.

In the mid-1960s, a third Russian nationalist group emerged on the Soviet political scene: the radical nationalists. Despite the fact that their writings explicitly challenged the official ideology, this group was exceptionally well suited for the role of articulated audience because they fiercely opposed the liberalization of Soviet politics and harshly attacked the reform-supporting intelligentsia, which had coalesced around the literary journal *Novy mir.* This stance explains why the representatives of this group were permitted, and even encouraged, to articulate their ideas freely. When, at the end of the 1960s, Soviet leaders decided that the radical nationalists had moved beyond the role assigned to them, the chief editor of their major publication, the literary journal *Molodaya gvardiya,* was dismissed from his position.

I will argue that the 1970s and the early 1980s were the years in which inclusion was one of most important means of legitimizing the political status quo. While driving many prominent members of the liberal intelligentsia into the ranks of dissidents and often into exile, the Soviet regime not only allowed Russian nationalist intellectuals to articulate their ideas with unprecedented freedom, but also permitted their exceptionally wide distribution. Between 1971 and 1982, the circulation of the journal *Nash sovremennik,* the most important Russian nationalist publication of the period, grew by 236 percent, and that of *Molodaya gvardiya* rose by 176 percent. Moreover, village prose was elevated to the position of the most powerful literary movement. Eleven of its members were awarded the most prestigious Soviet literary prizes, and their books were published in millions of copies and adapted for film, television and theater. This treatment was not limited to village prose writers. Between 1971 and 1982, another fifteen Russian nationalist writers and literary critics received similar recognition, publishing runs, and adaptation for film.

Inclusionary politics clearly made Russian nationalist intellectuals the most prominent and widely known group among the Soviet intelligentsia. However, it failed to transform them into an obedient and controlled articulated audience. Leonid Brezhnev and his chief ideologue, Mikhail Suslov, greatly miscalculated in thinking that they could control Russian nationalists by giving them a material stake in the system without satisfying their principal concerns. Russian nationalists were especially frustrated with the party's inability or lack of desire to reverse the process of the depopulation of the countryside, protect the architectural legacy of pre-revolutionary Russia, enforce environmental laws, or stop the moral corruption of Russian society and the progressive penetration of Western social and cultural influences. This built-up frustration finally erupted in the early 1980s when Russian nationalists began harshly criticizing the party on each of these issues. This lashing out at the regime marked the failure of inclusionary politics, and it was finally abandoned during the Andropov era.

The politics of inclusion had one major legacy: it transformed Russian nationalist intellectuals into a major force within the Soviet intelligentsia. Not only did many Russian nationalist writers become popular cultural icons, but they were also awarded control over such important cultural institutions as the RSFSR Writers' Union and several major Moscow and provincial literary journals.

Despite the prominent status Russian nationalist intellectuals acquired during the Brezhnev era, they failed to translate this advantage into a powerful political movement capable of shaping Russian politics during the era of Gorbachev's reforms. This was neither a consequence of the weakness of primordial sentiments of ethnic Russians, nor a result of a cost-benefit analysis carried by Russian elites but a direct outcome of Russian nationalist response to the political, economic, and cultural reforms Gorbachev initiated. This response, in turn, was conditioned by the social and political ideas that Russian nationalists developed in the decades preceding *perestroika*.

The Gorbachev reforms were so radical that they forced all Russian nationalist groups to make a clear choice of supporting or opposing them. Liberal nationalists, who were ideologically committed to radical reform, merged with other nonnationalist supporters of perestroika and subsequently lost their separate political identity. Opposition to perestroika, however, significantly obliterated the differences between conservative and radical nationalist groups, effectively paving the way to a close political alliance between the two. The rejection of democratic institutions and a market economy and the preservation of the empire provided the ideological basis of this alliance and pushed to the side their ideological differences.

Between 1987 and 1990, Russian nationalist opposition to the course of the reforms was largely limited to harsh attacks on perestroika and glasnost by the leaders of the RSFSR Writers' Union, which emerged as the most important cultural institution of the Russian nationalist intelligentsia, as well as a relentless antiglasnost and antiperestroika campaign in such leading Russian nationalist publications as *Nash sovremennik, Molodaya gvardiya,* and *Literaturnaya Rossiya.* However, already in this period Russian nationalist political organizations and movements began to emerge and to spread the political, social, cultural, and economic ideas articulated by Russian nationalist intellectuals since the 1960s. Some of these organizations and movements were led by prominent Russian nationalist intellectuals; others, like Pamyat, the first Russian nationalist organization to stage a street demonstration, were led by people who did not belong to the intellectual elite of the Brezhnev and early Gorbachev periods.

In 1990–1991, as politics was increasingly shifting from the realm of culture to the halls of parliaments and the streets, the importance of such Russian nationalist cultural institutions as the RSFSR Writers' Union and the literary journals began to decline. However, Russian nationalists were sorely unprepared to make the transition from the A-B to C stage, from politics, by culture to electoral politics. The Russian nationalist electoral alliance, the Bloc of Social-Patriotic Movements of Russia, was soundly defeated in the spring 1990 election to the RSFSR Congress of People's Deputies. This defeat fully revealed the weakness of the alliance of conservative and radical Russian nationalists and showed their inability to become a major political force.

Their failure had three main causes. First, their deep-seated distaste for the rules of democratic politics resulted in weak organizational structures and half-hearted efforts during the 1990 electoral campaign. Second, they insisted on reiterating their vision of a nonmarket, anti-Western, authoritarian, and imperial Russia at a time when this vision had lost its attractiveness for the majority of ordinary Russians. And finally, Yeltsin and his main organizational backbone, the social movement Democratic Russia, were able to articulate a popular alternative set of ideas that envisioned Russia as a strong democratic country with a Western-type market economy. An important part of this vision was its vaguely anti-imperial stand. Although Yeltsin never explicitly called for the dissolution of the USSR, his insistence on the principle of Russian sovereignty, his rhetoric against continuing Russian subsidies to the other republics, and his harsh condemnation of the Soviet government's efforts to preserve the territorial integrity of the USSR through the use of force constituted, in effect, a rejection of the imperial principle. Yeltsin's landslide victory in the June 1991 Russian presidential election was decisive proof that this vision of Russia appealed to the Russian people.

Recognizing their failure to become a major force in Russian politics, conservative and radical Russian nationalists were left with few alternatives but to hope that the main institutional pillars of the Soviet state, especially the CPSU, KGB, and the military, would embrace their vision of Russia's future and act decisively to prevent the dissolution of the empire and the transformation of Russia into a democratic market-oriented state. Since the elites within these institutions were deeply split on many key issues, conservative and radical Russian nationalists sought to ally themselves with the most conservative elements within these state elites and offer to them an ideological platform for action. This meant articulating an ideological justification for a political coup d'état, the desire for which was growing within the conservative wing of the Soviet establishment in the early 1990s.

The eagerness of conservative and radical Russian nationalists to provide ideological support to the conservative members of the Soviet political establishment was by no means a one-way process. In fact, Russian nationalist ideas looked increasingly attractive to the conservative elements within the Soviet political elite, particularly as their own power was decisively threatened by secessionist movements in the non-Russian republics and by Yeltsin and the liberal-democratic movement within Russia itself. Moreover, the conservatives within the Soviet political elite clearly realized that since neither orthodox communist ideas calling for a return to the policies of the Stalin era nor arguments for the continuation of the status quo had significant popular appeal, the only set of potentially popular ideas that defended the empire and the authoritarian nature of the Soviet state were articulated by the conservative and radical Russian nationalists.

This process of the progressive embrace of Russian nationalist ideology by the conservative forces within the Soviet political elite was especially evident in the politics of the antireform factions within the USSR and RSFSR parliaments, as well as in the actions of several leaders of the Russian Communist Party controlled by party conservatives. In many ways, this was the logical conclusion to the inclusionary politics of the Brezhnev era. What was cultivated as a substitute state ideology in the 1960s and 1970s, was to become an official ideology of the Soviet state in the 1990s, provided that Gorbachev and Yeltsin could be removed from their posts.

By August 1991, the process of the nationalization of the conservative elements within the Soviet political elite had not reached the CPSU's Politburo, which explains why the August 1991 coup plotters, all top-ranking party and government officials, largely eschewed Russian nationalist rhetoric in their official statements. The coup's failure and the subsequent ban of the CPSU, followed by the peaceful dismantling of the USSR, marked an end to the conservative and radical Russian nationalist dream of an imperial, authoritarian, and anti-Western Russia.

The coup also interrupted another potentially important avenue for the evolution of Russian nationalism articulated by Vladimir Zhirinovsky. His stunning success in the June 1991 Russian presidential election—a third-place finish and the support of nearly 8 percent of the vote—highlighted the potential for the popular appeal of conservative and radical Russian nationalist ideas when they are reduced to a set of populist slogans and adapted for the era of media-influenced electoral politics. If nationalist ideas, as articulated by the established conservative and radical Russian nationalist intellectuals, were particularly appealing to the conservative members of the political elite, Zhirinovsky's brand of nationalism clearly resonated with the masses.

Zhirinovsky espoused what he considered to be the essential part of the conservative and radical nationalist ideology: the preservation of the imperial nature of the Russian state and its anti-Western orientation. At the same time, by denouncing the CPSU and expressing support for market economics, private property, and a multiparty system of government, he was able to break the association between his brand of Russian nationalism and the old political, social, and economic institutions of the Soviet state, so completely and irreversibly discredited by 1991. The potential of Zhirinovsky's brand of Russian nationalism fully manifested itself in the postcommunist period when Zhirinovsky, following the stunning success of his Liberal Democratic Party of Russia in the December 1993 parliamentary election, became a major political player.

Although Russian nationalists failed to gain power in the first seven years of the postcommunist era, their electoral successes in parliamentary, presidential, and regional elections, as well as their ability to place their key ideological concerns on the political agenda, constitute a clear sign of the movement's strength. Khazanov, echoing the view of many other scholars, argues that this situation was inevitable, since "under the conditions of social and economic instability of postcommunist transition, when most social identities are lost or inflated, people turn to ethnicity as an identity of last resort."[35] My explanation, however, emphasizes the crucial importance of developments within the Russian political elite. In other words, the success of Russian nationalism in the postcommunist period was a consequence of the wide spread of conservative and radical Russian nationalist ideas within the Russian political elite.

In the postcommunist period, Russian nationalist ideas were consistently embraced by those members of the Russian political elite who opposed the policies of Yeltsin's government. The reason for their embrace of the imperial, anti-Western, antimarket, and authoritarian vision of Russia is rooted in the fact that this vision constituted the only well-articulated ideological alternative to the process of political and economic reform currently underway in Russia. This is true even in the case of the reconstituted Communist Party of the Russian Federation, which under the leadership of Gennady Zyuganov effectively abandoned most tenets of communist ideology in favor of a form of radical Russian nationalism.

The strong appeal of conservative and radical nationalist ideas was also a consequence of the ideological vacuum that emerged when the ruling elite was unable to develop a liberal nationalist ideology suitable to the new political and economic environment. Particularly glaring was their inability to develop a liberal-democratic conception of the postcommunist Russian nation-state with its civic definition of membership and nonimperial territorial boundaries. Opposition parties and politicians successfully filled this ideological vacuum with their own authoritarian, anti-Western, and imperial conceptions of a Russian nation and state, which helped them to seize control of public discourse on these issues and to emerge as a major political force. The Russian nationalist electoral success at the polls was the inevitable outcome of their ability to seize control of public discourse.

Structure of the Book

Chapter 2 traces the roots of the Russian nationalist movement from the mid-1950s and mid-1960s, when intellectuals began searching for a new political identity in the wake of the Twentieth Party Congress. Because many had their roots in rural Russia, their fictional and nonfictional analyses of the political, social, economic, and cultural realities prevailing in the Russian countryside became intellectual vehicles for establishing such an identity.

The work of this group of village-born intellectuals became known as the "village prose." In the last years of the Khrushchev era, "village prose" writers were established as the prominent members of Soviet intelligentsia and were the core of the Russian nationalist movement up to the Gorbachev era. During the Khrushchev era, all members of the "village prose" belonged to a broad anti-Stalinist alliance within the Russian intelligentsia that coalesced around the literary journal *Novy mir*. At the same time, the first signs of ideological division within the school developed between its liberals, who emphasized elimination of the sociopolitical consequences of the Stalinist legacy in the countryside, and the conservatives, who stressed the primacy of the preservation of the moral values of the traditional Russian peasantry.

Chapter 3 analyzes the reasons Soviet leadership adopted inclusionary politics in the mid-1960s. Village prose writers were targeted for inclusion to provide an ideological justification for Brezhnev's policies of high investment in the agricultural sector of the economy. Also, in the mid-1960s, other Russian nationalist group was targeted for inclusion. This group of intellectuals was associated with the literary journal *Molodaya gvardiya*, and was selected for inclusion because of its ardent rejection of the Western-oriented path of Russia's development and for its calls for the creation of a powerful authoritarian state similar to that which had existed under Stalin. Because of their ideas, the *Molodaya gvardiya* intellectuals were called "radical nationalists."

Inclusionary politics allowed both village prose writers and the radical nationalists of *Molodaya gvardiya* a relative freedom to express their main political beliefs, which became the subject of intense political debate within the intellectual community and the Soviet political establishment. These debates ultimately led to a crackdown on *Molodaya gvardiya* and a partial suspension of inclusionary politics in 1970.

Chapter 4 analyzes the interrelations between Russian nationalists and the Soviet regime from 1971 to 1985. Enforcement of inclusionary politics resumed in full force in the early 1970s and lasted until 1982, during which time Russian nationalist intellectuals enjoyed an unprecedented freedom to articulate their main sociopolitical ideas, saw an increase in the circulation of Russian nationalist publications, received prestigious literary prizes, and were rewarded with massive print runs of their books.

Despite their privileged position in Soviet society, the Russian nationalist intelligentsia did not obediently serve the regime's goals. In fact, quite the opposite occurred: By the early 1980s, all ideological groupings within the Russian nationalist intelligentsia had become harsh critics of the government's policies, contributing to the suspension of these policies soon after Brezhnev's death in late 1982.

Chapter 5 explores the main reasons the Russian nationalists did not become a regime-supporting group. As a result of the implementation of inclusionary politics, Russian nationalists became prestigious and popular in Russian society, creating high expectations that the regime would address their principal social, political, and cultural concerns. Yet, inclusionary politics was never intended to give Russian nationalist intellectuals any real influence on the policy process. Angered by the regime's environmental, agricultural, and social policies, Russian nationalists emerged as major critics of the Soviet government in the early 1980s.

Chapter 6 discusses the main political debates of the 1970s and early 1980s involving the Russian nationalist intellectuals. These debates were, in effect, debates about Russian national identity and about the political, social, economic, and cultural arrangements most suitable for Russia. They clearly revealed the continuing commitment of the members of the liberal trend in the village prose movement to radical economic and political reform and the further weakening of such a commitment from its conservative wing. The debates also fully revealed the radical nationalists' continuing commitment to the transformation of the Soviet Union into a militantly anti-Western, authoritarian state.

Chapter 7 examines the nature of Russian nationalist politics in the first four years of the Gorbachev era. Gorbachev's commitment to radical reform eliminated the raison d'être of inclusionary policy. Instead, Gorbachev and his allies in the political establishment assisted those forces within the intelligentsia supportive of perestroika. The attitudes toward Gorbachev's policies in general, and his cultural policies in particular, fully revealed the political implications of the long-held ideological beliefs of various elements in the Russian nationalist movement. Liberal nationalist intellectuals joined the coalition of perestroika supporters, while conservative and radical nationalists formed a Russian nationalist alliance calling for an end to reform.

Thus, Russian nationalists of the Khrushchev and Brezhnev era developed political beliefs that provide the key for understanding their Gorbachev-era politics. On the one hand, liberal nationalist intellectuals who consistently viewed radical political and economic reforms necessary for the preservation of Russian national culture and traditions ended up as full-fledged supporters of perestroika. On the other, fierce opposition to reforms on the part of radical nationalists was a logical consequence of the core belief that Russia must be transformed into an aggressively anti-Western authoritarian state. Conservative village prose writers' opposition to reform was not a reversal of their prior beliefs, but rather it was a direct result of their decades-long belief in the preservation of the traditional moral values and the isolation of Russia from Western social and cultural influences.

The common rejection of the Gorbachev reform policies effectively erased the previous ideological differences between conservative and radical nationalist intellectuals and paved the way for a formation of a Russian nationalist anti-perestroika alliance. Moreover, rejection of a market economy and political democracy combined with a commitment to the preservation of the imperial nature of the Soviet state led this alliance to support conservative forces the Soviet political establishment they criticized so harshly only few years earlier.

Chapter 8 analyzes Russian nationalist attempts to become a third major force in Russian politics (in addition to the CPSU and the liberal-democratic movement) in the era of electoral politics. Russian nationalists failed to become such a force following their poor showing in the 1989 elections to the Congress of People's Deputies of the USSR, and especially after the defeat of the Russian nationalist electoral alliances in the 1990 election to the Congress of People's Deputies of the RSFSR. This failure was a consequence of poor organizational and campaign skill, as well as the antidemocratic and antimarket orientation of the Russian nationalist electoral platform.

Failure to emerge as an independent force in Russian politics led the Russian nationalist intelligentsia to throw their full-fledged support behind the conservative forces within the Soviet political and military establishment, in the hope that these forces would be able to stop the democratization process and remove Gorbachev and Yeltsin from power. At the same time, the embattled antireform forces within the Soviet political elite began adopting Russian nationalist ideas as their own.

This process occurred in the CPSU, the Russian legislature, and, especially, in the Russian Communist Party (RCP). The August coup attempt and the subsequent ban of the CPSU and the RCP interrupted this process.

Finally, Vladimir Zhirinovsky advocated the emergence of an alternative brand of Russian nationalism in the waning days of the Communist regime. Coming out of nowhere to finish third in the June 1991 Russian presidential election, Zhirinovsky had shown that a nonliberal version of Russian nationalism could have a strong popular appeal if it were dissociated from its link to communist political and economic institutions. As in the case of the CPSU and the RCP, this process was also interrupted by the August 1991 coup attempt.

Thus, by mid-1991, the contours of postcommunist era Russian nationalism were already present. In the subsequent years, the reconstituted Communist Party of the Russian Federation under Zyuganov's leadership completed the process of transformation into a nationalist party with remnants of communist phraseology, while Zhirinovsky adjusted his ideological message to the postcommunist political, social, and economic realities. Both would become major players in postcommunist Russian politics.

In the final analysis, this book is about ideas and how they shape politics. The rise of Russian nationalism in the post-Stalinist era and its collapse along with the communist regime is impossible to understand without understanding its message. Moreover, the essence of this message continues to play a major role in the postcommunist era. The difficulties Russian democracy has encountered in consolidating itself are not merely a result of the failure of radical economic reform, but they also are the consequence of the ascendance of imperial and authoritarian nationalist ideas in Russian political discourse since 1992. Russia's success as a democracy ultimately depends on the ability of democratic-minded members of the political and intellectual elite to reinvent their country to foster a strong commitment to democratic government.

The Emergence of Politics by Culture, 1953–1964

Explaining Ethnonationalism in the Post-Stalin Era

Significant scholarly effort has been devoted to the development of theories explaining the rise of nationalist movements in the post-Stalin period. Rakowska-Harmstone expressed the prevailing scholarly consensus when she asserted in 1974 that since Stalin's death, "not only has the traditional sense of a separate identity on the part of major ethnic groups failed to disappear, but it has begun to transform itself into modern nationalism."[1] Scholars deeply disagree, however, on the roots and causes of this nationalism. Rakowska-Harmstone advances a theory which explains the rise of nationalism among minority ethnic groups as a consequence of modernization. She argues that the modernization of Soviet society created new native elites, who often felt themselves the victims of discrimination by the Russians. This sense of victimization merged with traditional ethnic antagonisms to give birth to national movements among many of the ethnic minorities.[2]

Krawchenko and Zaslavsky provide a socioeconomic explanation that is in essence similar to Rakowska-Harmstone's. According to Krawchenko, Ukrainian nationalism rose in the 1960s as a result of limited opportunities for upward social mobility—a combined result of Ukraine's failure to keep pace with Russia in overall levels of socioeconomic development after World War II, the russification of Ukraine's educational system, and an intense competition for positions of power and prestige in Ukraine because of a sizable increase in Russian immigration.[3] For Zaslavsky, the rise of Russian nationalism was a consequence of the discontent "generated by diminished social mobility in the large cities, by the [worsening] economic situation, by the scarcity of consumer goods . . . in a context of the atomization of the working class and limited communication between workers and specialists."[4]

Motyl, on the other hand, rejects socioeconomic explanations for the rise of ethnic nationalism in general and of Ukrainian nationalism in particular. He argues that, contrary to Krawchenko's assertion, post–World War II Ukraine did not lag behind Russia socioeconomically. Moreover, the leading figures of the Ukrainian nationalist movement were not losers in the socioeconomic competition with the Russians, but rather were highly successful members of the Ukrainian intellectual elite.

Motyl regards modernization merely as a necessary condition (the "base-type factor," in his terms) for the rise of nationalism. According to this explanation, political factors—the de-Stalinization policies of Khrushchev and their subsequent reversal by Brezhnev—were the main causes for the emergence of the Ukrainian nationalist movement in the 1960s. As he puts it, "modernization and social mobilization affected the range of political options that were open to the non-Russian elites and populations. But none of these base-type factors would have been operative had the state not made a number of political decisions—de-Stalinization and partial re-Stalinization—that first tolerated and then condemned incipient non-conformist activity."[5]

Suny and Connor attempt to balance the weighting of social and political factors. In explaining the rise of Georgian nationalism in the post-Stalin era, Suny argues that economic development and social change "had not been accompanied in Georgia by a significant democratization of the political superstructure . . . New generations of educated young people with broad intellectual interests came up against immovable restrictions on expression and the exercise of power." This situation led many frustrated young Georgians to embrace the nationalist creed.[6]

Connor comes to an essentially similar conclusion in his explanation of the emergence of dissent in the USSR. In his view, dissent, including ethnic nationalist dissent in the Soviet Union, arose "out of the interplay between the growing complexity, or differentiation, of a rapidly modernizing Soviet society, on the one hand, and the persistent reliance by the regime on what have been termed 'command-centralist' modes of integrating the differentiated segments of society in the face of rising demands for autonomy on the part of these segments, on the other."[7]

At the opposite end from Rakowska-Harmstone's and Krawchenko's theories stands what might be called an ideological explanation, espoused by Dunlop. Like many other scholars, he views modernization as a necessary condition—the "catalyst," in his words—for the rise of ethnic nationalism in the Soviet Union. Yet Dunlop presents the disillusionment of the intellectual elite from the Marxist-Leninist ideology in the aftermath of the Twentieth Party Congress as the main cause for the emergence of Russian nationalism.[8]

This chapter develops an explanation that places primary importance on a combination of social and political factors. It points to the contradictory nature of Khrushchev's policies in several areas, especially agriculture and religion, as factors heavily contributing to the emergence of Russian nationalism. In addition, the analysis of the backgrounds of the participants in the Russian nationalist movement indicates the importance of such factors as age, education, and social background.

De-Stalinization and Its Effect on the Intellectual Elite

Although Russian nationalism did not become a prominent force in Soviet society until the mid-1970s, a decade after Khrushchev's fall from power, the period between 1953 and 1964 was crucial to its formation. It was the de-Stalinization process, and especially the end of the terror, that created the necessary conditions for the emergence of Russian nationalism as a significant political and intellectual movement. Khrushchev did more than simply discontinue the terror; he eliminated it from the range of policy options available to the leadership. He accomplished this by dramatically denouncing Stalinism at the Twentieth and Twenty-second Party Congresses, dismantling the gulag system and releasing millions of prisoners from the labor camps, and drastically curtailing the size and power of the internal security apparatus, subordinating it to tight party control.[9]

The terror was rejected on an ideological basis as well. Stalin's theoretical justification of terror—the notion that the class struggle intensifies, the closer the dictatorship of the proletariat is to communism—was rejected. The new party program unveiled at the Twenty-second Party Congress in 1961, proclaimed the Soviet Union to be the "all-people's state" (obshchenarodnoe gosudarstvo). According to the program, the Soviet Union had passed the stage of the dictatorship of the proletariat and had become a new sociopolitical entity that encompassed all members of society. As a consequence, there was no place for notions of class struggle and class enemies.[10]

The elimination of the terror had a profound effect on the nature of state-society relations. In the absence of terror, there was no longer a force that could effectively prevent the social elites from developing a wide range of sociopolitical orientations. Moreover, under Khrushchev a variety of such orientations was openly expressed in the official press. Some scholars see individuals' openly articulating these orientations merely as spokesmen for competing factions in the leadership, with their views indicative of the intense struggle for power taking place in the Kremlin.[11] The truth is that these views were manifestations of the intense sociopolitical debate between antagonistic ideological groups within the social elites themselves.

During Khrushchev's years in power, the intellectual elite became the most outspoken and articulate element among the different social groupings, expressing positions critical of official policies and appearing in the pages of officially sponsored publications. Soon after Stalin's death, the most important of these publications were the mass circulation Moscow literary monthlies, which were issued in hundreds of thousands of copies. Also known as "thick journals" (tolstye zhurnaly), these periodicals published poetry, prose, literary criticism, and memoirs, as well as essays on history, economics and politics. By the late 1950s, because of the highly politicized content of Russian literature and literary criticism in the post-Stalin era, the Russian intellectual elite had resurrected the prerevolutionary Russian intelligentsia's tradition of using the thick journals as their main forum for political expression. Khrushchev's policy of creating and reviving scores of thick journals also contributed to a rejuvenation of this political tradition.[12]

By the mid-1960s, the Russian intellectual elite was divided into two main ideological camps, each of which controlled a major Moscow thick journal and had as its undisputed leader the editor of its journal. By the late 1950s, Novy mir had become the leading journal of the camp that promoted a continuation of de-Stalinization. The poet Aleksandr Tvardovsky (1910–1971), chief editor of Novy mir from 1950 to 1954 and again from 1958 to 1970, was responsible for the journal's high political and social status.

From 1961, the main publication of the Stalinist opposition to Khrushchev's reforms was a literary monthly, Oktyabr. As in the case of Novy mir, the journal's preeminence was largely due to the efforts of its chief editor from 1961 to 1973, the novelist Vsevolod Kochetov (1912–1973). Although their goals were diametrically opposed, we shall see later that together *Novy mir* and *Oktyabr* formed the institutional basis of the emerging Russian nationalist movement.[13]

The government allowed the thick journals to publish material that challenged its policies or its official descriptions of social reality in the first post-Stalin decade for four reasons.[14] First, Khrushchev and other members of the political elite may have come to the conclusion that it was impossible to suppress these ideas effectively, especially if they reflected real or potential discontent in the society at large. Because the political elite was unified in its determination to prevent the use of terror as a political tool, the government may have felt powerless to suppress such views.

Second, the scope of the views prevailing among members of the political elite was very similar, if not identical, to those prevailing among members of the intellectual elite.[15] Therefore, competing political leaders could view the sociopolitical debate among members of the intellectual elite as an important extension of their own debates.

This brings us to the third reason for Khrushchev's toleration of sociopolitical debate in the thick journals: Khrushchev's own strategy of mobilizing social support. That Khrushchev's efforts to carry out a radical transformation of the Soviet system met with stubborn opposition within the political elite is well documented. In order to succeed, he needed, and did not hesitate to mobilize, social support for his reform agenda by allowing open debate on key social issues among members of the intellectual elite.[16]

An integral part of this strategy was to encourage reformist members of the intellectual elite to express their views on a wide range of political, social, economic, and cultural issues. Khrushchev's personal decision to permit the publication of Solzhenitsyn's *One Day in the Life of Ivan Denisovich* in *Novy mir,* and his subsequent use of the novel, is the best-known example. Khrushchev allowed Solzhenitsyn's critical views of the Stalinist terror to be published in order to create an appropriate environment to undermine the opposition to de-Stalinization within the establishment.[17]

Political conservatives followed Khrushchev's example by using like-minded members of the intellectual elite to mobilize popular support against the same reforms. In other words, unable to prevent *Novy mir* from promoting political and economic reforms, the conservatives had a vested interest in protecting *Oktyabr*'s continued ability to voice ideas opposing these reforms, even though they did not always share Kochetov's blatantly Stalinist views.[18] Thus, within the political elite, both supporters and opponents of reform acquired a vital interest in protecting the ability of intellectuals to articulate their positions in officially sponsored journals, even though these journals often expressed ideas with which they did not fully agree.

Fourth, both Tvardovsky and Kochetov were, to use Tucker's concept, the "nonconstituted leaders" of two antagonistic ideological camps within the Soviet intellectual elite. According to Tucker, nonconstituted leaders are individuals who "have been or are now political leaders without possessing power or occupying high political office."[19] Tvardovsky and Kochetov acquired this status by being not only highly respected and trusted members of the Soviet cultural establishment, but also members of the political elite. In addition to being secretaries of the USSR Writers' Union, both held prestigious positions in the party: Kochetov as a member of the Appeals Commission of the Central Committee and Tvardovsky as a candidate member of the Central Committee. Tvardovsky was supported by Khrushchev, and Kochetov enjoyed the support of Khrushchev's rivals, Suslov and Kozlov.[20] This dual membership, in the cultural establishment and the political elite, gave Tvardovsky and Kochetov the power to protect the relative autonomy of their journals from pressures to conform to the prevailing political line.

The Russian intellectual elite emerged in the Khrushchev era as a major contributor to the ongoing political debate. As a result, Russian nationalist members of the intellectual elite found themselves strategically well positioned to become important contributors to the political debate. By itself, however, this strategic position explains neither the growth in popularity of Russian nationalism among members of the Russian social elites in the first post-Stalin decade, nor the particular ideas this nationalism would adopt. The answer to this can be found in an examination of the social profile of members of the Russian nationalist movement and their reaction to Khrushchev's contradictory policies.

A Social Profile of the Membership of Russian Nationalist Groups

An analysis of the biographies of leading figures of the Russian nationalist movement in the 1960s and 1970s focuses on three important factors: age, education, and social background. Smith argues that nationalist movements usually start as cultural movements of literati and become a political force by attracting members from such liberal professions as medicine, law, and journalism.[21] As he points out elsewhere, this social stratum is "the most relevant group in exploring the emergence of nationalism."[22]

Russian nationalism of the post-Stalin era was in no way exceptional in this respect. It started as a cultural movement among members of a new Russian intellectual elite, which had appeared on the Soviet social scene in the Khrushchev era. This elite was relatively young and extremely well educated. The main social difference between nationalist and nonnationalist members of this elite was their social origin. Most Russian nationalists were born and raised in the countryside and small towns.

Mannheim states that the concept of generation "is one of the indispensable guides to an understanding of the structure of social and intellectual movements."[23] He subdivides members of the same generation into "generational units." What separates members of one generational unit from another is a different sociopolitical interpretation of their common experience.[24]

A great majority of the Russian nationalists who stepped into the political arena between 1953 and 1964 represented two distinct generational units of two consecutive generations—the wartime generation, born between 1920 and 1925 and the postwar generation, born between 1926 and 1938.[25] In fact, of 152 prominent Russian nationalist intellectuals active between 1953 and 1991, 98 belonged to these two generational groups (see Table 2.1). In 1953, the year of Stalin's death, the youngest members were in their mid- to late teens, and the oldest were in their early thirties, in 1964, at the end of the period, they were in their mid- to late twenties to early forties. It is not surprising, therefore, that none of them was a publicly known figure before 1953 and that most became known only during the Khrushchev or Brezhnev eras.[26]

Perhaps more important, the political worldview of the war and postwar generations to which the Russian nationalists belonged was largely shaped by de-Stalinization. The poet Evgeny Evtushenko, himself a member of the postwar generation (b. 1933), called this new intellectual elite "the children of the Twentieth Party Congress." De-Stalinization released a whole range of new social, political, and philosophical questions for public debate and provided a strong impetus for members of the war and postwar generations to search for convincing answers to these questions. Nationalism would be one of the solutions chosen.

Table 2.1 Geographical Origins and Educational Achievements of Russian Nationalist Intellectuals Active Between 1953 and 1991

Generation Years of Birth	Place of Birth					Education		
	Village	City with Population of 100,000 and Below	City with Population of 100,000 to 500,000	City with Population of 500,000 and Above	Moscow and Leningrad	University Level (Moscow and Leningrad)	University Level (Provinces)	Less Than Complete University Level
1900–1919	10	3	1	—	3	7	7	3
1920–1925	20	1	2	—	2	15	6	4
1926–1938	38	8	7	8	12	54	13	6
1939–	7	10	6	3	11	26	9	2
Total	75	22	16	11	28	102	35	15

Note: The number of Russian nationalist intellectuals active between 1953 and 1991 exceeded the 152 listed here. For some, however, such biographical data as year and place of birth and type of education they received could not be found. They therefore were not included in the table.

Those members of the war and postwar generations who searched for new forms of Russian nationalism were assisted by the Russian nationalists who belonged to the Brezhnev (people born between 1900 and 1909) and purge generations (people born between 1910 and 1919). I have identified seventeen members who fall within these two age groups. Through their writings, these authors established themselves as mentors of and role models for nationalists of the war and postwar generations. For a variety of reasons, most of them became publicly known only during the Khrushchev era. The writers Oleg Volkov (b. 1900) and Aleksandr Solzhenitsyn (b. 1918) joined the intellectual elite only in the 1960s, having spent years in Stalin's concentration camps and in internal exile. On the other hand, such well-known Russian nationalists as Gavriil Troepolsky (b. 1905) and Sergei Zalygin (b. 1913) were not members of the intellectual elite before 1953 because writing was not their main occupation during the Stalinist period.[27]

Few Russian nationalists of the Brezhnev and purge generations were well-known members of the intellectual elite during Stalin's time. What distinguished them from the rest of the members of the old Stalinist intellectual elite which remained in control of the Soviet cultural establishment in the Khrushchev era, was their profound ideological transformation in the post-Stalin period. The writer Aleksandr Yashin (1913–1968), for example, was the Stalin Prize recipient in 1950 for his regime-glorifying poetry. His writings from the Khrushchev era, on the other hand, set the standard for Russian nationalist criticism of party policies in the countryside.

The majority of Russian nationalist writers, journalists, historians, literary scholars, and critics, especially those belonging to the postwar generation, studied at the highly prestigious Gorky Literary Institute in Moscow, Moscow or Leningrad universities, or other prestigious Soviet institutions of higher education. In fact, of 152 Russian nationalist intellectuals active between 1953 and 1991, 102 (67 percent) received their university-level education in Moscow and Leningrad (see Table 2.1). Moreover, a number earned the Soviet equivalent of the doctorate, primarily in the fields of history or literature. A good education in the humanities meant, especially after 1953, exposure to a wide variety of intellectual influences, including prerevolutionary Russian nationalist thought.

By the Khrushchev era, many Russian nationalist intellectuals held research or teaching positions in elite Soviet universities and research institutes, or were staff members of or regular contributors to important newspapers, magazines, and literary journals. Russian nationalist writers, movie directors, or painters earned national recognition between 1956 and 1964. The success of this group clearly indicates that Russian nationalism in the post-Stalin era was not a manifestation of frustration caused by increased competition from members of other ethnic groups or blocked career opportunities.[28]

An analysis of the geographic distribution of educational institutions and employment locations of members of the Russian nationalist movement and, especially, their social origins, supports this argument. Almost all Russian nationalists were educated and employed in the Russian regions of the RSFSR. Therefore, they were unlikely to face discrimination in education and employment in favor of other ethnic groups, a practice that did exist in non-Russian republics and the autonomous republics within the RSFSR in order to create and promote native elites. In fact, they were often the beneficiaries of post–World War II discriminatory policies aimed at restricting the Jewish presence in the Soviet intellectual, cultural, and scientific elites.

An analysis of their social origins reveals that 97 of 152 (64 percent) Russian nationalist intellectuals were born in either the countryside or small and highly rural towns (see Table 2.1) and moved to medium-sized and big cities during their late teens to early twenties. In most cases they moved in the decade immediately following World War II. Their ability to obtain a good education and secure prestigious positions in society was a truly remarkable achievement given the extremely limited opportunities for social mobility open to the children of peasants or small town residents at that time.

The link between the process of rapid urbanization and the rise of Russian nationalism is highlighted by the fact that most Russian nationalists were first-generation city residents. Russian nationalists whose origins were in countryside and in small towns represented only the tip of the iceberg of the massive influx of people into rapidly expanding Soviet cities. It started with the migration of millions of peasants to the cities during the collectivization and industrialization campaigns. In the 1930s, almost 27 million peasants resettled in urban areas, effectively doubling the size of the urban population. This trend continued after World War II, and between 1939 and 1959 another 24 million peasants migrated to urban areas.[29] Primarily as a result of this migration, the RSFSR was the most urbanized region of the Soviet Union, excluding the Baltic republics of Latvia and Estonia. Fifty-two percent of the RSFSR's population lived in towns. Eleven years later, 62 percent lived in cities.[30]

Thus, one of the prevailing features of Russian urban society of the late 1950s to mid-1960s was a massive concentration in the cities of former peasants, most of whom joined the working class.[31] These new urbanites had been brought up in traditional Russian villages or small towns, in which an extremely conservative social morality, characterized by patriarchal family relations and strong religious beliefs, prevailed. As Moshe Lewin points out, "The rural mind, way of life, and culture are extremely tenacious. It may take some three generations for the peasant outlook and mentality to disappear and for a true urbanite to emerge."[32] The persistence of this mentality, combined with the extremely harsh living conditions that these migrants experienced in the cities, made adaptation to urban life a painful experience.[33] Indeed, from Soviet fiction we know how harsh life was for these workers and how difficult and painful was their adjustment to an urban lifestyle.[34]

Analyzing the social consequences of rapid Soviet urbanization, Lewin argues that the tremendous influx of peasants into the cities led to "a massive uprooting, and cultural and psychological shock, causing widespread disorientation, a crisis of values, and the concomitant phenomena of delinquency, hooliganism, cynicism, mass anomie, and the attraction of not too palatable countercultures."[35] The theories of Halperin, Huntington, and Kornhauser emphasize the link between the psychological effects of modernization and a rise of nationalism, and suggest that the conditions Lewin describes should have led to the even greater popularity of Russian nationalist ideas among the recently urbanized members of the Soviet society.[36]

The Soviet regime could effectively prevent the spread of nationalist ideas among the newly urbanized masses, but it could not prevent the members of the intellectual elite who had come from the countryside and small towns from developing a set of nationalist ideas as a response to their identity crisis. Because of their high level of education, they experienced a more identity-threatening culture shock than the vast majority of former peasants who were poorly educated and joined the ranks of the working class. This education usually took place in the major urban centers of the Soviet Union, especially in Moscow and Leningrad—the most Westernized cities of the RSFSR and the first to experience the penetration of a wide variety of Western influences, in the arts, fashion, literature, and philosophy. After Stalin's death, the penetration of these influences greatly accelerated.[37]

An important benchmark in this penetration was the World Youth Festival held in Moscow in summer 1957. For the first time in decades, the festival brought to the Soviet Union thousands of young foreigners, including jazz musicians, beat poets, and avant-garde artists. Aleksei Kozlov, the famous Soviet jazz musician, later recalled that "during the Festival we all became convinced that our style and our music and our idols all belonged to the distant past."[38] Kozlov's impressions accurately represent the prevailing view in the 1950s among the younger city-born members of the intelligentsia. The impact of Western culture on students and young professionals born in the countryside had to be even more shocking. Their traditional peasant values were tested to the limit in the intellectual milieu of major Russian cities.

Remember that the rapid penetration of Western cultural influences took place at the same time as the highly intense sociopolitical debates over the nature of the Stalinist legacy. Thus, this crisis of personal identity coincided with the search for a political identity. And where these two quests merged, as in the case of the village-born intellectuals, the contradictory nature of Khrushchev's policies assumed crucial importance in the formation of their political worldview.

Social and Political Sources of Discontent

Discontent with Khrushchev's policies in agriculture, nationalities, ecology, and religion played a major role in driving Russian intellectuals to develop a nationalist worldview. Newly urbanized intellectuals, particularly those of the war and postwar generations, were especially sensitive to shifts in agricultural policies. They had high expectations that Khrushchev would eradicate the Stalinist legacy in the countryside. Although most of them were too young to remember collectivization, the great hardships experienced by the Russian peasantry as a result of Stalin's war and postwar agricultural policies were fresh in their minds.

During the Khrushchev period, the lot of the Russian peasantry dramatically improved. Taxation on private plots, introduced in 1948, was abolished in August 1953. In September 1953, procurement prices for grain and meat were increased by 500 percent and for dairy products by 200 percent. Procurement prices continued to increase throughout the Khrushchev era.[39] In 1958 the state abolished its procurement quotas on the produce of private plots. The abolition of taxation and the steady increase in procurement prices were instrumental in greatly improving the peasants' standard of living: peasants' total income doubled between 1953 and 1964, at the same time that the peasant population fell by 10 percent.[40]

Such a radical improvement in living standards should have transformed newly urbanized members of the intellectual elite into firm Khrushchev supporters. In fact, the effect was the opposite; by the late 1950s and early 1960s, this new intelligentsia was losing its faith in Khrushchev because of his inability to fulfill the high expectations fueled by his de-Stalinization campaign and policies to improve living standards. Moreover, several of Khrushchev's agricultural policies in the late 1950s and early 1960s in particular alienated the newly urbanized intellectual elite because they saw in them a return to the Stalinist approach.

One example is Khrushchev's campaign against private plots, which he denounced as one of the main causes of the low productivity of collective farms. Simultaneously, peasants were coerced into selling their livestock to collective farms in order to fulfill the greatly increased state quotas for meat and to satisfy plan targets for extraordinary growth in the size of kolkhoz (collective farm) livestock herds, all components of Khrushchev's plan to overtake the United States in meat production. The result of this policy was that by 1963, the number of privately owned cattle, pigs, sheep, goats, and poultry had fallen by several million.

Another agricultural policy that contributed to growing alienation was Khrushchev's policy aimed at radically increasing the acreage under corn cultivation. Collective farms all over the Soviet Union were ordered to grow corn, without taking into account the suitability of the region in this crop.[41] Often corn was substituted for rye, the traditional main crop in central and northern Russia. The corn campaign was a dramatic failure and contributed significantly to the agricultural disaster of 1963, when the Soviet Union was forced for the first time to import grain, meat, and dairy products from the West.[42]

The newly urbanized intelligentsia also strongly disapproved of Khrushchev's merging small collective farms into giant conglomerates, a policy later denounced as a "second collectivization."[43] Vigorously carried out between 1957 and 1960, it reduced the number of kolkhozes from 91,000 in 1955 to 39,000 in 1963.[44] The giant kolkhoz, however, turned out to be a much less efficient economic unit than its smaller counterpart. Moreover, in the small kolkhoz, the peasants had been able to preserve to a large extent the sense of intimacy and solidarity of the old village that had helped them to survive the difficult war and postwar years. Intimacy and solidarity were not possible in the giant, highly bureaucratized collective farms, and this contributed to a weakening of the peasants' attachment to the land.

At the same time, large numbers of collective farms—15,020 between 1955 and 1960—were converted into state farms.[45] This transformation meant that the number of traditional peasants sharply declined, while the number of agricultural workers grew significantly. Agricultural workers had much smaller private plots, lived a more urban lifestyle, and felt much less emotional attachment to the land than did the peasants of small kolkhozes.

Finally, despite significant improvements in the rural standard of living, newly urbanized members of intellectual elite felt that Khrushchev continued Stalin's discriminatory social policies. The Stalinist practice of denying internal passports to peasants, a policy that effectively made them second-class citizens, was not abolished. And while pensions for urban residents were significantly increased, peasants on collective farms continued to be denied state pensions. In addition, the government refused to provide disability pensions in the case of labor-related accidents, did not provide sick leave or maternity benefits, and collective farm peasants were not eligible for state-subsidized housing.[46]

The newly urbanized intelligentsia regarded all of these policies as instrumental in the continued migration of peasants to the cities—between 1954 and 1958 an annual average of 140,000, rising to about 340,000 to 350,000 between 1959 and the mid-1960s.[47] Indeed, the Russian countryside was being progressively depopulated. A Western scholar observed in 1963 that while the non-Russian agricultural areas of the Transcaucasus and Central Asia had labor surpluses, in such traditional peasant regions of Russia as Smolensk Oblast and Siberia, the only untapped resources of agricultural labor remained mothers of young children and severely disabled persons.[48]

Although themselves beneficiaries of this migration, the newly urbanized intelligentsia regarded the depopulation of their native villages with horror. They sought a revitalization of village life, not its decay, because the village provided them with a sense of identity and intimacy that no city could. They did not feel at home in the large Westernized cities and saw themselves as the voice not of the millions of workers of peasant origins, but of those unaffected by Westernization—traditional rural Russia and its peasants, which they increasingly identified with the Russian nation. Many cherished the dream of returning to their native village, and, indeed, from the 1970s on, some would start living in their native village for four to five months each year. For most of them, however, the return would be not literal but literary.

The abandonment of Stalin's nationality policies had different implications for Russian and non-Russian ethnic groups. For non-Russian minorities, de-Stalinization meant halting the deportation of small nationalities from their homelands; ending crude policies of forced russification and the systematic destruction of native elites; adopting flexible language, culture, and education policies which would contribute to the growth of new, non-russified indigenous social elites; and ending ethnic Russian domination of the party and state apparatuses of the non-Russian republics, and initiating policies of recruitment and promotion of members of indigenous ethnic groups to these positions.

A change in nationality policies for the Russian ethnic majority meant first and foremost a retreat by Stalin's successors from the extremely xenophobic domestic policies of the post–World War II period. The rabid anti-Semitic campaign, masked as a campaign against "rootless cosmopolitans," was discontinued, and its apogee, the doctors' plot, was publicly denounced as a fabrication.[49] Alongside state-sponsored anti-Semitism, Khrushchev rejected extreme anti-Westernism and Great Russian chauvinism as state policy. The campaign against "kowtowing to the West" (nizkopoklonstvo pered zapadom), the unqualified praise of everything Russian, the glorification of the military and diplomatic achievements of tsarist Russia, and especially, the cult of the state-building efforts of Peter the Great and Ivan the Terrible all came to an end.[50]

The unifying slogan of Khrushchev's reforms was "Back to Lenin's Path." Khrushchev perceived the rejection of Stalinist nationalism as it was applied to both Russian and non-Russian ethnic groups as an integral part of an effort to revive Lenin's nationality policies. He probably thought that Stalinist nationalism was the main hurdle to overcome on the path to achieving the bolshevik dream of the conclusive elimination of the nationality problem. The new party program, indeed, solemnly declared to have solved this problem in the Soviet Union.[51]

The program also promoted the new idea of a Soviet national identity—the formation of the Soviet nation-state *(sovetskaya natsionalnaya gosudarstvennost)* and the supra-ethnic "Soviet people" *(sovetskii narod)*. A shared belief in socialism and a pride in the industrial, scientific, and cultural achievements of the Soviet state were supposed to give the members of different ethnic groups a sense of common civic identity. This idea was grounded in a theory of the dynamics of ethnic relations in the Soviet state. According to this theory, the federal structure of the Soviet Union was becoming increasingly obsolete because Soviet people of different nationalities developed similar fundamental concerns and common spiritual features in the process of building socialism. The theory postulated that "full scale construction of communism constitutes a new stage in the development of national relations in the USSR in which the nations will draw still closer together, and their complete unity will be achieved."[52]

This attempt to promote the idea of a Soviet national identity did more than fail to win popular support among Russian and non-Russian social elites. In fact, it contributed to a rise of ethnic nationalism because the non-Russian elites suspected that behind such vague statements the "obsolete nature" of the federal structure, and the "drawing closer together" and "complete unity" of ethnic groups stood a renewed effort to russify. The party program gave the non-Russian elites sufficient reason for such fears since it contained such Stalinist euphemisms for continued Russian domination as "the help of the great Russian people" to non-Russian nationalities in their modernization, a condemnation of "national egoism," and an emphasis on the learning of Russian because it was both the lingua franca of the state and the language that linked Soviet nationalities to world culture.[53]

The idea of a new Soviet identity also alienated the newly urbanized members of the Russian intellectual elite because it was too abstract and too unrelated to their own life experiences. It glorified modernization while ignoring the problems that accompanied the transition from a rural way of life to that of an urban, industrial society. Finally, it left unanswered the crucial question of the nature of the cultural dimension of the new national identity. In short, it could not provide answers to the problems of identity that so preoccupied these new Russian intellectuals during the Khrushchev era.

Khrushchev's religious policies were an integral part of his overall effort to impose a new Soviet national identity on the various ethnic groups.

Religion, often an important component of traditional ethnic identity, was perceived as a formidable barrier to the adoption of a new secular, nonethnic Soviet national identity. In 1959, the CPSU launched a militant antireligious campaign which lasted until Khrushchev's removal from power in 1964. This campaign brought to an end the conciliatory policy toward the Russian Orthodox Church practiced in the last decade of Stalin's reign.[54]

In many ways Khrushchev's antireligious drive was a revival of the militant antireligious campaign that had accompanied the First Five-Year Plan (1929–1932). Although massive arrests of clergy did not take place during the Khrushchev campaign, large number of churches, monasteries, and theological seminaries shut their doors. In Moscow, about twelve of fifty churches were closed down and six of them demolished. Out of sixty-nine monasteries and convents functioning in the USSR in 1958, only approximately sixteen remained open by the end of 1964. Five of eight theological seminaries and about ten thousand churches, many of them in rural areas, were closed down as well.[55]

During this campaign, the government imposed a series of restrictions aimed at reducing the influence of the Orthodox Church. All church services, private and public, outside church walls were outlawed. In many places in the countryside, a ban was imposed on day services and on the ringing of church bells from May through October. The Orthodox Church was also forbidden to allow young people under the age of eighteen to attend services or to be given any religious instruction.[56]

Special effort was made to reduce the number of baptisms by ordering their official registration. The government issued a directive that forbade priests to administer the baptism of a child without the written consent of both parents. The parish executive committee had to register the names of all baptized children and their parents in its record books, which were monitored by the authorities. Thus, parents who had their children baptized were easily identified and could be reported to their place of work, where punitive measures against them might be taken.[57]

This persecution of both the Orthodox Church and believers alienated members of the intellectual elite from rural backgrounds, even though they were not personally affected. A sociological profile of Russian Orthodox believers shows that most of them are elderly, poorly educated, nonskilled, collective farmers.[58] This profile, however, fits very well with what we know about the relatives of Russian nationalist intellectuals. In the countryside, the antireligious campaign meant the closure of churches and the harassment of believers, some of whom were related to the newly urbanized intellectual elite. They could not and did not ignore the campaign and perceived it as yet another dimension of Khrushchev's assault on the peasantry and its traditions.

One of the consequences of Khrushchev's policies toward religion was the growth in awareness among most intellectuals of the fate of the ancient Russian churches closed under Stalin and Khrushchev. Many of these churches were crumbling due to a lack of maintenance or repairs. The growth of a preservationist consciousness among members of the Russian intellectual elite was fueled by the fact that the antireligious campaign coincided with several major building projects associated with the name of Khrushchev's favorite architect, Mikhail Posokhin. Between 1959 and 1961, the Palace of Congresses, a modern-looking convention center and concert hall was built inside the Kremlin walls in complete disregard to its historic surroundings. In 1958, construction of the new Kalinin Avenue began in the heart of the Moscow historic downtown, causing demolition of many of Moscow's old secular buildings. The end result was a thoroughfare 1.2 miles long and 264 feet wide with high-rise office buildings on both sides and a terrible disfigurement of the historic Arbat neighborhood.[59]

The destruction of prerevolutionary architectural monuments and unsuccessful efforts to prevent it triggered demands for the creation of a voluntary preservationist society. Khrushchev, however, harshly rejected an appeal by members of the Russian intellectual elite for the formation of such a society.[60] After Khrushchev's overthrow, efforts to create an institutional framework for the protection of Russia's ancient monuments became the first public priority of the emerging Russian nationalist movement.

The growth of preservation awareness coincided with a rise in ecological consciousness, fueled by Khrushchev's continuation of Stalinist industrial development. Industrial pollution that poisoned the air and water and the progressive disappearance of Russian forests and subsequent land erosion attracted the attention of the intellectual elite. This awareness was in part heightened by the observation of environmental destruction as the intelligentsia in the second half of the 1950s took to hiking and bicycling in the Russian countryside.[61]

In the same period, the Russian intelligentsia became aware of the human costs resulting from the construction of giant hydroelectric stations to harness the energy potential of the Russian rivers. In the late 1950s, the construction of the Krasnoyarsk power station on the Enisei River began, and in 1958 and 1961, respectively, the Irkutsk and Bratsk power stations on the Angara River came on line. To construct these stations, huge territories were flooded, and thousands of peasants dislocated.

By the early 1960s, feelings of discontent and frustration about the state of the environment were widespread among members of the intellectual elite. A spark was needed to translate this discontent into action. This spark was provided by the decision, announced in 1958, to establish a cellulose plant on the banks of Lake Baikal.[62]

On December 21, 1961, *Komsomolskaya pravda* published a letter from the director of the Limnological Institute of the Siberian branch of the Soviet Academy of Sciences, in which he warned of the grave ecological danger the cellulose plant posed to the lake. Lake Baikal, the largest and deepest fresh-water lake in the world, was an important symbol of Russia and its natural bounty in Russian folklore, music and literature. The defense of the lake against industrial pollution was an important rallying point, and linked the emerging Russian nationalist movement and environmentalism.

Thus, discontent within the newly urbanized Russian intelligentsia was fanned by a number of Khrushchev's critical policy decisions. The high expectations of the intelligentsia were destroyed as policies in the areas of agriculture, nationalities, religion, and the environment proved to be far less progressive than anticipated. This disappointment was a key factor in the emergence of Russian nationalism in the Khrushchev era.

Village Prose Nationalism in the Khrushchev Era

Gustafson argues that under Khrushchev and Brezhnev, specialists were able to influence the formation of Soviet agricultural and environmental policies only when the political leadership was changing its policy priorities or when it perceived the situation in these areas as being critical. In such situations, the leadership would "open a window," permitting public debate on the policy in question.[63] The concept of "opening a window" also can help to explain the content and form of Russian nationalism in the Khrushchev and Brezhnev eras.

The two open windows—that is, the two major subjects approved for open public debate in the Khrushchev era—were the state of agriculture and Stalinism. Since Khrushchev had great personal interest in agriculture

and sought every means available to improve its extremely poor performance in the postwar years, it is hardly surprising that agriculture became
the first major issue open to public discussion. In fact, the open debate on
the state of Russian agriculture had begun in the final year of Stalin's reign.
The September 1952 issue of *Novy mir* contained Valentin Ovechkin's
(1904–1968) semifictional essay, "District Weekdays" *(Raionnye budni)*, in
which, through the portrayal of a confrontation between a Stalinist local
bully, the district party secretary Borzov, and his reform-minded deputy
Martynov, Ovechkin blasted Stalinist agricultural management.[64]

A few months after Stalin's death, his successors signaled to the intellectual elite that the public debate on agriculture could be continued. On July
23, 1953, *Pravda* printed Ovechkin's essay, "On the Front Line" *(Na pered-
nem krae)*, which was a follow-up to "District Weekdays." Tvardovsky, the
editor of *Novy mir* at the time, was the first to grasp that open debate on
agriculture provided an opportunity for a broad sociopolitical debate. In
1953 and 1954, *Novy mir* published a series of fictional, semifictional, and
nonfictional works sharply critical of various aspects of the Stalinist agricultural legacy. As Spechler points out, "When taken together, these works
represented a thoroughgoing assault by the journal on the Soviet system of
rule and administration in the economic sphere."[65]

This policy of pressing the boundaries of acceptable debate was continued by Konstantin Simonov, the chief editor of *Novy mir* from 1954 to
1958, and by the editors of other thick journals and literary almanacs. By
1956, a distinct group of social critics had emerged; known at the time as
"essayists" *(ocherkisty)* and later as "village prose writers" *(derevenshchiki)*,
they actively campaigned for a radical change in party policy in the countryside.[66] This village prose became the voice of Russian nationalist sentiment and a starting point for the development of the Russian nationalist
movement.

During the Khrushchev era, village prose was written primarily by members of the intellectual elite from the purge and war generations. This
literature addressed many of the concerns of intellectuals from a rural
background who belonged to the postwar generation, and thus it became
their ideological guide. In the last years of the Khrushchev era, the newly
urbanized members of the Russian intellectual elite began to make their
own contributions to this literature.

There were two distinct phases in the development of village prose
during the Khrushchev era, with the year 1956 separating the two. The first

phase was dominated by the writings of Ovechkin, who continued his "District Weekdays" with two additional installments: "In the Same District" *(V tom zhe raione)* and "A Hard Spring" *(Trudnaya vesna)*. Both were published in *Novy mir,* and each was a more radical criticism of Soviet rural bureaucracy than its predecessor.[67]

Other leading village prose writers in this period who developed Ovechkin's ideas were Troepolsky, Tendryakov, Dorosh, and Yashin. Like Ovechkin's essays, most of their work also was published in *Novy mir.* Gavriil Troepolsky (b. 1905) ridiculed district party secretaries, kolkhoz chairmen, village demagogues and thieves in his satirical collection of short stories, *Notes of an Agronomist (Zapiski agronoma).*[68] Tendryakov (1923–1984), in *The Fall of Ivan Chuprov (Padenie Ivana Chuprova),* portrayed the moral bankruptcy of Stalinist methods of agricultural administration through a description of the fall of a kolkhoz chairman who built his career practicing these methods.[69]

Two works published in 1956, in the second and what would prove to be the last issue of the literary almanac *Literaturnaya Moskva,* represented both the continuity of Ovechkin's tradition and a significant departure from it. These works were the first manifestations of Russian nationalism in the post-Stalin era. Efim Dorosh (1908–1972) showed in *A Village Diary (Derevensky dnevnik),* in Ovechkin-like fashion, that the core of the problems facing the hard-working kolkhoz chairman Ivan Fedoseevich were rooted in Stalinist methods of agricultural management.[70] What made *A Village Diary* different from the writings of Ovechkin and other rural essayists was the muted criticism of half-hearted Soviet preservationist policies. Dorosh spoke with pain about crumbling and decaying ancient churches and portrayed them as a vital part of the rural Russian landscape.[71]

The second work of village prose that appeared in *Literaturnaya Moskva,* and was to become a landmark in the development of Russian nationalism in the Khrushchev era, was Aleksandr Yashin's (1913–1968) short story, *Levers (Rychagi).* This work was one of the strongest condemnations of the Stalinist legacy in the countryside to appear in the official Soviet press before the Gorbachev era. It was a powerful indictment of the principle of the party's right to control peasants' lives. This indictment, combined with a vivid description of the gap between official propaganda and the harsh reality of northern Russian village life in the post-Stalin years, provoked the condemnation of *Levers* by Khrushchev himself and led to the suppression of *Literaturnaya Moskva.*[72]

The story portrays the behavior of four members of a kolkhoz party organization before, during, and after an official meeting of the cell. As they sit in on the party meeting, the gap between reality and party propaganda becomes painfully clear. The village in which the meeting is taking place has no electricity; the room in which the meeting is held is lit only by an oil lamp. The supply of basic food staples is very poor, and the peasants speak about the availability of sugar in the village store as an event. A conversation before the meeting also reveals that the peasants are poorly paid, though the district party secretary continues to reiterate the official lie that the peasants' well-being is constantly improving. The peasants say that the kolkhoz no longer has any cows, while the party secretary reports that the livestock herds of the Soviet kolkhozes are growing from year to year. Cultural life also exists only on paper. One peasant sums up the situation with a harsh remark: "In our district the truth is seated only in the honorary presidiums so it won't feel offended, and keeps mum."[73]

Yashin also shares with the reader the nature of the relationship between the party and the peasants. The party gives orders and demands unquestioning obedience, even if these orders are against the peasants' best interests. The party members of the village cell are treated merely as levers—enforcers of party orders at the local level. Indeed, the reason for the meeting of the cell is to provide a rubber stamp for the kolkhoz sowing plan, imposed from above. Although the members of the kolkhoz party organization are reduced to the status of levers, they are not ordinary peasants; all hold important positions in the kolkhoz. The story emphasizes that party membership is a prerequisite for entering the social elite of the village and that there are no party members among the ordinary peasants.

Yashin reveals the double life led by the village elite in his portrayal of the transformation that occurs at the moment the meeting of the party cell begins. Suddenly the participants stop criticizing party policies in the countryside and start speaking in dull, official cliché-ridden language. They even imitate the district party secretary, who only seconds before was the object of their ridicule. During the meeting they do not challenge party policies and approve, as is expected of them, the sowing plan. Yet as soon as the meeting comes to an end, the peasants resume the honest and sincere conversation that preceded the official meeting.

Dorosh's *A Village Diary* and Yashin's *Levers* represented two distinct types of the Russian nationalist argument, which firmly established a link between Russian nationalism and problems in the countryside. The period after the Twentieth Party Congress marked a growing elaboration of these two trends in the Russian nationalist argument and a strengthening of the link joining Russian nationalism, Russian national identity, and rural Russia. In addition to Dorosh and Yashin, both of whom continued to play a prominent role in the village prose, the writings of Abramov, Soloukhin, Solzhenitsyn, and Zalygin contributed most to the development of the two main trends in Russian nationalist writing in the years 1957 to 1964.

Fyodor Abramov (1920–1983) was the man whose ideas were conceptually closest to those expressed in Yashin's *Levers*. In the April 1954 issue of *Novy mir*, Abramov published an essay in which he brilliantly demonstrated that descriptions of the postwar Russian village as a place of happiness, plenty, and prosperity, so often found in the prose of official Stalinist writers, were gross lies.[74] In 1963, he published *Around and About (Vokrug da okolo)*, which, alongside *Levers*, was the most daring critique of the party's methods of administering agriculture and its treatment of Russian peasantry published in the Khrushchev era.[75]

The main thrust of Abramov's story was a condemnation of Khrushchev's policy of imposing severe restrictions on private agricultural plots. He presented these plots as the main source of peasant income and showed how restrictive policies undermined the motivation of the peasants to work on the collective farm. Abramov also urged the party to abandon the Stalinist policy of denying peasants internal passports. In the story, he portrays a hard-working peasant, Pavel Voronitsyn, who feels demoralized after a visit to the city and becomes an alcoholic after he recognizes the discrimination to which he is subjected as a peasant.[76]

Like *Levers*, *Around and About* provoked strong official reaction; it was harshly criticized in the press and literary journals as a slander of Soviet reality. As part of a smear campaign, the district party organization, under whose jurisdiction Abramov's native village fell, drew up a protest letter, forced the village peasants to sign it, and published it in the local and central press.[77]

Although collectivization was not a major theme in "Around and About," it was semiexplicitly attacked in the story. Abramov strongly implied that collective farms had been imposed on the peasantry by force, and that these farms were the ultimate source of all problems in Soviet agriculture. It was one of the first literary works published in the Soviet Union that condemned collectivization.

Abramov's attack on collectivization reflected the growing interest of village prose writers in the historical origins of collectivized agriculture.

This interest was a natural offshoot of the public debates about Stalinism taking place in historiography and fiction. Encouraged by Khrushchev, the debates intensified after the Twenty-second Party Congress at which Khrushchev openly condemned Stalin's terror of the 1930s.[78]

Novy mir led the anti-Stalinist campaign in the thick journals. Throughout 1961 and 1962, it published Iliya Ehrenburg's memoirs, which contained a devastating attack on Stalin. In the March through May 1962 issues, *Novy mir* published Yury Bondarev's novel, *Silence (Tishina)*, which portrayed the environment of terror in the postwar years. The December 1962 issue contained Solzhenitsyn's *One Day in the Life of Ivan Denisovich (Odin den iz zhizni Ivana Denisovicha)*, which combined the themes of the concentration camps with the persecution of the peasantry under Stalin. Solzhenitsyn accomplished this by choosing peasants as the two major protagonists of the novel. The main hero, Ivan Denisovich Shukhov, is not a former party functionary or a military officer but a simple Russian peasant. His friend and protector, the head of the prisoners' construction brigade, Andrei Tyurin, is a peasant who was arrested as the son of a kulak and sent to the camps in the 1930s. Through the character of Tyurin, Solzhenitsyn introduces the subject of the victimization of peasants during collectivization.

Although Abramov's and Solzhenitsyn's writings were groundbraking, Abramov's critique of collectivization was buried in an analysis of the problems of the contemporary Russian countryside, and Solzhenitsyn's description of peasant suffering was secondary to his account of camp life. It was Sergei Zalygin who made the subject of the collectivization drive the center of attention. The February 1964 issue of *Novy mir* contained his short novel, *By the Irtysh (Na Irtyshe)*, which was an explicit attempt to tell the true story of collectivization. It had a tremendous impact on the Russian intelligentsia.[79]

Zalygin portrayed the collectivization campaign as a highly coercive act, by means of which the state imposed its control over the lives of the peasantry. The novel makes it clear that "dekulakization" was directed not only against rich peasants but against any peasant who refused to obey the orders of the state. The Stalinist official Koryakin brands Chauzov, the hero of the novel, a "kulak" and exiles him from the village not because he is rich, but because he refuses to endorse an order to give up personal grain to meet the target of the kolkhoz sowing plan.

The writings of Abramov and Zalygin represented one direction in the development of village prose, similar in many respects to Yashin's "Levers." This liberal village prose formed the basis of the liberal wing within the emerging Russian nationalist movement.

Another direction in the development of village prose was articulated in Yashin's *Vologda Wedding*, Solzhenitsyn's *Matryona's House*, Soloukhin's *Vladimir's Country Roads*, the short stories of Likhonosov and Shukshin, and the poems of Rubtsov. These works represented not only a decisive departure from the tradition established by Ovechkin, but also from Yashin's and Dorosh's writings of the 1950s. This new village prose was very critical of the Stalinist legacy in the countryside and Khrushchev's agricultural policies. Yet it was not these subjects, but the traditions of the Russian peasantry—its way of life and its morality—that stood at the center of the concerns of the writers who represented this emerging trend—the conservative village prose. From mid-1960s on, it would be the dominant trend within the village prose movement.

The 1962 Yashin story, *Vologda Wedding (Vologodskaya svadba)*, is a typical example of the conservative village prose of the 1960s. The story depicts the festivities surrounding the wedding of a young peasant couple. Like *Levers*, it portrays the harsh reality of daily peasant life in the Russian northeast: the lack of electricity, food shortages, poor roads, a deficient educational system, and the complete subordination of the kolkhozes to the dictates of the district party organization and their economic exploitation by industrial enterprises.[80]

What makes *Vologda Wedding* different from *Levers* is Yashin's idealization of the traditional way of life of the Russian peasantry and his sharp criticism of the CPSU for destroying centuries-old peasant traditions. In *Vologda Wedding*, Yashin argued that party efforts to uproot ancient peasant traditions created a spiritual vacuum that led to the progressive moral corruption of the peasantry. This corruption was expressed in widespread alcoholism, which caused crime, wife beating, suicide, and the disintegration of peasant families.

Aleksandr Solzhenitsyn's 1963 story, *Matryona's House (Matryonin dvor)*, like *Vologda Wedding*, combined a highly idealized depiction of the traditional Russian peasantry and a criticism of the Stalinist legacy in agriculture, a fact that a Stalinist critic of both writers did not fail to notice.[81] Solzhenitsyn described how peasants were denied peat and were forced to steal in order to heat their houses in winter. He wrote about the extremely difficult living conditions of old peasants like Matryona Zakharova, the story's main protagonist. After twenty-five years of hard labor in the kolkhoz, she is denied a pension because kolkhoz members are not entitled to it; her tiny private plot is cut by almost half because she is no longer an active member of the kolkhoz; and she cannot afford to keep a cow because retired kolkhoz members are not allowed to feed their own animals with the grass grown on kolkhoz land. The local bureaucracy also makes the life of the old peasant miserable. In order to receive the tiny monthly pension of eight rubles for her husband, who was killed in World War II, Matryona is forced to spend two months collecting scores of certificates and signatures from different agencies.

Despite the powerful description of the realities of peasant life, *Matryona's House* was not intended to be exclusively, or even primarily, a criticism of the Stalinist legacy in the countryside. Rather it was an attempt to present the moral code of the traditional peasantry, which Matryona symbolized, as a Russian national virtue. Solzhenitsyn emphasized Matryona's deep religiosity and her utter selflessness and called her "a righteous person" *(pravednik),* the existence of which guarantees Russia's national survival.

Matryona's House was an important landmark in the ideological development of village prose. Solzhenitsyn elevated an old religious and uneducated peasant, unaffected by communist values or modern lifestyle, to a symbol of the Russian nation. By doing this, he became the first Russian writer in the post-Stalin era to combine an open criticism of party policies in the countryside, past and present, with an equally open challenge to the official cult of modernity and modern lifestyle. This combination became a distinctive mark of the ideology of the conservative wing of the village prose movement in the Brezhnev era.

One of the first clear indications that the newly urbanized intellectuals of the postwar generation were going to develop this particular trend of the village prose was in a short story by Viktor Likhonosov (b. 1936). Entitled *The Bryansk Folks (Bryanskie),* the story is an account of the lives of a couple of old peasants, as observed by a narrator who is a first-generation urbanite.[82] The hardships of peasant life under Stalin were mentioned, although only in passing. Most of the story was an idealization of the simple life of the traditional Russian peasantry. The narrator expresses his uneasiness with modern urban society and dreams of buying the old couple's house as a way of returning to the village. The story is permeated with a painful awareness that a permanent return to the land is no longer possible. What is left was an imagined, political homecoming.

The same intense desire for an imagined return to the highly idealized

Russian countryside was vividly expressed by another first-generation urbanite from the postwar generation—the poet Nikolai Rubtsov (1936–71).[83] In the poems "I will gallop the hills of my sleeping Motherland," "The star of the field," and "I will rush to the hill and fall on the grass," Rubtsov expressed his love of the Russian countryside, of its churches and crosses. To Rubtsov this rural landscape was the embodiment of Russia, its history and its traditions. The fact that Rubtsov's poetry appeared not in the anti-Stalinist *Novy mir*, where most of the village prose was published, but in the avowedly Stalinist *Oktyabr* suggests that as early as the Khrushchev era, some far-sighted Stalinists viewed village prose nationalists as potential partners in a political alliance aimed against the liberal reformers.[84]

Another sign of *Oktyabr*'s effort to attract postwar generation village prose writers into an antireformist alliance was the publication of six short stories by Vasily Shukshin (1929–1974) in 1961 and 1962.[85] Kochetov, *Oktyabr*'s chief editor, was attracted to these very early stories by Shukshin because of their anti-intellectual themes and tried to link them to the antireformist cause. Shukshin was, indeed, the first village prose writer whose idealized portrayal of village life contained clear antiurban and anti-intellectual elements. In *Lelya Selezneva from the School of Journalism* (*Lelya Selezneva s fakulteta zhurnalistiki*), Shukshin portrays a young urban university student who lacks any knowledge of the nature of rural life but nevertheless tries to interfere.[86]

Kochetov failed to bring village prose writers of the postwar generation into the anti-reformist camp. Shukshin's case was rather typical. None of his stories were published in *Oktyabr* after its May 1962 issue. From early 1963 to 1970, he published his stories almost exclusively in *Novy mir*, and in 1965 his village prose was harshly attacked in *Oktyabr*.[87] The anti-intellectualism of village prose was not yet of such overwhelming importance to its writers to compel them to join an antireformist coalition in which Stalinists played the major role. As much as Shukshin did not like the urban intellectuals, who occasionally disrupted the stable patterns of village life, his stories reveal an even greater dislike for the rural party bureaucracy that perpetuated Stalinist methods of administration.

Abramov and Zalygin, on the one hand, and Yashin, Solzhenitsyn, Likhonosov, and Shukshin, on the other, represented the two trends of village prose that developed out of Yashin's *Levers*. Vladimir Soloukhin's (1924–1997) *Vladimir's Country Roads* (*Vladimirskie prosyolki*) represented a significant revision of the type of village prose Dorosh established in *A Village Diary*. The work was written as a semifictional hiking diary in the villages and ancient towns of the author's native Vladimir province. Like Dorosh, Soloukhin attacked Stalin's and Khrushchev's policies in the countryside. The question of the peasants' plight was only a secondary concern. Soloukhin's ire was directed more toward the poisoning of the water and air by industrial enterprises and toward unrestrained logging, which led to deforestation. This ecological concern is combined with a sharp criticism of the scant efforts to preserve ancient churches, prerevolutionary manor houses, and parks and anguish over the depopulation of the Russian countryside and the disappearance of traditional peasant arts and crafts.[88]

The power of *Vladimir's Country Roads* was its blend of social criticism with the joy of the rediscovery by a former peasant of his own rural roots and the roots of his own nation. Soloukhin did not simply describe a village or a town he passed through, but quoted from a prerevolutionary book describing the place or related events associated with it from the distant past. In this fashion he created a sense of the uninterrupted continuity of the Russian national existence and gave new meaning to the Russian national identity, at the center of which stood the traditional Russian peasantry.

Vladimir's Country Roads developed a particular stream within the village prose that was highly sensitive to ecological issues. In the late 1950s, Soloukhin was virtually the only village prose writer interested in the issue. By the 1970s, ecological issues had become a dominant theme within the movement.

If Soloukhin was the first writer to link concerns about agricultural policies with preservationist and ecological causes, Vladimir Chivilikhin (1928–1984) turned ecology into one of the main Russian nationalist themes. In 1963, he published "The Bright Eye of Siberia" *(Svetloe oko Sibiri)*, an essay that called for a halt to the construction of the cellulose plant on Lake Baikal. Chivilikhin did not limit himself to a description of the dangers to the lake of industrial pollution, but also criticized Khrushchev's environmental record. In particular, he pointed to the grave ecological consequences of unrestricted logging in Siberia and implicitly argued against the policy of constructing power stations on Siberian rivers because it involved flooding Russian land.[89]

Chivilikhin was a well-known opponent of Khrushchev's de-Stalinization drive within the Soviet intellectual elite. "The Bright Eye of Siberia" was published in *Oktyabr* and probably was viewed by Kochetov as an integral part of the Stalinist effort to discredit the Khrushchev reforms. Nevertheless, Chivilikhin's essay helped to focus the attention of Russian intellectuals on environmental issues and, at the same time, link those issues to Russian nationalism. Moreover, the essay contributed to the rise in ecological awareness among conservative members of the intelligentsia and as such represented a significant turning point in the transformation of antireformist ideas in the post-Stalin era. Following Chivilikhin, conservative intellectuals increasingly separated the environmental issue from the issue of the nature of the Soviet political and economic system. In the Brezhnev era, intellectuals like Chivilikhin would add the preservation of Russia's historical monuments to their political platform in the creation of a radical Russian nationalism.

By end of 1964, all three main trends of the future Russian nationalist movement were present, although not in a fully developed form. The different types of village prose were not yet clearly demarcated. Because village prose writers published largely in *Novy mir*, which strongly promoted their works, they were viewed as committed liberal-reformers. On the other hand, Chivilikhin and other representatives of the emerging radical nationalism, because of their association with *Oktyabr*, were not distinguished from orthodox Stalinists like Kochetov.

Under Khrushchev, village prose writers were only one group among many reform-minded members of intellectual elite. Brezhnev's politics turned a group of nationalistically minded Russian intellectuals into the only officially permitted, and even encouraged, group in the Soviet Union. The next chapter analyzes why this happened and how different Russian nationalist trends crystallized into three main groups with fundamentally different views about the desirable direction of political, social, and economic change in the Soviet Union.

CHAPTER

3

The First Phase of Inclusionary Politics, 1965–1970

An initial look at the period 1965 to 1970 seems to reveal a paradox. On the one hand, it was a time of clear retreat from Khrushchev's de-Stalinization policies and the partial rehabilitation of Stalin and his legacy, with increasing suppression of the liberal-reformist intelligentsia and the emergence of an articulate dissident movement. On the other hand, it was a period of unprecedented sociopolitical debate in the censored press, and the major subject of this debate was Russian nationalism. Village prose, ecology, the preservation of historic monuments, the contemporary relevance of the Slavophile legacy, and the nature of East-West relations were all intensely discussed in a fashion unimaginable just a few years earlier.

Yanov, himself an active participant in the political debates of the late 1960s and a writer on Russian nationalism, does not address the question of why Brezhnev and his colleagues in the political leadership decided to open a window to Russian nationalists.[1] Dunlop notes in passing that "from 1964 to 1970 the regime generally maintained a 'hands off policy' in order to concentrate on its opponents within the Democratic Movement and in order to separate itself clearly from the policies of Khrushchev."[2] In reality, however, these debates were not simply a hands-off policy but a consequence of the introduction of inclusionary politics, which, while gradually restricting the freedom of expression enjoyed by the liberal-reformist intelligentsia, allowed Russian nationalist intellectuals to articulate their ideas with unprecedented freedom.

The Politics of Inclusion

By the end of the 1960s, Russian nationalist intellectuals had become a significant force in Soviet society and culture. This happened not because

57

the post-Khrushchev leadership concentrated its efforts on crushing the emerging dissident movement, but because what Dunlop portrays as a hands-off policy was, in fact, an integral part of what might be called the Brezhnev program. This program consisted of four policy priorities: high budgetary allocations to the agricultural and defense sectors of the economy; improved living standards, especially those of the peasantry and the working class; the decisive rejection of radical social, political, and economic reform of the existing system; and efforts to incorporate into the system those members of the intellectual elite whose political ideas might assist, even if indirectly and unintentionally, in enhancing both the legitimacy of the Soviet regime and Brezhnev's main domestic policy priorities.

The radical improvement of Soviet agriculture was the highest domestic priority of the Brezhnev program. As Gorbachev points out, "Leonid Ilyich gave priority to two sectors [of the economy], agriculture and the military, in that order." This became clear within six months after Brezhnev came to power.[3] At the March 1965 plenum of the Central Committee, Brezhnev unveiled his program for the long-term development of Soviet agriculture. He blamed Khrushchev's agricultural policies rather than the system of collectivized agriculture for poor agricultural productivity. Consistent with Brezhnev's determination to avoid major structural reforms, his program called for large investments in the troubled agricultural sector.

The April 1, 1965, Central Committee and USSR Council of Ministers resolutions allocated 41 billion rubles for construction and the acquisition of machinery by collective and state farms, wrote off 2,010 million rubles of kolkhoz debt and all debt resulting from the acquisition of the Machine-Tractor Stations (MTS) in 1958, and deferred until 1970 the payment of an additional 120 million rubles owed by state and collective farms to the state. In the same year, 2 billion rubles in subsidies were given to collective and state farms in the form of sharp increases in procurement prices for agricultural goods. Altogether, from 1965 and 1970, Soviet procurement price subsidies for agricultural products rose from 3.5 billion to 14.3 billion rubles.[4]

New measures to improve the welfare and living standard of collective farm workers were also intended to contribute to the better performance of Soviet agriculture. In November 1964, the Khrushchev-era restrictions on the cultivation of private plots were abolished.[5] In 1965, maternity and state retirement benefits were extended to cover collective farm workers, and, finally, a May 16, 1966, Central Committee resolution established guaranteed cash payments for collective farm workers. All of these policies contributed to an increase of approximately 30 percent (about 34 percent in RSFSR) in the personal income of collective farm workers between 1965 and 1970.[6]

Breslauer and Gustafson show that initially Brezhnev's belief in the need to invest heavily in the rural sector of the economy did not enjoy unanimous support in the Politburo and was challenged by Kosygin. Only by 1968, they argue, did Brezhnev's approach to agriculture decisively prevail. They claim that Brezhnev's success was primarily due to his ability to appoint his supporters to key positions and to build a coalition with representatives of the military and heavy industry.[7]

What Breslauer and Gustafson overlook, however, is Brezhnev's efforts to create public support for his agricultural policies. It is not a coincidence that village prose flourished in the years 1965 to 1970. Brezhnev well understood that the village prose representation of the Russian peasantry as the bearer of Russian national traditions, combined with graphic descriptions of rural poverty and the lack of social justice in the countryside, could be used to manipulate public opinion in favor of supporting heavy investments in agriculture.

The need to create public support for his investment priorities, important as it was, constituted only one factor in Brezhnev's decision to co-opt the village prose writers. A far more important reason was a steep decline in the mobilizational power of the Marxist-Leninist ideology and the concurrent erosion of the ideological basis of the regime's legitimacy. As Huntington points out, this decline in the mobilizational power of ideology is inevitable in the evolution of revolutionary one-party regimes. During the revolutionary phase, he notes, ideology is crucial to a radical party because "it defines the goal, identifies the enemy, and justifies the struggle." After society settles down, "the need for ideology declines and the ideology itself begins to erode."[8]

Indeed, realizing that Marxist-Leninist ideology had irrecoverably lost its mobilizational power, the Soviet political elite under Brezhnev attempted only minor ideological innovations, embedded in the theories of the scientific-technological revolution and the scientific management of society, known, respectively under their Russian acronyms of NTR (*nauchno-tekhnicheskaya revolutsiya*) and NUO (*nauchnoe upravlenie obshchestva*). Although couched in Marxist-Leninist phraseology, these theories essentially postulated bureaucratic efficiency as the highest goal of the CPSU.

As Remington correctly points out, by reducing politics to administration, these concepts attempted to justify Brezhnev's determination to avoid meaningful political and economic reform.[9]

Huntington was perhaps premature in concluding that "it may, indeed, become increasingly in the interests of the (revolutionary one-party) regime to promote this decline (of the mobilizational power of ideology)."[10] The Brezhnev program's attempt to co-opt village prose and other Russian nationalist intellectuals was a direct response to the decline of the mobilizational power of the official Marxist-Leninist ideology and an attempt to strengthen the regime's legitimacy and its mobilizational power.

In the second half of the 1960s, reinforcing nationalist sentiments was considered particularly urgent because of deteriorating Soviet-Chinese relations and the resulting increased tension on the Soviet-Chinese border; the emergence of a reform communism in Czechoslovakia, which posed a threat to Brezhnev's concept of the nature of the communist regime; and a desire to isolate the reform-minded, Western-oriented intelligentsia, much encouraged by the direction of the reform process in Czechoslovakia, from the rest of Soviet society.

Co-optation of Russian nationalist intellectuals in general, and village prose writers in particular, was achieved through inclusionary policies. These politics strove to turn Russian nationalist members of the intellectual elite into an articulated audience that supported the regime and its policies. Thus, inclusionary politics was aimed at increasing popular support for Brezhnev's plan for the revitalization of Soviet agriculture and to regain the Stalin-era ability to politically mobilize the most important Soviet nationality, ethnic Russians.

Brezhnev may have calculated that heavy investment in the countryside and improved rural living standards would blunt the oppositionary edge of village prose nationalism and turn it into a regime-supporting force. If village prose writers could be turned into such a force, Brezhnev could also achieve his aim of splitting the coalition of the reform-oriented intelligentsia and isolating its pro-Western wing.

The policy of inclusionary politics helps us to understand why the heightened censorship that started again in 1965 and touched all areas of Soviet cultural life, including literature, did not seriously affect village prose. These writers, however, were not the only group of Russian nationalist intellectuals targeted for co-optation. Another group, mostly contributors to and members of the editorial board of *Molodaya gvardiya*, the thick journal of the Komsomol Central Committee, also enjoyed virtually unrestricted freedom to articulate their ideas in the official press. Behind the efforts to co-opt the *Molodaya gvardiya* writers stood high-ranking neo-Stalinist members of the party apparat, especially in the Propaganda and Cultural Departments of the Central Committee and the Central Committee of the Komsomol.

The Russian nationalism articulated by *Molodaya gvardiya* constituted an eclectic blend of a highly idealized view of prerevolutionary Russian history, a genuine concern for the lack of protection for the architectural monuments of tsarist Russia, a glorification of the virtues of the Russian peasantry as portrayed by the village prose writers, and an extremely anti-Western, anti-intellectual, anti-urban, and anti-Semitic orientation. On the question of Stalinism, the views of *Molodaya gvardiya*'s contributors varied from complete indifference to fervent reverence.

The neo-Stalinist party officials initiating the inclusion of *Molodaya gvardiya*'s writers did so as part of Brezhnev's effort to justify significant increase in defense spending and, more significantly, as a part of their own effort to achieve the official rehabilitation of Stalin and his legacy.[11] They needed intellectuals who could present to young Russians their own model of Stalinism as an attractive political, economic, social, and cultural alternative to Khrushchev's reformism, a task the orthodox communist contributors to *Oktyabr* were incapable of achieving. At the same time, they could discredit and isolate the reformist cause and its most important intellectual base, the journal *Novy mir*. Thus, the neo-Stalinist members of the party ideological apparatus shared with Brezhnev the belief that the inclusion of Russian nationalist intellectuals was necessary in order to win wider public support for their programs and to undermine those of the reformers. As did Brezhnev, these officials hoped to use Russian nationalism as an effective mobilizational tool.

The December 1965 plenum of the Komsomol Central Committee was important to the development of inclusionary politics. During the plenum, the neo-Stalinist Komsomol leadership finally concluded that a new Soviet ideology must emphasize nationalism and militarism rather than Marxism-Leninism. Led by Komsomol First Secretary Sergei Pavlov, speakers viciously attacked the "unpatriotic nature" of the articles appearing in the youth-oriented thick journal, *Yunost,* especially the works of liberal-reformist writers like Evtushenko, Gladilin, and Pristavkin. Yury Verchenko, director of the Molodaya gvardiya publishing house, went even further and openly accused literary works that raised the subject of Stalin's concentration camps and the fate of Soviet prisoners of war of undermining national morale. Verchenko echoed the views of the rest of the participants when he condemned the "universal humanism" of liberal-reformers and demanded intensified patriotic and paramilitary education, which would teach Soviet youth to love Russia and hate its enemies.[12]

The plenum's resolution very clearly indicated a strong desire to turn back the reforms of the Khrushchev era and transform the Soviet Union into a state that combined late-Stalin-era xenophobic Russian nationalism with an extreme militarization of society. The resolution accused the West and its media of attempting to undermine the morale of Soviet youth by preaching the "ideas of pacifism, abstract humanism, . . . (and) peaceful coexistence in the realm of ideology." It explicitly used language of the late-Stalin era to condemn "kowtowing [nizkopoklonstvo] before bourgeois culture" and accused liberal-reformist writers and movie directors of being antipatriotic for "belittling the great feats of our nation (and) refusing to glorify (our) heroic reality." Finally, the resolution called for a strengthening of nationalist sentiments among Soviet youth by using all available means of "ideological and emotional influence," intensifying a "patriotic education" and paramilitary training of youth, and strengthening the cooperation between local Komsomol organizations and the Soviet military.[13]

In October 1966, at a large conference attended by high party and government officials in charge of culture and ideology, the secretaries of the unions of the creative intelligentsia, heads of publishing houses, and editors of the literary journals (excluding Novy mir), neo-Stalinist party officials reiterated their demand for an intensification of the military education of youth as a way of strengthening nationalist sentiments. At the same time, however, they acknowledged that the de-Stalinization drive had created complex social realities that required new, more sophisticated forms of political mobilization—an implicit justification of inclusionary politics. This acknowledgment was best articulated in the remarks of Vladimir Stepakov, who in May 1966 had been appointed head of the Propaganda Department of the Central Committee and was a former editor of the newspaper Izvestiya.

According to an account of the conference in Roy Medvedev's Political Diary, Stepakov accused the liberal-reformist intelligentsia of being antipatriotic since it engaged in the "deglorification" (degeroizatsia) of Soviet history through its criticism of the Stalin era. In a vein similar to the resolution of the December 1965 plenum of the Komsomol, Stepakov complained that Soviet youth was "infected with skepticism and has shown instability in the face of Western propaganda" and called for an increase in "military patriotic propaganda." Yet he also acknowledged that party propaganda in the mass media was outdated and ineffective. In order to transform party propaganda into an effective mobilizational tool, it had to be based on a thorough knowledge of the complexity of Soviet society. His statement was an indirect admission of the need to adopt a program that would include Russian nationalist intellectuals because they constituted that part of the social complex that could be manipulated to aid the party in achieving its goals.[14]

Another speaker at the conference was Vasily Shauro, who was appointed the head of the Cultural Department of the Central Committee in November 1965.[15] Shauro, who had previously served as secretary for ideology of the Central Committee of the Belorussian Communist Party, was joined in May 1966 by Yury Melentiev, a former Komsomol functionary who was appointed Shauro's first deputy. In their official capacity as overseers of Soviet cultural life, Shauro and Melentiev fleshed out and implemented the policy of inclusion. They were, however, more than simply executioners of policy developed by Brezhnev; in particular, they promoted the inclusion of radical nationalist intellectuals associated with *Molodaya gvardiya.*

In order to implement their inclusionary program, Shauro and Melentiev had to secure strong support from the Propaganda Department of the Central Committee, which also had a significant role in the supervision of cultural life.[16] Stepakov, the head of the Propaganda Department, occupied a higher position than Shauro in the party hierarchy; Stepakov was a full member of the Central Committee, while Shauro was only a candidate. According to *Political Diary,* however, the Propaganda Department was very critical of *Molodaya gvardiya*'s editorial policy and made a serious effort to place the issue on the Politburo's agenda.[17] Apparently a split of opinion in the Propaganda Department between Stepakov, who supported *Molodaya gvardiya,* and his first deputy, Aleksandr Yakovlev, who opposed it, allowed the heads of the Cultural Department to defend the editorial line of *Molodaya gvardiya* between 1966 and 1970.

Stepakov, Shauro, and Melentiev were able to convince Mikhail Suslov, the Politburo member and senior party secretary in charge of ideology, of the necessity of cultivating *Molodaya gvardiya*'s intellectuals. Suslov, in turn, convinced Brezhnev to accept the policies of his subordinates. Brezhnev probably agreed because he was building his personal authority and did not want a confrontation with other powerful forces within the party apparatus. He may also have believed that the radical nationalist variant of inclusion would ultimately support his own policy goals. After all, the *Molodaya gvardiya* intellectuals could influence village prose writers, Brezhnev's own target for inclusion, and thus break the reformist alliance around *Novy mir.*

The policy of inclusionary politics began in early 1966. The timing of the introduction of the program was probably in response to the strong reaction on the part of the liberal-reformist intelligentsia to the regime's campaign to rehabilitate Stalin and to the arrest and trial of Andrei Sinyavsky and Yuly Daniel. Sinyavsky and Daniel were arrested in mid-September 1965 and tried in February 1966 for writing works critical of the Soviet regime and publishing them in the West. Both men were contributors to *Novy mir,* and Sinyavsky was one of the leading participants in the journal's anti-Stalinist campaign. The December 1964 issue of *Novy mir* contained one of Sinyavsky's last essays for the journal, a devastating review of Ivan Shevtsov's rabidly anti-intellectual, Stalinist novel, *The Louse (Tlya).*[18]

The arrest and public trial of the writers was probably masterminded by conservative forces in the party apparatus and the KGB in order to discredit the liberal-reformist intelligentsia as anti-Soviet and thus prepare the ground for *Novy mir*'s suppression.[19] The trial was also a major signal by the political leadership to liberal-reformist members of the intellectual elite that the de-Stalinization drive was over and that they would no longer be allowed to speak out and shape public opinion in favor of continuing de-Stalinization. Shortly after the trial, an additional step was taken to prepare for *Novy mir*'s suppression. The journal was harshly attacked at the Twenty-third Party Congress (March 29–April 8, 1966), and its chief editor, Tvardovsky, was not reelected as a candidate member of the Central Committee. The expulsion of Tvardovsky from the Central Committee limited his ability to protect the autonomy of the journal and to resist growing pressure from the conservative forces in the political and cultural establishments.

The political leadership, however, miscalculated when it thought that the liberal-reformist intelligentsia would surrender without a struggle the position it had acquired during the Khrushchev era. In the absence of the terror, it could not be intimidated into quiet acquiescence, particularly in

the light of what its editors perceived as the dangerous threat of the rehabilitation of Stalinism. On December 5, 1966, two hundred people gathered in Pushkin Square in Moscow to protest the upcoming trial of Sinyavsky and Daniel, an event that marked the beginning of the dissident
movement. On the eve of the Twenty-third Party Congress, twenty-five
leading Soviet intellectuals, from all realms of letters, arts, and sciences,
sent a collective letter to Brezhnev demanding that he not abandon the
anti-Stalinist resolutions of the Twentieth and Twenty-second Party Congresses.[20]

This letter was followed by scores of similar letters and petitions published in samizdat. In the less than two years since Khrushchev's overthrow,
samizdat had rapidly grown from being on the periphery of Soviet cultural
life to a major means of circulating uncensored material. In *Novy mir*,
Tvardovsky defiantly continued to publish anti-Stalinist works of fiction
and nonfiction, as well as works critical of contemporary Soviet life. Thus,
by mid-1966, Soviet leaders found themselves facing open opposition to
their policies from the liberal-reformist intelligentsia. Since there was a
strong consensus within the leadership to abandon terror as a means of
social control, the chosen response combined the persecution of the most
active dissidents, the tightening of censorship on the publication of anti-
Stalinist material, and a deliberate loosening of censorship on the issues of
primary concern to Russian nationalist intellectuals. This reduction in the
effective censorship of the Russian nationalists was one of the main manifestations of inclusionary politics from 1965 to 1970.

The fact that inclusionary politics peaked in 1968 and 1969 was by no
means coincidental. The year 1968 marked the rise and suppression of
reform communism in Czechoslovakia, and in 1969, the growing tension
in Soviet-Chinese relations led to military clashes on the common border.
These events, and the concurrent rise of the dissident movement, appear to
have been exploited by Stepakov and Shauro to argue to Suslov and Brezhnev for the immediate strengthening of nationalist sentiments among ethnic Russians. They apparently convinced the two senior Politburo members that a more broadly applied inclusionary politics was appropriate.

As a result, the institutional base for Russian nationalists within Soviet
culture was significantly expanded, and they were allowed to publish virtually unfettered. A number of conservative members of the cultural establishment, many with strong personal ties to village prose writers and literary critics of *Molodaya gvardiya*, were appointed the chief editors of several

important literary journals—an effort aimed at co-opting both village prose writers and *Molodaya gvardiya* critics while ensuring their wide access to Soviet literary publications. The first manifestation of this change appeared in 1966 when the Saratov literary monthly, *Volga,* headed by the novelist Nikolai Shundik, began to appear. Starting in 1967, *Volga* regularly published important contributions to the ongoing political debate by a number of literary critics closely associated with *Molodaya gvardiya.*[21]

In 1968, two important appointments were made: novelist Mikhail Alekseev was appointed as chief editor of the literary journal *Moskva,* and the poet Sergei Vikulov became chief editor of another Moscow literary monthly, *Nash sovremennik.* Alekseev immediately brought to *Moskva* such village prose writers and poets as Fyodor Abramov, Olga Fokina, Sergei Krutilin, Vladimir Soloukhin, Nikolai Tryapkin, Vladimir Tendrykov, Aleksandr Yashin, and Sergei Zalygin, in addition to such *Molodaya gvardiya*–based writers and literary critics as Aleksandr Baigushev, Pavel Glinkin, and Anatoly Lanshchikov.[22]

Vikulov's appointment would turn out to be of far greater political importance than that of Alekseev. Within two years of his appointment, Vikvlov had turned *Nash sovremennik* into the leading institutional base of Russian nationalist politics. A native of the Russian Northeast, Vikulov had strong personal ties with many *Novy mir*–affiliated village prose writers from the area. At the same time, as the former deputy editor of *Molodaya gvardiya,* he was in close contact with the leading writers of that journal. In August 1968, he took over *Nash sovremennik* and completely revamped its editorial board; out of twelve members of the old board, he retained only two, and thirteen new members were added, including Viktor Astafiev and Evgeny Nosov, two leading conservative village prose writers publishing in *Novy mir.*[23] More important, Vikulov appointed Viktor Chalmaev, a prominent contributor to *Molodaya gvardiya* and a central figure in the ongoing political controversy, as the deputy chief editor of the journal.

Immediately after his appointment, Vikulov began to use *Nash sovremennik* to build an ideological bridge between the village prose writers and the *Molodaya gvardiya* literary critics. From Vikulov's point of view, which coincided with those of the architects of inclusionary politics in the Central Committee Secretariat, uniting all Russian nationalist intellectuals in one major journal would strengthen the antireformist elements of the village prose writers and precipitate their departure from the *Novy mir*–based coalition of reformist intelligentsia. With the rapidly growing popularity of village prose, this departure could effectively undermine the reformers' ability to shape public opinion without forcing the regime to suppress *Novy mir, Yunost,* or other publications associated with the reformers.

The goal of creating an alliance of the various factions of the Russian nationalist intelligentsia was reflected not only in the composition of *Nash sovremennik*'s editorial board, but especially in its publication policies from 1968 to 1970. The journal opened its pages to village prose writers—to those already associated with *Novy mir* (Astafiev, Belov, Likhonosov, Nosov, Tkachenko) and to those who were not (Fokina, Frolov, Rasputin, Rubtsov). In fact, during this period it published more village prose authors than any other journal, including *Novy mir*.[24] The prose and poetry sections of the journal published liberal and conservative village prose authors, and other sections of the journal published essays by such prominent poets, literary critics, and historians, all closely associated with *Molodaya gvardiya,* as Chalmaev, Lobanov, Mikhailov, Kunyaev, and Semanov.[25]

Vikulov's strategy clearly had the approval of the Cultural Department of the Central Committee, which supervised the journals. This approval was manifest in the rapid increase in circulation—from 60,000 copies in October 1968, the last issue of the pre-Vikulov era, to 145,000 copies in May 1969.[26]

Up to the end of the Brezhnev era, the party's ideological establishment would continue to support the efforts of *Nash Sovremennik*'s editors to make the journal one of the main vehicles of the politics of inclusion. As long as inclusion was pursued, the circulation of the journal would continue to rise. But each time the party leadership felt that Russian nationalists violated the terms of political behavior prescribed by the politics of inclusion, the circulation of *Nash Sovremennik* would be sharply curtailed in retaliation.

The Campaign for Preserving Historic Monuments

The first public attempt to raise the issue of preservation of historic monuments in the Soviet political debate of the post-Stalin era took place in March 1962 with the publication in the thick journal *Moskva* of an article by a group of Russian intellectuals protesting the ongoing destruction of historic buildings in the city of Moscow. Reflecting Khrushchev's strongly negative attitude toward the preservation cause, the attempt was nipped in the bud when, on May 10 and May 11, 1962, *Pravda* published harshly worded criticisms of the *Moskva* essay.[27]

The 1962 debacle did not weaken the desire to turn the issue of preservation of historic monuments into a legitimate issue of public concern and a rightful cause to champion. In fact, two years after the publication of *Pravda*'s rebuttal, the preservation cause had acquired organized grass-roots support. In May 1964, six months before Khrushchev's downfall, the Rodina (Motherland) Club was founded in Moscow at the initiative of local students "to promote the study of historic monuments, to study ancient art and history . . . (and to) organize exhibitions and lectures in rural areas and at working clubs."[28] Rodina also collected contributions to undertake the restoration of ancient churches. At the end of 1965, apparently the high point of its activity, Rodina had approximately five hundred members. The first organization of its kind, Rodina was entirely an initiative from below. Its independence from the party and Komsomol meant that it would never be allowed to develop into a mass organization. Rodina disappeared from the Russian political arena in the early 1970s.

Despite its small size, Rodina was highly visible, endorsed by such well-known members of the Soviet cultural establishment as the painter Pavel Korin, the sculptor Sergei Konnenkov, the writer Leonid Leonov, and the aircraft designer Oleg Antonov. More important, support for its activities was expressed at the December 1965 plenum of the Komsomol Central Committee. The journalist Vasily Peskov, one of the plenum's speakers, not only condemned the destruction of churches but openly called on Komsomol to encourage its members to participate in Rodina's activities.[29]

The public pressure to create an official organization in charge of the preservation of historic monuments greatly increased with the publication of a letter signed by Konnenkov, Korin, and Leonov, in the May 1965 issue of *Molodaya gvardiya*. Entitled "Preserve Our Sacred Place!" *(Beregite svyatynuy nashy!)*, the letter harshly condemned the ongoing demolition of churches throughout Russia, and especially in Moscow.

The authors emphasized the political significance of preserving ancient Russian churches, which were not the "opium of the people" but the "foundation stones around which national consciousness is built." The churches were viewed as the most important element in the formation of the Russian patriotism that had played such a crucial role in the defeat of Nazi Germany.[30]

It was not accidental that the letter was published at the same time the Soviet Union was celebrating the twentieth anniversary of its victory over Nazi Germany. Konnenkov, Korin, and Leonov used the occasion to remind Soviet leaders that at a historic time of great political and national trial, Russian nationalism proved to be the ultimate source of regime support. The ongoing demolition of churches, they warned implicitly, weakens the nationalist sentiments and thus undermined the strength of the Soviet state.

In July 1965, two months after the publication of the "Letter of the Three," as the document became known, the RSFSR Council of Ministers officially announced its intention to convene an organizing committee entrusted with preparing for the formation of the All-Russian Society for the Preservation of Historic and Cultural Monuments (*Vserossiiskoe Obshchestvo Okhrany Pamyatnikov Istorii i Kultury*—VOOPIK]. The creation of VOOPIK was the culmination of mounting pressure by Russian nationalist intellectuals for action on the issue of historic preservation and a clear reversal of Khrushchev's policies in this area. At the same time, the creation of the society suggests that conservatives in the party apparat had finally succeeded in convincing Brezhnev and Suslov to sanction inclusionary politics. Thus, making the preservation issue a legitimate cause to champion, the establishment of VOOPIK constituted an important element in the strategy of the conservative forces in the party elite to transform the Russian nationalist intelligentsia into an articulated audience serving the regime's goals without acquiring an autonomous institutional base or effectively influencing the policy process.

That the party's intention was to make VOOPIK a mass, largely powerless, bureaucratic organization controlled by party officials became clear during the preparation for the society's first congress. On October 30, 1965, *Literaturnaya gazeta* published a letter signed by a large group of Russian intellectuals, including prominent Russian nationalists such as Efim Dorosh, Sergei Konnekov, Pavel Korin, Vladimir Soloukhin, Oleg Volkov, and Aleksandr Yashin, expressing their outrage that people selected to represent the city of Moscow on VOOPIK's organizing committee were almost entirely senior officials of various bureaucratic agencies rather than members of the intelligentsia who fought for the formation of the society. The society, staffed by bureaucrats, warned the authors of the letter, would not be an effective champion of the preservationist cause.[31]

In June 1966, at VOOPIK's first congress, Vyacheslav Kochemasov, a deputy chairman of the RSFSR Council of Ministers, was elected chairman, a clear signal that the party was determined to retain firm control of the society. In addition, VOOPIK was not allowed to have a regular publication of its own, a fact that angered many nationalist rank-and-file members.[32]

That VOOPIK never fulfilled Russian nationalist expectations is not surprising. Despite its huge and constantly growing membership (7 million by 1972, 12 million by 1977, and 15 million by 1985), it did not provide Russian nationalists with an institutional framework for influencing policy on key issues, including the preservation of monuments. Nevertheless, the founding of VOOPIK was of great significance to Soviet politics in the late 1960s and beyond. It created a public forum for discussing a whole range of policies and practices related to the preservation of historic monuments, which led to the legitimation of a variety of Russian nationalist issues that could not otherwise be discussed.

The Rise of Molodaya gvardiya–based Radical Nationalism

Molodaya gvardiya played a key role in the evolution of Russian nationalism in the second half of the 1960s. An undistinguished literary journal until the mid-1960s, it was transformed by chief editor Anatoly Nikonov. He brought to its editorial board such leading Russian nationalist intellectuals as Vladimir Soloukhin, Vladimir Chivilikhin, Mikhail Lobanov, Sergei Vysotsky, Valery Ganichev, and Sergei Vikulov.

In the aftermath of the publication of the "Letter of the Three," Nikonov and his colleagues transformed *Molodaya gvardiya* into an aggressive Russian nationalist journal that used preservationism to promote a variety of Russian nationalist causes. Encouraged by an avalanche of readers' letters expressing solidarity with Konnenkov, Korin, and Leonov, *Molodaya gvardiya* started a new column, bearing the title of their letter, in its July 1965 issue. The writers of the "Preserve Our Sacred Place" column used it to link the subject of the preservation of historic monuments to a key Russian nationalist cause, the rehabilitation of the Russian Orthodox Church.[33] In addition, they criticized a variety of issues ranging from Soviet urban planning to avant-garde art. The essays of Vladislav Shoshin and Dmitry Balashov are excellent examples in this respect.

Alongside descriptions of demolished or neglected ancient churches in the Russian Northeast and a call to protect Russian religious art and architecture, Shoshin's essay contained an open apology to the Russian Orthodox Church. Its historical record, he argued, defied the accusations of antireligious writers who accused it of being the "opium of the people." Shoshin viewed the Orthodox Church as an important national institution that played a significant role in the defense of the Russian state and the colonization of its northern territories.[34]

While Shoshin emphasized the contributions of the Orthodox Church to the state-building process, Balashev stressed the Orthodox Church's cultural and spiritual role in Russian history. Demolition of churches, he claimed, was tantamount to the destruction of Russian national culture because the Orthodox Church perpetuated centuries-old Russian national traditions.[35] He also linked the preservation issue to contemporary urban planning and development. Russian national traditions were destroyed in addition by the construction of high-rise buildings and other modern structures near the remaining churches. What made the situation particularly deplorable, he charged, was that modern Soviet architecture blindly imitated Western models, thus ignoring Russian architectural traditions, national lifestyle, and even climatic conditions. Balashev's criticism of Soviet urban planning extended to the size of cities. He postulates that the optimal size of a city should not exceed half a million inhabitants, and he criticized Soviet urban planners for creating giant metropolises.[36]

In 1965 and 1966, *Molodaya gvardiya* promoted Russian nationalist ideas in two other featured series—serialized essays by the painter Iliya Glazunov and the writer Vladimir Soloukhin.

Glazunov's essays, entitled *The Path to You (Doroga k tebe)*, had a tremendous impact because they effectively merged most of the issues on the Russian nationalist agenda: the preservation of monuments, the rehabilitation of the Orthodox Church, a glorification of prerevolutionary Russia and a condemnation of the October Revolution, a rejection of Western political and cultural models, and an attack on the liberal-reformist intelligentsia that admired these models.[37]

Published in the September and October 1966 issues of *Molodaya gvardiya*, Soloukhin's *Letters from the Russian Museum (Pisma iz Russkogo muzeya)* developed many of Glazunov's ideas and as a result had an even stronger resonance among the Russian nationalist intelligentsia.[38] Like *The Path to You*, *Letters* used the issue of historic preservation to promote a wide variety of Russian nationalist concerns. Soloukin strongly denounced the destruction of Moscow churches in the 1930s. He focused on the 1931 demolition of the Church of Christ the Savior, the city's largest church, and the subsequent use of its site as an outdoor swimming pool. Built to commemorate the Russian victory in the War of 1812 and decorated by famous Russian painters of the time, this church was the major symbol of the Orthodox Church's ability to rally mass support and inspire the Russian people at critical points in history. Soloukhin reminded readers of this fact and warned, in a fashion similar to the "Letter of the Three," that the suppression of religion and the demolition of churches had weakened the power of the Russian patriotic appeal and thus significantly undermined the commitment of Russians to defend their country.[39]

Like Balashev, Soloukhin invoked the preservation issue to attack contemporary Soviet architecture in general and Moscow city planning in particular. He charged that Moscow had been criminally destroyed. The ugly, stereotypical Western city that had been created in its place was due not only to the demolition of churches, but also to the eagerness of contemporary Soviet architects to built Western-style steel and glass high rises in the heart of the old city.

Soloukhin's work was a landmark in the evolution of the preservationist movement because it significantly extended the notion of preservationism. The preservation of ancient churches was merely one component of what might be called Soloukhin's campaign for the preservation of Russian national memory. This campaign was aimed at Russian national traditions and Russian national art and culture, and advancing a new Russian nationalist interpretation of Russian history. His preservationist argument was accompanied by a highly idealized description of prerevolutionary Russia, a condemnation of the radical tradition of the Russian intelligentsia, and an appeal to restore old, prerevolutionary names to all renamed Russian cities.[40]

By the end of 1966, *Molodaya gvardiya*'s editors began to move beyond the mere preservation of Russian national art and culture, now promoting a view of Russian history and Russian national culture that sharply contradicted the official version. The essence of Russian history was no longer the class struggle but an unending struggle of the Russian people as a whole, led by the tsars and the princes of the Orthodox Church, against foreign domination. The official Leninist theory of two cultures, proletarian and bourgeois, as two distinct components of every national culture, was rejected.[41] What was advanced instead became known as the "single stream" *(ediny potok)* theory of Russian culture: that there is one Russian national culture, and therefore one Russian national tradition, in which the spiritual values of the Orthodox Church and the sociopolitical ideals of prerevolutionary Russian nationalist writers and thinkers play a prominent role.

Essays written by such eminent literary critics and historians as Viktor Chalmaev, Pavel Glinkin, Leonid Ershov, Yury Ivanov, Vadim Kozhinov, Anatoly Lanshchikov, Mikhail Lobanov, Oleg Mikhailov, Pyotr Palievsky, Sergei Semanov, Vladimir Semenov, and Dmitry Zhukov presented a new type of Russian nationalist ideology, which can be called "radical nationalism." The ideological worldview of this group of intellectuals can be linked to their social origins. Contrary to the village prose writers, most of the *Molodaya gvardiya*'s contributors were born into intelligentsia families in major Russian cities and graduated from either the School of Journalism or the Faculty of Slavic Languages and Literatures at Moscow University during the mid- to late 1950s. In the early 1960s, most belonged to circles of the Moscow reform-oriented intelligentsia, and some even regularly contributed to *Novy mir*.[42]

Disappointed by Khrushchev and the reform communism he represented, they began to search for an ideological alternative. By the mid-1960s, they discovered the Russian peasantry, the Russian Orthodox Church, and anti-Western and antiliberal Russian nationalism through reading the emerging village prose and prerevolutionary Russian nationalist and religious thinkers. This discovery led them to break from the Western-oriented intelligentsia and present their evolving ideas as an ideological alternative to both orthodox communism and Western-oriented liberalism and reform communism.

The core of their radical nationalist ideology was the argument that Russia has a long tradition of a strong authoritarian state with an anti-Western orientation and that this tradition must be revived.[43] This argument went hand in hand with an elaboration of Russian national identity, characterized in part by a strong anti-Western and anti-intellectual dimension. Radical nationalists proclaimed the traditional Russian peasantry and its norms and values, which they idealized and often simply invented, as embodying Russian national identity. Glinkin presented the traditional peasantry as the guardian of moral virtues and national sociopolitical traditions and juxtaposed it to the urban liberal-reformist intelligentsia. The most extreme form of this juxtaposition appeared in his essay appropriately titled "The Land and the Asphalt" *(Zemlya i asfalt).* Here the peasants—"the Land"—were portrayed as guardians of the spiritual values of the nation. The urban liberal-reformist intelligentsia—"the Asphalt"—articulated Western individualistic and existentialist ideas, which he called alien to Russian national traditions and thus "infertile."[44]

Glinkin's arguments were developed by and acquired programmatic status in work by Lobanov and Chalmaev. In a series of essays published in *Molodaya gvardiya* between 1965 and 1968, Lobanov spelled out the primary ideological principles of radical Russian nationalism.[45] In the first four essays, he declared that the "spiritual renaissance" of the nation was of greater importance than economic efficiency. He asserted that Russian social and political structures should be original *(samobytnye)*, reflecting the uniqueness of Russian culture and traditions, and not imitating Western bourgeois democracy. In addition, he insisted that the preservation of the traditional peasantry was crucial for Russian national survival.

Lobanov harshly attacked the liberal-reformist intelligentsia for its efforts to spread Western sociopolitical and cultural ideas in Russia. His fifth essay, "Educated Philistines" *(Prosveshchennoe meshchanstvo)*, combined a forceful and explicit argument against Western-oriented political and economic reform with an assertion of the inevitability of a military-ideological confrontation with the West. Finally, it outlined the course of action he saw as necessary to reconstitute the Soviet Union as a vigorous, authoritarian Russian state.[46]

Central to the essay was Lobanov's reassertion of the primacy of Russia's "spiritual revival" over reforms that promised a more Western political system and a higher standard of living—two objectives he viewed as irreconcilable. In fact, he called Western-oriented radical political and economic reforms dangerous to Russia because "there is no greater enemy to the nation than the temptation of bourgeois well-being. It means the paralysis of the nation's creative genius" brought about by "the Americanization of the spirit." This would mean domination by the political and cultural values of a modern Western consumer society and the disappearance of Russia as a unique spiritual, cultural, and political entity.

Lobanov rejected modern capitalist, industrial society because it brought about a total economic, political, and cultural integration devoid of national differences. He compared such a society to a Babylon-like international train station, which by its nature is very cosmopolitan. "Sooner or later," he asserted, "a deadly confrontation will take place between these two irreconcilable forces, the moral distinctiveness (of Russia) and the Americanization of the spirit." Lobanov's "deadly confrontation" meant more than an apocalyptic vision of the military-ideological clash between the Soviet Union and the United States; first and foremost was a domestic confrontation between forces promoting Western-oriented political and economic reform, who "like, the bark-beetle, . . . eats away at the healthy body of the nation," and the Russian nationalist forces fighting for Russia's spiritual revival.[47]

Identical ideas were articulated by Viktor Chalmaev in three essays published in *Molodaya gvardiya* in 1967 and 1968. In the first, "Philosophy of Patriotism" *(Filosofiya patriotizma)*, he harshly attacked modern Western industrial society for its philistinism and consumerism and its philosophical principles of rationalism and individualism. Modern bourgeois society, he asserted in language almost identical to that of Lobanov, caused: "the standardization of lifestyles, rampant consumerism, . . . (and) the dissipation of religious, communal, and family ties . . . which, in turn, leads to the disappearance of the patriotic spirit and a transformation of the concept of 'Motherland' into an abstract, vague and useless idea."

Consumer society, Chalmaev continued, created "well-to-do philistines," merely the "patriots of their cars and refrigerators."[48] He identified the alternative to bourgeois democracy and consumer society as a powerful authoritarian nationalist state that would foster Russian spiritual values and national culture, protect the environment, and preserve ancient churches and other historic monuments.[49]

"The Great Strivings" *(Velikie iskaniya)*, Chalmaev's second major essay, elaborated on the radical nationalist rejection of the Western model as an ideal that all societies should strive to achieve. The West, in his view, was "suffocating from callousness, from a surplus of hatred, from the rationalism of the philistines, from the cult of the crowd, (and) from the terror of immoral public opinion created by the mercenary press."[50]

Finally, Chalmaev reminded the reformist intelligentsia that the Revolution of 1917 was an expression of "the universal Russian rejection of capitalism and a national protest against the imposition of capitalist 'prosperity' on the Russian homeland."[51] In other words, the hatred of a Western socioeconomic and political system was so deeply seated in the Russian soul that any attempt to reintroduce this order through radical reform would encounter strong national resistance.

Published a few weeks after the Soviet invasion of Czechoslovakia, "Inevitability" *(Neizbezhnost)*, Chalmaev's third and most important essay, synthesized the main ideas of his early essays and incorporated the ideas of other leading radical nationalists. He structured the essay around the question of why the party should adopt the Russian nationalist ideology. He began with the argument that the transformation of the Soviet Union into a Western-type consumer society would have neither legitimacy nor the support of the Russian people. Russians would not sacrifice their lives so that the motherland could become the "society of satiety" and the "kingdom of pleasures." What Russia needed was an ideology that would inspire and unify the nation and prepare it for the inevitable confrontation with the bourgeois-democratic West. He pointed out that "once in every hundred years, the Russian nation faces the Poltava battle or the Stalingrad confrontation."[52]

Chalmaev presented Russian nationalist ideology as the most potent weapon to combat "Americanism"—the spread of Western, especially American, political, economic, and cultural ideas in Russian society. "Americanism" constituted the most immediate danger to the Soviet state because it would lead to the destruction of the historically unique spiritual essence of Russian civilization—the "civilization of the soul" in his words—and the imposition of the Western values of crude materialism, brute force, and immorality.[53]

In order to preserve Russia's "civilization of the soul," nationalist ideology must teach all Russians about their centuries-old national heritage and the great contributions to Russian history made by the Moscow grand princes, Russian tsars, and the Orthodox Church. The Orthodox Church would take up its historic role as the spiritual guide of the nation. By drawing analogies from Russian history, Russian nationalist ideology would educate people to see that a strong, authoritarian regime was the most conducive to a flourishing of national culture.[54]

Finally, by adopting Russian nationalist ideology as its philosophical base, the party would recognize the Russian peasantry, rather than the urban working class or the intelligentsia, as the guardian of national traditions and moral values, and the social foundation of the nation. Thus, the party would commit itself to revitalizing the traditional Russian peasantry by resettling abandoned villages and encouraging the spread of conservative peasant moral values throughout society. The revitalization of the traditional peasantry was the key to Russia's survival because the peasantry had defended the state in the past and would defend it in the future.[55]

The Two Faces of Village Prose Nationalism

Radical nationalist exaltation of the virtues of the traditional Russian peasantry was a direct consequence of the growing influence of village prose ideas. By the mid-1960s, village prose was quickly becoming the most influential Soviet intellectual movement. Scores of village prose works appeared in *Novy mir* and in such provincial Russian journals as *Sever* and *Sibirskie ogni* and attracted wide public attention. By the late 1960s, *Nash sovremennik* and *Moskva* had become major forums for "village prose ideas. In 1968, the party acknowledged the importance of village prose by awarding novelist Sergei Zalygin, one of most prominent village prose writers, the USSR State Prize for literature.

In the years 1965 to 1970, village prose writers continued to explore the historical, political, and sociological dimensions of the peasant existence. The novels, stories, and essays portrayed the role of the peasantry in Russian history from the time of the Civil War to the post–World War II years, depicted the Stalinist legacy in the countryside, and analyzed the social and psychological trends prevalent among the contemporary Russian peasantry. In 1969, Zalygin summed up the nature of the village prose mission:

> I feel that the roots of my nation are, indeed, in the village, in the ploughed field, in daily bread. Furthermore, it seems that our generation will have been the last to see with its own eyes the one-thousand-year-old (peasant) way of life, in which each of us grew up. If we do not tell about it and about its radical alteration in a short period of time [the collectivization], who will?[56]

Despite their common project, village prose writers continued to be ideologically divided into liberal and conservative wings, which in effect constituted the core of liberal and conservative wings of the Russian nationalist movement.[57] Abramov, Mozhaev, Tendryakov, Troepolsky and Zalygin, the leading representatives of the liberal trend between 1965 and 1970, emphasized the social, economic, and legal dimensions of peasant life through harsh critique of Stalinist agricultural policies and the legacy of these policies in the countryside.

Boris Mozhaev's novel, *From the Life of Ivan Kuzkin (Iz zhizni Ivana Kuzkina)*, better known as *Alive (Zhivoi)*, is a typical example of the liberal nationalist village prose argument. It follows the life of a simple peasant Fyodor Kuzkin, after his decision to leave the kolkhoz and stay on in the village as an independent peasant. He decides on this radical step because he sees that his income as a kolkhoz member is not sufficient to feed his wife and five children. This is an act of rebellion against the system of collectivized agriculture by a simple Russian peasant. It is also Mozhaev's literary device by which he portrays how powerful the Stalinist legacy in the countryside remained years after Stalin's death.[58]

The Stalinist bureaucracy is the target of Mozhaev's criticism. These bureaucrats perceive Kuzkin's decision to leave the kolkhoz as an attempt to undermine the system of collectivized agriculture, and they are determined to defend the system at all cost. Since they can no longer use the classic Stalinist methods of arrest and exile, they try to drive Kuzkin out of the village and into jail.

Kuzkin survives all attempts by the Stalinist bureaucrats to drive him away, and his resistance symbolizes the unbroken spirit of the Russian peasantry and its determination to be the master of its own fate. Although Mozhaev does not spell it out explicitly, the political message of the novel is clear: the revival of Russian agriculture will happen only when peasants are liberated from the iron grip of the Stalinist bureaucracy.[59]

Conservative nationalist village prose writers rejected the liberal village prose emphasis on the primacy of socioeconomic reforms in favor of an emphasis on the moral values of the traditional Russian peasantry and viewed the regeneration of these values as key to the regeneration of the Russian countryside, and thus the Russian nation as a whole. They blamed the disappearance of the peasantry not on party policies alone but also on the impact of modernization. In particular, they singled out the corruptive influences of such agents of modernity as Westernized cities.

Vasily Belov's novel, *An Ordinary Thing (Privychnoe delo)*, was the most important ideological statement of conservative village prose in this period. Set in the early 1960s in a northeastern Russian village, *An Ordinary Thing* describes events in the life of a simple middle-aged peasant, Ivan Afrikanovich Drynov. The novel does not ignore the socioeconomic dimensions of peasant life, and Belov sharply criticizes Khrushchev's agricultural policies, as well as the continuing legal and social inequality of Russian peasants.[60]

Through this novel, Belov emerged as a strong and vocal opponent of Khrushchev's campaign against private plot agriculture. He showed how peasants were denied the right to cut the kolkhoz grass in order to feed their private cows, the main source of their income. In *An Ordinary Thing*, Ivan Afrikanovich secretly cuts grass at night for the family cow, grass that the kolkhoz is not going to use anyway. When the authorities discover his "crime," he is threatened with prosecution unless he denounces all other kolkhoz members who do the same.

Belov also exposed the pervasiveness of legal and social discrimination against the peasantry. He argues that the peasants were paid so poorly for their work that they are unable to sustain their traditionally large families. In addition, they are treated as second-class citizens who are not even permitted to choose their own place of residence. Katerina, the wife of Ivan Afrikanovich, is forced to take on additional assignments at the kolkhoz's dairy farm in an effort to feed her nine children. Her health deteriorates as a result, and she dies. For the same reason, Ivan Afrikanovich attempts to leave the village for a better-paid job in the city. But since peasants do not have internal passports and are not free to leave the kolkhoz, he resorts to violence in order to convince the kolkhoz chairman to issue him a passport.

The prevailing socioeconomic conditions in the countryside are ultimately of secondary importance in *An Ordinary Thing*. The novel's main argument is that Russia's future is dependent on the revival of the habits, norms, and moral values of the traditional peasantry. Belov portrays Ivan Afrikanovich and Katerina, representatives of the traditional peasantry, as honest and hard working, with a strong sense of communal solidarity and as the custodians of the institution of the traditional Russian family. Their nine children are presented as an example of the ideal size for Russian families.

Traditional peasants tend not only to have large families but are also deeply rooted in the land and therefore not easily tempted to leave the village in search of an easier life in the city. In the novel, this virtue is illustrated through the juxtaposition of Ivan Afrikanovich and his brother-in-law, Dmitry, who leaves the village for the city. Ivan Afrikanovich is a traditional peasant whose commitment to the land binds him to the village in spite of the social injustices he must endure. It is highly symbolic that Dmitry's efforts to convince Ivan Afrikanovich to leave the village ultimately fail; after three days in the city, Ivan Afrikanovich returns home because he feels a strong emotional and spiritual bond to his native village.

If Ivan Afrikanovich is a symbolic representation of the traditional Russian peasantry, Dmitry represents the first-generation urbanite who rejected village traditions and values in favor of the greedy, materialistic, and morally corrupt lifestyle of the city. Money, women, and alcohol are the things Dmitry values most. He peppers his language with urban slang, demonstrates his sexual promiscuity by showing a prescription for a contraceptive as his identification card, and believes that "money buys everything," be it a woman for a night or a passport for Ivan Afrikanovich. Belov presents Dmitry as a perfect example of how city life corrupts the Russian peasant, and he argues that the traditional village is threatened not only by party policies in the countryside but also by the culture and values of Westernized cities.

As *The Ordinary Thing* clearly shows, both reformist critics of the official socioeconomic policies in the countryside and the radical nationalists who idealized the moral virtues of the traditional Russian peasantry could find in the message of the conservative village prose elements consistent with their ideological positions. For this reason, its message would become a major issue in political debates.

Political Debates of the Late 1960s

The debate on the issues raised by village prose writers and *Molodaya gvardiya*'s literary critics became the subject of public discourse in late November 1968, when *Literaturnaya gazeta* initiated a discussion entitled, "On Certain Tendencies of Contemporary Russian Prose" *(O nekotorykh tendentsiyakh sovremennoi russkoi prozy)*. The first contributor to the discussion, literary critic Viktor Kamyanov, harshly criticized the idealization of the traditional Russian peasantry by several village prose writers.[61]

In January 1968, Fyodor Levin attempted to present a balanced evaluation of the ideological message of both the village prose and *Molodaya gvardiya*'s contributors. He recognized their shared fundamental precept that the peasantry serves as the guardian of Russian national tradition. He also acknowledged the validity of Russian nationalist criticism of the lack of appreciation for Russian religious art and the government's failure to preserve Russian historic monuments and the environment. Levin, however, criticized *Molodaya gvardiya*'s contributors for their inadequate knowledge of prerevolutionary Russian national culture. He also cautioned them not to idealize the traditional peasantry, which was not only the bearer of national tradition but also the stronghold of superstition, submissiveness to authority, the subjugation of women, and a deep-seated social conservatism. Levin argued that the way of life and morality of the traditional Russian peasantry could hardly provide workable solutions to the political, cultural, and moral problems facing modern Soviet society.[62]

Two weeks after the appearance of Levin's essay, it was challenged by Vadim Kozhinov, one of *Molodaya gvardiya*'s leading radical nationalist thinkers. Analyzing Belov's *An Ordinary Thing*, the most debated village prose novel of the late 1960s, Kozhinov reasserted the radical nationalist vision of the traditional Russian peasantry. He presented it as the social group whose existence was most necessary for the continued vitality of the Russian nation. To support this argument, Kozhinov borrowed the nineteenth-century Slavophile concept that the way of life of traditional peasants caused them to exhibit a wholeness *(tselnost)* of being and consciousness, a unity of thought, action, and moral behavior, that no member of any other social stratum could attain. At a time when the intelligentsia was searching for the political ideals embodied in Russian culture, he concluded, it should look to traditional peasant values and way of life as a guide to the answer.[63]

Although Kozhinov did not fully elaborate his ideas, their meaning was clear to Vladimir Gusev, Alexander Yanov, and Vladimir Voronov, the liberal-reformist participants of the debate. The traditional Russian peasantry portrayed in *An Ordinary Thing*, existed more in Belov's imagination than in reality, argued Gusev. Agricultural reform was needed to stop the real Russian peasantry from fleeing its idealized being for a better life in the cities. Kozhinov's idealization of the traditional peasantry, he concluded, had more to do with *Molodaya gvardiya*'s efforts to present the liberal-reformist intelligentsia as elitist and alienated from the true representatives of the Russian nation, than with any genuine concern for the fate of the peasantry.[64]

Yanov defended the liberal-reformist intelligentsia and challenged Kozhinov's vision of Russian society. The driving forces of the modern era, he argued, were technology and science, which made the creative intelligentsia the most vital social force of the nation. An anti-intellectual crusade was an integral part of Kozhinov's apocalyptic vision, and its adoption as party policy would condemn Soviet society to backwardness, ignorance, and stagnation.[65]

Voronov's contribution to the *Literaturnaya gazeta* debate, as well as his essay in the February 1968 issue of *Yunost*, was also a defense of the liberal-reformist intelligentsia—its beliefs, values, and culture. Like Gusev, Voronov accused Kozhinov and other literary critics of *Molodaya gvardiya*, whom he called the "Slavophile epigones," of ignoring both the Stalinist legacy in the countryside and the essence of village prose's description of this legacy. The *Molodaya gvardiya* idealization of peasant virtues was an effort to discredit the liberal-reformist intelligentsia, and its campaign to protect historic monuments was a tool for advocating Great Russian chauvinism *(rusopyatsvo)* and promoting the discredited theory the messianic role of the Russian people.[66]

The *Literaturnaya gazeta* debate was only a prelude to the heated political discussion that followed the publication of the essays by Chalmaev and Lobanov in *Molodaya gvardiya,* analyzed in the preceding section of this chapter. These essays triggered critical responses by such liberal-reformist members of the intelligentsia as Vladimir Borshchugov and Vadim Kovsky.[67] At the same time, they were joined by the orthodox Stalinist literary critics Pyotr Strokov (the deputy editor of *Oktyabr*), Igor Motyashov, and Aleksandr Metchenko, as well as literary critics Yury Surovtsev and Fyodor Chapchakhov, leading members of the Soviet literary establishment, all of whom viewed these essays as a gross deviation from the official ideological canon. Chalmaev especially was criticized for his nationalist rather than class struggle approach to Russian history and for his effort to rehabilitate the legacy of Russian nationalist thinkers of the late nineteenth and early twentieth centuries.[68] These attacks provoked equally passionate defenses of Lobanov and Chalmaev by the *Molodaya gvardiya* editorial board and other radical nationalists.[69]

The debate on the Lobanov and Chalmaev essays and the questions they raised intensified with the January 7, 1969, Central Committee decree with the cumbersome title, "On the Increase of Responsibility of Heads of Institutions of Printed Media, Radio, Television, Cinema, and Institutions of Culture and Arts for the Ideological-Political Content of the Published Materials and Repertoire" *(O povyshenii otvetstvennosti rukovoditelei organov pechati, radio, televideniya, kinematografii, uchrezhdeny kultury i iskusstva za ideino-politichesky uroven publikuemykh materialov i repertuara).* The decree explicitly made heads of cultural institutions responsible for the ideological content of works their institutions published or produced. Thus the decree gave the party formal justification for the dismissal of the heads of the literary journals if the content of their publications did not reflect the party line—clearly a warning to *Novy mir* and *Molodaya gvardiya* to stop challenging party ideology and policies.[70]

The decree provided the opponents of *Molodaya gvardiya* with a new and powerful weapon. It was hardly a coincidence that only ten days after the decree, Lobanov's and Chalmaev's essays were discussed at a meeting of the Moscow party organization of the USSR Writers' Union. The literary critics Fyodor Levin and Vladimir Sutyrin denounced Chalmaev's "Inevitability" as anti-Marxist and anti-Leninist.[71] On April 25, 1969, critics and defenders of Lobanov and Chalmaev clashed over broad issues related to their articles at a USSR Writers' Union–sponsored meeting of the leading Soviet literary critics. The *Molodaya gvardiya*–affiliated radical nationalists Kozhinov and Lanshchikov reiterated the position of their colleagues. What the Russian nation needed now, Lanshchikov asserted, was a new national ideal. This ideal could not be the liberal-reformers' repeated criticism of Stalin's cult of personality.

Feliks Kuznetsov, speaking for the liberal-reformers, claimed that the Russian nationalist intellectuals affiliated with *Molodaya gvardiya* and *Nash sovremennik* were reviving Slavophile arguments in order to create an ideological alternative to both the liberal-reformist *Novy mir* and the Stalinist *Oktyabr*. This alternative, however, was politically wrong; the wheel of history could not be turned back. Russia's political, socioeconomic, and moral problems were the result of being not European enough and not socialist enough rather than the opposite. Moreover, the radical nationalists were not knowledgeable about how Russian peasants actually lived and distorted the political message of the village prose writers.[72]

In March and April 1969, *Novy mir*, until then silent on the issue, joined the debate with an essay by literary critic Igor Dedkov that defended the reformist credentials of village prose and criticized its reinterpretation by the radical nationalists of *Molodaya gvardiya*. He conceded the existence of elements of the idealization of village life in some works of the village prose writers. However, he added that Solzhenitsyn's *Matryona's House* and Belov's *An Ordinary Thing* followed the progressive tradition of prerevolutionary Russian literature in portraying the harsh realities of the village and the negative aspects of peasant life. These works had nothing in common with Chalmaev's, Lobanov's, and Glinkin's rhetoric on the messianic role of the Russian soul.[73]

Aleksandr Dementiev's essay, "On Traditions and Nationalism" (*O traditsiyakh i narodnosti*), published in the April 1969 issue of *Novy mir*, was an even harsher attack on *Molodaya gvardiya*. Dementiev, *Novy mir's* senior literary critic and its deputy chief editor until early 1967, adopted the arguments of both the nineteenth-century radical intelligentsia and Lenin against Russian nationalism in his criticism of Chalmaev's and Lobanov's works, and other works of poetry, prose, and literary criticism published in *Molodaya gvardiya*. The essay assailed the *Molodaya gvardiya* idealization of the reactionary dimensions of prerevolutionary Russian history and especially Chalmaev's glorification of Russian conservative thinkers, politicians, and the Orthodox Church leaders. Dementiev condemned the *Molodaya gvardiya* assertion of Russian national superiority over the West and emphasized that the differences between the two were not national but socioeconomic.

He portrayed attacks by Lobanov and other *Molodaya gvardiya* contributors on the liberal-reformist intelligentsia as an effort to impose the politics of cultural and political isolation on the country. He dismissed their warnings of the "Americanization" of Soviet culture and lifestyle and argued that the adoption of radical nationalist ideas as state policy constituted a much greater danger.

Dementiev reiterated the arguments of other liberal-reformist intellectuals in his criticism of *Molodaya gvardiya*'s idealization of the village. In sharp contrast to the village prose writers, he argued, contributors to *Molodaya gvardiya* did not care about rural socioeconomic realities. Their village was merely a symbol of national "roots" and "traditions," spiritual health and inspiration. Finally, Dementiev pointed out that *Molodaya gvardiya*'s call for a return to Russia's roots was often accompanied by demands for the political rehabilitation of Stalin and Stalinism.[74]

Dementiev's essay provided an opportunity for the conservative members of the Soviet literary establishment and the party apparat to come out openly in defense of *Molodaya gvardiya*'s nationalists and argue for the suppression of *Novy mir*. The July 26, 1969 issue of the popular weekly *Ogonyok* contained a letter entitled "Against What Is 'Novy mir' Protesting?" *(Protiv chego vystupaet 'Novy mir'?),* which was signed by eleven members of the Soviet literary establishment, including Alekseev, Vikulov, and Shundik, the chief editors of *Moskva, Nash sovremennik,* and *Volga,* respectively.

The "Letter of the Eleven," as the document became known, contained, along with harsh criticism of Dementiev's essay, the most explicit plea ever made to the Soviet leadership to continue the inclusionary politics toward the radical nationalists of *Molodaya gvardiya*. The authors asserted that the gravest danger facing the Soviet Union was the continuing penetration of Western ideological influences. The "Letter" argued that the essays by Lobanov and Chalmaev, as well as other Russian nationalist essays, poems, and novels published in *Molodaya gvardiya,* provided the most effective weapons for fighting the penetration of Western political ideas among Soviet youth.

While vigorously defending *Molodaya gvardiya*, the "Letter" accused the reformers, and *Novy mir* in particular, of preaching the politics of ideological coexistence. They especially singled out Dementiev's plea not to overestimate the danger of Western ideological influences as proof of *Novy mir*'s campaign to spread Western political ideas in Soviet society and reminded Soviet leaders that the spread of these influences in Czechoslovakia had forced them to resort to military intervention.[75]

Novy mir responded to the "Letter of the Eleven" in its July 1969 issue. In the editorial statement, *Novy mir*'s editors emphasized the journal's liberal nationalist credentials by presenting it as the main publisher of village prose. At the same time, they supported Dementiev's essay and repeated his argument that Soviet society was endangered most by the kind of Russian nationalist tendencies articulated in *Molodaya gvardiya*.[76]

In 1969, debate on the issues raised by the village prose and *Molodaya gvardiya* essays was not limited to a confrontation between *Novy mir* and the conservative members of the Soviet cultural establishment. In fact, from May 1969 on, the debate continued in *Literaturnaya gazeta*, the scholarly journal *Voprosy literatury*, and even in the party journal *Kommunist*. In May 1969, *Literaturnaya gazeta* initiated a new discussion, "On the National and International in Russian Literature" *(O natsionalnom i internatsionalnom v russkoi literature)*, that centered on a confrontation between a representative of the party apparat, who appeared under the pseudonym "V. Ivanov," and Vadim Kozhinov.

Ivanov's essay, which started the discussion, was the first open intervention by opponents of inclusionary politics within the party apparat in the year-long dispute.[77] Ivanov was clearly conveying an official view of both the arguments of the liberal-reformers and of the Russian nationalist participants in the debate. He reiterated the official theory of the existence of two antagonistic components, the bourgeois and the proletariat, in any national culture as part of his criticism of Chalmaev and other *Molodaya gvardiya* contributors. He declared the radical nationalist vision politically wrong, particularly Chalmaev's insistence that the peasantry's moral values were more important than its standard of living. Ivanov reminded Chalmaev that Lenin viewed a rise in the living standard of the masses as the top goal of socialism.

Accompanying his condemnation of Chalmaev, Ivanov deplored the works of several conservative village prose writers for their idealized portrayal of the traditional Russian peasantry. In describing the contemporary countryside, he asserted, they ignored the positive changes in the character of the Russian peasantry since collectivization. Ivanov did not criticize the works of such liberal village prose writers as Abramov, Mozhaev, or Tendryakov, which focused primarily on the Stalinist legacy in the countryside.

This conspicuously gentle treatment of the liberal village prose writers suggests more a desire to co-opt this particular group than to support the liberal-reformist intelligentsia in general. In fact, Ivanov harshly attacked the latter, especially their criticism of *Molodaya gvardiya*. He accused Vasily Aksyonov and Anatoly Gladilin, two leading liberal-reformist writers and frequent targets of *Molodaya gvardiya* attacks, of borrowing Western ideas of "nihilistic skepticism and cold egoism." Moreover, he censured the *Yunost* essay by Voronov for its negative depiction of Russian nationalism, especially for diminishing its importance by the use of the derogatory term "Great Russian chauvinism."

Ivanov's official status did not deter radical nationalists from responding to his attacks. They must have been aware of support for their ideas in the apparat of the Central Committee and of the enormous organizational effort that culminated in the publication of the "Letter of the Eleven." This probably explains the timing of Kozhinov's reply to Ivanov, published in *Literaturnaya gazeta* on July 23, 1969, just three days before the appearance of the "Letter" in *Ogonyok*.[78]

Kozhinov did not confront Ivanov directly, instead challenging the underlying Marxist-Leninist assumptions of his essay. World history, Kozhinov asserted, was not one of class struggle but of the rise and fall of national civilizations. In order for Russian civilization to play a major role in world history, the Russian nation must rediscover its national past, and its "sources" [*istoki*] and "roots" [*korni*] of strength, all embodied in its thousand-year-old national traditions.

In the *Literaturnaya gazeta* debate, Kozhinov touched on the traditions he wanted to revive; it was only in the debate over the Slavophile legacy that took place on the pages of *Voprosy literatury* that he was able to elaborate his views. This debate, from May through December 1969, was an explicit effort to analyze the political legacy of nineteenth-century Russian nationalist thought with the implicit agenda of pronouncing judgment on the radical nationalism of *Molodaya gvardiya*. The debate involved, in addition to Kozhinov, Anatoly Ivanov, a future leading Russian nationalist dissident; Alexander Yanov, the liberal-reformist participant of earlier debates; Aleksandr Dementiev, the author of the *Novy mir* essay just analyzed; and Vasily

Kuleshov and Sergei Pokrovsky, orthodox communist members of the Soviet academic establishment and well-known scholars of the culture and literature of nineteenth-century Russia.[79]

Yanov's essay opened the debate and provided the frame of reference for the other participants. He argued that Russian nationalism evolved from liberal Slavophile opposition to the autocracy in the 1840s to reactionary support of the regime in the 1880s and 1900s. In fact, the Slavophile vision itself provides powerful inner logic for this evolution. The Slavophiles attempted to provide a political and social alternative to both the Westernizers' dream of a democratic Russia and the desire of the autocracy to preserve the status quo. Political reality, however, made a third alternative infeasible and forced members of the intelligentsia to make a choice between supporting the Westernization and democratization of Russia or autocracy. The antidemocratic and anti-Western core of the Slavophile vision effectively dictated that its followers support autocracy.[80]

As Yanov later acknowledged in his Western publications, he implicitly argued that the contemporary Russian nationalists who attempted to resurrect the Slavophile political legacy were bound to repeat the historical path of their "ideological fathers." Once again, the Russian intelligentsia would have to choose between supporting forces advocating major political and economic reform or joining the ranks of members of the political elite who advocated a return to Stalinism. Since the *Molodaya gvardiya* nationalists and conservative village prose writers idealized the traditional village and vehemently argued against the introduction of Western-type political, economic, and cultural models, they would eventually find themselves joining the orthodox communist opposition to reform.

Yanov's argument was supported to a large extent by Boris Egorov, Leonid Frizman, Evgeny Maimin, and Sergei Dmitriev, all liberal-reformist scholars of nineteenth-century Russian intellectual history. They did not idealize or condemn the Slavophile legacy simply on the grounds of its being antirevolutionary but analyzed and evaluated it without preconceived ideological clichés.[81] The use of these clichés marks the essays of Pokrovsky, Kuleshov, Dementiev, and, to a lesser degree, Sergei Mashinsky, the scholar who summed up the discussion. They all rejected Yanov's argument and reiterated the orthodox Marxist-Leninist interpretation of the Slavophile legacy, presented in their essays as a reactionary doctrine of the Russian landed gentry, which needed little analysis and must not be revived under any circumstances. In fact, Pokrovsky provided the crudest and most doctrinaire view of Slavophilism and openly condemned Chalmaev for his effort to use the Slavophiles as the philosophical basis of a new Russian national ideology.[82]

At the opposite end of the political spectrum from Yanov stood the radical nationalists Ivanov and Kozhinov, who were openly sympathetic to the Slavophiles. Ivanov presented the Slavophiles as being the first to see the collectivistic spirit of the Russian people and juxtaposed it to the "individualism and egoism of the bourgeois West." Kozhinov extended Ivanov's thesis and argued that the Slavophiles' true achievement was to rediscover that Russia's historical development, culture, and thought made it fundamentally different from both the West and the East. By reasserting the principle of Russia's uniqueness, the Slavophiles continued a great political tradition, which could be traced back to the eleventh century. This tradition strove to permeate Russian culture and politics with a uniquely Russian content.[83]

The political debates of 1968 and 1969 highlighted the reality that Russian nationalist ideas, and the politics of inclusion that promoted them, faced strong opposition within the Soviet intellectual elite. That these debates were allowed to take place also indicated that inclusionary politics was encountering an equally strong resistance within the party ideological establishment. Given the fierce nature of the debate over inclusionary politics, it was inevitable that Brezhnev and Suslov would intervene in the controversy.

The End of the First Phase of Inclusionary Politics

The debate on the Slavophile legacy was the last major one of the late 1960s. The struggle in the Central Committee apparatus between supporters and opponents of inclusionary politics clearly intensified throughout 1969. Ivanov's essay in *Literaturnaya gazeta* was the first signal that the opponents of inclusion were gaining ground in the struggle. The second, and probably more important signal was an essay by Yury Barabash, a leading figure in the Soviet literary establishment and a member of the editorial board of the party's main theoretical journal, *Kommunist.*

Although Barabash attempted to present himself as a balanced critic of both liberal reformers and Russian nationalists, the latter were the focus of his attack. Like "Ivanov," he censured the essays in *Novy mir* and *Yunost* that attacked Russian nationalism because they tacitly advocated Western political ideas. At the same time, Barabash harshly criticized Chalmaev for his deviation from the official Marxist-Leninist theory of the class nature of national traditions.[84]

Although by no means a liberal-reformer, Barabash came close to stating explicitly that radical Russian nationalist intellectuals presented a greater danger to Brezhnev's political goals than did the liberal-reformers. This argument apparently carried some weight in debates in the Central Committee apparat. However, as long as Stepakov, Shauro, and Melentiev staunchly defended the *Molodaya gvardiya* nationalists, Brezhnev and Suslov could not be convinced to abandon the politics of inclusion. In fact, in 1969, the supporters of inclusion strengthened the Russian nationalist institutional ability to shape Russian public opinion by appointing Valery Ganichev, a radical nationalist writer and deputy editor of *Molodaya gvardiya,* to head the Molodaya gvardiya publishing house, one of the leading Soviet publishing houses. Ganichev immediately appointed radical nationalist historian Sergei Semanov as chief editor of Molodaya gvardiya's popular semifictional biographical series, "Lives of Remarkable People" *(Zhizn zamechatnykh luydei).*

By early 1970, the arguments put forward by the opponents of inclusionary politics became effective enough to force a temporary compromise; the victim was not *Molodaya gvardiya* itself but another nationalist journal, *Nash sovremennik,* and its deputy editor, Chalmaev. In December 1969, circulation of *Nash Sovremennik* fell from 145,000 to 130,000 copies. A month later the circulation was cut almost by a half, to 70,000—a clear signal to the journal to dismiss Chalmaev from his position. Chalmaev's name was removed from the list of members of the editorial board in the February 1970 issue of the journal.[85] In the same month, the circulation of *Nash sovremennik* increased to 110,000 copies.

The January–February 1970 compromise between opponents and supporters of inclusionary politics in the Central Committee apparatus turned out to be short-lived. In late February the editorial board of *Novy mir* was purged, forcing Tvardovsky to resign. This was the culmination of a year-long effort by the conservative members of the political and cultural establishments to deny the liberal-reformist intelligentsia its most important institutional base.[86] Paradoxically, the *Novy mir* purge made it easier to suppress its main Russian nationalist opponent, *Molodaya gvardiya.* Protectors of the journal in the party apparatus often defended it as a tool necessary to fight the liberal-reformist ideas articulated in *Novy mir*. From March 1970 on, this argument could no longer protect *Molodaya gvardiya*.

A much more significant development precipitated the suppression of *Molodaya gvardiya*—the dismissal of Stepakov, a leading supporter of inclusionary politics in the Central Committee apparatus. In March 1970, Stepakov, the head of the Propaganda Department, was removed from his position and sent to Yugoslavia as the Soviet ambassador.[87] His post was left vacant, thus elevating Aleksandr Yakovlev, Stepakov's deputy and a staunch opponent of Russian nationalism, to acting head of the department. This change was apparently significant enough to shift the balance of power between supporters and opponents of inclusionary politics in the Central Committee Secretariat in favor of the latter.

The struggle in the Central Committee apparatus over inclusionary politics in general, and the fate of *Molodaya gvardiya* in particular, greatly intensified after the publication in early 1970 of the rabidly anti-intellectual, anti-Semitic, and anti-Western novel by orthodox Stalinist writer Ivan Shevtsov, *In the Name of the Father and the Son (Vo imya ottsa i syna)*.[88] Suslov greatly disliked the book's anti-intellectualism and plea for the restoration of Stalinism. At a special meeting of the Central Committee Secretariat, he called the novel a damaging work that criticized Soviet society from a Maoist position and undermined party efforts to bring together different social groups. Suslov ordered that no positive reviews of the novel appear in the main Soviet newspapers. Yet on April 24, 1970, a glowing review of the novel appeared in *Sovetskaya Rossiya*.[89] Suslov immediately ordered an investigation into the matter, and it was revealed that the newspaper's editor in chief had received conflicting instructions from the Propaganda Department. Although Yakovlev strongly opposed the publication of the review, his deputy, Anatoly Dmitryuk, demanded its publication. The affair resulted in the dismissal of two of the deputy editors of *Sovetskaya Rossiya* in June 1970. More important, it strengthened Yakovlev's position in the debate within the party ideological establishment regarding the continuation of the politics of inclusion.[90]

In less than two months after the end of the *Sovetskaya Rossiya* affair, Yakovlev received the ammunition he needed to intensify the argument against the continuation of inclusionary politics. The August issue of *Molodaya gvardiya* contained an essay by Sergei Semanov, "On Relative and Eternal Values" *(O tsennostyakh otnositelnykh i vechnykh)*, that presented the Stalinist creation of a powerful and socially monolithic state, imbued by Russian nationalism, as the greatest achievement of Russian history. In particular, he hailed Stalin's suppression of the antinationalist attitudes that prevailed in the party up to the 1930s.

Semanov argued that de-Stalinization had caused "a recurrence of grumbling nihilism." The dismantling of the Stalinist state allowed Western-oriented liberal-reformers to depict Russian history and traditions in a negative light and write off the achievements of the Stalin era. In addition, Russian national lifestyle and morality were threatened by the values of "the sexual revolution" and the hippie movement penetrating from the West. In other words, Russian nationalists must push for the reconstitution of a neo-Stalinist state that would purge the country of liberal-reformers and isolate Russia from the West. Only in this fashion could they protect the unique sociopolitical nature of the Russian-Soviet state, its national lifestyle, and its conservative moral values.[91]

Semanov's aggressive demand for the restoration of the Stalinist state provoked almost immediate reaction by the opponents of *Molodaya gvardiya* within the Soviet cultural establishment. On September 2, 1970, less than a month after its appearance, the essay was criticized in a *Literaturnaya gazeta* editorial.[92] More important, this essay, appearing shortly after the harsh condemnation of Shevtsov's novel by Suslov, assisted Yakovlev in his efforts to convince the Soviet leadership that inclusionary politics threatened the post-Khrushchev ideological status quo. By November 1970, Yakovlev and other opponents of inclusionary politics in the Central Committee were finally able to turn the tide.

Apparently between September and November 1970 the supporters of inclusionary politics in the Central Committee apparatus suffered a major setback. Yury Melentiev, one of the most ardent advocates of this policy, was dismissed as the first deputy head of the Cultural Department and replaced by Albert Belyaev, a man with a worldview similar to that of Aleksandr Yakovlev. According to Yanov, Melentiev was dismissed in the aftermath of a meeting with Brezhnev during which he urged the introduction of militaristic and Russian nationalist education courses, minimized contacts with the West, and the imposition of tight ideological control on the reform-minded members of the intelligentsia and the party apparat.[93]

Even if Yanov's account of the meeting is incorrect, we still can safely assume that Melentiev tried to convince Brezhnev not to retreat from the inclusionary program. It is also likely that even before the meeting, Brezhnev had decided to redefine the terms of inclusionary politics. He was determined to do this because he had been persuaded that *Molodaya gvardiya* was sowing too much discord in the party apparat and challenging his policy of maintaining the ideological status quo. Moreover, the Soviet invasion of Czechoslovakia and the subsequent stabilization of the situation there eliminated one of the immediate causes for the introduction of inclusionary politics.

Victory for the opponents of inclusionary politics found its first expression in a long article, "Socialism and Cultural Heritage" *(Sotsializm i kulturnoe nasledie),* published in the November issue of *Kommunist.* Written by a high-ranking party official who again used the pen name V. Ivanov, the essay was the harshest criticism of Russian nationalism published in the party press.[94] Like all previous official interventions in the ongoing political debate, this attack on Russian nationalism was combined with criticism of the liberal-reformist intelligentsia. Ivanov criticized liberal-reformers for underestimating the danger of bourgeois ideological influences, lacking an understanding of the Leninist notion of proletarian internationalism, and expressing contempt for the patriotic feelings of Russians.

The main thrust of Ivanov's argument was directed against *Molodaya gvardiya.* Ivanov accused the journal of systematically publishing works that challenged the Leninist two cultures theory, dismissing the notion of the "Soviet people," and refusing to recognize the achievements of the new socialist culture. He rejected *Molodaya gvardiya*'s depiction of the West immersed in consumerism and lacking spirituality, and warned the journal not to ignore the existence of progressive elements in Western culture and society.

Ivanov singled out the essays of Viktor Chalmaev, Yury Ivanov, and Sergei Semanov for his harshest criticism. He condemned Chalmaev's glorification of the conservative thinkers of prerevolutionary Russia and Ivanov's depiction of the nineteenth-century revolutionary movement as Western oriented and therefore anti-Russian. Finally, Ivanov scolded Semanov for trying to "cast doubt on questions long solved and clear," that is, his attempt to challenge the resolutions of the Twentieth and Twenty-second Party Congresses condemning Stalinism.

The *Kommunist* attack coincided with an assault on *Nash sovremennik.* On November 18, 1970, Andrei Kandrenkov, the first secretary of Kaluga regional party organization, sent a letter to the Central Committee Secretariat accusing the journal of publishing in its April 1970 issue a novel by village prose writer Anatoly Tkachenko. Kandrenkov claimed that the novel constituted a highly distorted and inaccurate portrayal of the socioeconomic reality of his region.[95]

Ivanov's essay and Kandrenkov's complaint could easily have served as grounds for the dismissal of the chief editors of *Molodaya gvardiya* and *Nash sovremennik*. However, the ensuing actions against both journals reflected the desire of the party leadership to retain those elements of inclusionary politics that cultivated the village prose writers. Sergei Vikulov was summoned to the Cultural Department, where he was severely reprimanded for publishing a novel full of "ideological deficiencies." This reprimand, however, was a mere slap on the wrist, since he retained his position as editor in chief of *Nash sovremennik*.

The accusation that *Molodaya gvardiya* was consistently attacking the ideological and political foundations of the Brezhnev regime was much more serious than the charges leveled against *Nash sovremennik*. In December 1970, Suslov called a special meeting of the Secretariat to discuss the content of *Molodaya gvardiya*. The *Kommunist* article appears to have signaled Suslov's position on the issue on the eve of the meeting. This meeting of the Central Committee Secretariat, which Brezhnev personally attended, resulted in the dismissal of Anatoly Nikonov from his position as the chief editor of *Molodaya gvardiya*.[96]

Nikonov's dismissal did not herald the end of the politics of inclusion; it was merely redefined and more closely managed. Brezhnev and Suslov were still determined to turn Russian nationalist intellectuals into an articulated audience serving the interests of the regime. Therefore, Russian nationalists were allowed to retain control of *Molodaya gvardiya*, *Nash sovremennik*, and *Moskva*, the provincial journals *Sever* and *Volga*, and the Molodaya gvardiya publishing house and its "Lives of Remarkable People" series. In fact, Semanov remained in charge of the series, despite being harshly censured by *Kommunist*.

The dismissal of Nikonov taught Russian nationalist intellectuals that the politics of inclusion had limits. The party wanted them to perform an important political function but was not yet ready to permit an open challenge to its policies or ideological foundations. At the same time, it taught Brezhnev and Suslov and the lower-ranking supporters of inclusion that such policies would encounter serious resistance in the party apparat. In the 1970s, Brezhnev and Suslov broke the opposition to inclusionary politics in the party apparat, while Russian nationalist intellectuals appeared to accept the role of an articulated audience, not challenging party policy or its ideological foundations.

The Rise and Fall of Inclusionary
Politics, 1971–1985

The years 1971 to 1982, the era of "mature Brezhnevism," witnessed a continuation of the party policies and social and intellectual trends that had evolved or were present by the late 1960s. The political practice of the inclusion of groups of Russian nationalist intellectuals in public political and social debates was no exception. This inclusionary policy lasted until 1982, and then was largely abandoned. Why these policies lasted another eleven years, what effect they had on the development of the political views of Russian nationalist intellectuals, and why they were discontinued are the main questions explored in this chapter.

Aleksandr Yakovlev and the Struggle over the Politics of Inclusion

Events that took place between 1971 and 1973 aptly illustrate that the struggle among members of the Soviet political establishment over the continuation of the inclusionary policy toward Russian nationalist intellectuals was far from resolved. Aleksandr Yakovlev and other opponents of Russian nationalism probably viewed the removal from the party apparat of Stepakov and Melentiev, ardent advocates of Russian nationalist inclusion, in addition to the Politburo's condemnation of *Molodaya gvardiya*, and the dismissal of its chief editor, Nikonov, in December 1970, as signs that Brezhnev and Suslov were reconsidering their positions on the politics of inclusion.

In early 1971, thinking that a retreat from the politics of inclusion was forthcoming, its opponents within the party ideological establishment, led by Yakovlev, launched a campaign aimed at discrediting Russian nationalist intellectuals and their sympathizers within the party apparat. It was probably Yakovlev who, in late 1970 or early 1971, commissioned a special report by the Academy of Social Sciences of the Central Committee of the CPSU that examined the role of religion in works of literature and art. The report, dated January 28, 1971, harshly attacked Soloukhin's "Letters from the Russian Museum," as well as essays by Chalmaev and other contributors to *Molodaya gvardiya*. The report had clear policy implications since the note attached to the report and signed by Yakovlev and his deputy, Vadim Medvedev, indicates that it was used in formulating the July 1971 Central Committee decree on strengthening atheistic education. This decree was probably designed to lay the foundation for a further attack on Russian nationalist intellectuals.[1] Almost immediately following this Central Committee decree on the strengthening of atheistic education, Yakovlev published an essay in *Kommunist* critical of Russian nationalism. Without mentioning specific names but clearly aimed at *Molodaya gvardiya* contributors, he condemned writings on national history that ignored the Marxist-Leninist class approach.[2]

On October 15, 1971, sensing the intensification of the antinationalist campaign, Pavel Romanov, the head of Glavlit and a staunch opponent of inclusionary politics, sent a memorandum to the Central Committee Secretariat denouncing works by Soloukhin, Likhonosov, Shukshin, and other Russian nationalist writers published in the journals *Nash sovremennik, Moskva,* and *Druzhba narodov* in 1970 and 1971.[3]

One of main achievements of this campaign was a January 21, 1972, Central Committee decree entitled "On Literary Criticism" *(O literaturno-khudozhestvennoi kritike),* designed to be the ideological guideline for institutions responsible for Soviet cultural life. It expressly criticized the *Molodaya gvardiya* type of Russian nationalism in the same way as in the Academy of Social Sciences report, Yakovlev's essay, and Romanov's memorandum. Implicitly attacking Soloukhin's "Letters from the Russian Museum," it spoke about publications that "present an incorrect picture of the history of Soviet and prerevolutionary art." Aimed at Chalmaev's essays on Russian national culture and history, the resolution also demanded a return to the Leninist approach to national culture.

The decree supplemented the January 7, 1969, Central Committee resolution that had ordered the chief editors of newspapers, literary journals, and heads of cultural and artistic institutions to prevent the publication or exhibition of ideologically flawed works. The 1969 resolution was aimed at both the liberal-reformist and nationalist intelligentsia and provided justification for the subsequent crackdown on *Novy mir* and *Molodaya gvardiya;* the 1972 resolution was aimed primarily at the Russian nationalist intelligentsia. As the acting head of the Propaganda Department of the Central Committee, Yakovlev probably played a major role in the drafting of this document. [4]

Within days of the decree's appearance, Russian nationalist intellectuals and their journals became targets of sharp criticism by their opponents in the Soviet cultural establishment. On January 26, *Literaturnaya gazeta* published an essay by Valentin Oskotsky in which he attacked the journal *Nash sovremennik* for publishing essays portraying the westernized Russian intelligentsia as detached from the roots of the Russian national culture. On the same day, at the meeting of the Governing Board of the USSR Writers' Union, Vitaly Ozerov, the chief editor of the journal *Voprosy literatury* and a prominent member of the Soviet cultural establishment, harshly attacked *Molodaya gvardiya* for its idealization of traditional peasantry and for the effort to challenge the official interpretation of the prerevolutionary Russian history and culture.[5]

By October 1972, the Yakovlev-led offensive against Russian nationalism had had only a negligible effect. Although the circulation of *Nash sovremennik* remained frozen at its February 1970 level of 110,000 copies and some Russian nationalist writers had difficulty getting their books published, Russian nationalist editors remained at the helm of their thick journals and publishing houses and continued to promote Russian nationalist authors.[6] Moreover, with Feliks Ovcharenko's death in 1972, *Molodaya gvardiya*'s chief editor became Anatoly Ivanov, a radical nationalist writer and one of the signatories of the 1969 "Letter of the Eleven." As expected, Ivanov preserved the journal as a major Russian nationalist publication.[7]

This succession could not have taken place without the strong support and manipulation of Vasily Shauro, an ardent advocate of inclusionary policy in the party apparat, who held the position of head of the Cultural Department of the Central Committee for an astounding twenty-one years (1965–1986). Shauro was a bureaucrat with an astute sense of Suslov's and Brezhnev's policy preferences regarding culture. He understood that Brezhnev and Suslov wanted to continue the politics of inclusion of Russian nationalist intellectuals despite the experience of the late 1960s. As a result, he continued to protect the privileged status of Russian nationalist intellectuals among the Soviet intelligentsia.

This privileged position became even more conspicuous in 1972, when the reformist intelligentsia lost control of their last major institutional stronghold, the Institute for Concrete Social Research. Founded in 1968 and headed by Aleksei Rumyantsev, a leading reformist party intellectual and a former editor of *Pravda*, the institute played a role in the social sciences similar to that of *Novy mir* in literature. In 1971, Rumyantsev was removed from the directorship of the institute and replaced by Mikhail Rutkevich, an orthodox communist sociologist who quickly began purging the Institute of reform-minded scholars.[8]

The purge of *Novy mir* in 1970 and the Institute for Concrete Social Research in 1972 were clear signals to liberal-reformist members of the intellectual elite that their control of major literary or scholarly institutions was over. Moreover, in 1972 the Politburo sent a clear message that the practice of inclusionary politics in the non-Russian republics, practiced in the late 1960s and early 1970s, would no longer be tolerated. In May 1972, Pyotr Shelest, the First Secretary of the Ukrainian Communist Party, was removed from office, and in September 1972, Vasily Mzhavanadze, the First Secretary of the Georgian Communist Party, suffered the same fate. In each case, support of nationalist tendencies within the native intelligentsia was a major factor in the Politburo decision.[9]

Yet it was not clear what the Politburo position on Russian nationalism was to be. The Central Committee apparat was strongly divided on the issue. While the Yakovlev-led opponents of inclusion attacked Russian nationalist intellectuals, Shauro and other party apparat supporters of inclusion effectively protected them. Moreover, in January 1971, dissident Russian nationalist intellectual Vladimir Osipov openly began to publish a samizdat journal entitled *Veche*, which provided a forum for representatives from across the Russian nationalist spectrum. Although the KGB attempted to suppress the liberal-reformist dissident journals as soon as they appeared, it allowed Osipov to circulate six issues of *Veche* between January 1971 and October 1972. We can assume that the KGB received instructions to allow the journal to publish during this period. But the KGB moved quickly to suppress the journal in 1973, when this protection was apparently revoked.[10]

The fact that Brezhnev's and Suslov's policy preferences concerning Russian nationalist intellectuals were vague and open to interpretation by opposing groups in the party apparat made each group believe that its position represented the official line. It may have been Yakovlev's ambition to preside over a complete rout of the supporters of inclusionary politics in the Central Committee apparatus and thus earn promotion to the position of permanent head of the Propaganda Department. On October 30, 1972, he sent to the Politburo a long memorandum in which he harshly criticized the party's main theoretical journal, *Kommunist*, for failing to address the issue of nationalism in non-Russian republics and among the Russian intelligentsia.[11]

Yakovlev was not content with limiting his campaign to the confines of the Central Committee apparatus, and he decided to make a public assault on Russian nationalists. On November 15, 1972, two weeks after he sent his memorandum to the Politburo, *Literaturnaya gazeta* printed his two-page essay entitled "Against Anti-Historicism" *(Protiv antiistorizma)*, the harshest criticism of Russian nationalism and, by implication, of the politics of inclusion, written by an important functionary of the Central Committee since the 1920s. The essay appears to have been the opening statement in a final confrontation with the supporters of inclusion.[12]

Yakovlev explicitly and implicitly assailed the views of sixteen Russian nationalist writers, poets, literary critics, and historians, focusing on the works of such well-known figures as Vadim Kozhinov, Anatoly Lanshchikov, Mikhail Lobanov, Oleg Mikhailov, and Sergei Semanov. He attacked Russian nationalists on four main issues. First, while carefully avoiding any overt criticism of the village prose writers, he denounced the idealization of the traditional Russian village, citing Lenin's views on the prerevolutionary Russian peasantry as his justification, as well as the anti-urbanism and anti-intellectualism prevailing in many Russian nationalist writings.

Second, the essay criticized Russian nationalist rewriting of history, which presented in a highly idealized fashion the institution of autocracy, the Russian Orthodox Church, the tsarist generals, and Slavophile thought. The ongoing campaign for the preservation of historic monuments, he wrote, must not be exploited to whitewash the reactionary nature of the tsarist regime. Third, Yakovlev accused Russian nationalist intellectuals of advancing a nonclass approach to nationalism and national culture and thus challenging Lenin's views on this issue.

Finally, he rejected the idea, prevalent among Russian nationalists and their supporters in the party apparat, that Russia and the West were irreconcilable enemies. Yakovlev called this a false dichotomy that completely ignored the existence of strong democratic and progressive traditions in the West and had no basis in Marxist ideology. Although the essay did not dwell on this issue as fully as on others, this was probably Yakovlev's most important argument because it conveyed a clear message of a fundamental contradiction between the recently launched policy of détente, symbolized by the May 1972 visit of President Nixon to Moscow, and the regime's commitment to Russian nationalist inclusion.

The immediate consequence of the essay was the imposition of a publication ban on the works of the authors whom Yakovlev criticized. This ban was not a result of a Central Committee order, but rather the initiative of numerous editors of Soviet newspapers, journals, and publishing houses who interpreted the essay as the Politburo directive. Nevertheless, Yakovlev failed to achieve his main aim of triggering a frontal attack on Russian nationalist intellectuals and the politics of inclusion. No articles endorsing his essay appeared in any official Soviet publication, a clear indication that a direct Central Committee order forbid debate on the essay.[13]

The unprecedented length of Yakovlev's essay and the nature of his accusations were bound to force the Politburo to clarify its position on the issue of Russian nationalist inclusion.[14] Many letters sent to the Central Committee by respected members of the Soviet cultural establishment strongly protesting the content of the essay had certainly been taken into account.[15] Clearly the Politburo had not authorized the essay and was taken aback when it appeared.[16] Moreover, Yakovlev's subsequent effort to appease the Russian nationalist intellectuals he had criticized suggests that the Politburo let him know that it did not approve of the essay and perhaps suggested that his own position as the acting head of the Propaganda Department was in jeopardy.

Yakovlev's efforts to save his post included meetings with Lanshchikov, Lobanov, Mikhailov, and Semanov, the four writers attacked in the essay. These meetings were arranged through the mediation of the radical nationalist painter, Ilya Glazunov, and took place in early 1973. Lobanov, Mikhailov, and Semanov met individually with Yakovlev, and Lanshchikov met Yakovlev's assistant, Aleksandrov. The intent of the essay, Yakovlev argued, was grossly misunderstood. It was merely an attempt to provoke an intellectual debate about the ideas prevailing among the Russian intelligentsia and was not intended to suppress Russian nationalism. Finally, he claimed that there was no Central Committee ban on the publication of their works, and he personally offered to facilitate their quick publication.[17]

Yakovlev's gross miscalculation of the anticipated Politburo reaction to the publication of "Against Anti-Historicism" also undermined his campaign against the editors of *Kommunist*, whom he implicitly accused of being sympathetic to the Russian nationalists. In fact, on November 11, 1972, the chief editor of *Kommunist*, Anatoly Egorov, sent a memorandum to Suslov in which he rebutted Yakovlev's accusations against the journal. In the margins of the Egorov memo is a note by a Central Committee official indicating that Suslov reviewed both the Yakovlev and Egorov memorandums and found Yakovlev's accusations against *Kommunist* "unconvincing."[18]

The note mentioning Suslov's decision was dated February 26, 1973. At the April 1973 plenum of the Central Committee, the Politburo effectively outlined the party's policies for the rest of the decade: a commitment to the principle of détente in foreign policy and inclusionary politics in the domestic arena. In the early 1980s, the invasion of Afghanistan and growing Russian nationalist discontent led to a major revision in foreign and domestic policy orientations.[19]

The April 1973 plenum marked the beginning of a three-year period of personnel change in the Soviet ideological establishment.[20] Shortly after it, Yakovlev was relieved of his Central Committee post and appointed Soviet ambassador to Canada.[21] In October 1974, his immediate superior, the party secretary in charge of ideology, Pyotr Demichev, was removed from his position and appointed the USSR minister of culture. In 1976, the chief editor of *Pravda*, Mikhail Zimyanin, became Demichev's replacement as party secretary in charge of ideology. Finally, in May 1977, Evgeny Tyazhelnikov, the first secretary of the Komsomol, was appointed head of the Propaganda Department of the Central Committee.

Zimyanin, like his predecessor, Demichev, was hardly a committed supporter of inclusionary politics, but he enforced it as long as this policy constituted the party's official line. Tyazhelnikov, on the other hand, was a strong supporter of the politics of inclusion, and his sympathetic approach to the Russian nationalists was clearly manifested in his toleration of *Molodaya gvardiya*'s aggressive promotion of Russian nationalist causes in the late 1960s and the appointment of prominent Russian nationalist intellectuals to key positions in the Komsomol-controlled cultural institutions in the 1970s.[22] One of the first major appointments under Tyazhelnikov was the 1978 appointment of Valery Ganichev, a prominent radical nationalist writer who headed the Molodaya gvardiya publishing house, as the chief editor of the major daily newspaper, *Komsomolskaya pravda*. Given his support of the Russian nationalists, it is hardly surprising that Tyazhelnikov would be the first high party official to be dismissed shortly after inclusionary politics was finally abandoned in late 1982.

The overhaul of the leadership of the party ideological establishment did not affect Vasily Shauro, an ardent supporter of inclusionary politics within the party apparat. He continued to hold his post as head of the Cultural Department of the Central Committee, and so from 1977 to 1982, the Propaganda and Cultural departments were headed by officials sympathetic to Russian nationalists.

Russian nationalist intellectuals viewed Yakovlev's departure for Canada as punishment for "Against Anti-Historicism." Throughout the 1970s, they believed that their ideas enjoyed significant support at the highest levels of the Soviet government. This illustrates the success of inclusionary politics to create among Russian nationalist intellectuals the impression of their power and influence rather than to concede to their concrete social, political, and cultural demands.[23]

The question is why the Politburo rejected Yakovlev's argument that inclusionary politics and the politics of détente were incompatible. The answer is probably that Suslov and Brezhnev's reasoning was the opposite of Yakovlev's. In their view, the opening up of Soviet society to greater Western influence, one of détente's unavoidable consequences, required that they effectively combat these influences by means other than official propaganda. The inward orientation of all segments of the Russian nationalist spectrum and the strong anti-Western ideas held by many of its leading representatives made Russian nationalist intellectuals a powerful weapon in combating Western influences "from within."[24]

Finally, the decision to reinforce the politics of inclusion rather than crack down on Russian nationalists was probably also an outcome of the realization by Brezhnev and other leading members of the Politburo of growing anti-Russian sentiment in the non-Russian republics. In 1972, a memorandum prepared for the Politburo by a senior Central Committee official, Leon Onikov, warned the Soviet leadership about the rise of anti-Russian sentiment and a possible backlash by ethnic Russians. Moreover, Chernyaev reported that in 1972, the Politburo discussed the rise of nationalist sentiments in the non-Russian republics and the role of local political elites in fanning those sentiments.[25]

The removal of Shelest and Mzhavanadze from their high positions in May and September 1972, respectively, was clearly an attempt to combat the rise of nationalism in non-Russian republics. While cracking down on nationalism in the periphery, Brezhnev and Suslov felt that they needed inclusionary politics in order to strengthen their support among ethnic Russians, the ethnic backbone of the Soviet state.

Inclusion as a Success Story

In addition to détente and rise of the anti-Russian sentiment in the non-Russian republics, there were two other compelling reasons for the continuation of inclusionary politics in the 1970s. First, inclusion from the beginning was a substitute for radical social, political, and economic reform in the Soviet Union. In the 1970s, the Brezhnev-led leadership was even less inclined to experiment with reform. The last economic reform left over from the 1960s was dismantled in 1973. In that same year, the final effort to implement the so-called link reform in agriculture was defeated and its chief promoter, Ivan Khudenko, was arrested.[26]

Second, in the late 1960s Brezhnev needed village prose to foster public support for large investments in agriculture. In the 1970s, he continued the pattern of investment established in the late 1960s, which gave extremely high priority to investments in agriculture at the expense of light industry. From 1970 to 1983, procurement price subsidies alone ballooned from 14.3 billion to 54.6 billion rubles. Gustafson even speaks of the existence of the "post-1968 consensus" in the Politburo on the issue of investments in agriculture. Moreover, as Breslauer points out, most of these investments went to Siberia, the Far East and the Non–Black Earth Zone, (the agricultural regions of the Russian Republic).[27]

Among these projects, the revival of the Non–Black Earth Zone was the most ambitious. Initiated on March 20, 1974, the project attempted to revitalize the progressively failing agriculture of Russia's heartland and halt its rapid depopulation by 1990. The government wrote off 202 million rubles of debt incurred by area collective farms and postponed the payment of another 494 million, a de facto write-off. Moreover, the Central Committee decree gave collective farms of the region a direct subsidy of 12 billion rubles and assigned another 23 billion for land reclamation, construction, and the improvement of social services in the Russian countryside, all to be spent between 1976 and 1980.[28]

The role that public opinion played in the adoption of this program is not clear. Its purposes, however, coincided with many of the principal concerns of the liberal and conservative representatives of village prose.

Brezhnev therefore could present the project as a sign that the party was addressing the issues raised by the Russian nationalist intelligentsia. At the same time, he could skillfully use the village prose writers and other Russian nationalist intellectuals to create a public opinion highly supportive of such enormous budgetary allocations. Such public opinion could be used to silence any potential opposition to the project from those sectors of the economy or non-Russian republics adversely affected by the budgetary redistribution. Thus, as in the 1960s, inclusionary politics in the 1970s was an important means of manipulating public opinion in support of Brezhnev's policy of high budgetary allocations to agriculture.[29]

Inclusionary politics as it fully emerged from 1973 on put a high premium on political behavior within the limits defined as acceptable by the party and severely punished those who went beyond them. The suppression of "independent from the state" political groups, even if they expressed Russian nationalist ideas, was reaffirmed after Yakovlev's removal. In 1973 the KGB was apparently given an order to suppress the dissident Russian nationalist journal *Veche*, and in March 1974, Osipov was forced to suspend the publication. In November 1974, he was arrested and a year later was sentenced to an eight-year prison term. Finally, in February 1974, Alexander Solzhenitsyn, the leading Russian nationalist dissident, was deported from the Soviet Union after publication of *The Gulag Archipelago* in the West. Thus, by late 1974, the KGB had effectively eliminated the possibility of an "independent from the state" Russian nationalist movement by suppressing its most important institution, the journal *Veche*, and expelling from the country its chief ideologue and potential leader, Solzhenitsyn.

Soon after suppressing the dissident wing of the movement, the state began to elevate village prose as the most prestigious Soviet literary movement. In the 1960s, Sergei Zalygin had been the only village prose writer awarded the USSR State Prize for literature; between 1971 and 1982, eleven village prose writers were honored with four highest Soviet literary awards: the Lenin Prize (the most prestigious Soviet award), the USSR State Prize, the Gorky Prize (the highest literary award given to RSFSR writers), and the Komsomol Prize.[30] Only Boris Mozhaev, the leading member of the liberal wing of the village prose and the most outspoken critic of Soviet agricultural policies, was not awarded any major prize during the entire Brezhnev era.

The official awards brought village prose writers not only honor but significant financial rewards as well. A Lenin Prize winner received 10,000 rubles, a USSR State Prize winner received 5,000 rubles, and a Gorky Prize winner was awarded 2,500 rubles, all significant sums by Soviet standards of the time.[31] More important, the prizes effectively guaranteed their recipients publication in multiple editions totaling in the high hundreds of thousands and even millions of copies. As Table 4.1 shows, between 1971 and 1982, Abramov, Astafiev, Belov, Nosov, Rasputin, Shukshin, Soloukhin, Troepolsky, and Zalygin, the village prose recipients of the Lenin, State, and Gorky prizes, amassed significant fortunes as a result of their each publishing over 2.5 million books. Moreover, their work was published in the widely read bi-weekly *Roman-gazeta,* which had a circulation of 2.5 million copies. And their works were often adapted for theater, television, and cinema, thus further spreading the ideas they contained.

The state bestowed its honors on and enriched not only Russian nationalist intellectuals affiliated with the village prose. Between 1971 and 1982, fourteen conservative and radical nationalist writers, poets, and literary critics were rewarded with prestigious literary prizes for propagating anti-Western and antireformist ideas in their works. Their books too were published in hundreds of thousands and even millions of copies, serialized in the *Roman-gazeta* series, and adapted for theater, television, and the cinema.

Village prose and other Russian nationalist writers who did not receive an official prize in the Brezhnev era published smaller numbers of books, and their works more rarely appeared in *Roman-gazeta,* but they too enjoyed the fruits of the inclusionary politics in the form of very large print runs for their works. Seventeen of these writers saw print runs of books ranging from 450,000 to 2.1 million copies. All in all, forty-three Russian nationalist writers, poets, and critics saw their books published in print runs of more than 450,000 copies, including twenty-three writers who saw their books published in more than a million copies, and twenty writers saw their work serialized in *Roman-gazeta.*

Another important dimension of inclusionary policy was the sharp rise in the circulation of three of the main Russian nationalist thick journals—*Nash sovremennik, Molodaya gvardiya,* and *Moskva.* As Table 4.2 shows, between 1971 and 1982, all three of these journals increased their circulation by more than 100 percent; *Nash sovremennik* led, with an impressive 236 percent increase in circulation. In comparison, only one of six major Moscow and Leningrad thick journals that either published primarily liberal-reformist writers or did not have a distinct ideological profile saw its

Table 4.1 Regime Beneficiaries: Print Runs of Books by Major Russian Nationalist Authors and State Awards Received, 1971–1982

Author	Total Books Published	Awards	Roman-gazeta Publications
Viktor Astafiev (vp)	13,737,840	USSR State Prize, 1978; Gorky Prize, 1975	4
Evgeny Nosov (vp)	6,640,150	Gorky Prize, 1975	2
Yury Bondarev	6,627,780	Lenin Prize, 1972; USSR State Prize 1977; Gorky Prize, 1975	4
Vasily Shukshin (vp)	6,537,500	Lenin Prize, 1976*	1
Mikhail Alekseev	5,642,810	USSR State Prize, 1976	4
Fyodor Abramov (vp)	5,061,000	USSR State Prize, 1975	1
Sergei Voronin	4,226,000	Gorky Prize, 1975	
Vasily Belov (vp)	4,006,000	USSR State Prize, 1981	2
Gavriil Troepolsky (vp)	3,609,000	USSR State Prize, 1975	1
Valentin Rasputin (vp)	3,478,600	USSR State Prize, 1977	3
Anatoly Ivanov	3,446,000	USSR Prize 1979; Gorky Prize, 1971; Komsomol Prize, 1980	7
Vladimir Soloukhin (vp)	3,060,760	Gorky Prize, 1979	
Piotr Proskurin	2,955,250	USSR State Prize 1974, 1979; Gorky Prize, 1974	7
Sergei Zalygin (vp)	2,521,270		2
Valentin Pikul	2,165,000		
Oleg Mikhailov	1,495,000		
Nikolai Rubtsov (vp)	1,495,000		
Yury Prokushev	1,361,180	Gorky Prize, 1977	
Vladimir Chivilikhin	1,114,200	USSR State Prize, 1982; Gorky Prize, 1977	
Aleksei Yugov	1,100,000	Gorky Prize, 1972	2

Table 4.1 (continued)

Author	Total Books Published	Awards	Roman-gazeta Publication
Nikolai Shundik	1,093,360	Gorky Prize, 1979	4
Aleksandr Yashin (vp)	1,024,000		
Semyon Shurtakov	1,005,000		
Sergei Vysotsky	970,000		
Anatoly Tkachenko (vp)	839,000		1
Viktor Likhonosov (vp)	835,000		
Boris Mozhaev (vp)	797,000		
Dmitry Balashov	795,000		
Vladimir Lichutin (vp)	779,000		1
Aleksandr Prokhanov	730,000	Komsomol Prize, 1982	1
Sergei Vikulov	715,000	Gorky Prize, 1974	
Egor Isaev	747,330	Lenin Prize, 1980	
Yury Borodkin	695,000		2
Georgy Semenov	650,000	Gorky Prize, 1981	1
Anatoly Znamensky	613,000		
Sergei Semanov	555,000		
Viktor Potanin (vp)	545,000	Komsomol Prize, 1978	1
Viktor Petelin	515,000		
Olga Fokina (vp)	505,000	Gorky Prize, 1976	
Vladimir Firsov	463,000	Gorky Prize, 1976	
Oleg Shestinsky	462,000		
Yury Loshchits	450,000		
Evgeny Ivanov	450,000		

Note: vp = village prose; * = awarded posthumously.
Sources: *Bolshaya Sovetskaya Entsiklopediya; Ezhegodnik knigi SSSR, 1971–1982.*

Table 4.2 Circulation of Main Russian Thick Journals, 1971–1982

Journal	1971 Monthly Circulation	1982 Monthly Circulation	Percentage Increase, 1971–1982
Russian nationalist			
Nash sovremennik	100,000	336,000	236
Molodaya gvardiya	315,000	870,000	176
Moskva	240,000	500,000	108
Liberal-reformist or without distinct ideological profile			
Druzhba narodov	80,000	240,000	200
Novy mir	178,000	350,000	97
Yunost	1,800,000	3,150,000	75
Oktyabr[a]	160,000	218,000	36
Neva	270,000	333,000	23
Znamya	150,000	170,000	13

[a]After Kochetov's death in 1973, *Oktyabr* lost its status as the mouthpiece of ultraorthodox communism in Soviet cultural life. Under its new editor, Anatoly Ananiev, *Oktyabr* lost its clear ideological orientation and published authors of all political persuasions.

circulation increased by 100 percent or more during the same period. Since the circulation level of the journals was determined by the Propaganda and Cultural departments rather than by public demand, these figures clearly indicate party preferences.[32]

Political inclusion and its benefits were not restricted to the leading Russian nationalist writers and literary critics but extended to the fine arts as well. The case of Ilya Glazunov, a painter who expressed radical nationalist ideas in his work, is an example of how inclusionary politics was manifested in the realm of the fine arts. In the 1970s, while the Soviet government literally bulldozed unofficial exhibitions of avant-garde art, and forced well-known avant-garde artists such as the sculptor Ernst Neizvestny and the painter Mikhail Shamyakin to emigrate, Glazunov's career flourished. His openly nationalist views, expressed in his rabidly anti-urban painting "The Return of the Prodigal Son" or paintings glorifying the role of the Russian Orthodox Church and its princes in Russian history, generated significant controversy in the Soviet political elite, and at some point in the mid-1970s, the KGB was drawn into this controversy. On October 8, 1976, the head of the KGB, Yury Andropov, sent a memorandum to the Central Committee Secretariat containing a recommendation on how to treat the artist. Andropov acknowledged that Glazunov "often degenerate[d] to openly anti-Semitic positions," which many people found repulsive, yet in the spirit of the politics of inclusion, Andropov did not recommend alienating Glazunov. Quite the opposite, he recommended to the party that they cultivate the artist by involving him in the founding of a museum devoted to the history of Russian furniture.[33]

Although this museum was never opened, Glazunov continued to be treated as one of the most privileged men of Soviet art. An officially sponsored personal exhibit was one of the greatest privileges given to a Soviet artist; between 1972 and 1982, Glazunov staged seven such exhibits in the USSR and nine abroad.[34] Among the exhibits, those that took place in Moscow in June 1978 and Leningrad in October 1979 turned out to be major events in Soviet cultural life. Both took place in the city's most important exhibition hall, lasted one month, and attracted about 600,000 visitors in Moscow and about 1 million in Leningrad. In both cases, approximately 400 of Glazunov's paintings were shown, including many with such Russian nationalist themes as anti-urbanism and an idealization of prerevolutionary Russian history.[35] Moreover, such major Soviet museums as the Moscow Tretiyakov Gallery and the Leningrad Russian Museum purchased his paintings, and in 1980 he was elevated to the status of "People's Artist of the USSR," the most prestigious title awarded to a Soviet artist.

Glazunov's treatment was only slightly exceptional. Aleksandr Shilov and Yury Raksha, two younger prominent Russian nationalist painters, were also beneficiaries of inclusionary policy. In 1977, Shilov (b. 1943) was awarded the Komsomol Prize, the most prestigious award given to a young artist. Between 1978 and 1983, he staged four officially sponsored exhibits in Moscow and two abroad; he was sent to study in Italy by the Soviet Academy of Fine Arts in 1979; and in 1981 he was given the title of "People's Artist of the RSFSR."[36] Although Raksha died young (1937–1980) and was never awarded the title of "People's Artist," he nevertheless in 1980 was awarded a personal exhibit and another three in 1981, a year after his death.[37]

By the late 1970s, the most visible manifestations of the politics of inclusion—the state's active promotion of Russian nationalist literature, cinema, and fine arts and the transformation of Russian nationalist intellectuals into highly privileged individuals—seemed to yield the desired results. Russian nationalist writers enjoyed wide popularity among the reading public. A list of the twenty-four most popular contemporary Soviet authors, compiled by Klaus Mehnert, contains six members of the village prose school (Abramov, Astafiev, Belov, Rasputin, Shukshin, and Soloukhin) and four other Russian nationalist writers (Bondarev, Anatoly Ivanov, Pikul, and Proskurin).[38] Some Russian nationalist movies were enormously popular. For example, the 1974 film written and directed by Shukshin, *Snowball Berry Red (Kalina krasnaya)*, was seen by 62.5 million people.[39] In the fine arts, the Moscow and the Leningrad exhibits of Ilya Glazunov attracted over 1.5 million visitors.

Moreover, attempts to convince Suslov or Zimyanin to initiate a crackdown on Russian nationalist intellectuals were unsuccessful. For example, on January 20, 1977, the head of Glavlit, Pavel Romanov, sent a memorandum addressed to the party secretary in charge of ideology, Mikhail Zimyanin, in which he harshly criticized *Nash sovremennik*'s publication policy in 1976 and early 1977. Romanov especially singled out fiction by Astafiev, Rasputin, Belov, and Bondarev for their ideologically erroneous content. Romanov clearly hoped that his memorandum would lead to Central Committee action against the journal. It did not. The reply, signed by the deputy heads of the Propaganda and Cultural departments, Vladimir Sevruk and Albert Belyaev, on March 1, 1977, clearly indicated that *Nash sovremennik*'s editors effectively received a mere slap on the wrist. The punitive measures were restricted to a discussion of *Nash sovremennik*'s publication policy at a gathering of the Governing Board of the RSFSR Writers' Union and a meeting of officials of the Propaganda and Cultural departments with the journal's chief editor, Vikulov, at Central Committee headquarters. The authors of the reply explicitly stated that the Central Committee would not go beyond the adopted measures.[40]

By the late 1970s, the benefits that the inclusionary politics had bestowed on its recipients seemed to be achieving their goals. Russian nationalist intellectuals dutifully showed their political loyalty to the state. Such popular Russian nationalist writers as Evgeny Nosov and Yury Bondarev denounced the morally corrupt West and Aleksandr Solzhenitsyn at USSR and RSFSR Writers' Union Congresses. In the same years, Ilya Glazunov was painting portraits of Brezhnev and construction workers of the Baikal-Amur railway, the most publicized project of the Brezhnev era.[41]

The Decline and Demise of Inclusionary Politics

The relationship between Russian nationalist intellectuals and the Soviet state was harmonious only on the surface, covering the growing alienation of Russian nationalists from the Brezhnev regime. I will analyze in depth the main causes of this alienation in the next chapter. It is sufficient to say here that this alienation was an unavoidable consequence of inclusionary politics itself. It created high expectations within the Russian nationalist intelligentsia that the party would address their political, social, and cultural concerns, concerns that it was not capable of fulfilling.

As the 1970s unfolded, Russian nationalist intellectuals became increasingly frustrated with the state's continuing censorship of their works, which they rightly interpreted as demonstrating its unwillingness to allow the free articulation of their ideas. They grew impatient with Brezhnev's inability to address such major concerns as the destruction of the environment and the neglect of the prerevolutionary Russian architectural legacy. The progressive deterioration of the state of Russian agriculture and the accelerated depopulation of the Russian countryside were key concerns. The demographic decline of ethnic Russians, the disintegration of the traditional family, and an increase in the rates of divorce, alcoholism, and spiraling crime rates were all seen as dramatic indicators of the state of Soviet decline. Finally, the continuing penetration of Western influences and fads were for many an indication of a dubious future.

There remained opponents of Russian nationalism in the party apparat and the cultural establishment, even after Aleksandr Yakovlev's departure to Canada. They were powerless to challenge the politics of inclusion as long as Suslov and Brezhnev supported it, but they clearly were waiting for their opportunity. As Romanov's 1977 memorandum shows, they sought to exploit the brewing Russian nationalist discontent to convince the top leadership to abandon the politics of inclusion completely, or at least restrict its scope. The increased frustration among Russian nationalist intellectuals and the desire of their opponents to discredit them were bound to lead to a confrontation between the two and to force the Politburo to become involved.

The first sign of the forthcoming confrontation between the party and Russian nationalist intellectuals was the March 14, 1978, letter to Brezhnev written by Mikhail Sholokhov. Sholokhov, a Nobel Prize laureate and one of the most prominent figures in the Soviet cultural establishment, was sympathetic to many Russian nationalist causes and often acted at the request of Russian nationalist writers. In 1972, he had written a letter to Suslov protesting Yakovlev's "Against Anti-Historicism" essay. His 1978 letter was not directed against a particular party official but constituted a general complaint about the state of contemporary Russian culture. In particular, Sholokhov complained about the poor state of the preservation of historic monuments and protested an alleged policy of discrimination against Russian nationalist art and literature in favor of pro-Western and avant-garde culture. He demanded the "active defense of Russian national culture against anti-patriotic, anti-socialist forces, and the appropriate coverage of its historical role in the creation and development of the Russian state in the press, cinema and television."[42]

A strongly worded letter written by such a prominent member of the Soviet cultural establishment could not be left unanswered. On March 20, 1978, Zimyanin, probably acting on Brezhnev's and Suslov's orders, sent a memorandum to the Central Committee Secretariat in which he rejected Sholokhov's accusations, but at the same time he announced the creation of a panel of top party and government officials to investigate Sholokhov's complaints.[43] The panel's report, submitted to the Central Committee Secretariat on June 5, 1978, went to great lengths to show that Sholokhov's accusations were groundless.[44] The report went well beyond a rejection of Sholokhov's charges regarding the poor state of preservationist efforts and policies of preference for avant-garde and Western art at the expense of the Russian nationalists. It dealt as well with other long-standing Russian nationalist concerns, including the domination of non-Russians (i.e., Jews) in Russian cultural life and the absence in the RSFSR of such major cultural institutions as the Academy of Sciences and the Academy of Fine Arts, institutions that existed in all other Union republics.[45]

On each of these issues the report found no factual base for Russian nationalist complaints. It did concede, however, that the Russian nationalist intelligentsia was frustrated with the party's unwillingness to rehabilitate the Russian Orthodox Church and acknowledge the importance of the Slavophile legacy. Yet the report did not recommend a change of party policy on these issues.

The report faithfully reflected the principles of inclusionary politics. The extraordinary attention to Russian nationalist concerns went hand in hand with an unwillingness to recognize the validity of these concerns or introduce policy changes in the areas where these concerns appeared to be justified. Because of the high profile of the panel members, the report could have recommended the radical expansion of inclusionary politics to satisfy Russian nationalist concerns. Yet it recommended a continuation of the status quo. In the long run, this recommendation failed to satisfy the opponents of inclusionary politics and Russian nationalists themselves, effectively paving the way for both sides to try to change the status quo.

The first salvo in the confrontation was fired by the opponents of inclusion in May 1979, when *Kommunist* published an essay that ostensibly criticized the attempts of two minor Russian nationalist writers to portray Faddei Bulgarin, a reactionary journalist of the Pushkin era, in a highly positive light. The essay effectively warned Russian nationalists not to challenge the party's interpretation of Russian history.[46]

This essay was a long-awaited signal to *Literaturnaya gazeta,* the institutional base of the opponents of the politics of inclusion in the cultural establishment, to begin its attack on Russian nationalism.[47] In its June 13, 1979, issue, *Literaturnaya gazeta* reprinted the *Kommunist* essay, and three issues later (July 4, 1979) its editorial reiterated the *Kommunist* warning to Russian nationalists.[48]

The confrontation greatly escalated with the publication of Valentin Pikul's historical novel, *At the Brink of the Abyss (U poslednei cherty)* in the April through July 1979 issues of *Nash sovremennik.* In the novel, Pikul presented a rather unflattering portrait of Nicholas II's court and argued that Gregory Rasputin, and especially the Jews in his entourage, played a key role in the collapse of the monarchy. Despite the fact that the novel was heavily censored (even its title was changed), it was still perceived by the party's ideological establishment as a challenge it could not ignore.[49] It is not clear whether the true cause of the party's rage was Pikul's interpretation of historical events or, as the chief editor of *Nash Sovremennik,* Vikulov, would argue in his memoirs, a suspicion on the part of Brezhnev's wife and her entourage that the novel drew a rather thinly disguised parallel between Brezhnev's Russia in the late 1970s and that of the Romanovs on the eve of the Russian Revolution.[50]

Pikul's novel provided opponents of inclusionary politics in the party apparat and the cultural establishment an opportunity to raise the issue of its efficacy. The first action against Pikul and *Nash sovremennik* took place at the May 29, 1979 meeting of the Secretariat of the USSR Writers' Union. At the meeting, Vadim Kozhevnikov, a prominent member of the cultural establishment and the chief editor of the thick journal *Znamya*, accused Pikul of ignoring the class approach in interpreting historical events and in analyzing the nature of the tsarist regime. The head of the USSR Writers' Union, Georgy Markov, and his deputy, Yury Verchenko, held the editors of *Nash sovremennik* responsible for the publication of the ideologically flawed novel.[51]

Shauro, who was present the meeting, probably hoped that Zimyanin, his immediate superior, would be satisfied with the censure of *Nash sovremennik* and not order any additional action against the journal. Yet within few weeks of the Secretariat of the USSR Writers' Union meeting Zimyanin ordered the Propaganda and Cultural departments to get seriously involved in the Pikul affair.

The formal reason for the interference of the party apparat was a letter to Zimyanin written by a Moscow historian, Z. Mirsky. The letter, dated June 15, 1979, constituted a long and devastating review of Pikul's novel, the publication of which was not yet complete. Mirsky plainly accused Pikul of writing an anti-Soviet novel, which, by completely dismissing the role of the Bolshevik party in the revolutionary process, grossly contradicted the official interpretation of the Russian Revolution. He also pointed out that the rabidly anti-Semitic nature of the novel would be immediately noticed abroad and would seriously damage the Soviet Union in world public opinion.[52]

Since Mirsky was neither a member of the Soviet cultural establishment nor a prominent public figure, Zimyanin could have easily disregarded the letter. Yet, probably under pressure to take action from the opponents of inclusion within the party apparat, he forwarded the letter to Tyazhelnikov and Shauro with instructions to report the party response to the novel. Since Tyazhelnikov and Shauro were strong supporters of inclusionary politics, it is hardly surprising that they tried to limit reprisals against Pikul and *Nash sovremennik* to a mere reprimand of the journal's editors.

Tyazhelnikov and Shauro's memorandum, dated June 20, 1979, acknowledged the strong negative responses to the novel among the intelligentsia but at no point agreed with Mirsky's accusations. Moreover, the memorandum recommended that publication of the work not be halted but reconsidered after the appearance of the novel's last installment in the July issue of *Nash sovremennik*. In order to prevent charges of blatant favoritism toward Pikul and *Nash sovremennik,* Tyazhelnikov and Shauro reported that they called the journal's chief editor, Vikulov, to the Central Committee headquarters, where he was reprimanded and ordered to make changes in the novel's last installment. Finally, the authors of the memorandum proposed publishing a critical review of the novel in the weekly *Literaturnaya Rossiya* after publication of the last installment.[53]

Indeed, on July 27, 1979, *Literaturnaya Rossiya* printed an essay by historian Irina Pushkareva asserting that *At the Brink of the Abyss* advanced an ideologically incorrect conception of the causes of the Russian Revolution of 1917.[54] The Propaganda and Cultural departments lauded the essay for providing a detailed analysis of the novel and highlighting Pikul's ideological mistakes. Despite the publication of Pushkareva's essay, the supporters of inclusionary politics in the party apparat were not able to stop discussion of novel. In the two months following the publication of Pushkareva's essay, the opponents of inclusion were able to use the novel to convince Suslov to take stronger measures against the Russian nationalists than originally had been proposed by Tyazhelnikov and Shauro.

On October 8, 1979, *Pravda* published an article by the literary critic Valentin Oskotsky reiterating Pushkareva's charges.[55] Almost immediately after *Pravda's* condemnation of Pikul's novel, a meeting of the Secretariat of the RSFSR Writers' Union was convened. Since the Secretariat was controlled by Yury Bondarev and other leading Russian nationalist writers, the initiative to convene the meeting and condemn the novel must have originated in the Central Committee apparatus. Pushkareva spoke at the meeting and repeated her criticism. At the same time, none of the thirteen speakers called for Vikulov's dismissal, which clearly indicated that the party's ideological establishment was not willing to initiate a crackdown against the institutional stronghold of Russian nationalism. In a statement issued after the meeting, the Secretariat merely expressed its agreement with the criticism of the novel as voiced in *Literaturnaya Rossiya, Pravda,* and "many readers' letters" and asserted that the publication of the ideologically flawed novel had been a mistake. It instructed the editors of the republican thick journals to be more careful in examining the ideological nature of literary works submitted for publication. In other words, *Nash sovremennik's* editors received a slap on the wrist.[56]

The mere fact that the meeting was convened clearly signified an increase in the influence of the opponents of Russian nationalism in the party apparat. The latter did not lose time and used the Pikul case as an opportunity to issue a stern warning to other prominent Russian national-ist writers whose works they had viewed as particularly objectionable for a long time, but had not criticized openly. Moreover, they clearly were not satisfied by the outcome of the meeting of the Secretariat of the RSFSR Writers' Union and were greatly encouraged by a thinly veiled criticism of Russian nationalism by Suslov himself.

In mid-October 1979, speaking at a conference dedicated to ideological issues, Suslov, clearly alluding to Pikul and other prominent Russian na-tionalist writers, criticized "the distorted and ahistorical understanding of the past [and] strange interests in historical adventurers" found in recently published literature.[57] Shortly after Suslov's speech, an unsigned editorial in the October issue of *Kommunist* criticized the radical nationalist writer of semifictional biographies, Yury Loshchits, and the village prose writer Viktor Astafiev. Loshchits was accused of challenging Lenin's interpretation of nineteenth-century Russian society in his fictionalized biography of the novelist Ivan Goncharov, and Astafiev was accused of portraying contem-porary Soviet society as existing in a spiritual void in his short story "A Falling Leaf."[58]

The party-initiated condemnation of *Nash sovremennik,* the first serious action taken against a major Russian nationalist publication since the dis-missal of Anatoly Nikonov from *Molodaya gvardiya* in 1970, and the *Kom-munist* editorial were interpreted by the foes of Russian nationalism in the Soviet cultural establishment as clear signs that inclusionary politics was losing its support within the party apparat. This, in turn, encouraged them to sharpen their criticism of Russian nationalism. The December 5, 1979 editorial of *Literaturnaya gazeta* attacked another *Nash sovremennik* publi-cation on Russian history. Two weeks later, in its December 19 issue, *Litera-turnaya gazeta* published an essay sharply criticizing anti-urbanism and the idealization of the village in the works of minor Russian nationalist writers.[59]

Also in December 1979, Yury Surovtsev, a leading figure in the USSR Writers' Union and an active participant in the attack on *Molodaya gvardiya* in the late 1960s, sharply criticized the radical Russian nationalist poet Tatiyana Glushkova and several young Russian nationalist writers for promoting an anti-Leninist conception of the essence of national cul-ture. In February 1980, a *Literaturnaya gazeta* editorial explicitly endorsed Surovtsev's attack on Russian nationalist intellectuals.[60]

The December 5, 1979 *Literaturnaya gazeta* editorial provoked a sharp response from *Nash sovremennik*'s chief editor, Vikulov. On December 28, 1979, he sent a letter to Zimyanin protesting the *Literaturnaya gazeta* attack on the journal. However, the party response clearly suggested that supporters of inclusion were losing ground in the intra-apparat struggle. In March 1980, Vikulov was called to the Secretariat of the USSR Writers' Union and was told that his complaint had no merit.[61]

Suslov and Brezhnev, however, were not interested in ending inclusionary politics in 1980. The benefits it was yielding were still regarded as too valuable to justify its abandonment. Sergei Vikulov therefore remained *Nash sovremennik*'s chief editor, the journal's editorial board remained intact, and its overall circulation was not affected. The punishment was merely an attempt to discipline the journal; its subscription was frozen at its 1979 level.[62]

The campaign against Russian nationalism came to an end in the spring of 1980 and, with the single exception of the dismissal of Valery Ganichev from the post of chief editor of *Komsomolskaya pravda* in October 1980, no prominent Russian nationalist editor was fired from his post until April 1981, and no editorial board of any major Russian nationalist thick journal was purged until December 1981.[63] There were good reasons for the timing. The period between 1980 and 1982, the last two years of the Brezhnev era, shared one fundamental similarity with the period 1968 to 1970: the emergence of an external threat. In 1968–1970, the Czech reforms and military clashes on the Chinese border constituted a serious external threat; now the emerging threats were the war in Afghanistan triggered by the Soviet invasion in late December 1979 and the emergence of the anti-communist Solidarity movement in Poland in the spring of 1980. These crises of the early 1980s were much worse than those of the late 1960s because they occurred not in a period of economic growth but one of stagnation, which seriously affected Soviet living standards. As Colton points out, this stagnation opened a dangerous gap between the people's expectations of the steady improvement of their quality of life and the regime's capacity to fulfill these expectations.[64]

Unwilling to undertake radical economic reform to boost economic growth and facing two potent external threats, the political leadership was forced to seek support for its policies by appealing to the nationalist sentiments of the Russian population. Russian nationalist intellectuals were perceived as best able to rally ethnic Russian support for the war in Afghanistan and the continuation of the Soviet empire in Eastern Europe.

The party probably hoped that a high tide of Russian nationalist sentiment would make Russians willing to postpone or sacrifice the pursuit of improved material conditions.

Moreover, there was one major domestic reason for the continuation of the inclusionary politics in the early 1980s. The deepening crisis of Soviet agriculture in the early 1980s led to pressures for new massive budgetary allocations for the agrarian sector of the economy. The so-called "Food Program" called for 140 billion rubles of new investment in agriculture. However, as Gorbachev testifies in his memoirs, there was strong resistance in the Central Committee Secretariat for approval of such enormous investment in the continuously failing sector of the economy. As was the case in the 1960s and 1970s, public support of village prose writers was deemed crucial in order to facilitate acceptance of the major reallocation of resources that the Food Program required. Thus, in 1980 and 1981, the potential benefits of inclusionary politics still outweighed its liabilities.[65]

The year 1980 provided a special opportunity for Russian nationalist intellectuals to stir the patriotic feelings of ethnic Russians above and beyond what had previously been permitted; it was the six hundredth anniversary of the Russian victory over the Mongols at the Kulikovo Field Battle, one of the most spectacular events in Russian history. The celebrations of the anniversary provided Russian nationalists with the best opportunity yet to express the full depth of their discontent with the political, social, and cultural realities of Brezhnev's Russia.

The ideas articulated by Russian nationalist intellectuals during this event are thoroughly covered in Chapter 6. Meanwhile, it is sufficient to say that they openly extolled the virtues of Russian Orthodoxy and challenged the party's antireligious policies, demanded the restoration of churches and other historic monuments, and criticized the policies of détente and the opening up of Soviet society to Western cultural influences.

The intensity of this criticism apparently caught the Soviet leadership by surprise—probably the major reason that the party failed to respond in any significant way.[66] The lack of party action encouraged Russian nationalist intellectuals to intensify their criticism. The year 1981 gave them another excellent opportunity to do so. In the Russian cultural calendar, the year 1981 marked the 160th anniversary of the birth and the centenary of the death of Fyodor Dostoevsky, whom Russian nationalists regarded as their most important ideological predecessor.[67]

The March 1981 issue of *Nash sovremennik* contained a collection of

Vladimir Soloukhin's short reflections, entitled "Pebbles in the Palm" *(Kamushki na ladoni)*. In one story, he openly ridiculed atheistic materialist philosophy and asserted his belief in the existence of superior reason.[68] This articulation of a belief in God and his contempt for the principles of materialism was the logical follow-up to his 1980 essay in which he positively portrayed the contribution of the Optina Pustyn Monastery, one of the most important centers of prerevolutionary Orthodox monasticism, to Russian culture.

Both publications exposed him to the criticism of the opponents of the politics of inclusion in the party and the cultural establishments, seeking to regain the influence they had enjoyed at the end of 1979. Two factors worked in their favor: the stabilization of the situation in Poland after the imposition of martial law and the rapidly deteriorating health of both Brezhnev and Suslov and the ascendance of Andropov, the leading candidate to succeed Brezhnev. Andropov was planning radical reform and could not be swayed by arguments favoring a continuation of inclusionary politics.

From April through June 1981, the journal *Nauka i religiya* published an elaborate criticism of Soloukhin's idealization of Russian monasticism. In September 1981, the journal *Znamya* published a long essay by Surovtsev attacking "Pebbles in the Palm" together with other publications of *Nash sovremennik*. Surovtsev's criticism was quickly endorsed by *Literaturnaya gazeta*.[69]

In April 1981, a second prominent Russian nationalist intellectual was dismissed from his post. While the October 1980 dismissal of Ganichev from the post of chief editor of *Komsomolskaya pravda* was largely unrelated to the fact that he was a prominent Russian nationalist, the dismissal of Sergei Semanov from the post of chief editor of the journal *Chelovek i zakon,* a position he had held since 1976, was a direct result of his Russian nationalist activities. As recently published archival documents clearly indicate, Semanov's dismissal on April 17, 1981 was the consequence of a KGB report in which he was accused of maintaining close ties with a prominent Russian nationalist dissident, Anatoly Ivanov-Skuratov, who was arrested in August 1981, as well as Semanov's harsh criticism of foreign and domestic policies of the Soviet government, which he openly expressed among his entourage.[70] By sacking Semanov, the party apparat sent a clear warning that Semanov-type offenses constituted a violation of the unwritten terms of inclusionary politics and would not be tolerated.

This warning was ignored by Russian nationalist intellectuals. In November 1981, at the peak of the Dostoevsky anniversary celebrations, *Nash sovremennik* published an essay by Vadim Kozhinov entitled, "And Every Tongue Will Name Me" (*I nazovyet menya vsyak sushchy v nei yazyk*), in which Kozhinov openly declared the primacy of the national idea over a cosmopolitan (i.e., communist) one, attacked the permanent orientation of Russia toward the West, and reaffirmed Russia's close historical ties to Asia. Kozhinov also reminded readers of Dostoevsky's central idea of Russia's historical mission and implied that the spread of communism could not be accepted as being a part of this mission.[71]

The same issue of *Nash sovremennik* contained a novel by a young conservative village prose writer, Vladimir Krupin, entitled *The Fortieth Day (Sorokovoi den)*. The novel provided an unflattering account of a contemporary village in which a very low work ethic, moral corruption, and, especially, alcoholism were the dominant features of rural society. Krupin openly blamed the Soviet mass media, especially television, for heavily contributing to these negative social trends by incessantly beaming into peoples' homes "debauchery and violence, vulgarity and obscurantism."[72]

The challenge to party ideology and policies presented by Kozhinov and Krupin became an important weapon in the hands of the opponents of Russian nationalism in their efforts to force a review of the policy of inclusionary politics. In December 1981, on the order of the Central Committee, a special meeting of the Secretariat of the RSFSR Writers' Union was convened to discuss the November 1981 issue of *Nash sovremennik* and Krupin and Kozhinov's work.[73] The outcome of the meeting was an overhaul of the journal's editorial board. The first deputy chief editor, Yury Seleznev, was removed from his post, and five new members were added to the board. These changes, however, were hardly a victory for the opponents of Russian nationalism since the new board members were well-known Russian nationalist intellectuals. As long as Suslov was alive, the party probably was not willing to abandon its decade-long commitment to inclusionary politics.[74]

This situation changed dramatically after Suslov, the most important supporter of inclusionary politics in the party leadership, died on January 25, 1982. Now the scales within the party ideological establishment tipped in favor of the opponents of Russian nationalism. It was not a coincidence that an attack on Russian nationalism in the party press began on the eve of Suslov's death and was greatly intensified thereafter. The January 22, 1982 issue of *Sovetskaya kultura* contained an article by Feliks Kuznetsov, the head of the Moscow Writers' Union organization, in which he attacked Russian nationalists for flagrantly ignoring in their works the principles of the January 1972 Central Committee resolution on literary criticism. More important, the first issue of *Kommunist* to appear after Suslov's death contained letters from Mikhail Rutkevich, the prominent orthodox Communist sociologist, and S. Filippova, both of which sharply protested *Nash sovremennik*'s publication of Soloukhin's "Pebbles."[75]

On February 1, 1982, shortly after the *Kommunist* publication, *Pravda* published an article attacking Kozhinov's essay. The author was Vasily Kuleshov, a professor of Russian literature at Moscow University and a well-known opponent of Russian nationalism. This attack was effectively a synthesis of the accusations voiced by both Kuznetsov and Rutkevich. Kuleshov accused Kozhinov of articulating ideas that challenged the official interpretation of Russian history and culture. By doing this, Kuleshov asserted, Kozhinov blatantly violated the principles established by the 1972 Central Committee resolution on literary criticism.[76]

In March 1982, Surovtsev greatly elaborated Kuleshov's attack on Kozhinov. In a twenty-page essay published in the journal *Znamya*, Surovtsev accused Kozhinov of committing such grave ideological heresies as rejecting the Marxist class interpretation of world history, denying the importance of the revolutionary movement in Russian history, distorting the meaning of Lenin's texts through a selective choice of quotations, and ultimately challenging Lenin's conception of the class nature of every national culture.[77]

The letters in *Kommunist* and Kuleshov's *Pravda* article, as well as the unprecedented aggressiveness of Surovtsev, all point to the growing influence of the opponents of inclusionary politics in the winter and spring of 1982. In each case, *Nash sovremennik* was the target of attack, suggesting that the antinationalist opponents were lobbying to take over the most important institutional base of the Russian nationalists.

In April 1982, the Central Committee apparat called a meeting of *Nash sovremennik*'s party organization. At the meeting, attended by a representative of the Cultural Department, *Nash sovremennik*'s editors were told to accept the criticism leveled against the journal and revise its publication policy accordingly.[78] The main consequence of the meeting was a letter to *Kommunist*, sent by *Nash sovremennik*'s party organization and signed by the journal's chief editor, Sergei Vikulov, and a new board member, Aleksei Shitikov, in which the journal expressed its agreement with the contents of Rutkevich's and Filipova's criticism and promised not to publish ideologically incorrect works like those of Soloukhin.[79]

To the opponents of Russian nationalism, this contrition was hardly satisfactory. Moreover, they were emboldened by the May 1982 appointment of Andropov as Suslov's successor as the Politburo member in charge of ideology. The first to respond to this appointment was Glavlit's head, Romanov, who within days of Andropov's appointment sent a long memorandum to Zimyanin harshly denouncing *Nash sovremennik* for its publication policies between 1980 and mid-1982. Romanov deliberately avoided criticizing Soloukhin and Kozhinov, the targets of earlier attacks, and focused on other works in order to show that most of the journal's publications were in complete contradiction with party policies, and this forced incessant intervention by the censorship agency. In particular, Romanov lashed out against such prominent Russian nationalist writers and journalists as Mikhail Alekseev, Vasily Belov, Yury Bondarev, Vladimir Krupin, and Ivan Vasiliev.

Zimyanin, unsure whether a decisive change of opinion regarding Russian nationalists had indeed taken place in the Politburo and mindful of the 1972 Yakovlev incident, decided to proceed cautiously. He forwarded Romanov's memorandum to Tyazhelnikov and Shauro with the following note:

> The note of comrade Romanov justly highlights the serious flaws in the work of the journal *Nash sovremennik*. As you well know, there are many more of these flaws [than those mentioned by Romanov]. The journal invoked a great deal of criticism for ideological inconsistency, philistine grumbling and so on. We should consider measures . . . to explain with all seriousness to the editorial board of *Nash sovremennik* the nature of its obligation to the party.[80]

In the jargon of the party apparat, this note was an instruction to order the chief editor to stop criticizing party policies or its ideology. In other words, Zimyanin proposed yet another slap on the wrist, which Tyazhelnikov and Shauro dutifully carried out.

Although no further action was taken against *Nash sovremennik's* editors in the aftermath of Romanov's memorandum, the Andropov-led ideological establishment began preparation for the introduction of major changes in the nature of inclusionary politics. The first major signal of the imminent change in party policy toward Russian nationalist intellectuals was the July 23, 1982 Central Committee resolution on the thick journals. Entitled "On the Creative Links of Literary Journals with the Practice of Communist Construction" *(O tvorcheskikh svyazyakh literaturno-khudozhestvennykh zhurnalov s praktikoi kommunisticheskogo stroitelstva)*, the resolution was the first of its kind since January 1972. It cited the frequency of publications that ignored the class approach in the analysis of historical events, a clear allusion to recent *Nash sovremennik* articles. The resolution's insistence that the journals give firm support to the party's foreign and domestic policies was also an implicit criticism of the publication policy of the Russian nationalist journals since 1980.

The resolution was extremely frank in outlining how the party planned to restrict the scope of Russian nationalist criticism of its policies. The party organizations in the literary journals were given a greater role (vis-à-vis the chief editor) in approving works for publication and in hiring the journals' staff. In addition, the regional party committees and the Moscow party organization were ordered to monitor more closely the content of the journals appearing in their locales.[81]

The resolution was not followed by any action against *Nash sovremennik*, and this prompted the opponents of Russian nationalism to increase their pressure on Andropov to take action against Russian nationalists and their chief publication. On August 17, 1982, *Pravda* published Surovtsev's article in which he sharply denounced an essay by the radical nationalist historian Apollon Kuzmin, printed in the April issue of *Nash sovremennik*.[82]

On September 28, 1982, Romanov sent another memorandum to Zimyanin criticizing *Nash sovremennik* for its continuing attempts to publish works that the chief censor found unacceptable for one reason or another.[83] As in the previous case, Zimyanin's response was hardly one that Romanov and other opponents of inclusionary politics in the party apparat had hoped for. As long as Brezhnev was alive, Zimyanin was reluctant to undermine inclusionary politics by initiating a major crackdown on Russian nationalists and *Nash sovremennik*. In a note addressed to the heads of the Propaganda and Cultural departments, he laconically instructed both departments to order the USSR and RSFSR Writers' Unions to "take necessary measures" against the journal. From the October 19, 1982 reply of Tyazhelnikov and Shauro, we learn that "necessary measures" were confined to another slap on wrist: Vikulov was called to the offices of the

RSFSR Writers' Union, where one of its heads, Sergei Mikhalkov, chastised him for transgressions mentioned in Romanov's report and forced him to consent to Glavlit's demands to exclude several works from forthcoming issues of the journal.[84]

Thus, no serious action was taken against *Nash sovremennik* or any other Russian nationalist publication until late 1982. Moreover, on November 6, 1982, only four days before Brezhnev's death, the radical nationalist novelist Vladimir Chivilikhin was awarded the USSR State Prize for a rabidly nationalistic historical novel, *Memory (Pamyat)*, published in *Nash sovremennik* in 1980.[85] This may well have been the outcome of Andropov's effort in the last months of Brezhnev's life to ensure his succession to the post of the general secretary of the CPSU. Andropov wanted to reassure supporters of inclusionary politics in the Soviet political elite that he was not going to crack down on Russian nationalists or bow to the pressure of those forces demanding such a crackdown.

Andropov nevertheless began preparing for a radical shift in the party's policies toward Russian nationalists even in the last days of Brezhnev's life. In October 1982, he convened a meeting with Tyazhelnikov and all of his deputies in the Propaganda Department, telling them that he was dissatisfied with the department's work.[86] This was a clear warning to Tyazhelnikov that his days at the helm of the Propaganda Department were numbered. Indeed, only a few weeks after his assumption of power, Andropov sacked Tyazhelnikov and appointed him ambassador to Romania. His replacement, Boris Stukalin, the former head of the USSR State Committee on Publishing (Goskomizdat), was not sympathetic to Russian nationalist causes.

The sacking of Tyazhelnikov was a clear sign to Zimyanin that Andropov wanted to see more decisive action against those Russian nationalists who openly challenged the party. By December 1982, the party's ideological establishment had decided to demonstrate its new policy toward Russian nationalist intellectuals and their journals. The immediate objects of attack were the radical nationalist literary critic, Mikhail Lobanov, and the Saratov literary journal *Volga*.

The October 1982 issue of the journal contained Lobanov's essay, "Liberation" *(Osvobozhdenie)*, the most open Russian nationalist denunciation of communist ideology and the entire Soviet historical experience to appear in the censored Soviet press. Lobanov was especially critical of collectivization, which he portrayed as the greatest calamity to befall the Russian nation. Collectivization, he openly declared, had destroyed the backbone of the Russian nation, the traditional Russian peasantry. In short, Lobanov's essay, more than any other Russian nationalist publication in the past, made it absolutely clear that inclusionary politics had failed to achieve its goals.[87]

Published in the last days of the Brezhnev era, "Liberation" did not provoke an immediate response from the party apparat. However, Andropov viewed the attack on collectivization as a grave ideological offense, and shortly after his assumption of power ordered the ideological establishment into action.[88] In late December 1982, the chief editor of *Volga*, Nikolai Palkin, and his deputy, Boris Dedyukhin, were removed from their posts for publishing Lobanov's essay. Following this purge, *Volga* ceased to be a Russian nationalist publication. The treatment of *Nash sovremennik* was more sophisticated and was aimed at reducing the exposure of the Russian public to its ideas. In January 1983, *Nash sovremennik*'s circulation was cut by 33 percent (from 335,000 copies in December 1982 to 225,000 in January 1983) and the subscription quota was reduced by 135,000 subscribers, although the journal's chief editor and the editorial board remained intact.[89]

These measures were combined with a massive attack on Russian nationalism, sometimes disguised as criticism of Lobanov's ideas, in the Soviet press. The January 5, 1983 issue of *Literaturnaya gazeta* contained an essay by Pyotr Nikolaev, a literary critic and important member of the Soviet cultural establishment, that harshly attacked Lobanov and defended collectivization "as a historically necessary act of the revolutionary transformation of the peasant consciousness." On January 21, Oskotsky, writing in *Literaturnaya Rossiya*, accused Lobanov of historical voluntarism and excessive idealization of the traditional Russian peasantry, and declared that there was no return to the precollectivized village.

On February 6, *Literaturnaya gazeta*'s editorial praised Nikolaev's and Oskotsky's attacks on Lobanov and added to them criticism of the village prose as suffering from a "narrowness of vision" and failing to provide a new positive hero: the collective farmer who lives in the era of science and technology.[90]

On February 8, 1982, on the orders of the Cultural Department, Secretariat of the RSFSR Writers' Union was convened to discuss Lobanov's essay. The meeting duly issued a condemnation of Lobanov's ideas and called the publication of the essay an ideological error.[91] Following this condemnation, the new editors of *Volga* published an apology for print-ing an essay critical of collectivization and promised to follow the guide-lines established by the July 1982 Central Committee decree on literary criticism.[92]

Nash sovremennik and *Volga* were not the only targets of attacks by opponents of Russian nationalism in the Soviet cultural establishment during this period. On January 12, 1983, the Secretariat of the USSR Writ-ers' Union was convened to review the publication policy of the provincial Russian nationalist journal *Sever*. At the meeting, several members of the Secretariat harshly criticized the journal for publishing works of fiction and nonfiction that idealized prerevolutionary Russia, as well as for *Sever's* excessive preoccupation with rural themes. The apparent purpose of the meeting was merely to pressure the journal chief editor, Dmitry Gusarov, to drop *Sever's* nationalist orientation, because no further action against the journal was taken.[93]

The resolution of the RSFSR Writers' Union Secretariat and review of the *Sever* publication policy, however, did not produce any immediate results. *Nash sovremennik* and *Sever* continued to defy their opponents in the Central Committee apparatus and cultural establishment by publishing fiction and nonfiction works that defied the main tenets of the official ide-ology and criticized party policies. The February 13, 1983 issue of *Pravda* contained Surovtsev's essay accusing Lobanov and several *Sever* authors of promoting "ahistorical" and "nihilistic" ideas. The underlying message of Surovtsev's essay was an appeal to Andropov to adopt tougher measures against Russian nationalism.[94]

The June 1983 plenum of the Central Committee was aimed at clarifying the party's cultural policies, which could be used later to crack down on *Nash sovremennik*. Konstantin Chernenko, speaking at the plenum in his capacity as the Politburo member in charge of ideology, criticized the Russian nationalist denunciation of collectivization, the idealization of the traditional Russian peasantry, and the glorification of the Russian Ortho-dox Church, and demanded that the editors of the thick journals and publishing houses not publish such works. He also criticized the Cultural Department for its tolerance of works of literature and art that challenged official Marxist-Leninist ideology.[95]

The plenum's resolution faithfully reflected Chernenko's speech. It es-tablished the personal responsibility of the chief editors of journals and publishing houses for the ideological correctness of works they published.

It also implied that publication of Russian nationalist works that challenged the official ideology or interpretation of history would no longer be tolerated. Thus, the ground was prepared for a crackdown on *Nash sovremennik* and other Russian nationalist publications.[96]

The June 1983 resolution and the campaign preceding it in the press were the most visible signs of the planned crackdown on Russian nationalism but not the only ones. In late September and early October 1983, Andropov recalled Aleksandr Yakovlev from his post as the USSR ambassador to Canada and appointed him the head of the highly prestigious USSR Academy of Sciences Institute of World Economy and International Relations (IMEMO). The fact that the most outspoken opponent of inclusion in the party apparat in the early 1970s was back in Moscow and holding an important position was far more than a symbolic gesture that the Brezhnev-era policies in the realms of culture and ideology were over. It is quite possible that Andropov planned to involve Yakovlev in the crackdown on Russian nationalism.[97]

Yet this crackdown did not occur, and the Russian nationalists entered the Gorbachev era with their institutional base intact. The June 1983 resolution also remained a dead letter in the realm of book publication. As table 4.3 shows, seventeen prominent Russian nationalist writers, including Pikul and Soloukhin, the subjects of harsh party criticism in the late 1970s and early 1980s, saw their books published in 1 million or more copies between 1983 and 1985. Moreover, the state also continued to bestow high honors on leading Russian nationalist writers. In 1983, Yury Bondarev, the head of the RSFSR Writers' Union, was awarded his second USSR State Prize, and the radical nationalist poet Oleg Shestinsky was awarded the Komsomol Prize.

Undoubtedly Andropov's rapidly failing health in the second half of 1983 and his subsequent death on February 9, 1984, brought to a halt any decisive political action against a long-privileged and well-entrenched group of intelligentsia and led to the perpetuation of certain features of inclusionary politics. Yet there was a more important reason for the contradictory nature of Andropov's cultural policies in the second half of 1983 and early 1984. The consequences of inclusionary politics could not be undone overnight. The party had assisted Russian nationalist writers in gaining genuine popularity in Soviet society. Andropov realized that it was impossible to eradicate this popularity through purely repressive measures. Giving the liberal-reformist intellectuals the freedom to articulate and propagate their ideas, as well as the institutional bases from which to do so, was the best way of reducing the influence of Russian nationalist ideas. Andropov, however, hesitated to lift the tight censorship on the discussion of Stalinism and its legacy or a need for radical reforms, key subjects for liberal-reformist intellectuals, or to give them control of a major thick journal or newspaper. The reformist intellectuals remained equally alienated from the party. Thus, the party was left without any significant support in the Soviet intellectual and cultural community.[98]

Table 4.3 Book Publication by Prominent Russian Nationalist Intellectuals, 1983–1985

Author	Total Copies of Books Published, 1983–1985	Literary Prizes
Viktor Astafiev	5,459,260	
Yury Bondarev	3,200,890	USSR State Prize, 1983
Vasily Shukshin	2,860,160	
Valentin Rasputin	2,854,130	
Evgeny Nosov	2,601,740	
Mikhail Alekseev	1,922,000	
Pyotr Proskurin	1,880,000	
Gavriil Troepolsky	1,852,040	
Nikolai Rubtsov	1,824,000	
Fyodor Abramov	1,648,000	
Valentin Pikul	1,390,000	
Vladimir Soloukhin	1,254,210	
Sergei Voronin	1,225,000	
Aleksei Yugov	1,100,000	
Vladimir Chivilikhin	1,050,000	
Aleksandr Yashin	1,029,760	
Ivan Vasiliev	1,017,000	
Egor Isaev	977,000	

Table 4.3 (continued)

Author	Total Copies of Books Published, 1983–1985	Literary Prizes
Sergei Zalygin	925,000	
Anatoly Ivanov	794,650	
Vladimir Likhonosov	750,000	
Semyon Shurtakov	700,000	
Aleksandr Prokhanov	539,570	
Oleg Shestinsky	521,000	Komsomol Prize, 1983
Vladimir Krupin	500,000	
Anatoly Tkachenko	465,000	
Vasily Belov	507,970	
Georgy Semenov	417,280	
Stanislav Rybas	375,000	
Leonid Frolov	375,000	
Sergei Vysotsky	350,000	
Yury Borodkin	330,000	
Nikolai Shundik	309,000	
Boris Mozhaev	300,000	

Source: *Bolshaya Sovetskaya Entsiklopediya; Ezhegodnik knigi SSSR, 1983–1985.*

Reluctant to use coercive measures against Russian nationalists or to seek support among the liberal-reformist intelligentsia, Andropov was left with little choice but to present the party as the institution that no longer favored any particular ideological group within the Soviet intellectual elite. As in other policy areas, this solution was the postponement of a difficult decision and allowed the continuation of the status quo. As such, it perfectly suited the general policy framework preferred by Chernenko. This is the reason that Chernenko essentially continued the cultural policies shaped in late 1983, rather than attempt to revive the Brezhnev-era politics of inclusion.[99]

This postinclusion era cultural politics found its expression in the choice of recipients of the prestigious literary prizes, in the selection of deputies to the USSR Supreme Soviet, and in the choice of writers given state honors during the celebrations of the fiftieth anniversary of the USSR Writers' Union. Thus, in addition to Bondarev, the USSR State Prize in 1983 was awarded to the playwright Mikhail Shatrov, one of the most prominent liberal-reformist intellectuals. Another prominent liberal-reformist intellectual, the poet Evgeny Evtushenko, received the USSR State Prize in 1984. In 1983, the chief editor of the main liberal-reformist journal *Druzhba narodov*, Sergei Baruzdin, was awarded the Gorky Prize, and in 1984 the same prize was given to the radical nationalist poet Nikolai Starshinov.

In 1984, Bondarev and radical nationalist poet Egor Isaev were chosen to be deputies of the Soviet parliament, the USSR Supreme Soviet, a highly prestigious if politically powerless position. Along with Bondarev and Isaev, the list of deputies also included such outspoken critics of Russian nationalism as Aleksandr Yakovlev and the Kazakh poet Olzhas Suleimenov.[100]

The clearest expression that the party no longer favored Russian nationalists over their ideological foes among the intelligentsia was reflected in the politics of the state honors bestowed on members of the USSR Writers' Union during the celebration of the union's fiftieth anniversary in the fall of 1984. On this occasion, 297 writers, poets, and literary critics were awarded five prestigious state honors ranging from the Order of Hero of Socialist Labor, the highest civilian award, to the Order of the Mark of Honor *(Orden Znak Pocheta)*, the least prestigious in the honors hierarchy. Thirty-two Russian nationalist intellectuals were awarded the state honors. However, as Table 4.4 shows, in each honor category there was a balance between Russian nationalists and their opponents. At the same time, the party found a less than subtle way to express its displeasure with Russian nationalist thick journals and their editors. Thus, Sergei Vikulov and Mikhail Alekseev, the chief editors of *Nash sovremennik* and *Moskva*, were awarded the Order of the Friendship of the People, a less prestigious honor than the Order of the October Revolution, which was bestowed on Sergei Baruzdin and Andrei Dementiev, the chief editors of liberal-reformist journals *Druzhba narodov* and *Yunost.*[101]

Although the books of Russian nationalist authors continued to be published in hundreds of thousands of copies, the circulation of *Nash sovremennik* remained frozen at its 1983 level. Chernenko also continued Andropov's policy of allowing attacks on Russian nationalism to appear in the

Table 4.4 Awards Given at the Fiftieth Anniversary Celebration of the USSR Writers' Union, November 1984

Political Orientation	Order of the Hero of Socialist Labor	Order of Lenin	Order of the October Revolution	Order of the Red Banner of Labor	Order of the Friendship of the People	Order of the Mark of Honor
Russian nationalists	Anatoly Ivanov	Vasily Belov Egor Isaev Evgeny Nosov Pyotr Proskurin Valentin Rasputin	Oleg Shestinsky	Yury Borodkin Vladimir Firsov Olga Fokina Georgy Semenov Gavriil Troepolsky Vladimir Tsybin	Mikhail Alekseev Feliks Chuev Leonid Frolov Gleb Goryshin Vladimir Krupin Stanislav Kunyaev Valentin Pikul Vasily Roslyakov Valentin Sidorov Nikolai Shundik Nikolai Starshinov Sergei Vikulov	Viktor Likhonosov Oleg Mikhailov Boris Mozhaev Gary Nemchenko Valentin Sorokin Mikhail Vorfolameev Igor Zolotussky
Liberal-reformers and other opponents of Russian nationalism	Anatoly Ananiev	Daniil Granin Veniamin Kaverin Vitaly Ozerov Robert Rozhdestvensky	Sergei Baruzdin Andrei Dementiev Vitaly Korotich Feliks Kuznetsov Yury Surovtsev	Margarita Aliger Ivan Drach Ion Drutse Oles Honchar Olzhas Suleimenov Valentin Kataev	Chengiz Aitmatov Vladimir Amlinsky Bella Akhmadulina Georgy Berdnikov Otar Chiladze Mikhail Dudin Irina Grekova Leonard Lavlinsky Bulat Okudzhava Evgeny Sidorov Mikhail Shatrov	Igor Dedkov Sergei Chuprynin Vasily Kuleshov Vladimir Makanin Boris Nikolsky Anatoly Kim Svetlana Alekseevich

Source: *Literaturnaya gazeta*, November 21, 1994.

main party publications, although the intensity of these attacks was diminished. The harshest attack on Russian nationalists was the May 6, 1984, *Pravda* essay by Valentin Oskotsky. Entitled "In the Struggle against Antihistoricism" *(V borbe s antiistorizmom)*, an obvious paraphrase of "Against Antihistoricism," the title of Yakovlev's 1972 essay, Oskotsky's essay attacked Russian nationalists who idealized autocracy and the Russian Orthodox Church and rejected Lenin's concept of the class nature of national culture.[102]

Russian nationalists were able to publish a response to their critics only at the very end of the Chernenko period. The March 1985 issue of *Nash sovremennik* contained a lengthy essay by Apollon Kuzmin, a radical nationalist historian and member of the journal's editorial board. The essay harshly attacked Yury Surovtsev, the most consistent critic of Russian nationalism in the Soviet literary establishment. Kuzmin accused Surovtsev of advancing the Menshevik and Trotskyite rather than the Leninist concept of nationality and national culture, in his attacks on Russian nationalist intellectuals. After the October Revolution, Kuzmin asserted, Lenin fully embraced Russian nationalism as the key element in building the new socialist Russia.[103]

Kuzmin's essay attempted to do more than simply discredit his ideological opponents in the eyes of the party leadership. Appearing only days before Gorbachev became general secretary, the essay was an Aesopian way of calling upon Gorbachev to reform the Soviet state according to the ideological precepts of Russian nationalism and offering a justification for such a transformation. As we shall see in chapters 7 and 8, Gorbachev chose quite a different path of reform than that offered by Kuzmin and other radical nationalists.

Why, despite the privileges Russian nationalists enjoyed during the Brezhnev era, they rejected the unwritten terms of the politics of inclusion is the subject of the next chapter.

What Went Wrong with the Politics of Inclusion?

Unmet expectations created by the politics of inclusion led to the alienation of Russian nationalist intellectuals from the regime. The politics of inclusion were more a golden straitjacket than a policy initiative designed to co-opt Russian nationalists. Certainly, inclusion conferred on Russian nationalist intellectuals privileged social status, prestigious titles and awards, huge print runs of their books or exhibition of their works of art, and highly prized opportunities to travel abroad. This treatment raised their expectations that the party would lift tight censorship restrictions on the articulation of their ideas and seriously address their principal social concerns. But an effective response to these concerns would have required a radical structural change in the very nature of Soviet politics—unthinkable to the Brezhnev regime.

Between 1971 and 1985, Russian nationalists focused on such fundamental issues as the destruction of the environment, the preservation of historic monuments, the progressive deterioration of Russian agriculture and the accelerated depopulation of the Russian countryside, the demographic decline of ethnic Russians, the disintegration of the traditional family, growing alcoholism, and the continuing penetration of Western influences and fads. This chapter analyzes how Russian nationalists articulated their concerns on these issues, and the party's response and the impact this would have on the role of Russian nationalists as an articulated audience of the regime.

Censorship

Privileged social status went hand in hand with a continuation of tight control on Russian nationalists' activities. Strict censorship of books and

exhibits deemed to challenge Marxist-Leninist ideology, the official interpretation of history, or party policies on key social, economic, or political
issues remained in force. The experience of such prominent Russian nationalist writers as Yury Bondarev, Viktor Astafiev, Fyodor Abramov, Vasily
Belov, Valentin Rasputin, Mikhail Alekseev, and Boris Mozhaev effectively
illustrate this point.

Bondarev was deputy head of the RSFSR Writers' Union and thus a
prominent member of the Soviet cultural establishment. Between 1971 and
1985, he was awarded the Lenin Prize (1972), the USSR State Prize (1977
and 1983), and the Gorky Prize (1975), and more than 9.8 million copies
of his books were printed by various Soviet publishing houses. Yet despite
his privileged status, Bondarev was hardly exempt from the censors' harsh
scrutiny of his works. In 1977 and 1982, the censors banned the publication of his stories in *Nash sovremennik* on the grounds that they included
the Stalinist terror as an integral part of his story line. Again in 1982, the
censors forced Bondarev to soften his criticism of the moral corruption of
contemporary Soviet society, which was a key element in his story "Russian
Towns" *(Russkie gorodki).*[1]

Viktor Astafiev was the most published Russian nationalist writer of the
1970s and early 1980s. Between 1971 and 1985, more than 19 million
copies of his books were printed in the Soviet Union. He received the
Gorky Prize in 1975, and, in 1978, he received the USSR State Prize for a
collection of short stories on ecological issues entitled *The Queen Fish.*
Despite Astafiev's public recognition and immense popularity, Glavit head
Pavel Romanov harshly criticized *The Queen Fish* for its negative depiction
of Soviet life. Only a highly edited version of the story appeared in print.

Valentin Rasputin, probably the most influental village prose writer of
the 1970s and the 1977 laureate of the USSR State Prize, had a similar
experience. His most important work of the period, the 1976 ecological
novel *Farewell to Matyora,* was one of the most hotly debated literary works
of the Brezhnev era. In 1982, the screen version of the novel became a
popular Soviet movie, yet the novel appeared only in a highly censored
form on the grounds that Rasputin portrayed the Soviet government's
actions during the construction of a hydroelectric station in a "highly
repugnant fashion."[2]

Between 1971 and 1985, more than 6.6 million copies of Abramov's
books were published, and in 1975 he was awarded the USSR State Prize.
This recognition nevertheless did not protect him from the heavy censorship of his novels *Roads and Crossroads (Puti-pereputiya)* and *Home*

(Dom). In both cases, the censors removed major passages sharply critical of Stalinism, past and current policies in the countryside, and the mention of grain purchases from the United States.[3] In 1982, the censors banned the publication in *Nash sovremennik* of Abramov's recollections of village prose writer Aleksandr Yashin on the grounds that they contained Abramov's rejection of the "just party criticism" of Yashin's 1962 story "Vologda Wedding," and Abramov's own 1963 essay, "Around and About," both highly critical of the party's policies in the countryside.[4]

Between 1971 and 1985, about 4.5 million copies of Belov's books were printed, and in 1981 he was awarded the USSR State Prize. His novel *On the Eve (Kanuny)*, which was harshly critical of collectivization, was heavily edited by the censors. Moreover, in 1981, the censors excluded an essay on the important role played by the Orthodox Church in the peasant way of life from his book about peasant traditional lifestyle, entitled *Harmony (Lad)*.[5]

Mikhail Alekseev's novel *Pranksters (Drachuny)*, a part of which describes a Russian village at the time of the 1933 famine that accompanied collectivization, was published in *Nash sovremennik* in 1981 and nominated for the Lenin Prize in 1984. Alekseev, the USSR State Prize recipient in 1976 and chief editor of the thick journal *Moskva*, whose books were published in over 7.5 million copies between 1971 and 1985, was one of the most powerful figures in the Soviet cultural establishment. Yet he had serious difficulties in publishing *Pranksters*. Romanov, the head of Glavlit, demanded that Alekseev exclude from the novel any mention of the famine. Alekseev refused and agreed to make only minor revisions. Ultimately, he was able to use his highly placed connections in the Central Committee apparatus to force the censors to publish the novel, without drastic revisions. However, *Nash sovremennik* was not allowed to publish any readers' comments on the novel and Alekseev would be forced to wait until 1988 to publish a selection of readers' letters.[6]

If the leading Russian nationalist writers were subjected to such aggressive censorship, lesser figures in the movement faced even harsher scrutiny. Boris Mozhaev was a popular liberal village prose writer who had received recognition for his fictional and nonfictional critiques of Soviet agricultural and ecological policies. Between 1971 and 1985, almost a million copies of his books appeared in print. Yet his works appeared only three times in the thick journals, the most important and prestigious forum for literary publication. The first volume of his novel *The Country Folk*

(*Muzhiki i baby*), which contained sharp criticism of collectivization, appeared as a book only in 1976, four years after it was written. Despite the literary quality of the work, it was never serialized in a thick journal. The second volume of the novel, completed in 1980, was also rejected by all the thick journals and had to wait until 1987 for publication.[7]

The censors effectively prevented substantive public debate on fictional works exposing the horrors of collectivization. Although they permitted the publication of vaguely worded reviews of Alekseev, Belov, and Mozhaev's novels, the censors often caused substantial delays in the publication of these reviews. Because of the nature of Soviet society, literary works and the reviews and discussions that followed their publication were often the only public forum for discussion of important political and social issues. The party so feared public discussion of collectivization and its aftermath that the censors prohibited the publication of any reviews or readers' responses that might have sparked such debate. In May 1982, the Governing Board of the USSR Writers' Union, clearly on orders from the Central Committee, condemned attempts of village prose writers to challenge the official interpretation of collectivization.[8]

The editors of the journal *Volga* ignored this condemnation and attempted to launch a debate on the benefits and ills of collectivization in their October 1982 issue. Mikhail Lobanov's review of Alekseev's novel, explicitly critical of collectivization, was denounced and quickly suppressed.[9] Subsequently the journal's editors were dismissed, and the publication of Lobanov's essay was condemned in *Pravda* and, ultimately, by the RSFSR Writers' Union. A real debate on collectivization and its legacy would not begin until 1987, with the publication of the second volume of Mozhaev's *The Country Folk*.

The censors practiced similar policies in the realm of fine arts. Despite Glazunov's privileged status, an exhibit of his work planned for 1977 in Moscow was canceled because Glazunov was determined to show his giant painting, *The Mystery of the Twentieth Century*, despite the censors' ban of the work. This same ban, because of the painting's radical nationalist interpretation of twentieth-century Russian and world history, eliminated the painting from the 1978 Moscow and the 1979 Leningrad exhibits. Moreover, the Leningrad exhibition would have been cancelled if Glazunov had not agreed to place two other paintings in inconspicuous locations in the hall.[10] Glazunov was able to exhibit *The Mystery of the Twentieth Century* in public for the first time in 1988.

Censorship also restricted the dissemination and analysis of the works of prerevolutionary Russian nationalist thinkers regarded by many Russian nationalist intellectuals as their ideological predecessors. In the 1970s, Russian nationalists were not allowed to renew the 1969 discussion about the relevance of the Slavophile legacy.[11] At the same time, realizing the importance that Russian nationalists placed on the Slavophile movement, the party allowed scholarly analysis of the Slavophiles and, in the late 1970s, a very selective publication of works by Slavophiles and other prerevolutionary Russian nationalists as an element of inclusion.[12]

In the late 1970s, Sovremennik publishing house, specializing in fictional and nonfictional works by village prose writers and other leading Russian nationalists, was allowed to launch a series, "To the Lovers of Russian Letters" *(Lyubitelyam Rossiiskoi slovesnosti),* featuring selected works by prerevolutionary Russian nationalists. In the late 1970s and early 1980s, other publishing houses, notably Iskusstvo, also published works by prerevolutionary Russian nationalist philosophers and literary critics.[13]

Russian nationalists enthusiastically greeted the publication of works by Slavophile thinkers and scholarly books on Slavophiles and their legacy.[14] Now their expectations grew that at least the most significant works of their prerevolutionary predecessors, and perhaps all of them, would be published. Yet the party's ideological apparatus, fearing that such an undertaking would constitute a threat to Marxism-Leninism, did not permit the republication of a number of important nineteenth-century classics, among them Nikolai Karamzin's monarchist *History of the Russian State,* the main philosophical works of the Slavophiles, and any of the early twentieth-century Russian religious thinkers. Even works approved for publication often appeared only in a highly censored form.

From the late 1970s, and especially during and immediately after the 1980 celebrations of the battle of Kulikovo, leading Russian nationalist intellectuals loudly demanded the publication of Karamzin's *History.*[15] The party ideological apparatus would not give in. The book's publication became one of the first Russian nationalist demands raised during the Gorbachev era, and finally appeared in 1988.

Environmental Protection

Throughout the 1970s, essays by such leading Russian nationalist environmentalists as Vladimir Chivilikhin, Pyotr Dudochkin, Aleksandr Malyshev, and Oleg Volkov, as well as fictional and nonfictional works by the village prose writers Viktor Astafiev, Boris Mozhaev, Valentin Rasputin, Vladimir Soloukhin, and Sergei Zalygin, were full of graphic descriptions of deforestation, the poisoning of air, land, and water, and numerous other manifestations of the wholesale destruction of nature. These writers warned not only about the dangerous ecological consequences, but also the social and moral consequences, of Soviet industrial and agricultural policies.[16] Throughout the 1970s, *Nash sovremennik* regularly published essays and reviews on ecology-related issues. And in his 1975 novel *Commission (Komissiya)*, Zalygin went so far as to argue that the party's legitimacy to rule was jeopardized by its wanton neglect of the environment.[17]

The party apparat's response was direct and heavy-handed. In late 1972, when the journal *Nauka i zhizn* published a series of essays by Soloukhin, entitled "Grass" *(Trava)*, that condemned the excessive use of chemical fertilizer in Soviet agriculture, a joint report of the Propaganda and Chemical Industry departments of the Central Committee labeled them politically and ideologically erroneous. The Znanie Society, the official publisher of *Nauka i zhizn*, and the journal's editors were severely reprimanded for allowing the publication of the essays.[18]

Despite the severe responses they occasionally provoked, Russian nationalist environmental writings may have played a role in the 1972 and 1978 Central Committee and Council of Ministers' decisions to improve environmental protection, as well as to increase budgetary allocations in this area from 857 million rubles in the years 1971 to 1972 to 9.3 billion rubles in the years between 1976 to 1980.[19]

These efforts, however, achieved little, and the destruction of nature continued unabated throughout the 1970s and early 1980s.[20] The fate of the cellulose plant that polluted Lake Baikal is a typical example. In the early 1960s, Russian nationalist intellectuals sought to stop the construction of the plant. In the 1970s and early 1980s, such leading Russian nationalist intellectuals as Volkov and Rasputin campaigned relentlessly to close down or relocate the plant away from the lake. Although they were allowed to publish on the issue in such authoritative party papers as *Pravda*, the cellulose plant continued to operate.[21]

Russian nationalists' frustration over the party's lack of response to their environmental concerns was further aggravated after the Politburo unveiled a plan in December 1978 to start preparatory work on a massive project to divert the Northern and Siberian rivers to Central Asia.[22] Even before this project was officially inaugurated, Russian nationalist journals published articles by scientific experts who opposed the plan on ecological grounds. By 1981, this project had become the primary focus of leading Russian nationalist intellectuals.[23] Nevertheless, at the October 1984 plenum of the Central Committee, the project was given its final approval.[24] In February 1985, *Nash sovremennik* published an essay by Fatei Shipunov, a prominent Russian nationalist scholar specializing in environmental issues, in which Shipunov blasted the river diversion project and presented it as a continuation on a grand scale of policies that had already led to the destruction of the best Soviet agricultural land, deforestation, and recurrent droughts.[25]

Shipunov's essay was a clear indicator of the strength of Russian nationalist outrage at the state's environmental policies on the eve of Gorbachev's accession to power. It also served as a clear signal to Gorbachev that Russian nationalist intellectuals were determined to fight vigorously for the cancellation of the river diversion project.

The Preservation of Historic Monuments

The demolition or neglect of ancient Russian churches, one of the key catalysts in the emergence of Russian nationalism in the 1960s, remained a fundamental concern of Russian nationalist intellectuals, a concern they openly and consistently voiced. Writing in 1972, Mikhail Alpatov, a prominent Russian nationalist historian, explained the Russian nationalists' drive to preserve and protect the architectural legacy of prerevolutionary Russia: "Protection of historic monuments is not a luxury one can live without. It is the gratification of a human need to see before his eyes historically formed features of the native region, city, home. The man of the future must find his place not only in space but also in time, in centuries."[26]

Political leaders were well aware of the significance of historic preservation in the eyes of Russian nationalists. In Moscow, the budget for the restoration of local historical monuments increased from 2 million rubles in 1965 to 25 million in 1984. Moreover, during the entire Brezhnev era, only three churches were demolished in the capital.[27] In 1976, a high-ranking committee was established in Moscow to prevent the demolition of historic buildings in the city. According to a Russian nationalist source, leading Russian nationalist intellectuals were invited to participate in the committee's work.[28] In October 1976, the USSR Supreme Soviet passed a law entitled "On the Protection and Use of Monuments of History and Culture" *(Ob okhrane i ispolzovanii pamyatnikov istorii i kultury)*, aimed at strengthening the state's protection of historic monuments. This law became operational in March 1977. The RSFSR Supreme Soviet passed an identical law in December 1978.

In a page-long interview that appeared in the June 21, 1978, issue of *Literaturnaya gazeta*, Mikhail Solomentsev, a candidate member of the Politburo and the chairman of the Council of Ministers of the RSFSR, attempted to show that the preservation of historic monuments was a high priority for the party. He described the large scope of restoration projects, the fourfold increase in budgetary allocations for preservation in the last ten years, the RSFSR Council of Ministers' order to several regional soviets to improve the maintenance of monuments in their locales, and the special attention that the Central and the Moscow Party Committees gave to preservation issues in determining construction in the center of the capital. He lavishly praised the activities of the All-Russian Society for the Preservation of Historical and Cultural Monuments (VOOPIK) and stressed that government agencies were ordered to consult with VOOPIK on projects that affected historic monuments.[29]

Solomentsev's assurances fell on deaf ears. Russian nationalist expectations were well beyond the government's ability or desire to carry out restoration projects. On September 13, 1978, *Literaturnaya gazeta* published an essay by the radical nationalist novelist Dmitry Zhukov that constituted an implicit Russian nationalist response to Solomentsev's description of the effectiveness of state restoration efforts. Taking an ancient Russian church near Moscow as an example, Zhukov argued that restoration work was carried out so poorly and over such a long period of time that the object under restoration was actually destroyed.[30]

In 1979, a series of essays published in the journal *Moskva* continued Russian nationalist criticism of the party's preservation record. A long essay by Vladimir Soloukhin in its January and February issues vividly described the ruins of the estate of Aleksandr Blok, one of the greatest twentieth-century Russian poets, and the unsuccessful efforts to restore it.[31] The July issue contained essays by architect Ivan Belokon and literary scholar Dmitry Likhachev. Belokon reminded readers of the destruction of such important Moscow landmarks of Russian culture as the Simonov Monastery, the Sukharev Tower, and the Kazan Church in the 1930s. He also pointed out that detailed proposals by VOOPIK's Architectural Department were routinely ignored by Moscow construction agencies. Likhachev went much further and accused the party of lacking commitment to what he termed the "ecology of culture" *(ekologiya kultury)*, that is, the comprehensive preservation of the nation's cultural heritage. He listed the destruction of the ancient city of Novgorod by construction agencies and the reluctance of state authorities to prosecute criminals who ruined priceless historic monuments as contemporary examples of the party's insensitivity to the ecology of culture.[32]

Writings by Zhukov, Soloukhin, Belokon, and Likhachev clearly expressed the depth of the Russian nationalist frustration with the state of preservation of historic monuments in Russia in general and in the city of Moscow in particular. The case of Moscow clearly shows that Russian nationalist complaints were based on the real facts. Thus, Colton points out that despite significant increases in the Moscow preservation budgets in the 1970s, these budgets "were drops in the bucket of true needs and were under 0.5 percent of the capital investment in the city." The lack of budgets created the situation in which "hundreds of designated landmarks ended up with no help at all. And caring for the some did not help the average state of old Moscow from worsening by reason of past mistreatment, the careless property management that goes with public ownership, and technical blunders. In the mid-1980s, Moscow had about 1,200 architectural landmarks. However, despite 1,100 applications, no new buildings were added to the registry after 1974. The result was a destruction of more 2,200 historic monuments."[33]

Solomentsev's endorsement of VOOPIK's activities could hardly dispel the Russian nationalist intelligentsia's view of the party as evincing little interest in historic preservation. After all, verbal support for VOOPIK by an important member of the political elite was in line with one of the main principles of the politics of inclusion. He presented VOOPIK an institution with a large Russian nationalist rank and file membership, as playing an important role in the decision-making process, while in reality it was impotent. In his memoirs, Oleg Volkov, one of VOOPIK's early activists, confessed that in the 1970s he quit the organization because of its total failure to influence the decision-making process on such issues as city planning and monuments preservation.[34]

Although they detested the bureaucratic nature of VOOPIK, the Russian nationalist intelligentsia was still frustrated by the fact that the society did not have a regular publication of its own.[35] They viewed this as an indication of the party's true attitude toward the preservationist movement. Indeed, as archival documents reveal, the Central Committee rejected repeated requests by VOOPIK's head, Vyacheslav Kochemasov, to allow the organization to publish a mass-circulation monthly or bi-monthly journal.[36] In the 1970s, VOOPIK was able to publish only four collections of essays on preservation-related issues entitled *Monuments of the Fatherland* (*Pamyatniki Otechestva*).[37] By April 1979, the RSFSR Council of Ministers had sensed growing Russian nationalist discontent and allowed VOOPIK to upgrade (beginning in 1980) its biannual collection to a semiannual almanac, also titled *Monuments of the Fatherland*.[38]

In many ways this was too little too late. During the year-long celebration of the six hundredth anniversary of the Kulikovo Field Battle, Russian nationalists harshly attacked the party's preservationist record. In February 1980, the journal *Moskva* published an essay by Vladimir Soloukhin, "The Time to Gather the Stones" (*Vremya sobirat kamni*), in which he described the ruins of the Optina Pustyn Monastery, one of the most important centers of Russian Orthodoxy before the October Revolution, and the unsuccessful attempts to restore it.[39]

In 1981, the Russian nationalist attack on the state's preservation policies continued in the journal *Sever*. Its July issue contained an essay by Vyacheslav Orfinsky, chairman of the department of architecture at Petrozovodsk University and a VOOPIK activist, in which he exposed the ongoing destruction of historic monuments in northern Russia. Bringing to the light recent examples of the demolition of ancient churches, Orfinsky accused the tourist organizations, local soviets, militia, and even the VOOPIK bureaucracy of tolerating this state of affairs. The harshness of the accusations forced local tourist and VOOPIK officials to defend the preservationist record of their agencies in the January 1982 issue of the journal.[40]

In the same month that *Sever* published the official response to Orfinsky's essay, *Nash sovremennik* published Soloukhin's concluding note to his preservationist writings of the 1970s in which he expressed the full extent of Russian nationalist despair at their inability to change state preservationist policies. Despite the decrees, Soloukhin asserted, local authorities continued to destroy the cultural heritage of Russia. Nor did they pay any attention to Russian nationalist writings on historic preservation. As he bluntly put it: "My previous book could have contained not four [preservationist] essays but twenty-four. I suspect, however, that the effect would have been the same."[41]

In July 1982, Dmitry Likhachev intensified his criticism. In an interview published in the popular weekly *Ogonyok*, he claimed that Russia contained at least 180,000 registered historic monuments, of which at best one-third were protected. He cited numerous examples of neglect and blamed VOOPIK, and state and local agencies. The interview attracted wide attention, and *Ogonyok* received hundreds of letters expressing support for Likhachev's views. Many contained descriptions of local neglect and suggestions on how to improve the protection of monuments.[42]

Russian nationalist discontent with the preservation of historic monuments was clearly expressed at the Fourth VOOPIK Congress, which took place in Novgorod between June 30 and July 1, 1982. The chairman of the RSFSR Council of Ministers, Mikhail Solomentsev, attended the meeting and reported to the Central Committee such complaints voiced by the delegates as the poor administration of organizations entrusted with the protection of historic monuments; the low quality of preservationist work, which often caused more damage to the historic monuments; insensitive urban planning, which destroyed historic districts of old Russian towns; and the small circulation and irregular timing of VOOPIK's publication, *Monuments of the Fatherland*. Finally, the delegates voiced forceful opposition to the river diversion project on the grounds that it would eliminate many historic Russian towns and villages.[43]

The VOOPIK Congress, as well as the campaign by Likhachev and other Russian nationalist intellectuals that preceded it, finally forced the government to action. The RSFSR Council of Ministers ordered its Ministry of Culture to take immediate additional measures to protect historic monuments. On July 22, 1982, the ministry issued a statement in which it acknowledged the accuracy of Likhachev's accusations and ordered the restoration and protection of numerous places he had cited. Yet by the end of 1982, a survey by *Ogonyok* reporters revealed that nothing had changed. In January 1983, the RSFSR Council of Ministers adopted yet another resolution aimed at improving the protection of historic monuments, but it would have taken far more than another resolution to convince Russian nationalist intellectuals that the party was capable of addressing one of their most significant grievances.

The Failure of Russian Agriculture

The fate of Russian agriculture continued to dominate the works of village prose writers. The ambitious 1974 project to revitalize agriculture in the

Non–Black Earth Zone had created high expectations among village prose writers, who now believed that the party had finally resolved to turn Russian agriculture around. The project failed on a grand scale. Despite enormous investments (36.8 billion rubles in the years 1976–1980), Russian agriculture continued to stagnate. In March 1981, a Central Committee and the USSR Council of Ministers' decree implicitly admitted the failure of the project and announced massive new budgetary allocations (39.3 billion rubles to be spent between 1981 and 1985) in the hopes of producing a turnaround.[44]

To the utter dismay of Russian nationalist intellectuals, it turned out that the project had actually accelerated the disappearance of many small Russian villages, the consequence of an attempt to resolve the acute problem of providing services to small and remote villages located in the Non–Black Earth Zone.[45] The government's solution now was to declare such villages as "having no future" (besperespektivnye), cutting all services to them, and relocating the peasants of such communities to bigger and more conveniently located villages. Nothing angered village prose writers more than policies that wiped out scores of Russian villages by declaring them as "having no future."[46] As archival evidence clearly points out, in the 1970s and 1980s, the censors heavily edited the works of Russian nationalist intellectuals who were critical of this government policy.[47] Critiques that did pass the censors relatively intact appeared in provincial journals and usually in the midst of a discussion of an entirely different subject. It was only during the Gorbachev era that the full intensity of Russian nationalist rage over this policy became fully evident.[48]

Throughout the period between 1971 and 1985, in their prose, poetry, and public appearances, leading Russian nationalist intellectuals openly denounced the continuing depopulation of the countryside in the Non–Black Earth Zone.[49] The failure of the project to revitalize this area greatly disappointed them. In an attempt to alleviate the resulting acute shortage of labor in the zone, the party issued a decree in May 1979 promising a range of special privileges to people working and living there. As with all previous measures, this also failed to reverse the process of outmigration.[50]

Throughout the 1970s, the rural population in the Non–Black Earth Zone continued to decline notably. Russian nationalist intellectuals could observe this trend on return visits to their native villages and from their extensive tours of the Russian countryside. Village prose writer Fyodor Abramov and his friend, the poet Antonin Chestyakov, toured the rural areas of the Novgorod region in northwestern Russia in 1978 and 1979.

Their travels resulted in two coauthored essays in which they described the abandoned villages they found and explicitly blamed the system of planned agriculture as the primary cause of the exodus.[51]

Other major sources of information about the depopulation of the Russian countryside were *Nash sovremennik* and *Literaturnaya gazeta*. Early in 1974, *Nash sovremennik* published two essays by a well-respected sociologist, Viktor Perevedentsev, that analyzed the social processes at work in the countryside. Basing his arguments on statistical data, Perevedentsev described the desertion of the Russian village by its best human component, the educated youth. He indicated that the rural population of ten oblasts in central and northwestern Russia had declined by over 25 percent between 1959 and 1970.[52]

Five years later, in the October 30, 1979 issue of *Literaturnaya gazeta*, Perevedentsev published his analysis of the preliminary results of the 1979 census. He pointed out that between 1970, the time of the previous census, and 1979, the rural population of the twenty-four oblasts of the RSFSR had decreased by 20 percent or more, with the RSFSR experiencing the highest decline of rural population in comparison to all other Soviet republics. This information would only exacerbate the frustrations of Russian nationalist intellectuals.[53]

Negative Social Trends

Social changes taking place in Russian society were another major component of the growing frustration of village prose writers. Russian nationalist intellectuals were especially disturbed by the party's inability to combat the growing incidence of alcoholism in Soviet society. In the 1971 story "Alka" *(Alka)*, Fyodor Abramov has his heroine proclaim: "Everybody drinks these days. In our town only those [people] do not drink who do not have money or are not being treated [for a drink by friends]."[54] A few months after Abramov's story was published, the government issued a decree aimed at combating alcoholism.[55] Nevertheless, the total consumption of alcohol in the Soviet Union, according to a Western calculation, rose by a staggering 149 percent between 1969 and 1979.[56]

Abramov was hardly alone in his attempts to convince the government to take radical measures to fight alcoholism. In the early 1970s, Vasily Belov indignantly exposed the practice of selling alcohol in the countryside to solve regional budgetary problems. In the mid-1970s, he described with unusual frankness the drinking habits of residents of his native village. He asserted that the peasants drank much more now than on the eve of World War II, despite a significant rise in rural living standards. In 1976, at the Sixth Congress of the USSR Writers' Union, another leading village prose writer, Viktor Astafiev, criticized the level of alcoholism and crime prevailing among peasants who moved to the city. Descriptions of crime and rampant alcoholism also dominate Astafiev's novel *The Queen Fish (Tsar-ryba)*, published in the same year. In 1978, the chief editor of *Nash sovremennik,* Sergei Vikulov, criticized the government for its policy of massive sales of low-quality alcohol in the countryside.[57]

On August 2, 1979, the Central Committee issued a decree implicitly acknowledging the staggering growth of alcoholism and crime and ordered additional measures to combat them. This decree and a December 7, 1979 instruction by the Soviet Supreme Court to lower courts to stiffen penalties for alcohol-related offenses failed to produce a noticeable improvement. In 1981, Russian nationalists' frustration with the government's inability to fight alcoholism found its first organized expression. In its June, August, and November issues, *Nash sovremennik* ran a series of essays and letters from readers that openly challenged the wisdom of using the sale of alcoholic beverages as an important source of state revenue and called for a total ban on their production and sales.[58]

The disintegration of the traditional family, an increase in divorce rates, the demographic decline of ethnic Russians, and the inability of the state to reverse these social trends were important sources of growing frustration in the 1970s, and *Nash sovremennik* played a major role in publicizing these social problems. Between 1973 and 1975, it published three essays by Perevedentsev that analyzed the nature and causes of these demographic changes in contemporary Soviet society. He identified the decline of fertility among ethnic Slavs as a consequence of urbanization, a rise in educational standards, the incorporation of women into the workforce, and a staggering increase in the divorce rate (from 67,000 in 1950 to 679,000 in 1973).[59]

Perevedentsev was not a Russian nationalist, but his *Nash sovremennik* readers were. They began to borrow some elements of his analysis and incorporated them into their own work. In 1977, *Nash sovremennik* published Vasily Belov's "The Morning Dates" *(Svidaniya po utram),* a story that established a pattern for Russian nationalist responses to the ongoing changes in the nature of the contemporary Russian family. In the story,

Belov blames the disintegration of the traditional family, the rise in the divorce rate, and the decline in birthrates on urban women and the state for its inability to enforce traditional moral values.[60]

In 1984, Belov's essay entitled "Milkmaid Required" (*Trebuetsya doyarka)*, extended his argument to the countryside, blaming the educational system and, particularly, the mass media for inculcating village girls with modern urban values. So swayed, he asserted, peasant women were not likely to remain in the village or to continue the tradition of having a large family.[61]

Belov's views on the moral corruption of rural society were widely shared by other village prose writers. This was the main theme of Abramov's 1978 novel *Home (Dom)*, and Krupin's 1981 novel, *The Fortieth Day (Sorokovoi den)*. In the latter, contemporary village life was completely dominated by alcoholism and an extremely low work ethic.[62]

Ivan Vasiliev, a prominent conservative nationalist journalist specializing in rural issues, provided the most elaborate nonfiction description of the moral corruption of the Russian peasantry in a series of essays published in *Nash sovremennik* in the late 1970s and early 1980s. Among these, his 1979 essay, "The Land of My Fathers" (*Zemlya moikh ottsov)*, stands out because it was among the first Russian nationalist works to blame urban culture for the moral corruption of rural women, whom he held responsible for the depopulation of the countryside. As such, it become a model for many subsequent essays on the same subject, including Belov's 1984 essay. Vasiliev argued that the values of young rural women were shaped by urban mass culture, which reached them through cinema and television. So indoctrinated, they refused to follow the steps of their mothers and did not want to accept hard menial jobs on the farm. Instead, they migrated to the cities and took jobs in the service sector. Even young women who chose to stay in the village had assimilated urban women's values, which included having a smaller number of children.[63]

Russian nationalist frustration over the nature of demographic trends reached new heights after the publication of the 1979 census, which showed a continued decline of ethnic Russians and the growth of Muslims in the Soviet population.[64] These frustrations and the resulting demand to take urgent action to reverse the direction of these demographic trends were aired in two Russian nationalist publications in 1981.

In its September issue, *Nash sovremennik* published an essay by journalist Boris Sporov that took the arguments of conservative village prose writers and essayists one step further. At the center of the essay stands the argument that "if the nation wants to . . . survive, if it wants to be healthy and prosperous, then it must care about the health of the family." Sporov denounced divorce as a crime and implicitly argued for the reintroduction of Stalin-era restrictions on divorce in order to reduce its incidence among Russians significantly. Citing statistical data that identified women as the initiators of most divorces, he called for an end to the equality that Soviet women had enjoyed as a result of the October Revolution, since this equality had led to women's "emancipation," which motivated them to divorce their husbands.[65]

The second major work to appear in 1981 also articulating Russian nationalist frustration and anger with the demographic trends was a book written by a legal scholar, Galina Litvinova. In *Law and Demographic Processes in the USSR (Pravo i demograficheskie protsessy v SSSR)*, she surveyed a whole range of factors affecting the demographic situation and appealed to the government to take urgent action. She called for the effective enforcement of the sixty-year-old ban on the employment of women in night shifts, greater governmental efforts to reduce the percentage of working women in the Slavic republics, the creation of hospital-based boards to advise women about alternatives to abortion, the stiffening of penalties for alcohol abuse, and the provision of greater power to local authorities to fight alcoholism. Finally, she wrote, the recruitment of industrial workers in the Russian countryside must be abandoned, and ecological issues must receive the highest priority in economic planning.[66]

What made Litvinova's book a particularly harsh attack on the policies of the Soviet state was its linkage of the demographic situation to another major source of Russian nationalist frustration—the perceived economic, social, and educational discrimination against the RSFSR in relation to other Union republics. Litvinova had broken new ground since this complaint had previously not been aired openly, largely due to censorship. She challenged the policies of state support for families with four or more children as an indirect way of subsidizing the Muslim population of Central Asia at the expense of the one- or two-child families in the RSFSR. Moreover, she argued, precisely because the Russian regions were experiencing labor shortages and population decline, they should be given much higher budgetary allocations than the Central Asian republics, which posted labor surpluses and faster population growth. Only scaling down the pace of the socioeconomic development of the Central Asian republics could slow down its population growth.

Litvinova also highlighted the educational discrimination practiced against residents of the RSFSR. Although most of the institutes of the USSR Academy of Sciences, universities, and research centers were located in the RSFSR, the percentage of the population with higher education was much lower in the Russian Republic in comparison to other republics.[67]

Finally, Russian nationalists' frustration with the social and demographic trends was inseparable from their concern over the state's inability to prevent the penetration of Western cultural values and fads. David K. Shipler, *The New York Times* correspondent in Moscow between 1977 and 1979, correctly observed that "in the decade of the 1970's the opening provided by détente exposed Soviet society to more Western, especially American, influence than at any other period since the Bolshevik Revolution."[68] In many Third World countries, intensive exposure to Western influences often led to the widespread rejection of everything associated with the West; in the Soviet Union the opposite occurred. The 1970s saw an unprecedented rise in the popularity of Western cinema, literature, fashion, and, especially, rock music among young urban Russians.[69] By the early 1980s, the popularity of rock music reached such heights that the party had to accept it as unavoidable reality.[70]

Many Russian nationalist intellectuals had held strongly anti-Western views even in the 1960s. In the 1970s and early 1980s, these views intensified, partly as a reaction to the unprecedented growth in the popularity of Western ideas and fads in Soviet society. Yury Bondarev's trilogy—*The Shore (Bereg)* (1974), *The Choice (Vybor)* (1980), and *The Game (Igra)* (1984)—explore the life of the Soviet intelligentsia and its encounters with the West and articulated anti-Western views. Bondarev portrayed the West as a morally corrupt civilization obsessed with "sport, sex, and television." He argued that Western consumerism transformed people into consumption machines and that traditional family values were abandoned during the sexual revolution of the 1960s, replaced by values that legitimized pornography, prostitution, and homosexuality. He believed that the middle class was philistine in its mentality and that intellectuals conformed to rather than fought moral corruption.[71]

In the late 1970s and early 1980s, the magnitude of Russian nationalist frustration and despair with the deepening Westernization of Russia became ever more visible. Sporov clearly expressed this despair:

One who thinks that external Western trends do not find their reflection in the spiritual life of [Soviet] society is grossly deluding himself. Be it mini-skirts or the 200-ruble jeans, vulgar popular songs or pornographic journals, alcoholism, mass smoking, or speculation with icons—all these [things] in the first place influence human morality, destroy it, and, therefore, the family as well, thus reducing the birth-rate and increasing the number of divorces.[72]

In an open letter to the residents of his native village, Fyodor Abramov complained that village youth had abandoned traditional peasant arts and crafts in favor of "primitive jazz rhythms and seizure-like Western dances." In 1982, Vladimir Soloukhin portrayed a New York discotheque as the modern incarnation of hell and lamented the penetration of the discotheque culture in provincial Russia. In the same year, Viktor Astafiev harshly criticized the leading Soviet rock band, Time Machine (*Mashina vremeni*) for its blind imitation of the Western rock culture, as well as for cynicism and lack of taste in their lyrics.[73]

As with many other issues, Vasily Belov expressed these feelings in an articulate and aggressive manner. In a series of essays written between 1979 and 1985, he attacked rock music, modern dance, and aerobics (which he considered a form of indecent exposure), as well as the party and state institutions in charge of cultural life, and Soviet mass media for actively promoting these western forms of entertainment and recreation.[74] In the early 1980s, the Soviet government attempted to undermine the popularity of rock music among Soviet youth through series of repressive measures which included a ban on the performance and distribution of 68 Western and 38 Soviet rock groups, a thorough check of the repertoire of the rock groups by the Ministry of Culture, and imposition of a tight censorship on publication of materials related to rock music.[75] Yet, all these measures failed to achieve their goal, and rock music entered the Gorbachev era dominating Soviet youth culture.

Chapter 7 explores the removal of the barriers to the penetration of Western cultural influences under Gorbachev, especially in the arts, and how this became one of the major issues that unified the different factions of the Russian nationalist intelligentsia in their opposition to perestroika.

What Is Russia, and Where Should It Go?
Political Debates, 1971–1985

Although the years 1971 to 1985 have rightly been called the "era of stagnation" by virtue of Brezhnev's determination to avoid radical political, social, and economic reforms, political debates within the Soviet intellectual elite continued unabated. They dealt, often for the first time, with issues that would dominate political discussions during the Gorbachev era, preparing the ground for perestroika.[1]

Because of their privileged status, Russian nationalist intellectuals could publish their views with relative ease, and thus they initiated or played a prominent role in many of the key ideological debates of the period. In an interesting twist, these debates were often not between Russian nationalists and their ideological opponents, but between members of various factions within the Russian nationalist movement itself. These discussions covered a wide range of subjects: village prose, agriculture, the political nature of ethnicity, scientific and technological progress, the message of nineteenth-century Russian literature, ancient and modern Russian history, and trends in contemporary Russian culture. Nevertheless, there was a common denominator to these seemingly unrelated and apolitical debates: they were all constituent parts of a greater effort by different ideologically oriented factions of the Russian intelligentsia to gain the support of both the political leadership and society at large for their vision of the Soviet state. Not coincidentally, we see the same Russian nationalists participating in most of these debates. In this chapter, we analyze seven such debates, each in one form or another addressing the issue of the nature of the Russian national identity and with major social, economic, cultural, and foreign policy implications.

Village Prose in the 1970s

The disappearance of the Russian peasantry did not mean the end of village prose. In fact, between 1971 and 1985, it was the dominant ideological current in Soviet intellectual life. Moreover, a new generation of Russian nationalist intellectuals had joined the village prose ranks. The most prominent among them were Boris Ekimov (b. 1938), Vladimir Krupin (b. 1941), and Vladimir Lichutin (b. 1940).[2] At the same time, Fyodor Abramov, Viktor Astafiev, Vasily Belov, Boris Mozhaev, Evgeny Nosov, Valentin Rasputin, and Vasily Shukshin, the founders of the movement in the late Khrushchev and early Brezhnev eras, remained the school's most popular and influential members. The appearance of their new works attracted significant attention and often provoked intense debates in the major newspapers and thick journals.[3]

During this period, the village prose writers became acutely aware of the decline and disappearance of the traditional villages and the transformation of Russia into a predominantly urban nation. This recognition was clearly articulated in Abramov's 1971 story, *Alka (Alka)*, and Shukshin's 1973 story, "Looking for a Village Residence" (*Vybirayu derevnyu na zhitelstvo*). In Abramov's story, Alka, the heroine, a young waitress, decides to return to her native village, but eventually succumbs to the temptations of city life and the glamour of becoming an Aeroflot flight attendant. In Shukshin's story, the hero is an aging storehouse manager who left his village over thirty years before yet every Saturday afternoon goes to the town's train station to talk to peasants passing through. He asks them about the prices of homes and the possibility of employment in their villages, and he carefully records every bit of information, even though he knows that his return to the countryside is impossible. Thus, the closest he comes to a village is the urban train station.[4]

This acknowledgment of the disappearance of Russian rural life as an irreversible social process came hand in hand with an awareness that village-based Russian national traditions were being lost. As Rasputin put it in 1980, "To come back to what is already lost is impossible. This is not a plane which could be turned around in mid-air in order to pick up forgotten luggage . . . We should not delude ourselves—we cannot retrieve many of the good old traditions. Now the question is how to preserve what is left."[5]

Although all village prose writers agreed that the traditional village was quickly disappearing, they were strongly divided on the issue of what the Russian nationalist political agenda should be. This disagreement reinforced the ideological division between the liberal and conservative wings of the village prose in the years 1971 to 1985. Abramov, Ekimov and Mozhaev, the most important liberal village prose writers during this period, argued that Russian agriculture and the path to its revival must continue to be the school's main concern.

Astafiev, Belov, Nosov, Rasputin, and Shukshin, the leading conservative village prose writers of the 1970s, on the other hand, found the liberal village prose writers' preoccupation with agriculture too narrow and considered it of secondary importance in the discussion of the underlying causes of moral decay of Russian society in general. In the 1970s, their fiction and nonfiction works presented a highly idealized portrayal of the traditional Russian peasantry—its ways of life, customs, and moral virtues—in order to criticize contemporary urban lifestyle, culture, and morality.[6]

While liberal village prose writers exhibited an ambivalence toward scientific and technological progress, their conservative counterparts clearly rejected its virtues. They insisted that the effects of ongoing technological progress contributed to Russia's deepening moral crisis. Their preoccupation with the subject of moral corruption, which Shukshin summed up in his famous 1973 question, "What is happening to us?" *(Chto s nami proiskhodit?)*, was also a vehicle for the argument that this issue was more important than the liquidation of the political and socioeconomic consequences of the Stalinist legacy in the countryside.[7]

The conservative emphasis on moral, rather than social, political, and economic, issues, already present in the late 1960s, became more and more forceful as the Brezhnev era drew to a close. Thus, the continuing Westernization of Soviet society in the years 1971 to 1985 further weakened conservative village prose support for radical economic and political reform. One of the manifestations of this weakened commitment to reform was the appearance of highly idealized descriptions of the Russian village in the Stalin era. The 1977 novel by Evgeny Nosov, *The Helmet Wearers of Usvyaty (Usvyatskie shlemonostsy)*, completely ignored the dreadful socioeconomic condition Russian peasants on the eve of World War II. Instead, in his portrayal of life in a Russian village during the first weeks of the war, he focused on the high moral virtues, strong work ethic, fervent patriotism, and harmony that prevailed among the traditional peasantry.[8]

Finally, it is important to recognize that the growing influence of the conservative wing of village prose nationalism continued in the 1970s. Almost all the writers who joined this school between 1971 and 1985 professed a conservative nationalist philosophy. Throughout the 1970s and 1980s, conservative village prose writers effectively left the 1960s coalition that had favored radical political and economic reform, without, however, joining the antireform radical nationalists. In this sense, inclusionary politics achieved its aim of splitting and weakening the pro-reformist forces within the Soviet intellectual elite.

The Debates about the Relevance of the Village Prose Message

The relevance of the social and political ideas of the village prose as a school, rather than of its individual members, to contemporary Soviet society was debated twice during the 1970s—first on the pages of the academic journal *Voprosy literatury* in 1972 and 1973 and then, and with much more heat on the pages of *Literaturnaya gazeta* in 1979.

Because of its timing, the *Voprosy literatury* debate was largely an attempt to draw conclusions from the village prose of the late 1960s. It began with the publication in the July 1972 issue of the journal of an essay by the liberal reformist literary critic Ekaterina Starikova, entitled "The Sociological Aspect of Contemporary 'Village Prose'" (*Sotsiologichesky aspekt sovremennoi 'derevenskoi prozy'*). The essay was largely a criticism of conservative village prose and revealed the first cracks in the 1960s reform alliance among the intelligentsia.

Using 1970 census data, Starikova pointed out that village prose became a major phenomenon in cultural life at the same time that Soviet society was becoming largely urbanized. Moreover, although village prose writers preferred to preoccupy themselves with the traditional Russian village, sociological studies showed that fundamental changes were taking place in the nature of the contemporary Russian peasantry. Peasants in the 1970s had a higher standard of living, were much better educated, and operated far more sophisticated machinery than peasants of the 1930s and 1940s. Yet instead of dealing with the problems of contemporary peasants, conservative village prose writers almost exclusively focused on traditional Russian peasants who survived only in the most remote villages. Starikova was warning conservative village prose writers that their flight from reality, harkening back to a village way of life that effectively no longer existed, dangerously weakened their commitment to the liquidation of the Stalinist legacy and in turn undermined the 1960s *Novy mir*–sponsored coalition.[9]

The issues that Starikova raised were discussed by four prominent writers, critics, and journalists in the March 1973 issue of *Voprosy literatury*. As in all debates of this kind, the ideological balance was carefully maintained among the participants. The literary critic Shamil Galimov and the novelist Semyon Shurtakov, the conservative Russian nationalist participants in the debate, vigorously defended the ideological orientation of the conservative village prose writers. Galimov agreed that Russian society was undergoing far-reaching social change. This change, however, was transforming Russia into a society in which "satiety" and "moral deafness" were becoming the dominant values and whose members were largely preoccupied with the pursuit of higher standards of living. This was precisely why the conservative village prose writers' call for the preservation of the non-materialist moral values of the traditional Russian peasantry was of such great importance.[10]

Galimov was restrained in his criticism of Starikova's argument; Shurtakov was not. The sociological studies on which Starikova had grounded her argument, he asserted, did not expose objective social processes but rather were the outcome of the deeply flawed planning system. Rather than recruiting industrial labor in the overpopulated Central Asia or the Caucasus, industrial recruitment concentrated on the Russian countryside, which was experiencing acute labor shortages. As a result, peasant youth left their Russian villages for the cities. By portraying disappearing villages and old peasant women, conservative village prose writers were protesting the irretrievable loss of national traditions and moral values in the process of urbanization. Shurtakov implicitly called for the conservative village prose writers to sever their ties with the liberal-reformist intelligentsia, since it supported government policies that were transforming Russia into an urban and, ultimately, Western-oriented society.[11]

Starikova's arguments were defended by Yury Galkin and Leonid Ivanov, members of the liberal wing of the village prose. They participated in the debate in an attempt to keep the entire village prose school in the reform alliance. Galkin agreed that the changes that the Russian countryside was undergoing were irreversible, but also admitted that he and his fellow village prose writers had failed to discover the contemporary village. Contrary to the village prose writers of the 1920s and the 1950s who accurately described the countryside of their time, the village prose writers of the 1960s attempted to preserve in public memory the village of their childhood. Galkin called on village prose to analyze the impact on contemporary Russian peasantry of the multitude of policy changes and experiments that Soviet agriculture had experienced since the 1940s. He challenged them to bring back to the center of their political agenda demands for radical reform in the countryside.[12]

Leonid Ivanov openly took issue with Shurtakov and elaborated Starikova's arguments about the nature of change in rural Russia. According to Ivanov, the traditional Russian peasants described by the conservative village prose writers had all but disappeared. Contemporary peasants wanted to live an urban lifestyle. Moreover, many people who lived in rural areas worked not in agriculture but in industry and services.

Shurtakov was wrong, he said, in claiming that the outmigration of rural youth and the depopulation of the Russian countryside was solely the result of industrial recruitment. He identified the real cause as the deplorable lack of adequate social services and the refusal of peasant youths to tolerate such deprivation. Ivanov challenged conservative village prose writers and their apologists, like Galimov and Shurtakov, that if they were truly concerned with the disappearance of the Russian village, they should address its socioeconomic and, ultimately, political causes.[13]

Despite the fact that *Voprosy literatury* promised to continue the debate in subsequent issues of the journal, no further contributions were published. Between September and December 1979, *Literaturnaya gazeta* renewed the debate on the village prose, focusing on the issue of the school's relevance to contemporary Soviet society. The debate revolved around the issues posed by the radical nationalist writer Aleksandr Prokhanov. Since all the participants were Russian nationalist intellectuals, the discussion was essentially an internal debate on the movement's ideology in the 1980s.

Although he was only one year younger than Rasputin, Prokhanov (b. 1938) was virtually unknown until the late 1970s. The 1979 debate was an important stepping-stone in his meteoric rise to a position as one of the most prominent figures in the Russian nationalist movement in the 1980s. Better than any other leading Russian nationalist intellectual at the time, Prokhanov understood that the changing nature of Russian society and global technological change required significant changes in Russian nationalist ideology. He believed that the urban, technologically educated intelligentsia held the key to Russia's ability to retain its superpower status. Russian nationalist ideology must therefore be attractive first and foremost to this social stratum, a goal that could not be achieved without ending the dominant position of the village prose within the movement. The *Literaturnaya gazeta*–sponsored discussion on the village prose gave Prokhanov the opportunity to do so in a powerful public forum.[14]

In his essay published in the September 12, 1979 issue of *Literaturnaya gazeta* and provocatively entitled "The Metaphor of the Present" (*Metafora sovremennosti*), Prokhanov asserted that a village prose that attempted to present itself as expressing the concerns of the majority of Russians was in fact elitist. He saw village prose as a group of members of the intellectual elite who preferred to idealize the disappearing traditional peasantry and were thus oblivious to the realities of the modern, technology-dominated world. The village prose school, Prokhanov argued, consisted of gloomy accounts of demographic and ecological problems rather than articulating a clear vision of Russian national goals on the eve of the twenty-first century. He did not specify the details of this new vision but merely declared that it must be able to show that a highly advanced society and traditional Russian moral values were indeed compatible. Russian national ideology, Prokhanov concluded, must be relevant to people who serve on nuclear submarines or sit in daily traffic jams. In other words, it must come to terms with, rather than reject, modernity.[15]

Prokhanov's challenge put village prose writers and their supporters on the defensive. The first to respond was the conservative village prose writer Vladimir Krupin. In his essay in the October 3, 1979 issue of *Literaturnaya gazeta*, he rejected Prokhanov's call to abandon the village prose version of Russian nationalist ideology. According to Krupin, the future of the Russian nation would depend not so much on the state of its technology, but on the moral values of Russians—their ability to reverse the process of the disintegration of the traditional family, preserve the historic memory of the nation, and put an end to the ongoing destruction of the environment. Prokhanov had not identified these key issues, but village prose placed them at the top of its agenda. Thus, technological progress did not diminish the relevance of the ideological message of village prose.[16]

Two weeks later, on October 17, 1979, Krupin's argument was elaborated by the conservative nationalist essayist Boris Anashenkov. The village prose preoccupation with ecological and moral issues was of great social and political importance, he wrote. Its writers brought to the attention of the nation the idea that technological progress required an even stronger emphasis on moral values since it gave humans a level of power they had never dreamed of before.[17]

The harshest criticism of Prokhanov's essay appeared in the October 31, 1979 issue of *Literaturnaya gazeta*. Boris Mozhaev rejected Prokhanov's two major claims that the village prose was elitist in its orientation and that Russian nationalist ideology must glorify technological progress because it strengthened the Russian state. Mozhaev argued that behind Prokhanov's criticism of the village prose stood his etatist disgust with the fact that the school focused on the lives of ordinary people, regarded by party leaders as "cogs" or "bricks," rather than on army generals or government bureaucrats.

Second, Prokhanov's linkage of technological progress and state power was faulty. Village prose contributed to the strength of the Russian state not by uncritically supporting technological progress, but by fighting to protect Russia from its consequences. It was the village prose, Mozhaev reminded his readers, that publicly raised such major environmental issues as the importance of the protection of rivers, forests, and meadows and the proper siting of polluting industrial enterprises, and called into question the wisdom of constructing hydroelectric power stations.[18]

The debate was concluded in the December 5, 1979 issue of *Literaturnaya gazeta* with the publication of responses to Prokhanov's essay by Valentin Kurbatov and Vladimir Bondarenko. The radical nationalist critic Vladimir Bondarenko was the only participant in the discussion who defended Prokhanov's ideas, but even this support was only partial. He agreed with Prokhanov that Russian nationalist ideology must focus on the dynamic elements in society rather than on the passive, traditional peasantry. Yet Russian national tradition was so intrinsically linked to the countryside that Prokhanov's effort to "urbanize" Russian nationalist ideology and focus it on the glorification of modern technology could sever the connection joining the national past, the present, and the future. The village prose emphasis on the inseparable bond between Russians and the land, and the moral values that this bond created, must remain at the core of Russian nationalist ideology. The task was to show that these bonds and values had not lost their relevance in the modern world.[19]

Conservative nationalist literary critic Valentin Kurbatov effectively endorsed Bondarenko's main argument. Village prose was correct, he argued, in connecting Russian national identity with the peasantry. The reason it focused on the traditional peasantry was rooted in the fact that the technological revolution in the countryside did not cause a rapid change in the nature of peasant moral values. Prokhanov failed to understand that the Russian countryside was in transition. The traditional peasantry and its moral values were dying out, but the contemporary peasantry and its character and moral values were only in the early stages of formation. When this transformation was completed, Kurbatov implied, the peasantry would regain its status as the spiritual backbone of the Russian nation. Prokhanov therefore was wrong in his attempt to displace the peasantry as the central element of Russian nationalist ideology.[20]

In many ways, Prokhanov's essay constituted the greatest challenge that village prose nationalism faced during the Brezhnev era. It was published when the school was at the peak of its popularity in Russian society. This probably explains why the 1979 debate was so one-sided and why no leading Russian nationalist intellectual openly expressed support for Prokhanov's ideas. As a result, the dominant position of village prose within the Russian nationalist movement, and its prominent status among the Soviet intelligentsia in general, remained intact. Nevertheless, this situation did not prevent serious discussion of the socioeconomic issues raised by village prose writers. In the next two sections, we examine two such discussions: the debates on Russian agriculture and on the virtues of scientific and technological progress.

Village Prose and Russian Agriculture

One of the most important political debates of the 1970s centered on Russian agriculture. Village prose writers disagreed about the causes of the declining performance of agriculture in the 1970s. On one side stood Fyodor Abramov, who argued that heavy monetary infusions into the rural sector of the economy not only failed to turn Russian agriculture around but also morally corrupted the Russian peasantry. He expressed this view in his 1978 novel, *Home (Dom)*, and in a 1979 open letter to the residents of his native northern Russian village, in which he asserted that a significant rise in the peasants' living standards was a consequence not of increased productivity but of heavy state subsidies.[21] Agriculture, he passionately argued, was stagnating because traditional peasant habits and values such as discipline, initiative, and hard work had been replaced by alcoholism, passivity, and indifference.[22]

This view was not accepted by all village prose writers. In particular, it was challenged by Boris Mozhaev, who throughout the 1970s had consistently argued that radical agrarian reform was the only solution to the problems of Russian agriculture.[23] Mozhaev could not accept Abramov's reasoning and in 1981 wrote a long programmatic essay elaborating his own position.

Mozhaev openly blamed the plight of Russian agriculture not on peasants but on the very nature of centralized agricultural planning. He exposed the ruinous effects of orders imposed from above and the success of farmers who dared to disregard the plan and adopted more economically sound decisions. The massive budgetary allocations to agriculture, asserted Mozhaev, were not invested to improve the quality of life in the countryside, but rather were squandered on senseless irrigation and construction projects.[24]

The Abramov-Mozhaev debate was an integral part of a larger debate about the present and future of the Russian peasantry and, thus, of Russian agriculture. This debate could have well been inspired by the 1972–1973 *Voprosy literatury* debate on the village prose. Abramov's speech at the Sixth Congress of the USSR Writers' Union in June 1976 effectively initiated the debate. In his address, he called for a discussion of the social and national consequences of the far-reaching technological and scientific revolution in the countryside, which was causing the disappearance of the traditional Russian village.[25] A year and half later, he openly rejected the views of the radical nationalists and conservative village prose writers who identified technological progress as the source of all evil in contemporary Soviet society. In an essay published in the March 22, 1978 issue of *Literaturnaya gazeta,* he proclaimed, "We should be saved not from the scientific-technological revolution but from the bureaucrat and the narrow-minded worker, the people indifferent to the machines and the land who are capable of destroying both."[26]

As if responding to Abramov's calls, *Nash sovremennik* in its March 1979 issue published a story by Boris Ekimov, "Kholyusha's Farm" *(Kholyushino podvoriye).* Ekimov's story portrays the life of Kholysha, a seventy-year-old one-legged peasant who works hard on his private plot. Driven by his own work ethic, he is able to turn the plot into a small farm with cattle, goats, sheep, pigs, turkeys, geese, and chickens, as well as a vegetable and fruit garden. Kholyusha's prosperity is the cause of envy and even hatred on the part of other village peasants, who do not want to work as hard as he does on their private plots.

The highly idealized portrait of Kholysha and his farm was a metaphor for the argument that efficient agriculture exists only on private plots and that only Kholysha-type peasants were capable of reviving Russian agriculture. That Ekimov could find no such work ethic among the young and educated peasants is represented in the story by Mitka, a young kolkhoz electrician who prefers to drink rather than to work hard on his plot and openly expresses his wish that Kholyusha be dispossessed of his property. The death of the old man at the end of the story was Ekimov's way of questioning the ability or desire of Mitka types to turn Russian agriculture around.[27]

In 1980 and 1981, the issues the story raised became the subject of a heated political debate within the pages of *Literaturnoe obozrenie* by six prominent journalists, economists, and literary critics of various ideological orientations who discussed "Kholysha's Farm." The debate, one of the most important of the Brezhnev era, began in the July 1980 issue with an analysis of the story by a conservative nationalist essayist, Boris Anashenkov, and a liberal-reformist economist Gennady Lisichkin. Anashenkov used Ekimov's story to argue that the future of the Russian peasantry, and Russian agriculture in general, depended on the ability of society to preserve the moral code of the traditional Russian peasantry, the code that guided Kholysha's behavior. Such a peasantry, he asserted, would compete effectively with American farmers. This traditional morality, however, could not be preserved in a society exposed to radical scientific and technological change because it created morally corrupt and alienated people such as Ekimov's Mitka, the electrician. The implications of Anashenkov's argument were clear: Russia must protect itself from the technological and scientific revolution and limit its exposure to the West, the primary source of this revolution.[28]

Lisichkin rejected Anashenkov's implications. It was illusion, he argued, to think that traditional the Kholysha-type peasants could save Russian agriculture. Tiny, primitive farms like those of Kholysha continue to exist in countries like Mexico, yet they were so inefficient that the state was forced to spend millions of dollars to import produce. The example of American agriculture taught that a massive infusion of modern technology would guarantee high productivity and freedom from food imports. The problem of Russian agriculture, and all of the Soviet economy, he stated, was its command structure, not the disappearance of traditional peasant morality. Mitka the electrician was alienated from the land and alcoholic not because he was the product of scientific and technological change but because of the command structure of the Soviet economy. Russia's future, he said, depended on its ability to carry out radical political and economic reform that would liquidate the Stalinist legacy rather than on a rejection of technological progress and the West.[29]

In January 1981, *Literaturnoe obozrenie* resumed the debate by publishing an essay by Anatoly Strelyany, an ardent proponent of radical political and economic reform. Strelyany challenged the veracity of Ekimov's story. Kholysha's farm, he asserted, existed only in the author's imagination; it could never survive in the real world of Russian agriculture. Like Lisichkin, Strelyany strongly rejected Anashenkov's views on the primacy of the preservation of traditional moral values. High productivity was not a function of morality, but of material incentives and general economic conditions. Only by giving full freedom to producers—that is, radical reform of the command economy—would Russian agriculture be turned around. The insistence on moral perfection was a thinly disguised attempt by Russian nationalists to preserve the political and economic system.[30]

Lisichkin's and Strelyany's harsh criticism of Anashenkov's ideas had an additional implication. Their essays constituted an open declaration by the most radical wing of the reform-minded intelligentsia that the 1960s reform coalition with the conservative village prose was no longer viable. Thus, what in 1972 had been merely a warning was reality in 1981.

In July 1981, Lisichkin and Strelyany's arguments were contested by agricultural journalist Vyacheslav Palman and literary critic A. Obertynsky, who supported Anashenkov's view of the importance of preserving traditional moral values. In their view, rational economic calculations were incapable of reviving Russian agriculture. Young Russian peasants must acquire an unbounded love of the land and the habit of hard work, the main elements of the traditional peasant morality, in order to make Russian agriculture productive again, stop the massive exodus of peasants to the cities, and halt the complete disappearance of the Russian countryside and, ultimately, the Russian nation.[31]

The discussion officially came to an end in the September 1981 issue of *Literaturnoe obozrenie* with an essay by Vsevolod Surganov, an orthodox communist literary critic specializing in the village prose. He rejected the Russian nationalist emphasis on moral issues because Marxism treats morality merely as a social and historical category. Surganov also refused to accept Ekimov's view that only private farming would turn around Russian agriculture. Private farming, he warned, is a slippery slope and would lead to the reintroduction of capitalism in Russia. Collectivization of agriculture was a historic necessity, and no one could turn the wheel of history backward. The key to the future of Russian agriculture was not radical economic reform, but the party's ability to make peasants as efficient on collective farms as they were on their private plots.[32]

Abramov, who called for the initiation of such a debate, ultimately had the last word. In October 1981, a month after the *Literaturnoe obozrenie* debate was closed, Abramov stated his own position on the future of Russian agriculture. Speaking on television, he outlined two possible directions for Russian agriculture and the Russian peasantry. The first direction was the Americanization of Russian agriculture, which he characterized as the total industrialization of agricultural production, the amalgamation of villages, and their transformation into agro-cities. He rejected this path because it would lead to the disappearance of the intimate links between people and the land, the moral foundation of the Russian national character. The alternative path, which Russia must choose, Abramov asserted, was the retention of this link through the preservation of villages and the avoidance of the total mechanization and industrialization of the countryside. Although Abramov ultimately came out in support of Ekimov's views, as his 1978 statement clearly suggests, he did not share the views of Anashenkov and other Russian nationalist participants in the debate.[33]

The debate on Russian agriculture did not—and could not—have had an immediate impact on Soviet agricultural policymaking. It did, however, become an important prelude to debates on the nature and direction of reform that unfolded under Gorbachev. It showed that conservative Russian nationalists would not support Western-oriented radical political and economic reform and might ultimately side with the opponents of reform in the Soviet political establishment, a fact that Strelyany did not fail to notice. It also revealed an important division among the liberal prose writers on the issue of radical political and economic reform; while Mozhaev emphasized its primacy, Abramov and Ekimov were more ambivalent.

Village Prose and Technological Progress

The debate on the virtues of technological progress, or the "scientific and technological revolution" as it was officially called, continued throughout the 1970s. It played a significant role in discussions on the village prose in general and about Russian agriculture in particular. The debate became especially heated when it acquired a strong ecological dimension in the aftermath of the publication in 1976 of Viktor Astafiev's novel, *The Queen Fish,* and Valentin Rasputin's novel, *Farewell to Matyora.*[34]

The Queen Fish (Tsar-ryba), a collection of twelve novellas, portrays the relationship between man and nature in Siberia. The book protested the construction of a network of hydroelectric stations on the Enisei, one of the largest Siberian rivers, and showed the damage caused by local poachers and visiting urban tourists to Siberia's natural environment. Through a depiction of the moral degradation and personal calamities that afflicted those who destroyed nature, the book conveyed the idea that policies aimed at reshaping the natural environment were leading to disastrous consequences for the Russian nation. At the same time, Astafiev called for the abandonment of urban, consumption-oriented morality and a revival of the moral values of the traditional Russian peasantry as necessary to save both the environment and the Russian nation.[35]

In October 1976, *Literaturnoe obozrenie* organized a roundtable discussion on the issues raised in *The Queen Fish.* Eleven writers, literary critics, and environmental scholars, as well as Astafiev himself, took part. Kim Shilin, an environmental scientist with liberal-reformist views, agreed with Astafiev that the ecological crisis was a consequence of the "existing cultural environment" (the official ideology), which led people to believe in the supremacy of economics and technology, and attempt to subjugate nature at any cost. At the same time, he challenged Astafiev's strong anti-intellectual and antimodern bias. The ecological balance that existed in the past, Astafiev's fundamental assumption, he dismissed as illusionary. Ecological crises occurred throughout history on the local and regional levels. Only science could create and maintain an ecological balance. The revival of traditional moral virtues could not substitute for science and scientific progress.

Shilin's ideas were reiterated by his colleague, Nikolai Svatkov. He agreed that the network of hydroelectric stations built on Siberian rivers had changed the ecology of the region and greatly encouraged poaching and, thus, moral corruption. On the other hand, Svetkov added, there was no real alternative to these stations. In principle, nuclear power stations could become an alternative to hydroelectric stations when the technology was developed. Only then would Russia be able to dismantle the hydroelectric stations and restore the ecological balance. In other words, only scientific and technological progress was ultimately capable of saving the environment. Literary critic Sergo Lominadze and literature teacher Lev Sobolev, two other liberal-reformers in the debate, also praised the novel but rejected Astafiev's attempt to add an anti-intellectual dimension to the ecological argument.

The environmental scientist Nikolai Reimers and the village prose writer Gleb Goryshin provided the most articulate defense of Astafiev's views. Reimers defended Astafiev against the criticism of the liberal-reformist scientists. He called on his colleagues to wake up from the dream that science and technology would solve environmental problems. Moreover, he argued, nature is worth much more than money, gold, precious stones, factories, or the machine tools on which traditional estimates of national wealth are calculated. From a strictly economic point of view, nature's roles in creating a livable environment was worth 40 to 280 times more than anything that could be extracted from it. Technological progress had little real value and must not be pursued. Reimers also endorsed Astafiev's anti-urban arguments. The urban tourist, the resident of "jungles of concrete," was ecologically illiterate and incapable of truly loving nature.

Goryshin rejected the liberal-reformist accusations that Astafiev was idealizing the past. Astafiev was right, Goryshin argued, to warn that by violating the ecological balance, technological progress was destroying a traditional moral code that governed the relationship between humans and nature. Technological progress was indeed causing the moral corruption of Russian society. Astafiev was also right in his insistence on the primacy of a moral revival. Here, according to Goryshin, Astafiev followed in the great moral tradition established by Dostoevsky.[36]

Although *Literaturnoe obozrenie* did not pursue the debate on the novel, it continued to publish essays on the issue of the virtues of technological progress. In March 1977, six months after the roundtable on *The Queen Fish*, the journal published an essay on the subject by Vadim Kozhinov. At the center of this radical nationalist programmatic essay stood harsh criticism of the official glorification of the virtues of scientific and technological progress, of an urban lifestyle, and, ultimately, of the West.[37]

Technological progress, Kozhinov asserted, liberates people from all forms of monotonous physical labor—certainly a positive process—yet it does not justify the glorification of all advancements in science and technology. The latter separated people from the immediate experience of nature by creating a second, artificial "nature." The West provided an excellent example of life in a completely man-made and artificial environment—instead of natural air, the air-conditioned environment; instead of natural fruits and vegetables, synthetic food created by the biochemical industry; instead of unmediated observation of the world, it was perceived only through the color television set; instead of a natural forest, plastic "trees" planted along American highways, and Disneylands populated by artificial "animals."

Moreover, technological progress made Marxist pronouncements about the "idiocy of rural life" obsolete. Because of noise, polluted air, and long hours wasted commuting, it was now much more appropriate to speak of the "idiocy of urban living." These realities, he concluded, require Russians to make a choice as to the appropriate way of life. The great achievement of the village prose was that it showed what the nation would lose if technological progress was allowed to shape its existence. Kozhinov called on the Russian people to prevent the transformation of Russia into a Western-type modern industrial society.[38]

Under different circumstances, such an essay would have provoked a variety of responses, including from the party itself. The politics of inclusion was aimed at preventing a confrontation between the party and the Russian nationalist intellectuals and could well be one reason that the party ideological establishment did not react. The reason the intellectual community did not attempt to launch a discussion was probably rooted in the fact that the publication of Kozhinov's essay coincided with the beginning of what turned out to be a prolonged discussion on similar issues. This was the debate on Rasputin's *Farewell to Matyora*.

Rasputin's novel synthesized the ecological argument of the conservative village prose writers with their other principal sociopolitical ideas and was to some extent a manifesto. *Farewell to Matyora (Proshchanie s Matyoroi)* describes the last months of Matyora, a three-hundred-year-old Siberian village due to be flooded as a consequence of the construction of the Bratsk hydroelectric station. Rasputin portrayed in detail the gradual abandonment of the village: the angry reactions of peasants to an attempt by the demolition crew to destroy the village cemetery, the last harvest, the burning of the houses, and the evacuation of the peasants from the island and their resettlement in an urban community.

The novel provided a highly idealized portrayal of the way of life and morality of the traditional Russian peasantry and juxtaposed it with the corrupt morality of city dwellers. It also openly challenged the virtues of technological progress and raised the question of its cost. These ideas were meant to support Rasputin's central argument that the flooding of Matyora was a symbolic representation of the nature of Russia's national tragedy—a sharp break in historic continuity caused by the sacrifice of national traditions and values in the process of modernization. The key to Russian national survival, he wrote, was the ability to reestablish the broken chain between the past, the present, and the future. As an eighty-year-old peasant woman, Dariya, the chief heroine of the novel and a personification of the national traditions which the Russian peasantry embodies, states, "The truth is in memory. He who has no memory, has no life."[39]

The debate on *Farewell to Matyora* began in late January 1977 with the publication in *Literaturnaya gazeta* of Evgeny Sidorov's review of the novel. Sidorov, a liberal-reformist literary critic, praised the work yet did not endorse its main theme. Rasputin's emotion-colored desire to preserve the traditions and values of the Russian peasantry in the age of technological progress was utopian, implied Sidorov.[40]

Less than a month later the journal *Voprosy literatury* published a discussion of Rasputin's prose, at the center of which was *Farewell to Matyora*. A lengthy essay by the liberal-reformist literary critic Oleg Salynsky, effectively an elaboration of Sidorov's position, opened the discussion and served as a frame of reference for the rest of the participants. Salynsky pointed out that Rasputin's protest against the abandonment of national traditions in the age of rapid technological change forced him to portray the peasants who willingly moved from Matyora as empty and morally corrupt. These ideological principles prevented Rasputin from attacking the real problems of contemporary Soviet society, which meant that he lacked commitment to radical political, social, and economic reform. Support of this sort of reform, Salynsky implied, was based not on the blind acceptance of the virtues of scientific progress but on the belief that the desire to move forward, to improve human knowledge and fate, is fundamental to human nature.[41]

Salynsky's criticism of the novel was shared by the liberal-reformist literary critic Valentin Oskotsky. The liberal-reformist literary critic Ekaterina Starikova, the radical nationalist critic Yury Seleznev, and the orthodox communist scholar of Russian literature Aleksandr Ovcharenko all rejected it. Oskotsky shared Salynsky's rejection of Rasputin's ideological framework—in particular, his failure to understand that progress by its very nature is a process through which something new is gained and something old is lost. He unfavorably compared *Farewell to Matyora* to *Memory of the Land (Pamyat zemli)*, the 1960s ecologically oriented novel by liberal village prose writer Vladimir Fomenko. The latter also dealt with the flooding of agricultural land, but focused instead on the social problems it caused. The reformers, Oskotsky asserted, should not be afraid to speak about technological progress, but should insist that it be carried out without destroying nature.[42]

Starikova was not as critical of Rasputin as one might have expected given her 1972 criticism of conservative village prose. She admitted that Rasputin was not dealing with the real social problems the Russian peasantry faced in the process of modernization. Rasputin, she argued, was a humanist who posed questions about the cost of progress without attempting to provide a simplistic answer. He therefore should not be considered an enemy of progress and a retrograde (i.e., an enemy of reform). By stressing Rasputin's humanism, Starikova attempted to argue that he was an ideological ally of the liberal-reformist intelligentsia.[43]

Seleznev and Ovcharenko defended Rasputin, but not because of his presumably universal humanist concerns. What Salynsky and Oskotsky perceived as Rasputin's weakness, Seleznev and Ovcharenko regarded as his strengths. Seleznev defended the novel because its central message was the preservation of centuries-old national traditions, which were conservative by their very nature. Rasputin's work should serve as a warning because these traditions were being abandoned by urban and Western-oriented Russians. Rasputin showed that a rejection of tradition would lead to the moral corruption of Russian society. Ovcharenko hailed the novel because its heroes, like old Dariya, unquestionably accepted the existing social and political reality, and preservation of a strong, authoritarian, socialist state required people like Dariya. Ovcharenko identified political passivity as a national moral virtue and treated Rasputin and the conservative village prose idealization of the traditional Russian peasantry as a basis for the rejection of radical political and economic reform.[44]

The *Voprosy literatury* debate did not end the public discussions of the questions raised by *Farewell to Matyora* but rather served as a frame of reference for a continuing discussion that lasted until early 1979. Although the novel articulated strongly antireformist ideas, the party's ideological establishment was hardly eager to embrace it. The main reason was probably the fact that the river diversion project, involving the flooding of an enormous territory in Siberia and the Russian Northeast, was already on the drawing board. This might explain why a review of the novel in *Pravda* was highly critical. Writing in the July 25, 1977 issue of the newspaper, literary critic Boris Pankin rhetorically asked Rasputin why he avoided giving a clear answer as to whether the flooding of the village was justified. If the answer was yes, as Pankin implied, then the benefit to an infinitely larger number of people was ultimately of higher social importance than the personal tragedy of Matyora's residents. In this case, Rasputin, without realizing it, wrote not a work of social criticism but an elegy to the past.[45]

Pankin's position was supported by Anatoly Ananiev, Kochetov's successor as the chief editor of *Oktyabr* and a prominent conservative, although an antinationalist member of the Soviet literary establishment. In the 1979 novel *Years without a War (Gody bez voiny)*, a character with Rasputin-like ideas is criticized by a hero as being out of touch with the true concerns of the Russian people and as a hypocrite for enjoying the fruits of technological progress while rejecting it in the name of moral salvation:

> You are going to return Russians back to huts without chimneys to their fire-places? But they do not like it. They are seeking another, new life and they are creating it. But you do not like it. You are indignant and ready to shout whenever possible that the very source of our national culture is being dried up! You want to take advantage of electricity but the view of electrical transmission lines disturbs you . . . You want to use electric railways and the subway but you are upset to think that one might need to dam the Enisei, the Angara or the Volga.[46]

Rasputin was not without supporters. In the same month that *Novy mir* published Ananiev's thinly veiled criticism of Rasputin, *Sever* published an essay by the critic Nikolai Yanovsky defending Rasputin's ecological arguments. *Sever* was in the forefront of the campaign against the just unveiled river diversion project (December 1978), and Yanovsky's essay was clearly part of this campaign. The essay declared that *Farewell to Matyora* made an important contribution to the village prose by showing the dire ecological consequences of projects that involve the construction of hydroelectric stations and the flooding of a huge territory. Yanovsky called on the party to heed Rasputin's warning and learn from the ecological devastation of the past.[47]

A few months after the *Pravda* review, a defense of the novel appeared in *Nash sovremennik*. The reviewer, Nina Podzorova, argued that Rasputin left enough evidence in the novel to conclude that the flooding of Matyora was necessary. Nevertheless, this did not mean that Pankin's argument must be accepted. The novel attempted to bring to the public's attention the idea that technological progress should not contradict the moral foundations of society. Rasputin did so by focusing on the bureaucrats in charge of the village evacuation, who ruthlessly did their job without paying any respect or attention to the wishes of Matyora's residents. That is why the flooding of the village was an immoral act, unjustifiable even in the name of higher social values.[48]

The debates on *Farewell to Matyora* showed the ambivalent position of the conservative village prose writers in Soviet politics. By no means a reformer, Rasputin nevertheless was courted by both opponents and supporters of radical reforms. At the same time, by the early 1980s, the conservative party apparatus and its supporters in the Soviet cultural establishment viewed Rasputin as a potentially dangerous opponent of its major policy initiatives. This situation continued until the Gorbachev era, when the inevitable finally happened. Facing the reality of radical political and economic reform and unable to accept it ideologically, Rasputin, Belov, Lichutin, Krupin, and other prominent conservative village prose writers firmly joined the conservative forces in the Soviet political elite in their opposition to change.

Stalinist Legacy in Russian Culture: The "Classics and We" Debate

Equally important to village prose inspired debates were debates on Russian culture and history, which were, in effect, about Russian national identity and the desired direction of social, political, economic, and cultural change.

The most significant of these debates took place on December 21, 1977, in Moscow's Central Hall of the Writer, with an audience of over one thousand people. The historical significance of the date was not lost to anyone: it was the ninety-eighth anniversary of Stalin's birth. Officially titled "The Classics and We: Artistic Values of the Past in Contemporary Science and Culture" *(Klassika i my. Khudozhestvennye tsennosti proshlogo v sovremennoi nauke i kulture)*, the real subject was the Stalinist legacy and its relevance to the present and future of Russia.

Eighteen prominent writers, poets, literary critics, and theater directors, representing the entire spectrum of political opinion, took part. The discussion began with a programmatic presentation by radical nationalist literary scholar Pyotr Palievsky, and this set the tone for the rest of the evening. Palievsky attempted to provide a justification for a Russian nationalist rehabilitation of Stalinism and made a thinly disguised demand for a return to Stalinist-type rule.

His argument was structured as a comparison of the cultural policies of the 1920s to those of the 1930s and 1940s. Palievsky portrayed the cultural policies of the 1920s as attempting to destroy Russian national culture, particularly Russian classical literature, theater, and music, and to force on Russian society the cosmopolitan tastes and values of the Western avant-garde. In contrast, the Stalinist cultural policies of the 1930s and 1940s rejected the cultural values of the avant-garde and restored Russian national culture to its former glory. Palievsky came close to justifying the purges by arguing that many of the avant-garde artists who had participated in the destruction of Russian national culture during the Revolution and the New Economic Policy (NEP) era had met their just fate under Stalin. The great achievement of the Stalin era was the revival of the classical national tradition in Russian culture and its popularization among the masses.

Palievsky extended his argument beyond history to the current situation. In the 1960s and 1970s, he asserted, the liberal-reformist intelligentsia attempted to exact revenge for its defeat in the 1930s by writing off the cultural achievements of the Stalin era. In opera, theater, and cinema, one could see an ongoing effort to revive the traditions of the avant-garde of the 1920s at the expense of the classical tradition. This process had to be stopped in order to preserve that tradition. Palievsky called for the restoration of the all-powerful, all-intrusive state as it had existed under Stalin in order to protect Russian national culture.

Palievsky's argument was endorsed and elaborated by Kunyaev, Lobanov, Seleznev, Kozhinov, and Kupriyanov. By emphasizing the Jewish origins of many leading representatives of the cultural avant-garde of the 1920s, Stanislav Kunyaev and Vadim Kozhinov added an anti-Semitic dimension to Palievsky's attack. Mikhail Lobanov accused the early avant-garde artists and their spiritual successors, the liberal-reformist intelligentsia of the 1970s, of showing a nihilistic attitude toward the lofty moral ideals at the core of Russian national culture and tradition. The spiritual ideals of the liberal-reformist intelligentsia, Lobanov asserted, were embodied in the novels of their most popular author, Franz Kafka, and consisted of the glorification of a morally corrupt society.

Yury Seleznev added a militant anti-Western aspect to Palievsky's argument by asserting that the cultural realm was the battlefield of an ideological world war. Its weapons, he proclaimed, were the Western cultural values that the liberal-reformist intelligentsia was attempting to foist on the Russian nation. The future of Russia hinged on victory in this war. Seleznev openly called for a return to the crude anti-Western and Russian nationalist cultural polices of the late Stalin era.

These efforts to rehabilitate the Stalinist legacy were strongly challenged by prominent liberals. Theater director Anatoly Efros asserted that calls to suppress cultural pluralism in the name of protecting classical Russian culture were nothing but a reactionary attempt to reimpose Stalinism in the cultural sphere. The poet Evgeny Evtushenko reminded Palievsky and his supporters that literary and artistic works created by the avant-garde artists in the 1920s had become an inseparable part of the Russian national cultural heritage. Moreover, it was not the radical nationalists but the liberal-reformist intelligentsia who were the true heirs of classical Russian culture because they were free from chauvinism and anti-Semitism and did not hesitate to borrow from the West. Radical Russian nationalism was a reactionary and isolationist nationalism soundly rejected by classical Russian culture. The nationalism of classical Russian culture was, in Evtushenko's words, "a nationalism of truth, a love of freedom and revolution."

Literary critics Aleksandr Borshchagovsky, Sergo Lominadze, and Igor Zolotussky challenged Palievsky's assertion that Russia had experienced a cultural renaissance in the 1930s and 1940s. They pointed out that Palievsky greatly distorted historical truth in order to have it fit his ideological framework; the terror had victimized not only avant-garde artists but millions of Russian peasants as well. In the 1930s, Zolotussky reminded the audience, classical Russian culture was locked into a tight, ideological straitjacket, which resulted in the condemnation of such Russian classical writers as Dostoevsky and Gogol. This Stalinist cultural legacy remained alive, Lominadze added, and was manifested in the continuing ban on the publication of any work by the great Russian writers that the party viewed as challenging official ideology. The literary critic Irina Rodnyanskaya suggested that the banned works, which embodied universal human values, had become world classics. Throughout the discussion, the opponents of the radical nationalists emphasized that the reimposition of a Stalinist-type regime could not be carried out in the name of Russian culture; a true Russian cultural renaissance could happen only as a consequence of the full liquidation of the Stalinist legacy.

The unprecedented frankness of the debate between the radical nationalists and the liberal-reformist and liberal-nationalist intellectuals prompted the party ideological establishment to forbid the publication of the transcript and the continuation of the discussion in official Soviet journals. Such a debate was not seen again until the glasnost era.[49]

The Debate on Olzhas Suleimenov's *Asia*

Until the party archives are fully opened, it will be impossible to determine to what extent the Politburo itself was involved in the political debates among the Soviet intelligentsia in the 1970s and 1980s. The only exception is the well-documented debate over the controversial work of the popular Kazakh poet Olzhas Suleimenov. Inspired in part by Lev Gumilev's theories about the Turkic origins of Russia, Suleimenov carried out a historical-linguistic analysis of the twelfth-century Russian epic, *The Lay of Igor's Campaign (Slovo o polku Igorove)*. The outcome was a Russian-language book provocatively entitled *Asia (Az i Ya)*, which appeared in Alma-Ata in 1975.[50]

The book challenged both the official interpretation of the epic and argued that the most celebrated piece of medieval Russian literature bore clear traces of heavy Turkic influence. This influence mirrored the historical role the Turkic language and culture played in twelfth-century Russia and was similar to the role that French language and culture would play seven centuries later. Suleimenov held that the text was heavily edited in the sixteenth and again the eighteenth centuries in order to eliminate any evidence of Turkic cultural influence on Russia, and thus it distorted the true history of Russia's relations with the Turkic nations on its Asian borders. He charged that Russian scholars did not want to admit to this editing of *The Lay of Igor's Campaign* because they were Russian nationalists who wished to create the myth of a medieval Russia with a highly developed literary culture of its own.[51]

Suleimenov was not a scholar, and the book's intentions were not scholarly but political; it was an attempt to refute official theories about the cultural backwardness of the Central Asian people and the great progress they had experienced as a result of Russian annexation.[52] By accusing Russian scholars of distorting historical truth to accommodate such deeply ingrained ideological beliefs as Russian cultural superiority over the other nations of the empire and the historical legitimacy of this, Suleimenov was bound to come under intense fire.

In December 1975, a review of the book appeared in *Molodaya gvardiya*, written by a radical nationalist historian of medieval Russia, Apollon Kuzmin. He not only dismissed the book as deeply flawed but also openly accused Suleimenov of advancing Kazakh nationalist and anti-Russian views. A month later, Suleimenov was harshly criticized by two Russian nationalist scholars in the scholarly journal *Russkaya literatura*. He was labeled ignorant of medieval Russian language, culture, and literature, unaware of important scholarly works on *The Lay of Igor's Campaign*, and without respect for Russia's cultural heritage.[53]

The *Molodaya gvardiya* and *Russkaya literatura* reviews apparently attracted wide Russian nationalist attention to Suleimenov's book. It is clear that leading Russian nationalist intellectuals took the issue all the way to the Central Committee apparatus. According to Suleimenov's own account of the publication of *Asia* and the ensuing controversy, soon after the appearance of the reviews, he was called to Central Committee headquarters in Moscow, where a certain party official censured him for intellectual arrogance. After he refused to repent, Suslov ordered the Science, Culture, and Propaganda departments of the Central Committee to prepare a policy recommendation on the subject. A denunciation of the book was even contemplated for inclusion in the text of Brezhnev's speech to the forthcoming Twenty-fifth Party Congress.

Alerted by the turn of events, the first secretary of the Kazakh Communist party, Dinmukhamed Kunaev, decided to read the book himself. Although he later admitted to Suleimenov that he failed to understand the argument, he was able to convince Brezhnev to read the book. When Kunaev telephoned Brezhnev and asked him whether the book preached Kazakh nationalism as charged, Brezhnev replied that he did not find *Asia* to be nationalist. His opinion effectively resolved the issue at the Politburo and Central Committee Secretariat levels.

This was hardly the end of the controversy, however. Eager to please angry Russian nationalist intellectuals, Suslov ordered an open discussion of the book in the USSR Academy of Sciences. On February 13, 1976, a special joint session of the History and Literature and Language Sections of the academy was held at which Suleimenov was subjected to eight hours of pounding attack by the most prominent Russian nationalist scholars. Academician Boris Rybakov, a leading specialist on medieval Russian history and one of the objects of Suleimenov's criticism, led the assault proclaiming the book to be an anti-Russian publication that grossly exaggerated Turkic influences on medieval Russian culture.

Although personally unable to attend, Dmitry Likhachev, another Russian nationalist scholar criticized in *Asia*, sent a harshly worded review of the book that was read publicly at the meeting. Likhachev defended the Russian nationalist scholarship of medieval Russian history, arguing that it gave a significant boost to the study of national culture rather than inhibiting objective historical research. He called Suleimenov's thesis about Turkic-Russian relations a "fiction," with no basis in Russian history or literature.

The director of the Institute of History of the USSR Academy of Sciences, academician Aleksei Narochnitsky, also defended Russian nationalist scholarship and accused Suleimenov of deliberately exaggerating the Turkic influences on Russian culture. Other Russian speakers, including the head of the Institute of Russian Language of the USSR Academy of Sciences and his deputy, as well as the authors of the *Molodaya gvardiya* and *Russkaya literatura* reviews of *Asia*, all attacked Suleimenov with arguments similar to those of Rybakov, Likhachev, and Narochnitsky.

Even the vice president of the Academy of Sciences of Kazakhstan, Akai Nusupbekov, was brought to the meeting to deliver a condemnation of Suleimenov's book. He effectively apologized for the publication of the book in Kazakhstan and assured the audience that Kazakh scholars did not share Suleimenov's views.

The only defense of the book came from one of the few non-Russian participants, Vasily Abaev, a well-respected scholar at the Institute of Linguistics of the USSR Academy of Sciences, who called on Russian scholars to explore in depth the nature of Russian-Turkic cultural ties. In his own statement, Suleimenov admitted the existence of some flaws in his book, but he emphatically rejected any accusations of a lack of respect for Russian culture and refused to recant his views.[54]

The Russian nationalist attack on Suleimenov continued after the meeting. The journal *Moskva*, in its March 1976 issue, printed an essay by Seleznev, entitled "Myths and Truths" (*Mify i istiny*), which was the crudest Russian nationalist condemnation of *Asia* to appear in print. Seleznev accused Suleimenov of being rabidly anti-Russian and a Turkic nationalist whose book attempted to create a myth of Turkic cultural superiority over Russia. As such, according to Seleznev, Suleimenov's Turkic nationalist myth was similar to the Nazi one: both proclaimed the cultural inferiority of the Slavs.[55]

By making an explicit comparison to Hitler's *Mein Kampf,* Seleznev made the most serious political accusation against Suleimenov and his book, thus exerting pressure on the Soviet ideological establishment to take action. Soon after the appearance of Seleznev's review and apparently wanting to end a potentially dangerous controversy, Kunaev convened a meeting of the Central Committee Secretariat of the Communist party of Kazakhstan and decided to ban the book, pulling it from republican librar-ies and book stores. This act was a clear sign that leaders of the non-Rus-sian republics had no desire to stand up to Russian nationalist intellectuals and their high-level supporters in the Soviet political establishment.

The decision to ban *Asia,* did not affect Suleimenov's status in the Kazakh social and intellectual elite. In fact, his bold stand against Russian nationalism made him a local hero. As long as inclusion was a clear party goal, Kunaev did not appoint Suleimenov to a position corresponding to his actual status in the republic, fearing that this would reopen the de-bate. In December 1983, however, after the demise of inclusionary poli-tics, Suleimenov was appointed First Secretary of the Union of Writers of Kazakhstan. In 1989, he was elected a deputy to the USSR Supreme Soviet. In the following year, *Asia* was reprinted.[56]

The Debate on the "Lives of Remarkable People" Series

The fictionalized biography of leading political or cultural figures of pre-revolutionary and Soviet Russia was an important literary genre in which political debate took place in the 1970s and early 1980s. In the period under consideration, two popular biographical series were published in the USSR. One of them, "Flaming Revolutionaries" (*Plammenye revolyutsion-ery*), published work by such prominent liberal-reformist intellectuals as Vasily Aksyonov, Yury Davydov, Anatoly Gladilin, Natan Eidelman, Bulat Okudzhava, Vladimir Voinovich, and Yury Trifonov. Their books, dedi-cated to the lives of the Decembrists and other important revolutionaries in Russian history, attempted to show the existence of a strong democratic tradition in Russia and tacitly argued that the main sociopolitical goal of the Russian revolutionary movement, Russia as a just and democratic society, was still far from being realized. Since the CPSU always represented itself as the heir of the Russian revolutionary and democratic tradition, the biographies effectively called on the party to be true to this tradition by renouncing the Stalinist legacy and undertaking political, social, and economic reforms.[57]

The second, and far more prestigious biographical series, entitled "The Lives of Remarkable People" (*Zhizn zamechatelnykh lyudei*), was controlled by Russian nationalists from the late 1960s. From the mid-1970s through the early 1980s, Seleznev was the chief editor of the series and was responsible for attracting the most prominent Russian nationalist intellectuals as contributors including well-known authors such as Viktor Chalmaev, Mikhail Lobanov, Yury Loshchits, Oleg Mikhailov, Viktor Petelin, Sergei Semanov, Nikolai Skatov, Dmitry Zhukov, and Igor Zolotussky. Like the "Flaming Revolutionaries" series, "Lives of Remarkable People" was much more about the present than about the past. Semanov, editor of the series until 1976, openly admitted this in 1980, when he asserted that the series' works "are achieving an important spiritual [i.e., political] task by interpreting the present through an understanding of the past."[58]

The purpose of many Russian nationalist historical biographies published in the "Lives" series was the opposite of those that appeared in the "Flaming Revolutionaries" series. Books on the lives of medieval Moscow princes, tsarist generals, and Stalinist ministers, as well as Russian writers of the nineteenth and twentieth centuries, attempted to portray Russian national culture, traditions, and history as requiring the creation of a powerful, anti-Western authoritarian state of the Stalinist type.[59] Moreover, Russian nationalist intellectuals often used reviews of books published in the series to endorse and reiterate the political message they contained.[60]

In the late 1970s, three biographies of nineteenth-century Russian writers in the "Lives" series attracted significant attention and triggered a major debate on the Russian nationalist interpretation of Russian culture and history: Loshchits's biography of the novelist Ivan Goncharov, Lobanov's biography of the playwright Aleksandr Ostrovsky, and Zolotussky's biography of Nikolai Gogol. All three books criticized the nineteenth-century radical intelligentsia's interpretation of the works of these writers. Since these interpretations had been incorporated into Lenin's criticism of the tsarist state and, subsequently, into official ideology, these biographies constituted a thinly veiled criticism of the latter.[61]

Loshchits's book triggered a major controversy because it contained a politically charged interpretation of Goncharov's famous novel, *Oblomov*. The Russian nobleman Oblomov, the novel's main protagonist, had been interpreted by the nineteenth-century radical Russian intelligentsia as symbolic of Russian laziness and backwardness. Lenin himself often used this interpretation, and eventually it became an integral part of the official interpretation of prerevolutionary Russian history. Loshchits, on the other hand, transformed Oblomov into a positive symbol of the Russian rejection of Western cultural values. In short, what was portrayed as backward was in reality merely non-Western. In this fashion, Loshchits boldly challenged the validity of official assertions about Russia's backwardness and the need for a revolution to overcome it.

Lobanov's book on Ostrovsky attracted attention for essentially similar reasons. The radical intelligentsia had hailed Ostrovsky's plays for their criticism of patriarchal morality and the denial of women's rights that prevailed in tsarist Russia. Official ideology had always presented women's equality as being one of the great achievements of the October Revolution. Lobanov, on the other hand, used Ostrovsky's plays to condemn the emancipation of women as leading to the destruction of the family and the disappearance of the moral values that sustain it. Thus, Lobanov implicitly presented the October Revolution as the fundamental cause of the breakup of the traditional family and the moral corruption prevailing in contemporary Soviet society.

Zolotussky's book challenged the official interpretation of Russian history by defending Gogol's political views, regarded by the radical Russian intelligentsia, and subsequently by the party's ideological establishment, as reactionary. Gogol emphatically rejected the transformation of Russia's political and social institutions in accordance with progressive Western models. In his biography, Zolotussky used Gogol's political ideas in order to criticize the Russian revolutionary tradition and revive the debate on the applicability of Slavophile-type ideas to the political and social realities of contemporary Russia.

The party was extremely sensitive to the political content of the books published in the "Lives" series because of their great popularity. Throughout most of the 1970s, however, the guidelines of inclusionary politics forced the party's ideological establishment to tolerate the Russian nationalist challenge to the official version of Russian history and culture. The growing tension between the party and the Russian nationalist intellectuals came to the fore in 1979 in connection with Valentin Pikul's challenge to the official interpretation of the Russian Revolution. The "Lives" series did not entirely escape party censure. An unsigned editorial in the October 1979 issue of *Kommunist* harshly criticized Loshchits's biography of Goncharov. The *Kommunist* editorial signaled to the opponents of inclusionary politics that the "Lives" series were no longer immune from criticism. In March 1980, Vasily Kuleshov, a prominent critic of Russian nationalism in the Soviet cultural establishment, harshly attacked Lobanov's biography of Ostrovsky in a lengthy article in *Literaturnaya gazeta*.[62]

The appearance of the *Kommunist* editorial and Kuleshov's article in *Literaturnaya gazeta* criticizing the "Lives" book series was interpreted by the editors of *Voprosy literatury* as creating an opportunity to stage a major debate about the Russian nationalist interpretation of Russian history promoted by the biographical series. This discussion was published in the September 1980 issue of the journal and focused primarily on the three books just discussed. Three literary critics defended the "Lives" series in general, and the ideological message of Loshchits, Lobanov, and Zolotussky, while five other participants in the debate harshly criticized the authors, as well as several other books published in the series.

Vsevolod Sakharov praised the series' books on the grounds that they illustrated the true path of the development of Russian national culture. In other words, Russian history as it was presented by the contributors to the series decisively proved that Western democratic institutions and values were alien to Russian national traditions. Nikolai Skatov defended the Russian nationalist challenge to the official history of prerevolutionary Russian culture and society as well. He conveyed this argument by asserting that Loshchits, Lobanov, and Zolotussky understood the essence of the works of Gogol, Ostrovsky, and Goncharov better than had the nineteenth-century revolutionary intelligentsia and contemporary intellectuals who repeated the same old arguments.

Seleznev, chief editor of the "Lives" series, proclaimed that Loshchits, Lobanov, and Zolotussky's books attempted to establish the existence of "positive elements in our cultural and historical legacy which . . . enrich the creative striving of our nation." These biographies were of national importance because they rehabilitated the prerevolutionary, anti-Western ideological tradition and presented it as the source of a solution for the sociopolitical problems of contemporary Russia. Seleznev could not ignore the repeated accusations that the "Lives" series rendition of Russian history stood in sharp contrast to the official account. He attempted to rebuff his opponents by accusing them of trying to resurrect the old bolshevik negative treatment of Russian culture and history, which the party had condemned as "vulgar sociologizing."[63]

The opponents of the nationalism promoted in the "Lives" series were led by Aleksandr Dementiev, deputy editor of *Novy mir* under Tvardovsky and a relentless critic of Russian nationalism since the 1960s. Dementiev defended the nineteenth-century radical intelligentsia's interpretation of Russian culture and history and argued that behind Russian nationalist claims to the rediscovery of precious national traditions stood the idealization of such negative aspects of prerevolutionary Russian social reality as xenophobia, passivity, and patriarchal moral values. Dementiev warned that the elevation of these characteristics to the status of national virtues that deserved revival was a dangerous attempt to take Russian culture and society backward rather than to advance it.[64]

Dementiev's arguments were elaborated by the literary critics Vladimir Zhdanov, Arkady Anastasiev, and Igor Dzeverin, who all accused Lobanov of distorting the meaning of Ostrovsky's plays in order to condemn the emancipation of women as a leading cause of the disintegration of the family and traditional moral values. Dzeverin insisted that the use of the Ostrovsky-coined concepts "accursed past" and "kingdom of darkness" was justified in a description of prerevolutionary Russian society. Anastasiev also pointed out that by presenting capitalism as an evil forced on Russia by the Jews, Lobanov added a strong anti-Semitic dimension to his already distorted account.

Ukrainian literary critic Pavlo Movchan focused his criticism on Zolotussky's biography of Gogol. He accused its author of lacking sensitivity to and knowledge of Ukrainian culture and history. Zolotussky, Movchan argued, provided a caricature-like description of Ukrainian life and presented the Ukrainian nation as lacking a history or distinguished cultural traditions of its own. Although Movchan did not say it explicitly, the thrust of his criticism conveyed the message that Russian nationalist intellectuals were providing a historical justification for the government's russification policies.

In their concluding note, the editors of *Voprosy literatury* sided fully with the critics of Russian nationalism. They proclaimed that the three biographies under discussion were examples of a subjective and arbitrary interpretation of Russian history. They sharply rebuked Seleznev for avoiding

the issues raised by Dementiev and other non–Russian nationalist participants of the panel, and reminded him that the Leninist theory of two
cultures in any national culture provided the guiding interpretive principle
for writing Russian cultural history and should not be challenged.[65]

This lengthy debate in *Voprosy literatury* did not end the discussion of
the "Lives" series interpretation of Russian history. Between 1981 and 1984,
three additional essays appeared in Russian thick journals that were highly
critical of the Russian nationalist interpretation of Russian history and
culture. Two of them were written by the head Moscow Writers' Union
organization, Feliks Kuznetsov, and the third belonged to the director of
the Institute of World Literature of the USSR Academy of Sciences, Georgy
Berdnikov.

Kuznetsov's essays, published in the journal *Moskva* in 1981 and 1984,
harshly criticized Loshchits's biography of Goncharov and Lobanov's biography of Ostrovsky. Kuznetsov was not simply elaborating the arguments
of the liberal-reformist participants of the *Voprosy literatury* debate, but he
was attempting to integrate the criticism of a "Lives" series book into an
interpretation of Russian history capable of reconciling both Russian nationalist intellectuals and the party's ideological establishment.

Kuznetsov sharply criticized Loshchits and Lobanov for their idealization of Russia's premodern past, in which patriarchal moral values prevailed, and for their rejection of the radical socialist ideologies of the
nineteenth century as inherently alien to Russian national tradition. If the
claim that revolutionary ideas had been imported from the West and were
alien to Russian national traditions was correct, how could anyone explain
rebellions that occurred throughout Russian history? Kuznetsov did not
use his defense of the Russian revolutionary tradition in order to justify
radical political reform, as Trifonov, Okudzhava, Eidelman, and other liberal-reformist contributors to the "Flaming Revolutionaries" biographical
series did. Quite the opposite, he defended the Russian Revolution to dele-
gitimize the call for democratic political reform. The Revolution of 1917,
Kuznetsov asserted, was national and anti-Western in its nature. It prevented Russia from becoming a philistine Western bourgeois democracy
and at the same time ensured the country political and economic independence. Following the path prescribed by the Slavophile ideology, on the
other hand, would have condemned Russia to political and economic backwardness with all its negative consequences. The implication of Kuznetsov's argument was clear: the Russian nationalist intelligentsia must stop

challenging the historical legitimacy of the existing sociopolitical order because it had achieved their most important goal—that of making Russia a powerful anti-Western state.[66]

Berdnikov's essay, which appeared in the August 1982 issue of the journal *Znamya,* examined the books of Lobanov and Zolotussky. Berdnikov essentially reiterated Kuznetsov's arguments and criticized both books for challenging the Leninist interpretation of Russian history and culture.[67]

It is not clear whether Kuznetsov and Berdnikov wanted to renew the debate or merely to pronounce the authoritative judgment on the issues discussed by the participants in the *Voprosy literatury* debate. No Russian nationalist response to Kuznetsov or Berdnikov's essays was published because of the determination of the party ideological apparatus not to give Russian nationalist intellectuals an additional opportunity to challenge the official interpretation of Russian history and culture. Kuznetsov's second essay was the final contribution to the debate on the Russian nationalist view of Russian history as it was advanced in the "Lives" biographies.

The Debate on the Anniversary of the Kulikovo Field Battle

The year 1980 marked the six-hundredth anniversary of the Russian victory over the Mongols at the Kulikovo Field Battle, traditionally regarded as one of the most celebrated events in Russian history. In 1963, Solzhenitsyn published a short story, "Zakhar the Pouch" *(Zakhar-kalita),* which described his pilgrimage to the Kulikovo Field. He presented the battle as the principal cultural symbol of Russian nationalism. In 1980, in an essay describing his own journey to the Kulikovo Field, Rasputin stated: "We talked about Russia, about our Motherland, and about her fate in the past and in the future. Where if not here, on the Kulikovo Field, can one talk about it?"[68]

Indeed, the anniversary was turned into a two-year (1980–1982) celebration of the main social, political, and cultural views held by the Russian nationalist intelligentsia. Since the liberal-reformist intellectuals largely abstained from challenging Russian nationalist ideas, the battle anniversary effectively became a political debate among the various factions within the Russian nationalist movement.

The party allowed, and encouraged, them to do so. Although the tensions between the party's ideological establishment and Russian nationalist intellectuals were growing in the late 1970s, the nationalists were granted virtually unrestricted freedom of expression during the year-long anniversary celebrations. Moreover, this freedom to articulate principal sociopolitical ideas came with the privilege of publishing an enormous volume of literature of all kinds, from scholarly monographs to popular fiction. In the anniversary year, Soviet publishing houses printed approximately 150 titles related in one way or another to the battle. Their total circulation could well be in the range of between 5 to 10 million copies.[69] This policy was fueled by the party's desire to ignite the nationalist sentiments of the Russian population after the invasion of Afghanistan and the emergence of the Solidarity movement in Poland.

This was the context of the Kulikovo debate. As far as its content was concerned, the debate was largely focused on two main issues: the role of the Orthodox Church in Russian history and its desired position in contemporary Soviet society, and the causes of the rise and decline of states and the historical relationship of Russia to the West, with both its major domestic and foreign policy implications.

The underlying motive for the debate on the Orthodox Church was whether Russian Orthodoxy was a true Russian nationalist alternative to communist ideology and whether the Orthodox Church as an institution was capable of revitalizing Russian society. Most Russian nationalist intellectuals viewed Orthodoxy as a viable spiritual alternative to communism and harshly criticized the party's antireligious policies. They did this primarily by portraying the Orthodox Church as the first and foremost Russian national institution, which had played a crucial role in the formation of the Russian state by providing spiritual guidance to its rulers and the population as a whole.

At the level of popular literature, this position was presented in several fictional accounts of the Kulikovo battle that appeared in 1980. The novels of Vladimir Lebedev, Vladimir Vozovikov, and Boris Dedyukhin portrayed Russian society of the 1380s as devoutly Orthodox Christian. Yury Loshchits, in his "Lives" series biography of Dmitry Donskoi, Grand Prince of Moscow and the commander of the Russian army at Kulikovo, went even further and depicted the battle itself as a battle in defense of the Christian faith because Orthodox Christianity and Russia could not be separated.[70]

In their efforts to portray the Orthodox Church as the spiritual mainstay of the Russian nation, Lebedev, Vozovikov, Dedyukhin, and Loshchits elevated St. Sergius of Rodonezh, a battle contemporary and major figure in the history of the Russian Orthodox Church, to the rank of a great national hero. They depicted him as tirelessly promoting the idea of national unity as the key to the liberation of Russia from Tatar domination and who at the crucial moment blessed Dmitry Donskoi to fight at Kulikovo.

The conservative nationalist philosopher Arseny Gulyga provided a theoretical justification of the ideas that had been expressed in fictional form. Human beings, he argued in an essay published in the journal *Litera-turnaya ucheba,* are first and foremost members of national communities. What effectively binds them together and gives them a sense of their communality is the living memory of a common past and a veneration of the things that national tradition has made most sacred. The Church entered the national memory as the institution that played a key role in Russian national history. The victory at Kulikovo, he asserted, was an illustration of the crucial importance of the Orthodox Church and its moral teachings and the role they played in one of the most spectacular achievements of the Russian nation. Gulyga argued that the party attempted to ignore the main lesson of the Kulikovo battle: Russian national greatness could not be achieved without the Orthodox Church. Only the Orthodox Church was capable of unifying the nation and bringing about its moral renewal.[71]

During the anniversary, Russian nationalist intellectuals repeatedly emphasized that the victory on the battlefield was a direct consequence of the Orthodox Church-inspired moral and spiritual revival that Russian society experienced in the fourteenth century. Dmitry Likhachev expressed this view in a succinct statement: "Victory and liberation from the foreign yoke was assured not only by the growing [economic and military] resources of the country but also by its spiritual and moral revival. The Kulikovo victory was no less the victory of ideas and new moral forces than a victory of arms and military organization."[72]

Liberal-nationalist historian Gelian Prokhorov emphasized that the main element of this revival was the spread of religious tenets that emphasized the moral rebirth of the individual. Others, like Likhachev, pointed out that fourteenth-century Russia was rediscovering its pre-Mongol past, thus suggesting the necessity of recovering the prerevolutionary cultural and spiritual legacy as a precondition of Russia's moral revival in the present. Gulyga went even further, implying that the rejection of this legacy by the CPSU was the cause of the moral corruption in Russian society.[73]

The Russian nationalist emphasis on the moral renewal of the nation, which only the Orthodox Church was capable of bringing about, was a clear message to the party leadership that the official ideology had failed to prevent the moral corruption of Russian society and had thus weakened the state. Indeed, the Kulikovo anniversary was exploited by Russian nationalists to criticize Russian moral degeneration. Russian nationalist fiction barely attempted to disguise its condemnation of the current moral corruption in descriptions of the events of the fourteenth-century. The main hero of Dedyukhin's novel declares drunkenness to be "an unforgivable disease, a fall lacking justification, the common shame of our people," and Vozovikov bluntly warned that "the corrupted urban plebeian proved [by history] to be a bad defender of the state."[74]

Russian nationalist intellectuals were not unanimous in their insistence that Orthodoxy must replace communist ideology and that the Orthodox Church-led spiritual renewal was the only solution to Russia's social crisis. Some advanced views that either assigned a secondary role to the Orthodox Church or were militantly anti-Christian. Among the latter, the radical nationalist historian Apollon Kuzmin stood out. Contrary to many other radical nationalists, Kuzmin used the anniversary to condemn Russian Orthodoxy rather than to extol its virtues. In an essay that appeared in a special issue of a scholarly periodical dedicated to the battle, Kuzmin rejected the argument that the Orthodox Church must be rehabilitated as a condition for Russian national renewal. Kuzmin did this by emphasizing the foreign nature of the Orthodox Church and its anti-Russian politics during the Kulikovo battle era.[75]

The real national religion of Russia, Kuzmin asserted, was not Orthodoxy but pre-Christian paganism. Moreover, the Christian creed that Russia originally adopted was not Greek Orthodoxy but Arian heresy. Russian princes accepted a heretic creed because it did not bring with it foreign domination. Greek Orthodox Christianity was effectively forced on Russia in the aftermath of the Mongol invasion when the state was weak. The transformation of the Russian Church into the Russian Orthodox Church spelled an end to the Church as a Russian national institution. The Orthodox Church's policies during the Kulikovo battle period were dictated exclusively by a desire to subjugate Russia to the authority of its Byzantine-based hierarchs. In order to do this, the Orthodox Church attempted to stop the process of Russian unification and to undermine the growing power of the princes of Moscow.[76]

Behind Kuzmin's rejection of the Russian Orthodox Church as an institution capable of revitalizing Russian society and his exaltation of paganism implicitly stood a proto-fascist vision of the ideal future: a powerful, highly coercive, and xenophobic (anti-Western and anti-Semitic) state that was no longer even formally inhibited by Christian moral values. The pagan element aside, Kuzmin's ideas bore close semblance to those of historians Vadim Kargalov and Fyodor Nesterov. During the Kulikovo anniversary, Kargalov insisted that the solution to Russia's social and moral problems was not an Orthodox Church-led spiritual renewal but the strengthening of the Russian state, which had become progressively weaker in the post-Stalin period. The lesson he thought should be drawn from the victory at Kulikovo was that only policies aimed at the creation of a strong state could unify the nation and inspire it to a heroic effort.[77]

This argument was developed into a manifesto-like statement by Nesterov in a book that appeared during the celebrations. Nesterov argued that Russian history teaches the lesson that only policies aimed at reconstituting the powerful state were capable of reawakening the nationalist sentiments of the Russian population and revitalizing Russian society.[78] He wrote that the Russian people accepted as legitimate only rulers who have proved themselves capable of keeping the state strong. The tsars enjoyed popular support as long as they continued the tradition of Dmitry Donskoi, of strengthening the Russian state. They lost their legitimacy and were overthrown in 1917 because they failed to prevent the domination of foreign capital, were unable to prepare Russia for World War I, and were responsible for the disintegration of the Russian state following the military defeat. The Communist party gained popular legitimacy because it was able to reverse the process of disintegration and create a powerful state. The underlying thrust of this argument was clear: the party would lose its right to govern the country, as the tsars had, if it failed to restore Russia to the powerful state it had been in the Stalin era. Nesterov openly admonished the party to reintroduce three fundamental tenets that from the time of the Kulikovo battle had made Russia a great state: "centralization, discipline, self-sacrifice." He even implicitly suggested that the party use the Orthodox Church in this endeavor. After all, in the past the Orthodox Church had helped the state to maintain the discipline and the morale of the Russian army.[79]

The debate on the nature of Russia's relationship with the West was an integral part of the argument on the appropriate policy necessary to revitalize the Russian state and society. The historian Prokhorov provided a liberal-nationalist defense of a continuation of Russia's openness to Western cultural and political influences. Russian cultural and religious traditions had their roots in Byzantium and were anti-Western in their nature. The borrowing of Western cultural traditions in the eighteenth and the nineteenth centuries, however, had transformed Russia into the only country that incorporated both Western and Eastern cultural legacies. This capability of representing truly universal human values was the source of Russia's strength. This was also why Russian society had to continue to be open to the Western world.

Prokhorov's ideas, however, were overwhelmingly rejected by Russian nationalists who used the Kulikovo anniversary to advance a thesis of the perennial hostility between Russia and the West. This thesis took the form of what might be called the "ungrateful West" argument. Russia's stubborn resistance to the Mongol invaders, Russian nationalist authors claimed, saved the West. The latter, however, instead of being eternally grateful, became the mortal enemy of Russia's existence by continuously invading it or supporting its enemies.[80]

Although most Russian nationalist intellectuals shared the view that the West threatened Russia politically and culturally, they clearly disagreed on the most appropriate policy toward the West. Rasputin expressed the conservative nationalist conviction when he called on the Soviet government to preserve some elements of détente in order to avoid military confrontation with the West.[81] The radical nationalists, on the other hand, did not hesitate to criticize Brezhnev's policies of détente and to call for the preparation of a total confrontation with the West. Nesterov proclaimed the historical inevitability of this confrontation on the grounds that from the thirteenth century to the present, "Russian land at least once in every one hundred years experienced devastating invasion, quite often from several directions simultaneously." Seleznev, in turn, saw the confrontation as inevitable; the Russian nation's will to maintain its own distinct political, economic, and cultural identity was irreconcilable with the Western cosmopolitan drive to impose bourgeois values and institutions on the whole world. Moreover, this confrontation had already begun in the realm of ideology and made military clash ultimately unavoidable.[82]

Among the Russian nationalist attacks on the West during the Kulikovo anniversary, Lev Gumilev's stood out because it provoked the most heated debate. Gumilev, a Leningrad historian and geographer, emerged in the 1970s as one of the most influential and controversial Russian nationalist thinkers. His ideas about the life cycle of nations and ethnic groups had provoked sharp criticism by many leading Soviet ethnographers because he challenged the official theories on the subject. His 1970 book, *In Search of the Imaginary Kingdom (Poiski vymyshlennogo tsarstva),* was harshly attacked by members of the Soviet historical establishment because it contested the official version of Russian history in the tenth to fourteenth centuries.[83]

The Kulikovo anniversary gave Gumilev an exceptional opportunity to popularize his ideas, which until then had been the domain of a small group of Russian intellectuals.[84] He did so in two essays that appeared in the magazine *Ogonyok* and the journal *Dekorotivnoe iskusstvo* in September and December 1980, respectively. While carefully avoiding the explicit linkage of his ideas to issues on the agenda of the ongoing sociopolitical debate, Gumilev nevertheless clearly attempted to provide a new historical and ideological justification for extreme anti-Western policies.[85]

Although Gumilev viciously attacked the West, he did not use the "ungrateful West" argument, which he regarded as failing to challenge the claim of liberal-reformers' that Russia's civilization was European in its nature. He openly proclaimed instead that "Eurocentricism is bad for Russia" and set out to prove that the West was the embodiment of evil and had attempted in the past (and, by implication, would try to do so again in the future) to impose on Russia its rationalist, urban, and capitalist civilization.[86]

Simplifying his rather complex theory of Russian and world history, he argued that three world civilizations (or "super-ethnic entities," in his terminology) had appeared in Eurasia since the end of antiquity: the civilization of Russian and Turkic ethnic groups of the Great Steppe, the civilizations of the Catholic West, and the Muslim East. The Russian–Great Steppe civilization differed from that of the Catholic West and the Muslim East in being rural, while the others were urban and dominated by a ruling class composed of the trading bourgeoisie. Russia, Gumilev claimed, had been forced throughout history to defend itself first and foremost against the West, which inscribed on its banners the twin goals of trade (even slave trade) and profit.

Following the arguments of the "Eurasian" émigré thinkers of the 1920s, Gumilev traced the emergence of the modern Russian nation and its civilization to the Mongol invasion of the thirteenth century and its aftermath.[87] The Mongols, who invaded from the Great Steppe, were pagans and Nestorian Christians and were not hostile to Russian Orthodoxy. Therefore, soon after their invasion, the Mongols became the defenders of Russia from

Western "Catholic aggression." The relations between Orthodox Russia and the pagan-Nestorian Golden Horde were, according Gumilev, so close and intense that he called them "symbiotic."

This Mongol-Russian symbiosis was the foundation of the Russian–Great Steppe civilization to which the West was extremely hostile. The first phase in the evolution of this civilization lasted until 1312, when the Mongol Khan Uzbek converted to Islam. This event had far-reaching consequences because a conversion to Islam meant that the Golden Horde became part of the Islamic civilization of the East and hostile to Russia. Mongols who remained loyal to the old tradition and refused to convert fled to Russia, further enriching it with the heritage of the Great Steppe. Thus, 1312 marked the beginning of the second phase in the development of the Russian–Great Steppe civilization.

At this stage, Russia had to acquire a new spiritual self-identity, and it did so as a result of the Kulikovo battle. The battle of Kulikovo was, in fact, a confrontation between Russia and universal, especially Western, capital, since the Tatar invasion in 1380 had been heavily subsidized by the West, the main beneficiary of a Tatar victory. By defeating the Tatars at Kulikovo, Russia effectively foiled the Western attempt to impose capitalism on it. The implication of this argument is rather clear: the identity of the Russian nation was shaped during an intense battle to defeat the efforts of the West to impose its institutions on Russia. Therefore, these same political, social, and economic institutions should not be accepted today.[88]

Gumilev also used his theory of the life cycle of nations to dismiss the arguments of liberal and conservative nationalist intellectuals who used the Kulikovo anniversary to emphasize the importance of a moral-religious revival as a precondition for the revitalization of the Russian state. This revival, he asserted, was not a precondition for the Kulikovo victory but the direct consequence of it. Each young ethnic civilization manifests its newly acquired spiritual self-identity in an unprecedented outburst of creative energy, which he called "passionateness" (*passionarnost*). In Russia, this outburst manifested itself in the religious renaissance of the fourteenth and fifteenth centuries. Although such outbursts are limited to the early stages of national life cycles, they continue to occur on the individual level. Such individuals ("passionaries" [*passionarii*] in his terminology) become the great leaders of the nation. One of the main implications of this argument was that what the Russian nation really needed most to overcome its crisis was not a spiritual revival but the emergence of a passionary leader.[89]

In 1981, the strongly anti-Western elements of Gumilev's theory were pushed to an even greater extreme by the philosopher Yury Borodai and the literary critic Kozhinov. Summarizing Gumilev's theory of world history in the September issue of the journal *Priroda*, Borodai declared Western civilization to be the spiritual heir of Manicheism. Emphasizing its Jewish origins, Borodai argued that Manicheism believed in the permanence of evil in the world and condoned murder, torture, lying, and debauchery. These ideas, he asserted, had found their way to the West via St. Augustine, himself a secret member of the Manichean sect, in the form of his theory that only a few people are predestined for salvation while the majority are doomed, and that the devil is acting on God's orders.

The Manichean ideas of St. Augustine had been revived by Calvin and became the essence of Protestantism and capitalism. The Protestant predestination doctrine constituted a reconciliation of God with the Devil, since it removed the freedom of choice between good and evil and granted the right to do anything without pangs of conscience. The philosophical theories that currently prevailed in the West, Borodai added, were, in effect, advocating the same principles. In other words, the Western economic, political, and cultural system was an embodiment of evil Jewish Manichean teachings. Borodai's argument had two clear implications. In the short run, Russia must be shielded from Western influences as much as possible, and in the long run, confrontation with the West was desirable since it would be a confrontation between good and evil.[90]

Borodai's essay created an uproar and provoked a strong reaction from the Soviet academic establishment. On November 11, 1981, the Presidium of the USSR Academy of Sciences convened a special session to discuss Borodai's essay and, by implication, Gumilev's theories. At the end of the meeting, the Presidium issued a resolution condemning the publication of the essay on the grounds that it spread ideologically harmful ideas about ethnicity and the ethnic formation processes. The main institutional consequence of the resolution was a purge of the editorial board of *Priroda* and the effective silencing of Gumilev and his followers until the glasnost era.[91]

The resolution of the Presidium of the USSR Academy of Sciences and the subsequent purge of *Priroda*'s editorial board did not deter *Nash sovremennik* from promoting Gumilev's interpretation of Russian history. Its November 1981 issue contained an article by Vadim Kozhinov that transformed Gumilev's theories on the Asian origins of Russia and its relationship with the West into a programmatic statement. Like Borodai, Kozhinov demonized the West, which did not accept the legitimate existence of civilizations that differed fundamentally from its own. The West either destroyed them, as the Spanish did in South America, or exploited them for its own ends, as the British did in India.

Kozhinov went on to argue that Russian national traditions were incompatible with Western traditions. The West elevated the freedom of the individual into its culminating cultural principle—a principle alien to Russian culture, which stressed the moral perfection of individuals. The efforts of the liberal forces in the Soviet political and intellectual elites to adopt Western cultural values and traditions were therefore bound to cause the destruction of Russian national culture. Russian society, he concluded, must free itself from a Western orientation and realize that its future lay not in adopting Western political, social, and cultural institutions and practices but rather in the recognition that Russia is part of Asia.

Kozhinov attempted to base his argument on Russian history. He identified the Western cultural domination of Russia in the eighteenth and nineteenth centuries as causing Russians to treat Asia and its traditions as alien and hostile. This was also the origin of the myth that presented the Kulikovo battle as a manifestation of the inevitable deadly confrontation of two hostile civilizations, Russia and Asia. In reality, the Kulikovo battle was a clash with the international forces of evil organized by the West. It therefore was the West, and not the East, that constituted Russia's historic mortal enemy.

The implications of Kozhinov's argument are clear. First, like Borodai, he viewed confrontation with the West as inevitable. Second, Asia was, first and foremost, a symbol of the principled renunciation of the primacy of Western political, socioeconomic, and cultural institutions. A fundamental change of cultural orientation would necessarily entail the decisive rejection of any thought of introducing Western-oriented liberal reforms in the Soviet Union.[92]

Kozhinov's essay constituted a major attack on the party's ideology and its foreign and domestic policies and it hastened the demise of the politics of inclusion. The Kulikovo anniversary had politics precipitated the last major political debate of the pre-Gorbachev period in which Russian nationalist intellectuals were given an opportunity to articulate their principal views on politics, history, and culture. Responses to the ideas of Nesterov, Kozhinov, Gumilev, and other participants in the Kulikovo anniversary discussion continued to appear between 1982 and 1985 and provided an important link to the political debates in the first years of the Gorbachev era.

Although the sociopolitical debates of the 1970s and early 1980s appear to have failed to influence the policymaking process, they played an important role in preparing Soviet society for the perestroika era. All the major Russian nationalist ideas expressed in these debates would be reiterated more explicitly and elaborately under Gorbachev, and ultimately they would be adopted by major political actors. Moreover, these ideas guided the politics of the Russian nationalist factions and individuals in the years 1985 to 1991 and beyond.

The Zenith of Politics by Culture, 1985–1989

Although the era of inclusionary politics ended in 1982, no clearly defined policy replaced it until 1986. The years 1983 to 1985 were years of temporary compromise. On the one hand, the party's ideological establishment waged a campaign of harsh criticism against Russian nationalist ideas in the official press, and this was accompanied by a substantial cut in the circulation of *Nash sovremennik* and a freeze in its subscription quota. On the other hand, both Andropov and Chernenko recognized that inclusionary politics had transformed Russian nationalists from being one among many groups within the Russian intellectual elite at the beginning of the Brezhnev era to the most influential group at its close. Russian nationalist intellectuals therefore continued to enjoy such important inclusion-era privileges as exceedingly large publication runs.

Inclusionary politics gave voice and status to the Russian nationalist intelligentsia, and this was a calculated substitute for radical political and economic reform. The decision to launch such reforms was bound to have an adverse effect on the status and power of the Russian nationalist intelligentsia. Policies aimed at introducing a Western-type market economy and democratizing the political system meant an end to the utility of favoring the Russian nationalists through an inclusionary strategy. It also meant the ultimate triumph of the ideas supported by liberal nationalists since the 1960s and a decisive rejection of the path of the sociopolitical development proposed by the conservative village prose writers and radical nationalists, the great majority of the Russian nationalist intelligentsia. Perestroika forced members of the Russian nationalist movement to make a clear choice between support of or opposition to the reform process. In each case, the decision was made based on the individual's personal identification with sociopolitical ideas that he or she had developed over a long period of time.[1]

Most Russian nationalist intellectuals found themselves actively opposing the direction of perestroika-engendered political, social, economic, and cultural reforms. In fact, perestroika united the conservative village prose writers and radical nationalists in their opposition to reform and drove them to abandon their Brezhnev-era disagreements and seek an alliance with antireformist forces within the political establishment.

The principal components of the politics of the Russian nationalist intellectuals in the Gorbachev era were their fundamental rejection of perestroika, their unwavering support for the preservation of the imperial nature of the Soviet state, and their ardent opposition to democratization and the introduction of a market economy. These positions left them with no other choice but to render full support to the conservative elements within the party, the army, and the KGB who were also fighting to preserve the multinational empire, an authoritarian form of government, and the command economy. Their political choices, however, were not generally popular and prevented Russian nationalists from institutionalizing themselves as a powerful political movement.

Russian Nationalist Intellectuals and Gorbachev: A Brief Alliance

In his February 1990 portrait of Egor Ligachev, the leader of the conservative opposition to Gorbachev in the Politburo, Russian journalist Vitaly Tretiyakov aptly remarked that if Ligachev's political career had come to an end in 1986, his name would have entered history as one of the initiators of perestroika.[2] This observation extends to the Russian nationalist intellectuals as well.

From the 1970s to the early 1980s, nationalist intellectuals loudly condemned social and economic decay of the Brezhnev era. Sensing impending radical change, they intensified their criticism almost immediately after Gorbachev came to power. As the best organized group of the Russian intelligentsia before 1985, they were better prepared for political action than the nonnationalist members of the Russian intelligentsia. In fact, it was the Russian nationalist agenda, as it had been molded up to 1985, that dominated the public political debates in the first year and a half of the Gorbachev era.[3]

As early as the summer of 1985, the Russian nationalist intelligentsia was able to turn ecology, and especially the river diversion project, into a major political issue. Opposition to the project was one of the few causes around which all Russian nationalists could rally. They were able to turn public opinion against the project and mobilize the support of leading intellectuals not already aligned with them.[4]

The campaign against the project began with the publication in the July 1985 issue of *Nash sovremennik* of a "roundtable," in which twelve highly respected Soviet scientists warned that the project not only would not bring the promised economic benefits but could lead to ecological disaster.[5] In December 1985, at the RSFSR Writers' Union Congress, and in June 1986 at the USSR Writers' Union Congress, the nationalist writers Belov, Bondarev, Proskurin, Rasputin, and Zalygin attacked the project as well as the unrestrained logging of the Russian forests and the industrial pollution of Lake Baikal.[6]

The publication in *Nash sovremennik* and the speeches of Russian nationalist writers at the RSFSR and the USSR Writers' Union Congresses were important milestones in a long campaign that ended on August 15, 1986, when the Politburo announced a halt to all fieldwork on the project in order to reevaluate its economic and ecological consequences. This was, in effect, the cancellation of the project. Moreover, opposition to the project appears to have been rewarded. One of the project's major opponents, the liberal-nationalist writer Sergei Zalygin, was appointed chief editor of *Novy mir* a week before the cancellation was announced.[7]

It is not clear how important the public pressure rallied by the Russian nationalist intellectuals was in influencing the Politburo decision, since there was also significant institutional opposition to the project.[8] Zalygin's appointment as the chief of the most prestigious Soviet intellectual journal and its timing, however, suggest that Gorbachev recognized the influence and prestige of the Russian nationalist intellectuals and wanted to use the cancellation of the project as an opportunity to mobilize Russian nationalist support in favor of the unfolding perestroika.

Zalygin's appointment appears also to have been a partial reward for his historical novel, *After the Storm (Posle buri),* the second part of which appeared in the July through September 1985 issues of the journal *Druzhba narodov.* The novel attacked Stalinism and introduced the liberal-nationalist rehabilitation of NEP as a political, socioeconomic model capable of reconciling the communist ideas of Lenin with Russian nationalist traditions. The work contained a thinly concealed argument that the proper path to political and economic reform should be a re-creation of NEP-type arrangements.[9]

Laudatory reviews of Zalygin's novel began to appear in the Soviet press in December 1985. In the aftermath of the Twenty-seventh Party Congress, such reviews appeared not only in major literary journals but also in *Pravda*, indicating that the book's ideas enjoyed the support of the top party leadership. Soon after the appearance of the essay in *Pravda*, the book was nominated for the Lenin Prize and dispelling any doubts about official support for Zalygin's ideas.[10]

Zalygin did not receive the prize for *After the Storm*. The honor went to another member of the village prose movement. In 1986, a member of the conservative wing of the movement, the rural journalist Ivan Vasiliev, received the Lenin Prize for his essays in the 1980s condemning mismanagement and moral corruption in the countryside.[11]

The award clearly signaled that the party shared Russian nationalist concerns about the moral crisis of Soviet society. Indeed, in the first year and a half of Gorbachev's tenure, fiction by three leading members of the village prose movement brought the subject of the moral corruption of Russian society to the heart of the political debate. Valentin Rasputin's novel *Fire (Pozhar)*, Viktor Astafiev's novel *The Sad Detective Story (Pechalny detektiv)* and a collection of short stories entitled *Place of Action (Mesto deistviya)*, and Vasily Belov's novel *Everything Lies Ahead (Vse vperedi)* all portrayed Russian society as morally corrupt and argued that without a revival of traditional moral values, Gorbachev's reforms were doomed to failure. They searched for the agents of moral corruption in Russian society and found them in the CPSU the urban intelligentsia, emancipated women, rock music, and national minorities, especially Jews and Georgians.[12]

Like the ecological campaign, these writings, despite their strong anti-communist undertones, complemented Gorbachev's pre–Twenty-seventh Party Congress strategy. During this period, Gorbachev continued many of Andropov's policies designed to fight widespread corruption and restore discipline in the workplace. On May 15, 1985, after strong lobbying by Ligachev, the Politburo launched an antialcohol campaign, unparalleled in scope, that included severe restrictions on the production and sale of alcoholic beverages. From the mid-1970s on, Russian nationalist intellectuals had loudly demanded strong government measures to fight the growing problem of alcoholism. Both Rasputin's *Fire* and Astafiev's *Sad Detec-*

tive Story contained condemnations of alcoholism, hitherto unprecedented in the censured press. The goals of the party leadership and those of the prominent Russian nationalist intellectuals dramatically coincided on this issue.[13]

Fire received wide public acclaim soon after its publication, and in 1987 Rasputin was awarded the USSR State Prize. The award was far more than the simple admission of the work's popularity or Rasputin's status as one of the leading reform-minded Soviet intellectuals. It constituted official acknowledgment that the party shared Russian nationalist concerns and gave tacit approval of their positions on these issues.

Nevertheless, it would be a mistake to assume that Russian nationalist activity during this period was limited to efforts to defeat the river diversion project, defend NEP, or criticize moral corruption, all positions supporting Gorbachev's reform agenda. The signs of future fierce Russian nationalist opposition to reform appeared early in Gorbachev's tenure. The June 1985 issue of *Nash sovremennik* contained a vicious radical nationalist attack on the liberalizing trends in Soviet cultural life that had emerged late in the Chernenko period. Theater critic Mark Lyubomudrov lashed out in an essay at those theater directors who staged plays that realistically portrayed Soviet life. Rather than giving Russia a clear national ideal to strive for, Lyubomudrov claimed, these plays were exclusively preoccupied with the darker sides of Soviet life. In many ways this article set the standard for all subsequent radical nationalist critiques of Gorbachev's glasnost policies.[14]

The radical nationalists also used the pages of *Nash sovremennik* to reiterate their rejection of any reforms that would include borrowing Western social, political, and cultural models—reforms, that is, aimed at the democratization of Soviet society. They warned that if Gorbachev guided the reforms in this direction, he and the party would lose their legitimacy, and hence their mandate to rule the country. Apollon Kuzmin outlined this argument in a discussion on the causes of the collapse of the tsarist regime. By adopting Western values and culture, he proclaimed, the post-Petrine autocracy and the aristocratic elite separated themselves from the rest of the Russian nation and became "rootless cosmopolites," bringing doom upon themselves. By using the concept "cosmopolites"—the euphemistic slogan of Stalin's anti-Semitic campaign—Kuzmin implied that politicians who wanted to introduce Western models to Russia were alien social elements, such as Jews, and should be treated the way Jews were in the late 1940s and early 1950s.[15]

Kuzmin's argument was supported and elaborated by another radical nationalist historian, Vadim Pigalev. He asserted that the Russian nation was antibourgeois and anticapitalist by nature. The only way to undermine its strength was to turn the Russian people into "consumerist-philistine cattle." In other words, to save Russia, Gorbachev had to be prevented from turning it into a Western-style consumer society.[16]

The Rise of Aleksandr Yakovlev and the End of the Alliance

The gap between Gorbachev's reform agenda and the great majority of Russian nationalist intellectuals began to widen in the aftermath of the Twenty-seventh Party Congress, and especially from the second half of 1986. This breach went hand in hand with the diminishing ability of Russian nationalist intellectuals to shape the agenda of the sociopolitical debate. This decline in their power stemmed from the meteoric rise in the Kremlin hierarchy of Aleksandr Yakovlev, a firm believer in radical reform and a long-time foe of Russian nationalism.

In July 1985, Yakovlev replaced Boris Stukalin at the helm of the Propaganda Department of the Central Committee. At the Twenty-seventh Party Congress in March 1986, he was promoted to the position of secretary of the Central Committee in charge of ideology and for the following ten months shared this post with Mikhail Zimyanin.[17] In January 1987, he became a candidate member of the Politburo and six months later a full member. From this time on, Yakovlev became, in effect, the chief ideologue of perestroika and the architect of Gorbachev's cultural policies.[18]

At the heart of Yakovlev's vision lay a firm belief that the success of perestroika depended on the complete and decisive eradication of the Stalinist legacy from all spheres of public life. This belief explains the critical role he attributed to the far-reaching liberalization of cultural life. Yakovlev realized that writers, literary critics, historians, artists, and movie and theater directors could reveal to millions of Russians the true nature of Stalinism and the onus of its legacy. He was also aware that in order to secure the firm support of the easily intimidated and much disappointed liberal intelligentsia, firm control of cultural life in the hands of the reformers was crucial. In order to achieve this, he made several key appointments over the course of 1986. Yury Voronov, the editor of *Komsomolskaya pravda* under Khrushchev, replaced Vasily Shauro, the staunch supporter of Russian nationalism in the party apparat, in the position of head of the Cultural Department of the Central Committee, and Vasily Zakharov replaced another of Brezhnev's early appointees, Pyotr Demichev, in the post of minister of culture of the USSR.

More important, Yakovlev appointed reform-minded intellectuals as the heads of several of Moscow's newspapers, popular weekly magazines, and thick journals, thus handing the reformist intelligentsia control over these publications. In retrospect, the most significant among these appointments were the replacement of the old Stalinist poet Anatoly Sofronov with Vitaly Korotich as chief editor of the mass-circulation weekly magazine, *Ogonyok;* the appointment of Egor Yakovlev as the chief editor of the newspaper *Moskovskie novosti;* and the selection of Albert Belyaev, the former deputy head of the Cultural Department of the Central Committee, as chief editor of the newspaper *Sovetskaya kultura.* Yakovlev also seized the opportunity provided by vacancies in the positions of chief editor of the journals *Znamya* and *Novy mir* to appoint Grigory Baklanov as the chief editor of *Znamya* and Sergei Zalygin as the chief editor of *Novy mir.* Finally, Yakovlev used his power to support the election of Elem Klimov as the first secretary of the Film Makers Union (May 1986) and of Kiril Lavrov as the first secretary of the newly created USSR Theater Workers' Union (December 1986), and thus helped the supporters of cultural liberalization to gain control of these two important unions.

These appointments signified the beginning of Gorbachev's political alliance with the liberal-reformist and liberal-nationalist members of the intelligentsia. Not only did they control important newspapers and journals, but the circulation of these publications was allowed to skyrocket while the circulation of *Nash sovremennik* essentially remained frozen at its 1983 level.[19]

The liberal-reformist intelligentsia was quick to use its newly acquired power; by early 1987, it was able to dictate the agenda of the sociopolitical debate: Stalinism, the Stalinist legacy, and the direction of political and economic reforms. At the same time, *Ogonyok, Znamya,* and *Novy mir* started publishing previously forbidden literary works of living and deceased Russian writers. Other major thick journals, such as *Yunost, Druzhba narodov, Oktyabr* and *Neva,* quickly followed their lead.

The winter of 1987 found Soviet society in the midst of what the poet Andrei Voznesensky termed "a revolution by culture." This revolution, which also became known as the "glasnost revolution," was expressed in the expanding range of permissible authors, subjects, styles, and genres in literature, theater, television, visual arts, and popular music. This liberalization created a pluralism of cultural forms and content, and undermined Marxist-Leninist orthodoxy, which viewed such plurality as dangerous to socialism.[20]

It also greatly emboldened the liberal-reformist critics of Russian nationalism to criticize openly the works of Astafiev and Belov published in early 1986. In journals and newspapers, they condemned Astafiev's and Belov's anti-urbanism, anti-intellectualism, antifeminism, and anti-Semitism. Natan Eidelman, the liberal-reformist writer of historical novels, criticized Astafiev's views in a letter he sent to the writer. Astafiev responded with a vicious anti-Semitic tirade in which he accused Jewish revolutionaries of murdering Tsar Nicholas II and his family and liberal Jewish intellectuals, like Eidelman, of opposing the contemporary Russian national revival. He warned that a victorious Russian nationalism would purge the Jews from all spheres of Russian cultural life.[21]

Astafiev's emotional outburst revealed the depth of Russian nationalist frustration over the profound impact of glasnost on Soviet culture. Moreover, many leading Russian nationalist intellectuals came to realize that their twenty years of privileged access to the mass media and literary publications was over. But they were not ready to accept the situation as a fait accompli. By early 1987, the Russian nationalist opponents of glasnost firmly controlled the RSFSR Writers' Union and its publication, the weekly *Literaturnaya Rossiya*. Despite the fact that Russian nationalist opponents of glasnost had lost *Ogonyok*, they were able to keep their three Moscow thick journals. The chief editors and editorial boards of *Moskva*, *Nash sovremennik*, and *Molodaya gvardiya* remained unscathed. Moreover, in the provinces, Russian nationalists continued to control many local branches of the RSFSR Writers' Union, as well as such important literary journals as *Don*, *Sever*, and *Sibirskie ogni*, and thus had the institutional ability to launch a frontal attack on Gorbachev's cultural policies.

The Politics of *Nash sovremennik* and *Molodaya gvardiya*

Russian nationalists reacted in different ways to these liberalizing developments. In fact, the period March 1987 to March 1988 was crucial in the development of their attitudes toward Gorbachev's reforms. Liberal nationalists like Likhachev, Zalygin, and Mozhaev became prominent members of the pro-Gorbachev coalition. At the other end of the Russian nationalist spectrum, conservative and radical nationalists formed an anti-perestroika alliance and fought hard against the liberalization of culture.

At the beginning of the period, leading conservative nationalist village prose writers such as Rasputin, Belov, and Astafiev took a position best described as political fence sitting. They supported some aspects of perestroika—the anti-Stalinist campaign, reform in the countryside, tough antialcohol policies, and the publication of previously forbidden works of literature—and opposed others—the opening up of Soviet society to Western cultural influences and, especially, the legitimation of rock music. Later they endorsed the views expressed by the deputy chairman of the Governing Board of the RSFSR Writers' Union, Yury Bondarev, who by March 1987 had established himself as the leader of the united nationalist opposition to Gorbachev's cultural policies.[22]

In early 1987, progressively losing the ability to shape the agenda of sociopolitical debate and increasingly repulsed by events in Soviet cultural life, the conservative nationalists and radical nationalists started preparing a frontal attack on Gorbachev's reforms, particularly his cultural policies. This assault on glasnost began in March 1987 at a meeting of the Secretariat of the RSFSR Writers' Union. On this occasion, Bondarev spoke of the "pseudo-democrats of literature, who have lit over an abyss the light of glasnost which they stole from justice and truth." He equated the situation of Russian national culture in 1987 to that of Russia in July 1941, when it was on the brink of defeat by Nazi Germany, and called on nationalist opponents of reform to rally for a "cultural Stalingrad." Other speakers at the meeting attacked *Ogonyok* and *Moskovskie novosti*, as well as the publication of previously forbidden literary works, including Pasternak's *Doctor Zhivago*.[23]

Shortly after the meeting, the prominent radical nationalist writer Pyotr Proskurin, in an article that appeared in *Pravda*, called the publication of the works of Pasternak and Nabokov "literary necrophilia."[24] The assault continued throughout the spring of 1987, and in May, at a meeting of the Secretariat of the USSR Writers' Union, nationalist writers repeated their attacks on the liberal-reformist intelligentsia and Gorbachev's cultural policies.[25]

In the months following the meeting of the RSFSR Writers' Union, the journal *Molodaya gvardiya* emerged as the forum for radical nationalists who opposed Gorbachev's reform efforts. The journal not only joined *Nash sovremennik* as a very important platform for Russian nationalist reaction to cultural liberalization but became the most important publication of the radical nationalists opposed to Gorbachev's reforms. With increasing intensity it assailed the publication of hitherto forbidden works of literature, the exhibition of avant-garde art, the liberalization of Soviet television, the acceptance of rock music, the liberal-reformist intelligentsia (especially its Jewish component), and newspapers and journals that supported the reforms.[26] The leading voice in this campaign was Vyacheslav Gorbachev, the deputy editor of the journal. In three essays published between March and August 1987, he defended Stalin, extolled traditional family values, criticized the publication of Nabokov's works and the exhibition of Chagall's paintings, and attacked Jews, rock music, and the liberal-reformist intelligentsia and such perestroika-supporting newspapers and magazines as *Ogonyok, Moskovskie novosti, Sovetskaya kultura,* and *Nedelya.*[27]

After *Ogonyok* responded sharply to Vyacheslav Gorbachev's vicious attack published in the July 1987 issue of *Molodaya gvardiya,* the party apparatus, fearing that the situation was spinning out of control, intervened to stop the bitter journal infighting In an article in *Pravda,* a high party official, who used the pseudonym "Vladimir Petrov," called on both *Molodaya gvardiya* and *Ogonyok* to restrain themselves. The radical nationalists of *Molodaya gvardiya* insisted, however, on having the last word in this confrontation. Its September 1987 issue allocated sixty-eight pages to twenty-two young radical nationalist historians, writers, and literary critics, who elaborated Vyacheslav Gorbachev's arguments against Mikhail Gorbachev's cultural policies. This was the strongest attack on Mikhail Gorbachev's reform program since his rise to power.[28]

In essay after essay, the contributors focused on six Russian nationalist themes: they assailed the Soviet press for its reports on drug addiction and prostitution; criticized rock music, the publication of forbidden works of literature, and the exhibition of avant-garde art; demanded the cessation of attacks on Stalin; and argued against the rehabilitation of Bukharin and Trotsky. Mikhail Gorbachev's belief that perestroika required the expression of differing social and political views was judged to be contradictory to Russian historical experience and its national traditions. As one of the contributors bluntly stated, "Cultural 'pluralism,' the uninterrupted "free competition" of different, [and] at the time, entirely contradictory points of view, tastes and predilections, implies a rejection of the main idea which unifies the Soviet people, of traditional spiritual values, and a deviation from the main path of our history."[29]

The principle of democratization was assailed as leading to social anarchy, and the liberal-reformist intelligentsia, which pressed for the democratization of Soviet politics, was accused of undermining the very foundation of the Russian state. What Russia needed was, another contributor asserted, "a strong and responsible state power, which knows the troubles and the needs of the nation."[30] In the next six issues of *Molodaya gvardiya* (October 1987 to March 1988), the attacks continued on various aspects of perestroika and glasnost, including the publication of Pasternak's *Doctor Zhivago* and works of fiction and literary criticism by liberal reformers, rock music, the content of Soviet television programs, and Nikolai Shmelev's proposals for radical economic reform.[31]

Nash sovremennik did not lag behind *Molodaya gvardiya* in its attacks on perestroika and glasnost. The line adopted by the editorial board of *Nash sovremennik* meant an end to the journal as a platform for all factions within the Russian nationalist movement. After late 1986, such prominent liberal nationalists as Dmitry Likhachev, Sergei Zalygin, and Boris Mozhaev no longer contributed to *Nash sovremennik*. It was *Novy mir*, after Zalygin's appointment as its chief editor, that became the main liberal nationalist journal.[32]

Contributors to *Nash sovremennik* saw an especially grave danger to the Russian national existence in the pluralism of cultural forms that Gorbachev encouraged. They pointed to the policy of removing all obstacles from the performance of rock music as an example of how perestroika was contributing to the spread of harmful Western political and cultural values among the Russian youth. And as in the case of *Molodaya gvardiya*, the attack on rock music as a symbol of Gorbachev's cultural policies went hand in hand in *Nash sovremennik* with vicious attacks on the liberal–reformist intelligentsia who defended cultural pluralism.[33]

Another device used by the contributors to *Nash sovremennik* to attack perestroika was to discredit Bukharin and his legacy, recently rehabilitated by Gorbachev. They portrayed Bukharin as a Trotskyite in disguise, a man who hated Russia, organized the persecution of leading representatives of Russian national culture, and even as an enemy of NEP and the Russian peasantry.[34]

Nash sovremennik tried to do more than simply criticize Soviet reformers. It attempted to concentrate on one policy area around which most Russian nationalists, as well as a broad section of the general public, could rally in order to exert strong pressure in favor of a major policy reversal. Thus, in 1985 and 1986, it campaigned for the cancellation of the river diversion project, and in 1987 and 1988, it lobbied for the imposition of a dry law in Soviet society.

The government had already launched an antialcohol campaign, including the creation of the All-Union Voluntary Society for the Struggle for Sobriety (*Vsesoyuznoe dobrovolnoe obshchestvo borby za trezvost*, VDOBT), which was to popularize sobriety. By mid-1987, it was clear that the campaign, initiated in May 1985, was not only failing to achieve its goals but was causing serious damage to the Soviet economy. In many places, local authorities quietly increased sales of alcoholic beverages, and prominent radical economists openly called for an end to the campaign. Moreover, instead of becoming an aggressive Russian nationalist organization as many Russian nationalist intellectuals had hoped, VDOBT (like VOOPIK in the past) turned out to be an ineffective institution staffed by ex-party and government bureaucrats.

These developments prompted leading Russian nationalist intellectuals to launch a campaign for the imposition of a total ban on the production and sale of alcohol. Belov, who in 1986 expressed his support for Gorbachev's antialcohol campaign, openly denounced it as inadequate and demanded the imposition of a dry law in 1987. Without this drastic measure, he declared, Gorbachev's reforms would never succeed: "Perestroika is inconceivable without a complete sobering up [of society]. Everyone has to understand this. Only a sober worker can reform himself."[35]

In July 1987, *Nash sovremennik* joined Belov's crusade by publishing a programmatic essay on the subject by Fyodor Uglov, a member of the Soviet Academy of Medical Sciences and the chief Russian nationalist spokesman on the problem of alcoholism. Uglov pinpointed two primary causes for the evident failure of the antialcohol campaign: the policies were at best half-measures, and there was a conspiracy between the bureaucrats who saw alcohol sales as the easiest way to generate revenues, and the ethnic non-Russians (the Jews) in the mass media, who opposed the idea of a sober Russian nation. He called for the reimposition of a complete ban on the production and sale of alcohol as had existed in Russia between 1914 and 1925, and for the transformation of VDOBT into a grass-roots movement led by prominent Russian nationalist advocates of the dry law policies—all in order to save the Russian nation from extinction.[36]

Uglov's ideas were defended and elaborated in two essays in the March 1988 issue of *Nash sovremennik*. In his article, Boris Lapchenko pointed out that the attempt to restrict the production and sales of alcohol was bound to be ineffective as long as there was an acute shortage of consumer goods. He called for a complete ban on alcohol production and sale, combined with a saturation of the market with consumer goods. In the second essay, A. Kovalenin, a member of the Novosibirsk chapter of VDOBT, proposed electing Uglov and other well-known Russian nationalists to head VDOBT, to undertake new elections in all regional chapters of the organization, and to impose a total ban on the production and sale of alcohol by December 19, 1989, the seventieth anniversary of the Bolsheviks' decision to continue prerevolutionary dry law policies.[37] This Russian nationalist campaign continued well into the summer of 1988 but utterly failed to achieve its aims.

The Emergence of Pamyat

A new form of Russian nationalist opposition to perestroika emerged between March 1987 and March 1988. Exploiting Gorbachev's policy of permitting the formation of nonofficial societies with political agendas, the nationalist and rabidly anti-Semitic Moscow organization calling itself Pamyat (Memory) was able to transform itself from a small cultural club into a highly visible, if not significant, factor in Soviet politics. Pamyat attracted worldwide attention on May 6, 1987, when four hundred of its members staged a demonstration in the center of Moscow demanding a halt to the construction of a World War II memorial, whose design they disapproved. They also called for the official recognition of their organization, and a meeting with Gorbachev and Yeltsin, then head of the Moscow Party organization.[38]

Although the leaders of Pamyat presented themselves as ardent supporters of perestroika, through their theories of a pervasive Judeo-Masonic conspiracy against Russia, they in fact challenged perestroika from the radical nationalist position taken to the extreme. Pamyat declared in its programmatic "Appeal to the Russian People [and] to the Patriots of All Countries and Nations" (*Vozzvanie patrioticheskogo obiedeneniya "Pamyat" k russkomy narody, k patriotam vsekh stran i natsii*) that the true goals of perestroika must be a revival of the traditional Russian village, the preservation of nature and historic monuments, an end to the persecution of the Russian Orthodox Church and a resumption of religious services in the Kremlin churches, and a relentless struggle against alcoholism, bureaucracy, and especially "Zionists" and "Free-Masons," the forces of evil behind Russia's economic and social problems.[39]

Pamyat's conception of glasnost consisted of demands to publish the *Protocols of the Elders of Zion,* excerpts of which were read at its meetings,[40] and to reveal to the Russian nation that the Jews were responsible for the murder of Tsar Nicholas II and his family, the administration of Stalin's labor camps, and the systematic destruction of ancient churches and other architectural remnants of prerevolutionary Russian culture. By 1988, Pamyat-like organizations had spread across the Soviet Union in such major cities as Leningrad, Chelyabinsk, Irkutsk, Novosibirsk, and Sverdlovsk. In June 1988, Pamyat-like organizations from Irkutsk, Sverdlovsk, Tyumen, Magnitogorsk, Chelyabinsk, and Zlatoust formed the Union of Patriotic Organizations of the Urals and Siberia *(Soyuz patrioticheskikh organizatsy Urala i Sibiri).* In October 1988, the Novosibirsk Pamyat organization joined the Union.[41]

These developments encouraged the leaders of Moscow's Pamyat society to present themselves as the leaders of a popular social movement in the making. In a series of interviews conducted between June and August 1988, the chairman of the Moscow Pamyat organization, the photographer Dmitry Vasiliev, claimed that Pamyat branches existed in thirty Russian cities, and he boasted that the number of Pamyat activists in Moscow had reached twenty thousand.[42]

The Pamyat phenomenon greatly alarmed the liberal-reformist intelligentsia, who perceived it as a grave threat to perestroika and sharply condemned it in *Ogonyok, Komsomolskaya pravda, Izvestiya,* and *Sovetskaya kultura.*[43] It was equally natural that *Nash sovremennik* would be the first journal to defend Pamyat and its platform. In October 1987, Vadim Kozhinov was the first to address the subject in *Nash sovremennik.* He rejected many of Pamyat's arguments because, in his words, they contained too much "ignorance" and "infantilism," which found its expression "in all kinds of symbols, myths [and] fantastic images." Nevertheless, he refused to condemn Pamyat, claiming that its extremism was an unavoidable by-product of the ongoing transformation of Russian nationalism into a mass movement.[44]

More important, Kozhinov's defense was seconded by Valentin Rasputin in the January 1988 issue of *Nash sovremennik.* Rasputin wrote about "the listed to the left press" which violated the principles of glasnost by attaching to Pamyat the derogatory label of the "Black Hundred" (a popular name for the Union of Russian People, an extreme right-wing, anti-Semitic party active in pre-revolutionary Russia) and by denying Pamyat the right to defend itself in print. Pamyat must be defended, Rasputin argued, because behind the attempts to discredit and crush the organization stood a desire to discredit and crush the entire Russian nationalist movement.[45]

The attention that both the proreform intelligentsia and its Russian nationalist opponents paid Pamyat in 1988 was above and beyond its actual popularity or influence. More important, Pamyat's popularity did not grow in succeeding years. By 1991, it had completely failed to transform itself into a mass movement and remained a marginal force, although quite a visible one, in Soviet political life.[46]

The Union of Patriotic Organizations of the Urals and Siberia, however, remained a successful example of a Pamyat-like society organized at the regional level. However, in 1989–1990, only one new organization joined the union, and by 1991 it was no longer functioning. A RSFSR- or USSR-level organization was never formed.

Vasiliev's figure of twenty thousand Pamyat activists in Moscow was a wild exaggeration. Independent Soviet estimates give much more reliable data: between two hundred and four hundred activists in Moscow and approximately one thousand more throughout the country in early 1990. Moreover, because of internal disagreements, the first split within Pamyat took place in late 1987. In the next three years, several additional splits took place, raising the number of rival Pamyat groups in Moscow to eight. Each of these groups was extremely small—about forty to fifty people in each.[47]

Nina Andreeva's Essay and Its Consequences

The March 13, 1988 issue of *Sovetskaya Rossiya* contained an essay by a Leningrad college teacher, Nina Andreeva, entitled "I Cannot Give Up [My] Principles" *(Ne mogu postupitsya s printsipami)*. Spread over a full page, it was a frontal attack on perestroika made from the orthodox Stalinist point of view. Andreeva defended Stalin as the leader who had turned Russia into a superpower, criticized glasnost policies, and accused the liberal-reformist writers Mikhail Shatrov and Anatoly Rybakov of falsifying Soviet history in their recently published works that contained harsh criticism of Stalin and Stalinism.

Andreeva made some clear overtures to Russian nationalist intellectuals by praising the writings of Prokhanov and making rabidly anti-Semitic statements. She emphasized Trotsky's Jewishness and even argued that Jews were a counterrevolutionary nation. The unprecedented length of the essay and the fact that it was reprinted in party newspapers throughout the Soviet Union and Eastern Europe clearly pointed to Egor Ligachev, the second-ranking Politburo member at the time, as the article's main sponsor.[48]

Despite an official rebuttal of Andreeva's essay in *Pravda,* publication of the essay made the editors of *Molodaya gvardiya* and *Nash sovremennik* adopt an even more aggressive approach in their assault on perestroika.[49] In its April 1988 issue, *Molodaya gvardiya* published an essay by the veteran Stalinist bureaucrat Mikhail Malakhov that was an outright statement of support for Stalinism, praising collectivization, industrialization, and the principles of Stalinist industrial management. Malakhov sharply criticized the de-Stalinization reforms of Khrushchev and warned that Gorbachev's renewed attacks on Stalinism would inevitably lead to anarchy and undermine socialism.[50]

Alongside Malakhov's essay, *Molodaya gvardiya* resorted to a strategy of selectively publishing readers' letters in order to create the impression of widespread public support for its campaign against the rehabilitation of Bukharin, private enterprise, rock music, and the publication of long-censored anti-Stalinist works of fiction. As before, the reformist intelligentsia bore the brunt of the attack. It was accused of undermining the national morale by filling literary journals with works that "attempt to prove that the last seventy years were the most dirty and disgusting in the history of our nation." It also was found guilty of weakening the Russian state by using the new freedom of expression to preach ideological rapprochement with the bourgeois West.[51]

Encouraged by Ligachev's support for Andreeva's attack on glasnost and perestroika, *Nash sovremennik* made a concerted effort to present leading conservative members of the political elite as leaders whose records showed a deep understanding of Russian nationalist concerns. The May 1988 issue of the journal contained an essay that examined the antialcohol policies of the Tomsk regional party secretaries, Ligachev, and his successor, Zorkaltsev. The essay claimed that in the 1970s, Ligachev had taken the initiative to restrict severely the number of alcohol sales outlets and their hours. As a result, the consumption of vodka in the Tomsk region fell by one-third between 1974 and 1984. After the introduction of antialcohol policies in

May 1985, Viktor Zorkaltsev closed several main alcohol-producing facilities in the region, left open only a few liquor stores and restaurants that served liquor, and banned deliveries of alcoholic beverages from outside the region. The message of the essay was clear: Ligachev and his followers in the party's apparat deserved the Russian nationalists' strong support.[52]

Along with promoting Ligachev, *Nash sovremennik*'s publication policies between April and June 1988 were aimed at strengthening the unity of the Russian nationalist opposition to perestroika on the eve of the Nineteenth Party Conference. As a symbolic act of solidarity with the editorial policy of *Molodaya gvardiya, Nash sovremennik*'s May 1988 issue carried a long interview with Anatoly Ivanov, the chief editor of *Molodaya gvardiya*, which contained a straightforward apology for Stalinism and a harsh attack on perestroika. Ivanov blamed the violence that accompanied collectivization, and the destruction of Moscow churches in the 1930s on Yakov Yakovlev and Lazar Kaganovich, Stalin's Jewish lieutenants, and justified the terror of the 1930s as a defensive act against internal enemies. The terror, he declared, saved the Soviet Union from a counterrevolution of the kind experienced by East Germany in 1953, Hungary in 1956, and Czechoslovakia in 1968. He sternly warned that the reforms were leading Russia to anarchy, just as they had in Eastern Europe.[53]

Ivanov's Stalinist and anti-Semitic assertions were seconded by radical nationalist Vadim Kozhinov. The April 1988 issue of the journal contained his programmatic essay in which he blamed the Jews for terrorizing the Russian peasantry during collectivization and for blowing up Moscow churches in the 1930s. Contrary to Ivanov, Kozhinov was not apologetic about Stalin. He presented Stalin as a good Leninist who perfected the machinery of terror that Lenin had built during the Civil War. Moreover, both Lenin and Stalin were only carrying out the will of the world communist movement, which was under Jewish domination.[54]

Russian Nationalist Opposition to Perestroika and the Nineteenth Party Conference

The publication of the articles by Ivanov and Kozhinov reflected the efforts of *Nash sovremennik*'s editors to turn anti-Semitism into the glue binding together nationalist opposition to the reforms. Indeed, in the months preceding the Nineteenth Party Conference, anti-Semitic attacks on perestroika reached an unprecedented level. *Nash sovremennik* now openly endorsed a theory of Judeo-Masonic conspiracy by publishing Viktor Ivanov's novel, *The Day of Judgment (Sudny den)*. The novel, of a type that had not appeared in print in the Soviet Union since Ivan Shevtsov's novels of the 1960s, portrayed the subversive activities of a Judeo-Masonic espionage network in the Soviet Union of the Khrushchev era.[55]

Nash sovremennik also rallied in defense of Vladimir Begun, the leading anti-Semitic theorist in the Soviet Union, who had been accused by liberal-reformers of plagiarizing Hitler's *Mein Kampf*. *Nash sovremennik*'s editors not only published a letter in defense of Begun but also endorsed his book in an editorial comment. By selectively quoting from Marx's *On the Jewish Question*, they argued that Begun was right about the vile nature of Jews.[56]

The anti-Semitic line of *Nash sovremennik* was quickly picked up by *Molodaya gvardiya*. Its July issue, which appeared during the party conference, carried a dialogue between Ivan Shevtsov and retired air force marshal Ivan Pstygo. They assailed "Zionism" and presented it as the most vicious enemy of the Soviet state. Moreover, they openly praised Pamyat for its efforts to make the public aware of the "Zionist" threat. Shevtsov and Pstygo went on to present Pamyat as a patriotic organization that deserved the open and unqualified support of the party and the military.[57]

That anti-Semitism was to unite Russian nationalist opponents to perestroika was conspicuously obvious in the coalition's first programmatic statement issued on the eve the conference. "Letter to the Soviet Government" *(Pismo sovetskom pravitelstvu)*, signed by many leading Russian nationalist intellectuals, claimed that "Zionists" (i.e., Jews) were spearheading a nationwide anti-Russian and anticommunist campaign aimed at undermining the Russian state and strengthening its Western enemies. It claimed that Jews were grossly overrepresented in Soviet media, science, and culture and demanded that proportional ethnic representation be adopted in the personnel selection for these institutions. Since the Jewish share of the Soviet population was officially 0.7 percent at the time, the "Letter" demanded a reduction in the number of Jews holding positions in the media, culture, and science to less than 1 percent.

The ten-point proposal included a call for an increase in the Central Committee's control over the mass media and press in order to prevent the promotion of Western cultural values and the performance of rock music, increase the "patriotic education of [Soviet] youth," and an end to the institutional discrimination against the RSFSR (with the creation of a RSFSR Central Committee, an RSFSR KGB, an RSFSR Academy of Sciences, and

Academy of Fine Arts). The "Letter" demanded that these institutions be staffed according to the principle of proportional ethnic representation to ensure that they served Russia's national interests.[58]

The proceedings of the Nineteenth Party Conference, held from June 28 to July 1, 1988, proved that Russian nationalist opposition to perestroika had substantial support inside the party. Such prominent opponents of perestroika as Yury Bondarev, Mikhail Alekseev, and Anatoly Ivanov were elected as delegates to the conference. Bondarev voiced the views of the nationalist opposition to reform in his speech before the conference by defending the publication policies of *Molodaya gvardiya* and *Nash sovremennik* and viciously attacking glasnost. He compared perestroika to an airplane that had been ordered to take off without knowing whether a landing strip existed at the destination point, implying that Gorbachev was leading the country to catastrophe. Bondarev went on to accuse reformist newspapers and journals of propagating national nihilism, immorality, and Western ideas and values, and warned that glasnost was destabilizing the Soviet state. These ideas clearly found resonance among many delegates who repeatedly interrupted his speech with boisterous applause, and who booed Baklanov, the editor of *Znamya,* who sharply criticized Bondarev's speech. Pro-perestroika publications such as *Ogonyok* and the policy of glasnost in general were attacked by five regional party secretaries. In his own appearance at the conference, Ligachev received enthusiastic applause from the audience while attacking the pro-reform press and explicitly endorsing Bondarev.[59]

Although it was clear that support for the Russian nationalist opposition to perestroika was evident among the conference delegates, this was not reflected in its resolutions. In fact, a resolution prepared by Yakovlev was a significant blow to efforts by party conservatives and their Russian nationalist allies to reverse the affects of glasnost. It implicitly condemned attempts by party conservatives to restrict glasnost, which the resolution proclaimed to be one of the most important conditions for the continuation of perestroika. The resolution also condemned "activities aimed at . . . stirring up national and racial hatred."[60]

The defeat at the party conference was soon followed by another: in September 1988, Gorbachev canceled the 1985 antialcohol campaign, thus completely disregarding intense Russian nationalist pressure to impose a total ban on alcohol production.[61]

Yet despite both setbacks, Russian nationalists were extremely encouraged by the hostility of the conference delegates toward the liberal-reformist Moscow intellectuals. To the nationalists, this was the best indicator of the views prevailing among the party elite. They also saw continuing signs of support from Ligachev. In late July 1988, his visit to a new exhibition of works by Ilya Glazunov was interpreted by nationalists as indicating his acceptance of the Russian nationalist message of Glazunov's paintings.[62] In late August, Ligachev reiterated his endorsement of Bondarev's party conference speech at a meeting with journalists in the city of Gorky. He used the occasion to assert that the party conference had rejected the reformers' attempts to portray Soviet history exclusively in negative terms and reminded the audience that it was during the Stalin and post-Stalin periods that the Soviet Union transformed itself from a backward country into a world superpower.[63]

Flexing Muscle: The Literaturnaya Rossiya and Sovetsky pisatel Affairs

At the September 1988 meeting of the Secretariat of the RSFSR Writers' Union, which took place in the city of Ryazan, a coalition of leading Russian nationalist opponents to perestroika, encouraged by Ligachev's support, began a new assault on Gorbachev's cultural and economic policies. It is worth pointing out here that the intensity of this assault did not diminish after Ligachev lost his position as the second-ranking Politburo member in the September 30, 1988 Politburo reshuffle.

At the Ryazan meeting, many key points of the "Letter to the Soviet Government" were elaborated. Rasputin, in the keynote address, spoke about the destructive impact of such Western imports as rock music, beauty contests, sex education, and the acceptance of homosexuality on Russia and its culture. The radical nationalist economist Mikhail Antonov attacked the legalization of joint ventures and moves toward integration into the world economy as leading to the transformation of Russia into a "colony of multinational corporations." Another prominent radical nationalist, the literary critic Anatoly Lanshchikov, supplemented Antonov's argument with a warning that Gorbachev's policies would cause Russia to fall victim to "Western 'peaceful' technological aggression and the equally 'peaceful' Eastern demographic aggression." He, as well as other participants, complained about the anti-Russian nature of *Ogonyok* and other leading reformist publications.[64]

The Ryazan meeting enjoyed the support of conservative elements in the party apparat, expressed in two ways: the second secretary of the Ryazan regional party organization, Vasily Popov, attended the meeting, and a positive report of the meeting, containing interviews with Bondarev, Rasputin, Antonov, and other participants, appeared in *Sovetskaya Rossiya*. Since the latter consistently endorsed Ligachev's views and those of perestroika opponents within the party apparat, the report was a signal that Ligachev approved of the ideas expressed at Ryazan.[65]

It is not surprising that an attack on ideas expressed at the Ryazan meeting was launched by *Kommunist*, a journal controlled and edited by the pro-perestroika supporters within the party. An unsigned editorial published in the November 1988 issue contained the harshest condemnation of Russian nationalism to appear in the party press since Gorbachev's rise to power. Going far beyond a mere response to the statements made in Ryazan, it stated that while the party and the nation had made the choice to embark upon the path of reform, Russian nationalists were trying to turn people away by blaming the West and Jews for the social and moral crisis of Soviet society and by frightening Russians with claims that rock music and beauty contests would destroy the nation. By doing this, they were attempting to revive pre–perestroika era cultural and political myths. Russian nationalists had to recognize, *Kommunist* added, that the Russian people had rejected their ideas by choosing to read and subscribe to the pro-perestroika press.[66]

The *Kommunist* essay was reprinted in the December 9, 1988 issue of *Literaturnaya Rossiya*. To reprint a *Pravda* or *Kommunist* essay critical of another publication in that very publication was still an established practice in 1988. But in addition, the publication of the essay sought to show the *Literaturnaya Rossiya* chief editor's disapproval of the RSFSR Writers' Union policy of militant opposition to perestroika. In particular, the newspaper was attempting to reassert its editorial independence from the mounting pressure of Yury Bondarev, who wanted to turn *Literaturnaya Rossiya* into an aggressive voice of the Russian nationalist opposition to perestroika. By republishing the *Kommunist* essay, however, chief editor Mikhail Kolosov gave Bondarev and his allies a powerful weapon for his own removal.[67]

Bondarev and other leading Russian nationalist intellectuals voiced the urgent need for a radical transformation of *Literaturnaya Rossiya*, particularly after they saw how an aggressive Russian nationalist editor could change a newspaper. In August 1988, Nikolai Doroshenko, a young radical nationalist writer, was appointed chief editor of *Moskovsky literator*, a small-circulation (1,500 copies) weekly published by the Moscow Writers' Union. With his arrival, *Moskovsky literator* became a Russian nationalist newspaper that viciously attacked the policies of perestroika and glasnost. Because of its small circulation and geographical limits (it was distributed only in Moscow), however, it could not effectively popularize Russian nationalist ideas throughout the country. The nationally circulated *Literaturnaya Rossiya*, on the other hand, could do this with the appropriate editor.

The political orientation of *Literaturnaya Rossiya* was one of the major issues discussed at the plenary meeting of the Governing Board of the RSFSR Writers' Union in late December 1988. While several speakers focused their attacks on *Ogonyok* and prominent perestroika supporters among intellectual elite, others like Vasily Belov, Vladimir Lichutin, and Valentin Sidorov, harshly criticized *Literaturnaya Rossiya*'s chief editor for reprinting the *Kommunist* essay. They called on Kolosov to resign from his post or to be removed if he refused to step down. Kolosov defended the newspaper's policies, claiming that it was merely following party guidelines. He also explicitly rejected the demands of his critics that he submit his resignation.[68]

Knowing that only the reformers in the party apparat would defend his position, Kolosov stepped up his criticism of the RSFSR Writers' Union and its politics. In an editorial postscript to the minutes of the meeting, he claimed that the roots of the current political, social, moral, and economic crisis were to be found in the politics of Stalin and Brezhnev. He condemned Russian nationalist attempts to find scapegoats as insulting to the Russian nation. Finally, his transition to the reformers' camp was completed with the publication of an open letter to Bondarev in *Ogonyok*, accusing Bondarev of attempting to transform *Literaturnaya Rossiya* into a tool for his political ambitions.[69]

Kolosov had overestimated the ability of party reformers to control Soviet cultural life, particularly after Yakovlev was replaced in September 1988 by the more cautious Vadim Medvedev as the party's chief ideologue. The *Ogonyok* letter was the last straw. On January 9, 1989, almost immediately after the appearance of the letter, the Secretariat of the RSFSR Writers' Union dismissed Kolosov from his post.

At this meeting, A. Tsvetkov, responsible for literature in the newly created Ideological Department of Central Committee, did not try to prevent

Kolosov's firing.[70] He did insist, however, that the party had the right to choose Kolosov's successor on the grounds that the position of *Literaturnaya Rossiya* chief editor was on the Central Committee nomenklatura list. Tsvetkov asked the Secretariat to approve the party nominee, Vladimir Malyutin, the Russian nationalist editor of the literary journal *Literaturnaya ucheba,* but not an active participant in the Russian nationalist opposition to perestroika. The Secretariat rejected this request as undemocratic and instead demanded a multicandidate secret ballot election for the position at a special joint meeting of Secretariats of the RSFSR Writers' Union and the Moscow Writers' Union, the official sponsors of *Literaturnaya Rossiya.*

On January 18, 1989, *Pravda* published a letter, signed by Mikhail Alekseev, Viktor Astafiev, Vasily Belov, Sergei Bondarchuk, Pyotr Proskurin, Valentin Rasputin, and Sergei Vikulov, that harshly denounced *Ogonyok* for publishing Kolosov's attack on Bondarev. They also attacked *Ogonyok* for its critical reporting of the Ryazan meeting. The publication of the letter by six prominent Russian nationalist intellectuals was a clear indication that the party ideological establishment favored the Russian nationalist intellectuals in the *Literaturnaya Rossiya* affair.[71]

In late February 1989, a special joint meeting of the Secretariats of the RSFSR Writers' Union and the Moscow Writers' Union did take place, but the secret ballot did not. Instead, Vladimir Egorov, deputy head of the Ideological Department of the Central Committee announced the appointment of conservative Russian nationalist writer Ernest Safonov as the new chief editor of *Literaturnaya Rossiya.* Clearly a compromise had been reached between the Russian nationalist leaders of the RSFSR Writers' Union and the Ideological Department. The latter was no longer interested in a proliferation of radical pro-perestroika publications of the *Ogonyok* and *Moskovskie novosti* type and could therefore accept a candidate chosen by the union. For its part, the union agreed that its candidate would be appointed by the Ideological Department rather than elected, thus not formally challenging the party's right to make the decision.[72]

This was a great tactical success for the Russian nationalist opposition to Gorbachev. As expected, Safonov purged the *Literaturnaya Rossiya* staff and quickly transformed the paper into the most important anti-perestroika weekly. Moreover, the affair showed Russian nationalist members of the Soviet literary establishment that Vadim Medvedev would not prevent them from taking over publications or publishing houses belonging the RSFSR or USSR Writers' Unions. In spring 1989, they took over

Sovetsky pisatel, the most important publishing house of the USSR Writers' Union.

Although the Sovetsky pisatel affair did not receive much attention, it was of equal importance to the events surrounding the purge of *Literaturnaya Rossiya*. In the fall of 1989, the position of director of the Sovetsky pisatel publishing house became vacant. Applying the 1987 law on state enterprise, publishing house employees held a multicandidate election to fill the vacancy and chose one of the most radical pro-perestroika intellectuals, Anatoly Strelyany, as the new director. On March 21–22, 1989, the Governing Board of the USSR Writers' Union, on which Russian nationalist writers had a significant representation, met and annulled the election as illegal. They argued that since Sovetsky pisatel was not a state enterprise but the property of the USSR Writers' Union, the employees had no right to apply the law on state enterprise and elect their own director.

A report on the events of the meeting published in *Literaturnaya gazeta* mentioned the presence of Vladimir Egorov, as well as the deputy head of the USSR State Committee on Publishing, Dmitry Mamleev. It does not mention that these representatives of the party ideological establishment in any way opposed the cancellation of Strelyany's election. They clearly were not interested in aiding the radical reformers to take control over one of the most important nonparty publishing houses. Their noninterference in effect gave a green light to the Russian nationalist takeover of Sovetsky pisatel.[73]

In late May 1989, the publishing house board elected Anatoly Zhukov, a party secretary of the Moscow Writers' Union organization and a well-known Russian nationalist opponent of perestroika, as the new director. *Literaturnaya Rossiya* immediately printed a page-long interview with Zhukov in which he condemned perestroika as "endless democratic talk, lack of power and action" that leads to the abyss.[74] The successful replacement of Strelyany by Zhukov was another significant boost to the Russian nationalist intellectuals. It convinced them that the party's treatment of the *Literaturnaya Rossiya* case was not an exception, but rather representative of a firm policy commitment.

NEP, Stalinism, Jews and Economic Reform

Russian nationalist publications would have liked to have avoided any extensive treatment of Stalinism, since this meant both an acceptance of the sociopolitical agenda set by the radical reformers and, more important, the danger of a potential breakdown of the Russian nationalist alliance against perestroika over this very issue. Stalinism and its political, social, and economic legacies indeed was neither mentioned in the "Letter to the Soviet Government" nor discussed during the September and December 1988 meetings of the Governing Board of the RSFSR Writers' Union. Russian nationalists, however, were dragged into this debate because of the extremely wide publicity that accompanied the publication of such anti-Stalinist works of fiction as Vasily Grossman's novel *Life and Fate* and Vladimir Voinovich's *Life and Adventures of Ivan Chonkin,* the founding in the fall of 1988 of the Memorial Society dedicated to commemorating the victims of Stalinism, and an intensification, due to the progressively worsening economic situation, of the debate on the long-term potential of the command economy and future economic reform.

Although the strategy of the Russian nationalist publications was to avoid dealing with Stalinism and the Stalinist legacy, they all heavily emphasized anti-intellectual and anti-Semitic elements in order to bind the Russian nationalist alliance together. *Molodaya gvardiya*'s policy was to publish essays and letters by orthodox Stalinists, be they simple workers, intellectuals, or former high party and government officials.[75] These Stalinists aggressively justified every aspect of Stalinism, including collectivization and the terror, as the price Russia had to pay to become a superpower. They supported the editor of *Molodaya gvardiya,* Anatoly Ivanov, in transferring the responsibility for the excesses of the terror from Stalin to his Jewish subordinates and to Jewish officers in the security police. Finally, their defense of Stalinism included a firm justification for and support of the command economy created by Stalin, and strong criticism of Khrushchev's reforms and their apologists among the liberal Moscow intelligentsia. These reforms, they argued, only undercut the vitality of the command economy by weakening discipline in the party and in society as a whole. The solution to the Soviet Union's economic problems was not a transition to a market economy but the strengthening of the work ethic and the selection of proper party cadres to supervise the command economy.[76]

Between the fall of 1988 and the summer of 1989, *Nash sovremennik* and *Moskovsky literator* adopted a far more sophisticated approach to dealing with Stalinism and its legacy. The orthodox communists' defense of collectivization, the terror, and the command economy was entirely absent from these publications. What they published instead were essays by conservative and radical nationalist intellectuals that attempted to discredit the reformers' view of Stalinism and its origins, the nature of the command economy, and the desired direction of economic reform. These essays effectively refuted Stalin's responsibility for collectivization and the terror by tracing the foundations of the Stalinist system back to the politics and ideas of the 1920s, and even to the revolution itself.

Vladimir Soloukhin and Anatoly Lanshchikov followed Solzhenitsyn's line and rejected reformers' attempts to attach the label of "Stalinist" to collectivization, the industrialization drive, and the terror. The "perestroika intellectuals" from *Ogonyok* and the Memorial Society, they asserted, employed the term *Stalinist* in order to whitewash the true record of their spiritual and biological fathers—the party intellectuals who had perished in the purges of the 1930s. The party intelligentsia, however, had been responsible for the murder of the tsar and his family, for the millions of victims of the Civil War, and for collectivization.

Soloukhin did not mention Lenin explicitly, but Lanshchikov did. It was Lenin, according to Lanshchikov, who first proposed the rapid collectivization of the Russian peasantry. This idea was ignored by the party during the NEP era, until Stalin reintroduced it. Nor was the breakneck pace of the industrialization Stalin's invention; rather, he borrowed it from Trotsky. There was no such thing as the Stalinist terror, Soloukhin and Lanshchikov argued, only a communist terror, which eventually justly victimized its architects. Attempts by the reformers to distinguish Stalinism from other forms of socialism, they implied, was merely a strategy to legitimize a Western-oriented socialism that combined political and cultural pluralism with market economics.[77]

Khatyushin, Kunyaev, and Kozhinov greatly elaborated this argument, and Kozhinov, together with Antonov and Kazintsev, linked it to the ongoing debate on economic reform. In his poems and essays, Stanislav Kunyaev aggressively promoted the idea that the terror of the 1930s was in fact fair retribution for the crimes against Russia that had been committed by Jewish communist intellectuals from the time of the revolution through collectivization. Moreover, the liberal-reformist intelligentsia of today must bear the responsibility for the crimes of their biological and spiritual fathers.

Trotsky, Bukharin, and other Jewish communists were the main targets of Kunyaev's diatribe. It was not Stalin, but Trotsky, whom he referred to as Leib Bronshtein to emphasize his Jewishness, who invented the concentration camp system in the early 1920s. Kunyaev carefully singled out all senior NKVD military officers in the early 1930s with Jewish-sounding names to assert that Jews played a key role in the emerging gulag system. Bukharin, the only non-Jewish communist attacked by Kunyaev, was found guilty of initiating the terror against Russian national culture in the 1920s.[78]

Trotsky, Zinoviev, Kamenev, Rykov, and especially Bukharin were virulently attacked by Valery Khatyushin. Like Kunyaev, he accused them of organizing the terror against Russian culture and society in the 1920s, and of thus providing the ideological justification for Stalin's policies in the 1930s. The attempt of pro-perestroika intellectuals to rehabilitate Bukharin's politics was therefore a gross falsification of his historical role as the party's chief ideologue whose plans Stalin merely executed.[79]

Bukharin and the NEP era in general were the principal objects of Kozhinov's criticism. In the 1920s, he argued, Bukharin had provided the ideological justification for a drive to transform Russian society radically and destroy centuries-old national traditions, as well as the intellectuals defending those traditions. There were no principal disagreements between Stalin and Bukharin over the collectivization of the peasantry, only disagreements about tactics. Bukharin, Kozhinov insisted, was concerned not with the fate of millions of peasants as such, but with the impact of the collectivization on the tempo of economic development and the stability of Soviet power.

Kozhinov's attack on Bukharin and the NEP era was not simply an academic effort to present Russian nationalist views on Soviet history. This was an integral part of the debate about the desired course of Gorbachev's economic reforms. In the 1920s, Bukharin had sought to destroy Russian national traditions; his modern followers attempted to use his ideas as a justification for the introduction of Western-type economic models and the American-style family farm, both alien to Russian national traditions. The Russian economy, concluded Kozhinov, ought to be reformed in accordance with centuries-old Russian national traditions.[80]

This linkage between Bukharin's ideas and the ongoing debate over the direction of economic reform was the central subject of Mikhail Antonov's writings during this period. Although his interpretation of Bukharin's ideas completely contradicted that of Kozhinov's, their conclusions were identical. According to Antonov, Bukharin interpreted the economic principles of NEP in a fundamentally different way than had Lenin. Lenin's conception of NEP had never envisioned the unrestricted development of market relations, but Bukharin's did. If his ideas had been accepted by the party, Antonov asserts, Russia soon would have fallen prey to Western economic imperialism.

Although he rejected Bukharin's idea of market socialism, Antonov did not accept the Stalinist model of the command economy. The latter, in addition to being an economic failure, was responsible for the systematic destruction of the environment and must be dismantled. The Stalinist command economy, however, should not be replaced by a contemporary version of Bukharin's ideas. Shmelev, Abalkin, Aganbegyan, Bogomolov, and other champions of market economics and Soviet integration into the world economy were wrong, Antonov argued, because their programs did not go beyond the narrow framework of Western economic theory. The primary purpose of economic reform must not be capitalist-level efficiency and productivity, or the growth of the gross national product, but the "real improvement of the physical and spiritual health of our compatriots and an increase in their well-being." The Russian national economic model should rely on neither command-administrative methods nor the market mechanism, but on "sociopolitical means based on spiritual and moral values which include both economic and administrative means."

Antonov did not go beyond this extremely vague statement or an equally ambiguous assertion that the Russian economic model should be based on millennium-old Russian national traditions. He also failed to explain how an economy based on national traditions ought to function or how it would be different from the existing system. However, he spared no effort in emphasizing that a market economy was an integral part of a plutocratic and individualistic Western democracy and that the introduction of such a system would effectively turn Russia into a Western colony.[81]

Antonov's attack on Bukharin's ideas and the "perestroika economists" stopped short of providing an answer to questions regarding the differences between his model of the future Russian economy and the current command system. This answer was provided by the deputy editor of *Nash sovremennik,* Aleksandr Kazintsev. He declared that a transition to a market economy and the growth of private business would be dangerous to the Russian people and their traditions. Russian nationalists therefore must make a painful choice between the bureaucratic command economy and the Western, socially unjust market system. Both were intolerable, but the former was definitely the lesser evil because Russian nationalists would be able to come to terms with the Russian bureaucrat but not with the emerging Soviet entrepreneur. Kozhinov's and Antonov's Russian national economic model was thus revealed as a mere variation of the existing command economy.[82]

The Emergence of Independence Movements

Kazintsev's justification for an alliance at all cost between Russian nationalist intellectuals and the antireform forces in the political elite, and his readiness to accept the essentials of the Soviet economic structure had yet another very important motivation: the fast growth of nationalist movements (which assumed the title of Popular Fronts in Support of Perestroika) in the Caucasus, Moldavia, and the Baltic republics in the second half of 1988 through the spring of 1989. Indeed, as nationalist movements in the Baltics grew in strength and became more aggressive in their demands, Russian nationalists increasingly challenged these claims and called for the strengthening of an alliance with the antireform wing of the party.

In 1987 and early 1988, Russian nationalist intellectuals showed little sensitivity to or understanding of the magnitude of the nationality problem in the Soviet Union. Instead, they complained about the discrimination suffered by the RSFSR in relation to other parts of the Union, the poor knowledge of the Russian language in the non-Russian republics, and the demographic decline of ethnic Russians. However, by November 1988, they acknowledged that ignorance of the native language on the part of local Russians living outside Russia constituted a legitimate basis for the natives' grievances. This admission was made under the assumption that the language question was the only aspect of the nationality problem that Russians were willing to recognize and discuss.[83]

The growing nationalist sentiments in the non-Russian areas was recognized at a December 1988 conference organized by Russian nationalist scholars and dedicated to the analysis of nationality problems. The statement issued at the end of the meeting clearly showed that Russian nationalists failed to comprehend the degree of resentment that prevailed among the non-Russian intelligentsia toward the official nationality policies. Complaints about russification policies in the non-Russian republics were rejected at the conference as attempts to discredit and vilify the Russian people. The statement's only concrete proposal for easing ethnic tension was a reiteration of the demand, first presented in the "Letter to the Soviet

Government," calling for the adoption of the principle of proportional ethnic representation at all levels of government.[84]

In January 1989, Apollon Kuzmin openly declared that the concepts "Russia hating" and "anti-Soviet activity" were one and the same and proclaimed the nationalist movements in the Baltics guilty of both. His statement made it clear that preserving the integrity of the Soviet state was a major concern of the Russian nationalist movement. It also provided a new rationale for Russian nationalist support of the anti-perestroika forces in the Soviet political establishment. After all, the preservation of the Soviet state was a principal issue for these groups as well.[85]

Finally, in April 1989, *Molodaya gvardiya* published a long essay on the situation in Lithuania that elaborated Kuzmin's argument. The author accused the local Communist party of bowing to the pressure of the Lithuanian nationalist movement, Sajudis, and of imposing discriminatory language requirements on the Russian-speaking population. The essay portrayed Sajudis as both an anti-Russian and anti-Soviet secessionist movement and implicitly called on the party in Moscow to suppress nationalist movements in the Baltic republics and restore to the Russian-speaking populations in those areas the privileges they had enjoyed prior to perestroika.[86]

The Growth of Russian Nationalist and Allied Organizations

Between 1987 and 1988, Russian nationalists chose largely to engage in cultural politics, the traditional form of their political activity. This lack of a desire to engage in the new politics, in itself a consequence of a deeply held mistrust of democratic politics, was responsible for the extremely small number of Russian nationalist organizations that appeared between the spring of 1988 and the spring of 1989. In comparison, in the same period, the pro-perestroika forces in Soviet society established scores of political clubs, associations, and societies throughout the country. By midsummer 1989, there were 372 unofficial political associations throughout the RSFSR, most with a democratic orientation.[87]

The Nineteenth Party Conference was the turning point in the history of unofficial Russian nationalist organizations. If virtually no new Russian nationalist organizations appeared between the spring of 1987 and the early fall of 1988, approximately seven were established within eight months after the conference. The main cause behind this substantial growth was the fact that at the party conference, Gorbachev had secured the party's approval for a further radicalization of the democratization process. In its most important act, the conference decided to shift the locus of political power in the country from the party to the soviets. In order to give the soviets popular legitimacy, free elections to the Congress of People's Deputies, the supreme legislative body of the USSR, were to take place in the spring of 1989. The Russian nationalist desire to have greater influence on the political process, and therefore a need to organize in order to participate in the electoral campaign, provided the impetus needed to create a variety of new organizational structures.

Among the first Russian nationalist organizations to emerge in the aftermath of the party conference was the Association of Russian Artists *(Tovar-ishchestvo russkikh khudozhnikov)*, founded in November 1988 by a group of Russian nationalist scholars, writers, painters, and movie directors whose professed aim was to engage in various cultural activities in order to "raise national consciousness" and "strengthen the nation's moral and spiritual forces." The association was hardly a cultural institution. Its program explicitly stated that the association's aim was to support political forces committed to the preservation of the Soviet state and its territorial integrity. In particular, the association proclaimed that it wanted to help the Soviet military and its political branch, the Main Political Administration, to foster a more militaristic spirit in society. In other words, the association sought to become an ally of the conservative forces within the Soviet military and political establishment.[88]

To foster an alliance between the Russian nationalist intelligentsia and the anti-perestroika forces within the political establishment was also the principal purpose of the Union for the Spiritual Rebirth of the Fatherland *(Soyuz dukhovnogo vozrozhdeniya Otechestva)* and Fatherland *(Otechestvo)* societies. Both were founded in March 1989 and were led by prominent Russian nationalist intellectuals: the Union by Mikhail Antonov and the Fatherland by Apollon Kuzmin. In his programmatic statement, Antonov proclaimed Russian nationalist ideology to be the only ideology capable of bringing about the moral rebirth of the Russian nation. The statement also clearly signaled the Union's desire to support the conservative forces within the political establishment. The declaration proclaimed socialism to be the only acceptable sociopolitical order appropriate for Russia and expressed the Union's commitment to the principle of the territorial integrity of the USSR.[89]

Kuzmin's Fatherland society had virtually the same ideology as the Union for the Spiritual Rebirth of the Fatherland. Like the latter, Fatherland declared socialism to be the sociopolitical order that suited Russia best and announced its support for the preservation of the territorial integrity of the USSR. The main difference between the two organizations was the explicitly militaristic nature of the Fatherland and its ardent desire to seek an alliance with the anti-perestroika forces within the Soviet military. Army officers and Russian nationalist writers specializing on military subjects spoke at the society's first conference. A hero of the war in Afghanistan, Colonel Aleksandr Rutskoi, became the society's deputy chairman. A resolution adopted by the conference condemned the pro-perestroika press as initiating a campaign aimed at discrediting the armed forces.[90]

The strong ecological concerns of the Russian nationalist intellectuals also found their institutional manifestation with the founding of the Public Committee to Save the Volga (*Obshchestvenny komitet spaseniya Volgi*) in late January 1989 and its Leningrad chapter, the Committee Neva-Ladoga-Onega (*Komitet 'Neva-Ladoga-Onega'*) in April 1989. Both societies chose prominent Russian nationalist intellectuals as their leaders; Vasily Belov was elected chairman of the Public Committee to Save the Volga, and Mark Lyubomudrov became the head of the Committee Neva-Ladoga-Onega. However, within a year after their creation, both organizations effectively abandoned their exclusive focus on ecological issues to oppose aggressively all aspects of perestroika.[91]

In contrast to these Russian nationalist societies, founded and led by leading members of the Russian nationalist establishment, the Christian Patriotic Union (*Khristiansko-patriotichesky soyuz*) was started by former members of a dissident faction of the movement. It held its first conference in mid-December 1988 and elected as its chairman Vladimir Osipov, who had spent eight years in Soviet labor camps for editing the samizdat Russian nationalist journal *Veche* in the early 1970s. Contrary to Antonov's and Kuzmin's societies, the Christian Patriotic Union did not proclaim socialism as the only acceptable sociopolitical form for Russia. On the contrary, it declared that Russians had the right to own land and engage in private farming. While remaining vague on the issues of the Soviet Union's territorial integrity and the desired nature of Russia's political and economic order, it emphasized the Orthodox nature of Russia and demanded that the Church be allowed to play a major role in the country's social, political, and cultural life.[92]

Like Pamyat, all of these organizations had limited membership. The Association of Russian Artists, the Union for the Spiritual Rebirth of the Fatherland, and Fatherland had about three hundred to five hundred members each, concentrated primarily in Moscow. Although literature on the new political associations does not provide data on the memberships of the Public Committee to Save the Volga, the Committee Neva-Ladoga-Onega, or the Christian Patriotic Union, all indications are that these organizations had even fewer members.

In addition to organizations that were clearly defined as Russian nationalist, one can observe the emergence of what might be called proto-Russian nationalist organizations between late 1988 and early 1989. These were organizations of Russian-speaking minorities in the non-Russian republics. Contrary to Russian nationalist societies, these organizations were more genuine social movements with significant popular support and were of greater political importance.

The rise of the nationalist movements in the Baltics and Moldavia provoked a strong reaction from the Russian-speaking populations in these regions. In November 1988, Russian-speaking Union-level industrial enterprises of Estonia founded the United Council of Labor Collectives (Obyedeneny sovet trudovukh kollektivov). In January 1989, the Russian-speaking opponents of the independence movements in Latvia and Moldavia created their own political movements, which they called the Intermovement (Internatsionalnoe dvizhenie); an Intermovement organization was founded in Estonia in March 1989. The Unity (Edinstvo) movement, the Lithuanian chapter of Intermovement, began its activities early in the winter of 1989 but institutionalized itself later than its Latvian and Estonian counterparts; its first conference took place in May 1989.[93]

The Intermovements were not Russian nationalist organizations but rather had a conservative communist orientation. However, their fierce calls for the preservation of the territorial integrity of the USSR, combined with their wholesale rejection of perestroika, made them natural allies of the Russian nationalists. In the fall of 1989, the Intermovements formed a political alliance with Russian nationalist organizations and individuals.

To summarize the main arguments of this chapter, between the spring of 1985 and spring of 1989, Gorbachev rejected the Brezhnev-era policy of co-opting Russian nationalist intellectuals. He and his allies in the intellectual community, however, had to deal with the consequences of the inclusionary politics. Firmly entrenched in various cultural institutions and possessing national name recognition, Russian nationalist intellectuals emerged as dangerous opponents to perestroika and glasnost. This opposition proved to be the glue that united different branches within the Russian nationalist movement, excluding only liberal nationalist intellectuals who sided with the reformers. This period was also marked by a strengthening of the ties between Russian nationalist intellectuals and the conservative forces within the Soviet political establishment. Finally, in this period we also observed the emergence of Russian nationalist organizations, as well as the proto-nationalist Intermovements in the non-Russian areas, which constituted their belated attempts to adapt to the rapidly changing political environment.

CHAPTER

8

The Demise of Politics by Culture, 1989–1991

The new era in Soviet politics in which elections and parliaments, rather than the CPSU Central Committee, became primary focal points of political activity began with the spring 1989 election for seats in the USSR Congress of People's Deputies and ended with the collapse of the Soviet system in the aftermath of the August 1991 coup attempt. As such, these years marked the transition from the A-B Phase of the development of Russian nationalist movement to the C Phase. In other words, the politics by culture, dominated by literati and their thick journals, was being replaced by electoral politics dominated by political parties, electoral alliances, and parliamentary factions.

During this period, Russian nationalists effectively abandoned all attempts to become major players in Russian politics and ultimately took on a new role as public defenders of those institutions and actors capable of preserving the empire and the authoritarian state. By choosing to ally themselves with those who wanted to preserve the Soviet political and economic order, Russian nationalists ultimately shared their same political fate.

The Spring 1989 Elections and the First Congress of USSR People's Deputies

Although they realized that the nature of the Soviet political system was undergoing fundamental change, Russian nationalists were completely unprepared for the 1989 elections to the USSR Supreme Soviet. Perhaps as a result of their contempt for democratic politics, they showed far less interest in the elections than their pro-perestroika opponents. Few prominent

Russian nationalist intellectuals agreed to run in the multicandidate races; no nationalist organization, with the exception of Pamyat, took an active role in the electoral campaign; and there was no Russian nationalist coordination of campaigns on the city or regional level. In comparison, the Moscow Popular Front *(Moskovsky narodny front)*, the umbrella organization of approximately forty Moscow democratic groups, societies, and clubs, actively participated in the electoral campaign by supporting sixteen pro-perestroika candidates in Moscow's twenty-seven electoral districts, twelve of whom were elected.[1]

Pamyat's participation in the electoral campaign was limited to several rallies, as well as a concerted effort to prevent the nomination of *Ogonyok*'s chief editor, Vitaly Korotich, as a candidate for one of Moscow's electoral districts. On January 9, 1989, a group of Pamyat activists heckled Korotich as he was speaking with the residents of his electoral district and forced him to leave the building. Facing the certain prospect of being harassed by Pamyat in any other Moscow electoral district, Korotich chose to seek nomination outside Moscow.[2]

Pamyat supported the candidacy of Mikhail Lemeshev, a prominent Russian nationalist environmental specialist who was running against one of the leaders of the Moscow Popular Front, the historian Sergei Stankevich. Realizing that a Pamyat endorsement was a liability rather than an asset, Lemeshev attempted to distance himself from Pamyat. This, however, did not help, and he was soundly defeated by Stankevich.[3] In addition to Lemeshev, such prominent Russian nationalist intellectuals as Mark Lyubomudrov and Yury Bondarev were defeated, the former in Leningrad and the latter in Volgograd.

Bondarev's defeat was particularly devastating for Russian nationalists. He was the unrefuted leader of the Russian nationalist opposition to perestroika, and, far more important, his defeat exposed the emptiness of their claims of strong support in provincial Russia. Bondarev's decision to run for the seat from Volgograd, rather than from Moscow or on the USSR Writers' Union list of deputies, was calculated to illustrate the depth of Russian nationalist support in the provinces. Bondarev was counting on the support of Vladimir Kalashnikov, the head of the regional party organization and an outspoken opponent of perestroika, who had appointed Bondarev to the Volgograd delegation to the Nineteenth Party Conference. Indeed, the regional party organization arranged Bondarev's meetings with faculty and students at Volgograd University, workers at a large factory, and local party and government bureaucrats. Bondarev campaigned on an openly anti-perestroika platform, calling for an end to glasnost and pledging to rename the city Stalingrad. However, his platform was rejected by Volgograd voters, who instead elected the second secretary of the local Komsomol organization, Aleksei Kiselev, who was running on a pro-perestroika platform.[4]

Russian nationalist intellectuals and their allies from the Intermovements did gain seats in the Congress of People's Deputies. Vasily Belov was elected on the CPSU list, Viktor Astafiev and Valentin Rasputin were elected on the USSR Writers' Union list, and Viktor Alksnis, Evgeny Kogan, Vladimir Yarovoi, and Yury Blokhin, the leaders of the Latvian, Estonian, and Moldavian Intermovements, were elected in the Russian-speaking districts of their own republics.[5] Moreover, despite the fact that pro-perestroika candidates swept the elections in several major cities, most deputies elected to the Congress were party functionaries, managers of large industrial enterprises, or officers of the Soviet military high command whose support for perestroika was halfhearted at best.[6]

The First Congress of People's Deputies of the USSR (May 25, 1989–June 9, 1989) heralded the emergence of an anti-perestroika alliance at the parliamentary level of Russian nationalist intellectuals, leaders of the various Intermovement groups, and leaders of the conservative wing of the political establishment. In his speech to the Congress, Belov harshly attacked "democratic" control of the mass media, cultural pluralism, the emerging private sector, and the opening up of the Soviet economy to Western entrepreneurs.[7]

Rasputin was even blunter in his remarks. He accused the democratic forces of imposing "upon the country the pluralism of morality which is more dangerous than any bomb"—in other words, of using glasnost policies to advocate Western social and moral values in order to undermine the strength of the Soviet state. Rasputin used the podium to declare that a powerful state was the ultimate goal of the Russian nationalist movement. Since the conservative wing of the party was also committed to this goal, Rasputin, although not a member, defended the CPSU and Ligachev against attacks by radical pro-perestroika deputies.[8]

At the Congress, strong support for anti-perestroika views in general, and Russian nationalist views in particular, was expressed in a variety of ways. The hall exploded with a standing ovation when Sergei Chervonopissky, an Afghan war veteran and the secretary of the Komsomol organization in the Ukrainian town of Cherkassy, ended his attack on Andrei Sakharov and the pro-independence movements in the Baltics and the Caucasus with a call for the defense of the powerful state *(derzhava)*, motherland, and communism. Similarly, the deputies greeted with prolonged applause the impassioned speech of General Igor Rodionov, the commander of the Transcaucasian Military District, who defended the bloody suppression of the peaceful demonstration in Tbilisi by his troops in April 1989.[9]

The elections to the USSR Supreme Soviet, which took place at the Congress, gave an even clearer indication of the political attitudes held by the majority of the deputies. The candidacy of Boris Yeltsin, the leader of the radical reformers, as well as those of such prominent members of the Moscow liberal-reformist intelligentsia as Yury Chernichenko, Arkady Murashov, Gavriil Popov, Sergei Stankevich, Vladimir Tikhonov, and Tatiyana Zaslavskaya, were all voted down by the Congress; Vasily Belov, on the other hand, easily won a seat in the Supreme Soviet.

Reaction to the Election Results

Faced with the impending elections to the RSFSR Supreme Soviet, Russian nationalists had to make important adjustments to their strategy in order to establish themselves as an influential political force. Between summer 1989 and spring 1990, they developed a strategy that included a purge of the editors of the main Russian nationalist journals, attempts to take control of major publications supporting perestroika, and the pursuit of an alliance with the conservative wing of the Soviet military establishment and the orthodox communist United Workers' Front of Russia, the most important anti-perestroika political movement to emerge in the summer of 1989.

Russian nationalists placed the blame for their 1989 electoral defeat directly on the policies of glasnost. Although realizing that these policies were not likely to be reversed any time soon, they nonetheless wanted to regain their ability to shape public opinion and thus devised a two-pronged strategy. The first aspect entailed replacing the aging chief editors of the main Russian nationalist journals with younger and more dynamic figures in order to make the journals much more attractive to Russian readers and radically increase their circulation.

In August 1989, the sixty-seven-year-old chief editor of *Nash sovremen-*

nik, Sergei Vikulov, succumbed to the pressure of the RSFSR Writers' Union Secretariat and announced his retirement. He was replaced by fifty-seven year-old radical nationalist poet Stanislav Kunyaev. The chief editor of *Moskva,* seventy-one-year-old Mikhail Alekseev, held out until February 1990, when he was finally replaced by forty-eight-year-old conservative village prose writer Vladimir Krupin.[10]

Russian nationalists, however, failed to comprehend that it was not the editors of the Russian nationalist publications, but the unpopular message they carried, that was the cause of their low subscription levels. Despite the change in editors, the main thick journals of the Russian nationalists proved incapable of competing against their liberal-reformist rivals in the battle for readers. In 1990, *Nash sovremennik, Moskva,* and *Molodaya gvardiya* had a total of 1.6 million subscribers, 23,000 fewer than in 1989. In comparison, in 1990, *Novy mir, Znamya,* and *Yunost,* the three most popular liberal-reformist thick journals, had a total of 6.6 million subscribers, an increase of 1.3 million over 1989.[11]

The second prong of the strategy aimed at improving the Russian nationalists' ability to shape public opinion by gaining control of publications previously not in their camp. Russian nationalist intellectuals understood all too well that merely changing the editors of their journals would not significantly improve their ability to influence public opinion unless this action was accompanied by an extension of control over such prestigious and widely read pro-perestroika Moscow thick journals as *Novy mir, Znamya, Yunost, Druzhba narodov,* and *Oktyabr.*

Among these journals, *Oktyabr* was the only one formally published under the auspices of the RSFSR Writers' Union. The Union leadership decided to replace its chief editor, Anatoly Ananiev, with a prominent Russian nationalist opponent of perestroika. The successful removal of Ananiev should have established a precedent that could be used to replace the chief editors of the other targeted journals.

On August 4, *Literaturnaya Rossiya* published a letter written by three prominent Russian nationalist intellectuals—economist Mikhail Antonov, sculptor Vyacheslav Klykov, and mathematician Igor Shafarevich—addressed to the Secretariat of the RSFSR Writers' Union. The letter accused *Oktyabr* of consistently pursuing an anti-Russian line that manifested itself in the publication of Andrei Sinyavsky's *Strolls with Pushkin* and Vasily Grossman's *Forever Flowing,* literary works long banned for their anticommunist content. Grossman's novel, the authors of the letter insisted, was permeated with a hatred of Russia because it presented the motherland as a nation with the soul of a slave. Citing the fact that *Oktyabr* was published under the auspices of the RSFSR Writers' Union, Antonov, Klykov, and Shafarevich asserted that it bore full responsibility for the content of *Oktyabr*'s pages. This was a thinly disguised demand for a purge of the journal.[12]

On November 29, after a month-long attack on *Oktyabr*'s publication record in *Literaturnaya Rossiya,* the RSFSR Writers' Union Secretariat officially dismissed Ananiev from his position as *Oktyabr*'s chief editor and appointed a militant Russian nationalist critic of perestroika, the village prose writer Vladimir Lichutin, as his successor.[13] The Russian nationalists, however, failed to enforce their decision. Ananiev refused to leave his office, and the powerful public outcry following the announcement of his firing made the conservative forces in the Soviet political establishment reluctant to give public support to the Russian nationalist effort to oust Ananiev. More important, in December 1989, the USSR Supreme Soviet notified the Secretariat of the RSFSR Writers' Union that Ananiev's status as a USSR People's Deputy made it illegal for the union to dismiss him without the Supreme Soviet's approval. This approval was never given, and Ananiev remained in his position as editor.[14]

The implications of the failure to remove Ananiev were far-reaching. It became clear that the Russian nationalist leadership of the RSFSR Writers' Union lacked sufficient political backing to take over any of the major pro-perestroika publications. Moreover, it fatally undermined the three-year-long effort of the Russian nationalist intelligentsia to transform the RSFSR Writers' Union into an important political player on its own right.[15]

Realizing their political weakness in the new era of electoral politics, the Russian nationalist intelligentsia now focused its post-1989 efforts on regaining its political significance by allying itself with major political actors, be they conservative forces within the Soviet military establishment or newly founded orthodox communist organizations supported by the conservatives within the party apparat.

In no other area was the effort to build an alliance between Russian nationalist intellectuals and anti-perestroika forces within the Soviet political establishment so open as in the case of the military. Russian nationalists hoped that their support of the military establishment, at that time subject to intense criticism from the reformers, would ultimately convince the military to adopt the Russian nationalist ideology as its own and use it as a guide to transforming the Soviet Union after the defeat of perestroika. The conservatives in the military establishment, for their part, entered the alliance because they clearly recognized the Russian nationalist intellectuals as the only group in the intellectual community willing both to defend the military against the reformers' attacks and support the military's opposition to Gorbachev's policies. Russian nationalist propaganda was also deemed invaluable in helping the conservatives within the military establishment fight off the penetration of reformist sentiments within the armed forces themselves.

One of the manifestations of this alliance was a series of meetings of prominent Russian nationalist intellectuals, the heads of the Ministry of Defense, and soldiers from various garrisons. Although only a few of these meetings were reported, their number was probably much higher.[16] Another sign of this emerging coalition was the transformation of several major journals published by the army's Main Political Administration (MPA) into Russian nationalist publications. This went hand in hand with a mobilization of the major Russian nationalist publications in defense of the military's actions in containing ethnic unrest and a harsh criticism of Gorbachev's military and foreign policies.

Transformation of the content of the military journals began before the 1989 elections and then intensified. Between 1987 and early 1989, the bimonthly journal *Sovetsky voin,* the primary publication of the MPA, regularly promoted Russian nationalist ideas. It published interviews with or works by prominent Russian nationalist intellectuals that extolled the military as "one of the pivotal axes which strengthens and supports the health of the nation," condemned glasnost policies as opening the gates to "Western cultural aggression," which attempted to "impose false values on Soviet youth," denounced true accounts of Soviet history as "painting our recent past black" and as "demagogic attempts to replace [the primacy of] sentiments of patriotic duty with those of human rights," and portrayed the emerging private sector of the economy as contributing only to a rise in crime and corruption.[17]

In order to widen the exposure of soldiers and officers to Russian nationalist ideas, MPA increased the circulation of *Sovetsky voin* from 250,000 copies in 1988 to 346,000 in 1989, and to 540,000 in 1990.[18] During this period, it continued to play the pivotal role assigned to it by the military establishment: it published interviews, essays, and editorials that attacked the reformers' proposal to create an all-volunteer army; criticized pro-perestroika publications for their contempt for patriotic sentiments; condemned the independence movements in the Baltic republics; and called for the preservation of a strong and unified Soviet state.

In 1989 and 1990, MPA expanded the number of major military journals promoting Russian nationalist ideology to include *Kommunist voruzhennykh sil* and *Voenno-istorichesky zhurnal*.[19] Starting in 1989, *Kommunist voruzhennykh sil (KVS)*, the most authoritative journal of the MPA, regularly published Russian nationalist essays that harshly attacked such major aspects of glasnost as the publication of anti-Stalinist and antimilitarist works of fiction written by prominent pro-perestroika intellectuals, and the publication of the previously forbidden works of Voinovich, Sinyavsky, and other émigré writers.

In early 1990, the journal mobilized Russian nationalist intellectuals to help the MPA wage an ideological battle against the growing secessionist movements in various parts of the country. In February, it printed an essay on the nationality problem in the USSR, written by Vladimir Fomichev, the chief editor of a new, rabidly anti-Semitic Russian nationalist newspaper, *Puls Tushina*. Fomichev rejected assertions regarding the exploitation and discrimination suffered by the minority nations. In reality, he proclaimed, Russia itself was discriminated against in favor of the non-Russian republics because it did not have such institutions as its own Communist party, trade unions, Academy of Sciences, or television and radio broadcasting services, and because Russia subsidized the other republics at its own expense. This Russian nationalist interpretation of the nationality problem appeared regularly on the pages of their publications in the Gorbachev era. However, this was the first time that an official journal of a Communist party organization in the Soviet military had published these arguments.[20]

In mid-1988, MPA appointed a radical nationalist army officer, Viktor Filatov, as the chief editor of *Voenno-istorichesky zhurnal (VIZ)*, a semischolarly journal dedicated to Soviet military history. Within a year, he had transformed it into the most aggressive publication controlled by the alliance of conservatives in the Soviet military and Russian nationalist intellectuals. In 1989, two major pieces illustrated *VIZ*'s new orientation. The first was a violent attack by radical nationalist literary critic Vladimir Bushin on Andrei Sakharov for his public criticism of Soviet military behavior in Afghanistan at the First Congress of People's Deputies. The second consisted of a series of seven essays, entitled "Army and Culture" *(Armiya i kultura)*, by radical nationalist writer Karem Rash on the role of the military in Russian culture and society. The series attracted substantial attention because it combined a harsh attack on the policies of glasnost and perestroika with the most elaborate Russian nationalist argument yet published for the thorough militarization and nationalization of Soviet society.

Rash condemned Gorbachev's reforms as undermining the "three pillars of the Soviet state: the family, the school, and the military." He claimed that glasnost policies "pollute the consciousness and increase confusion and panic in society," which contributed to loss of morale within the military. Proclaiming that a "love of the military . . . is the most reliable sign of a nation's health," Rash advanced his own vision of perestroika, which included the imposition of strict control over the mass media, the aggressive promotion of radical nationalist ideology, the militarization of the entire educational system, and the cultivation of a positive image of the military in society. The conservative military establishment hailed these essays, which became required reading for officers in many garrisons. Moreover, MPA appointed Rash to the editorial board of *VIZ*.[21]

While military publications were printing Russian nationalist attacks on glasnost and perestroika, Russian nationalist journals and newspapers were rallying in defense of the Soviet military and its policies. In late 1989 and early 1990, both *Molodaya gvardiya* and *Nash sovremennik* published abridged versions of Rash's work, as well as letters from army officers critical of Gorbachev's plan for a unilateral reduction in the size of the Soviet military and of the negative portrayal of military life in *Ogonyok, Komsolskaya pravda,* and other pro-perestroika publications.[22]

In the aftermath of the 1989 elections, support for the military establishment became one of the main editorial lines of *Literaturnaya Rossiya.* In its February 23, 1990 issue, the newspaper published an extensive interview with the head of MPA, General Aleksei Lizichev, in which he accused pro-perestroika publications of spreading antimilitary sentiments among the younger generation of Russians and warned that "the nation which refuses to feed its own army will be forced to feed the army of the enemy." Between May 1989 and May 1990, *Literaturnaya Rossiya* also printed essays justifying the army's bloody suppression of the demonstration in Tbilisi in April 1989, including one essay written by General Rodionov, the officer in charge at the time. This was accompanied by harsh criticism of the treatment of the Soviet military by *Ogonyok,* accusations that perestroika supporters in the mass media were fueling dangerous "pacifist hysteria," and rebuttals to reformers' proposals for a radical cutback in the size of the military.[23]

Among the essays printed by *Literaturnaya Rossiya* and supportive of the opponents to perestroika within the military establishment, those written by Yury Katasonov and Aleksandr Prokhanov contained the harshest condemnation of Gorbachev's military and foreign policies. Katasonov openly accused Gorbachev, his allies in the political leadership, and their supporters in the mass media and in the scholarly establishment of destroying the army and undermining the country's capacity to defend itself. Under Gorbachev, he asserted, Soviet foreign policy was no longer aimed at strengthening the USSR's military and political positions in the world, but rather at weakening them. In particular, the unilateral reduction of Soviet military power significantly altered the balance of forces in Europe in favor of the North Atlantic Treaty Organization, and Gorbachev's inability to link these cuts to the dismantling of the Strategic Defense Initiative constituted a "de-facto surrender to Washington." Moreover, all this was happening while perestroika's supporters in the mass media and the scholarly establishment were creating the dangerous political illusion of an end to the confrontation with the West, which could cause a "total political surrender and the loss of national independence."[24]

Prokhanov's essay "Sufficient Defense" (*Dostatochnaya oborona*), was a programmatic statement about the historical necessity of an alliance between Russian nationalist intellectuals and conservative forces within the military establishment. At its core stood an argument that such an alliance is crucial for the preservation of Russia as a great power:

> Today, the battle to preserve the military is the last struggle to preserve the state and the nation. The disintegration and destruction of the army makes us defenseless before plunderers seeking to dismember the USSR into easily digestible tidbits and to break the resistance of Russia who refuses . . . to become the basement in the economic and cultural hierarchy of cruel and pseudo-humanistic world civilizations.

Prokhanov openly accused Gorbachev of betraying Soviet national interests by launching a policy of unilateral disarmament and by surrendering Eastern Europe, which had provided a crucial buffer zone against Western invaders. He also blamed perestroika supporters in the mass media for creating an "antimilitary psychosis," which undermined the morale of the soldiers and destroyed the harmonious relationship between low-ranking officers and the high command. Finally, Prokhanov implored the latter to "cease preoccupying itself exclusively with military affairs, to join the sociopolitical process and announce to the people that it is ready to carry out a protective national mission." This was clearly the ideological justification for a military coup. In 1990, a defense of the military establishment would become an important element in the politics of the Russian nationalist electoral alliance.[25]

After the 1989 elections revealed just how unpopular the conservative Communist party apparatus was in some major cities of the RSFSR, its leading members began to search for new organizational structures that could rally the urban working class against perestroika in the forthcoming elections to the RSFSR Supreme Soviet and the local soviets. This was also the objective of many prominent orthodox communist intellectuals, such as philosopher Richard Kosolapov, the chief editor of *Kommunist* under Brezhnev, who in early 1989 organized like-minded intellectuals into the Association for Scientific Communism (*Assotsiatsiya nauchnogo kommunizma*).[26]

Strongly supported behind the scenes by the leadership of the Moscow and Leningrad party organizations, organizing committees of the new movement, which they called the United Workers' Front (*Obiedinenny front trudyashchikhsya*), were created in both cities.[27] In Leningrad, where the local party apparat was the most supportive of the United Workers' Front, the organizing committee convened its first regional conference on June 15, 1989, and elected a coordinating council that included workers, conservative communist intellectuals, and several local party functionaries. The conference adopted a program that combined Russian nationalist and orthodox communist rhetoric. It declared that the United Workers' Front would defend the socialist nature of the Soviet state and ensure that the working class would play a major role in governing the country. To achieve these goals, it proposed instituting working-class control over the mass media, to ensure the end of glasnost, and introducing tough measures against private enterprises designed to nip the emerging Soviet bourgeoisie in the bud.

The document shared key ideological principles with earlier Russian nationalist programs: an explicit promise to support Russia's national revival and fight against "mass culture" and the "dissemination of pornography" by the media, support for the armed forces and a vow to combat any effort by the reformers to weaken the military, and a pledge to oppose the transformation of the country from a superpower to a mere supplier of raw materials to capitalist countries.[28]

The United Workers' Front's crusade against a market economy rose to a dramatic climax during a major conference on the problems of radical economic reform in November 1989. The audience of hundreds of party, state, and trade union officials and heads of major industrial enterprises, which had coolly responded to proposals for radical reform, received Aleksei Sergeev's presentation of the United Workers' Front's economic program with wild applause, sending Gorbachev a clear message that the majority of the Soviet political establishment opposed the introduction of a market economy.[29]

Literaturnaya Rossiya carried a major essay on the conference and strongly endorsed Sergeev's plan.[30] This was a manifestation of the growing interests of Russian nationalists in the organization. Earlier, in August 1989, *Literaturnaya Rossiya* had published an essay on the United Workers' Front, presenting it as a genuine political movement of the Russian working class that could successfully challenge the pro-perestroika forces. The underlining message of the essay was clear: Russian nationalists must enter into a close alliance with the United Workers' Front in order to remain a meaningful political force.[31]

The alliance between the Russian nationalist intelligentsia and the United Workers' Front began to flourish in the fall of 1989. The October issue of the United Workers' Front journal, *Ekonomicheskie nauki*, published an essay by a secretary of RSFSR Writers' Union, Anatoly Salutsky, that attempted to discredit the ideas of Gavriil Popov, Nikolai Shmelev, and other supporters of radical economic reform. Publication coincided with the appearance in *Nash sovremennik* of the same author's interview with Aleksei Sergeev, in which he reiterated his main arguments against the introduction of a market economy.

Between November 1989 and April 1990, Russian nationalists effectively adopted the United Workers' Front economic program and eagerly promoted it on the pages of *Literaturnaya Rossiya, Moskovsky literator, Nash sovremennik,* and *Molodaya gvardiya.* Essays by Sergeev and the United Workers' Front's economists calling for monetary reform, a crackdown on the "shadow economy" (i.e., the private sector), and opposition to the creation of free economic zones in the Soviet Union regularly appeared in these publications.[32]

In fall 1989, the United Workers' Front and the Russian nationalist intelligentsia formed an anti-perestroika electoral alliance that participated in the spring 1990 elections to the RSFSR Supreme Soviet. After the elections, both groups played a significant role in helping the opponents of perestroika in the CPSU apparatus to create the Russian Communist Party.

The Formation of the Electoral Alliance

The alliance between the United Workers' Front and Russian nationalist intellectuals was of major importance because it was the first attempt to institutionalize a coalition of opponents to perestroika in Soviet society and to present itself as a viable alternative to both radical perestroika supporters organized in the electoral alliance Democratic Russia and the Gorbachev-led CPSU.

The first stage in the formation of this alliance took place on September 9, 1989, when the Association of Russian Artists sponsored a conference that brought together twelve leading Russian nationalist organizations, the Moscow and Leningrad United Workers' Front, and the Intermovements from the three Baltic republics and Moldavia. At the conference, a decision was made to create an institutional framework to coordinate the activities of the participating organizations and develop joint ideological programs as part of the preparation for the 1990 electoral campaign. This new institution was named United Council of Russia *(Assotsiatsiya 'Obyedenneny Sovet Rossii')*.

The conference participants elected a thirty-eight-member coordinating council, the association's ruling body, which included such prominent United Workers' Front and Russian nationalist figures as Mikhail Antonov, Stanislav Kunyaev, Mikhail Lemeshev, Aleksandr Prokhanov, Aleksei Sergeev, and Eduard Volodin. It then adopted a series of resolutions that, in effect, constituted an early draft of the alliance's electoral platform and would be the basis for all subsequent drafts. These documents represented a clear synthesis of various Russian nationalist and United Workers' Front programs and provided an ideological common ground for the emerging electoral alliance.

They also revealed the alliance's unwavering support for the conservative forces in the political and military establishments and its deep-seated hope that these forces would soon put an end to perestroika. They rejected Gorbachev's policy of radical reform on the grounds that "Russia must not become the testing ground for different political and economic models." In a thinly veiled declaration of support for the anti-perestroika wing of the party, the United Council of Russia proclaimed that socialism expressed the historical hopes and ideals of the Russian people and pronounced its readiness to back those forces within the party "capable of fighting for the socialist renewal of the Motherland." Hand in hand with this declaration came the accusation that perestroika's supporters were attempting to destroy the CPSU, the army, and the law enforcement agencies—those institutions entrusted with preserving the stability of the state, and thus greatly contributing to the growing political and economic disintegration of the USSR.

The military received substantial attention in the documents of the United Council of Russia. In this area, the organization fully accepted the ideas of the conservative forces in the military establishment. It rejected the reformers' proposals for the abolition of the draft and the creation of a professional army, called for a strengthening of the armed forces, demanded increased social prestige for the officer corps, and argued for broadening the paramilitary education of Soviet youth. This expression of support for the party and the military combined with a call for a more prominent political role for the Russian Orthodox Church. Behind this appeal stood the implicit argument that the Orthodox Church, given official recognition and support, would exert its influence to preserve the integrity of the Soviet state.

The alliance's program openly declared its opposition to any attempt to dismember the Soviet state, proposed giving Russian the status of the state language in all republics, called for the abolition of discriminatory language and election laws in the Baltics and Moldavia, and expressed support for the Intermovements in their struggle for "the political, economic, and cultural equality of the Russian and non-Russian populations" in these republics. The resolution concerning the status of the RSFSR demanded an end to Russia's institutional inequality and the creation of the political, economic, scientific, and cultural institutions found in other republics. Largely in an attempt to capitalize on the perceived strength of the anti-Jewish feelings in Russian society, the resolution revived the 1988 proposal of the "Letter to the Soviet Government," calling for the introduction of proportional ethnic representation in determining the composition of republic-level political, economic, and cultural institutions, although it did not specify how to implement the proposal.[33]

The economic section of the document was clearly influenced by the United Workers' Front. It declared that state-owned enterprises must remain the basis of the Soviet economic structure. Attempts to introduce a market economy were condemned as "leading directly to the impoverishment of the country and the open economic and political enslavement of the workers." Policies encouraging joint ventures and other measures aimed at integrating the Soviet Union into the world economy were denounced as turning the USSR into a Western colony of a new type—a place where Western countries would dump their industrial waste. The United Council of Russia also adopted the United Workers' Front's proposal to change the electoral system from territorial to enterprise-based districts. Although most of the other demands found their way into subsequent programs of the alliance, this particular proposal was tacitly dropped after the RSFSR Supreme Soviet rejected the idea in October.[34]

The second stage in the formation of the electoral alliance took place on October 21 and 22, 1989, when a group of fifty-one USSR People's Deputies, mostly from provincial Russian towns, met in the Siberian city of Tyumen. The guest speaker, Russian nationalist legal scholar Galina Litvinova, painted a dire picture of institutional, legal, and economic discrimination against the RSFSR in comparison with other republics.[35] These arguments were reiterated by Sergei Vasiliev, the USSR People's Deputy from Tyumen and the meeting's main organizer. Not all the participants shared the organizers' Russian nationalist agenda; in the end, only twenty-eight deputies signed a programmatic declaration, published first in the local paper and later reprinted in *Literaturnaya Rossiya*, *Moskovsky literator*, and *Nash sovremennik*.

Its style and content were strikingly similar to that of the 1988 "Letter to the Soviet Government" (see Chapter 7) and differed from the program of the United Council of Russia only in its emphasis. The Tyumen declaration protested the discrimination suffered by ethnic Russians in the Baltic republics and the Caucasus, and charged that the RSFSR's financial resources were being pumped into other republics. It expressed concern over reformers' efforts to discredit the military and denounced Gorbachev's disarmament policy. It called for an intensified effort to instill a commitment to the territorial integrity and strength of the Soviet state in Soviet youth and demanded the creation of an RSFSR Academy of Sciences, an RSFSR radio and television agency, and new newspapers and publishing houses in the RSFSR. In addition, it appealed for the adoption of new education and cadre policies based on the principle of proportional ethnic representation. Finally, citing the lack of action on these issues by the RSFSR Council of Ministers, the declaration called for the formation of a faction of People's

Deputies from the RSFSR that would defend the national interests of Russia in the USSR Supreme Soviet.[36]

This last idea was realized three days later. On October 24, 1989, the first meeting of the USSR People's Deputies and Voters Club Russia (Klub narodnykh deputatov SSSR i izbiratelei 'Rossiya') took place in Moscow and adopted the Tyumen declaration as the coalition's programmatic document. The Russia Club was more than a simple parliamentary faction; it was a coalition of People's Deputies who had signed the Tyumen declaration, organizations that had participated in the United Council of Russia, and such Russian nationalist and conservative communist institutions as the RSFSR Writers' Union, the journal Nash sovremennik, and the newspapers Sovetskaya Rossiya and Literaturnaya Rossiya. Veniyamin Yarin, USSR People's Deputy and one of United Workers' Front's leaders, was elected as the Russia Club chairman, and Viktor Astafiev, Vasily Belov, Yury Bondarev, and Stanislav Kunyaev were chosen as members of the executive board.[37]

In December 1989, at the Second Congress of USSR People's Deputies, approximately 150 deputies declared their affiliation with the Russia Club, thus making it a powerful parliamentary alternative to the Interregional Group of Deputies, the bloc supporting radical reform.[38] In February 1990, Yarin and other Russia Club deputies participated in the formation of the Soyuz (Union) parliamentary faction, which unified People's Deputies from all parts of the country who supported the preservation of the territorial integrity of the USSR and its strong anti-Western orientation. From the second half of 1990 until the coup attempt in August 1991, it was the most powerful faction in the Soviet parliament, with 561 members.[39]

Soyuz, as a faction in the USSR parliament, could not play a significant role in the spring 1990 republican elections. The Russia Club, on the other hand, became the organization responsible for Russian nationalist electoral campaigns to the RSFSR Supreme Soviet and regional and local soviets. In December 1989, the Russia Club, under the title of the Bloc of Social-Patriotic Movements of Russia (Blok obshchestevnno-patrioticheskikh dvizhenii Rossii) declared itself to be the official Russian nationalist and orthodox communist electoral alliance. In order to strengthen the bloc's electoral appeal, Pamyat was not invited to participate in its activities.[40]

On December 29, Literaturnaya Rossiya published the alliance's electoral program. This was the first electoral platform to appear in print; Democratic Russia's program was not published until early February 1990.[41] The bloc's program represented a combination of principles drawn from the documents of the United Council of Russia and the Tyumen declaration. At its center stood a solemn pledge to preserve Russia and the Soviet Union as a world superpower. The program promised that bloc deputies would defend the military, the KGB, and the police against the attacks of reformers and would work to strengthen military training and education of the country's youth.

In economics, the program reiterated the principal position of the Russian nationalists and United Workers' Front against the introduction of a market economy. It proclaimed that the underlying cause of the ongoing economic crisis lay in senseless efforts to destroy the existing economic structure and replace it with an unregulated market mechanism. The program declared that the bloc opposed the legalization of private property and demanded that the issue be subject to a national referendum. The opening up of free economic zones and the establishing of joint ventures with Western entrepreneurs were also condemned as policies that would turn Russia into a supplier of raw materials and a dump site for the nuclear and chemical waste of capitalist countries.

As an alternative to the introduction of a market economy and as a means to combat the shadow economy, the program advanced the United Workers' Front proposal for currency reform. According to the proposal, each individual could exchange 10,000 to 15,000 old rubles for new ones of the same value. A declaration on the sources of income would be required for those wishing to exchange amounts above this ceiling. The introduction of a progressive inheritance tax was proposed as a supplement to the monetary reform.

The Patriotic Bloc's program demanded the institutional equality of the RSFSR through the creation of a republic-level Communist party, Academy of Sciences, and research institutes similar to those of the USSR Academy of Sciences. The program repeated the Tyumen declaration's call for the creation of a separate RSFSR radio and television agency and supplemented this with a promise that the All-Union radio and television stations would stop broadcasting all but the news in the Russian republic because their programs propagated values of "immorality and individualism, pornography and violence." RSFSR radio and television would operate in accordance with a new RSFSR "law on morality," which would treat the propagation of immorality as a criminal offense.

In the realm of interrepublic relations, the program conceded for the first time the possibility of the secession of republics from the union. At the same time, however, it demanded reconsideration of the borders of those republics that wished to leave the union on the grounds that they had been arbitrarily established and changed from the 1920s on. Like the Tyumen document, the Patriotic Bloc's program promised that beginning in 1991, it would halt the RSFSR's subsidies to other republics and added to this a demand that All-Union organizations, ministries, and legislative organs located in the RSFSR be required to pay rent for the use of their facilities. Finally, the program proposed designating Moscow as the capital of the RSFSR and moving the All-Union capital elsewhere.[42]

The publication of the program was clearly intended to provide the basis for electoral alliances of Russian nationalist organizations and the United Workers' Front in all the major Russian cities where such organizations existed. In addition to Moscow, such blocs were formed in Leningrad, Sverdlovsk, Novosibirsk, Tyumen, and some smaller Siberian cities.[43] Moscow nevertheless remained the center of the Patriotic bloc's efforts and attention. The focus on Moscow was so great that the Bloc ultimately became a Moscow-based alliance whose members competed for seats in the RSFSR Supreme Soviet and the Moscow City Soviet.

The 1990 Electoral Campaign

With the printing of its program, *Literaturnaya Rossiya* became the alliance's primary newspaper.[44] On January 5, 1990, the newspaper launched the electoral campaign with the publication of Prokhanov's essay, "Tragedy of Centralism" (*Tragediya tsentralizma*), an impassioned indictment of perestroika. Perestroika, Prokhanov asserted, destroyed the socialist ideology and fatally weakened the centrally planned economy, the army, and the party—those very institutions that played a crucial role in securing the territorial integrity of the Soviet state. Perestroika had not improved the economic situation but had created a growing social inequality, which resulted in the emergence of a criminal private economy. Its emphasis on "new thinking" and the "primacy of universal human values" was a betrayal of Soviet national interests and had led to the unification of Germany and the loss of Eastern Europe, and ultimately had rendered the Soviet Union incapable of containing Western expansion in the Third World.[45]

In the following months, *Literaturnaya Rossiya* regularly printed interviews with the Patriotic Bloc's leading candidates in which they articulated their views on the political, social, economic, and cultural situation, as well as letters from readers expressing support for the bloc and criticizing its main opponent, Democratic Russia. In order to help voters identify Patriotic Bloc candidates to the RSFSR Supreme Soviet and the Moscow City Soviet, *Literaturnaya Rossiya* published their names and electoral districts in its February 23 and March 2 issues.[46]

Literaturnaya Rossiya's efforts were supported by the conservative communist daily, *Sovetskaya Rossiya*, which vigorously promoted the official CPSU candidates in various parts of the country. It also found the space to print a summary of the Patriotic Bloc's platform, as well as the electoral programs of several of the bloc's leading candidates.[47]

The electoral campaign strategy adopted by the Patriotic Bloc was amateurish. It relied primarily on promoting its candidates and ideas in *Literaturnaya Rossiya, Sovetskaya Rossiya,* and some smaller Russian nationalist publications, such as *Puls Tushina.* It entirely ignored the need for an effective street campaign, and during the three months of the campaign, it staged only one public rally, on January 27 near the Ostankino television center, which was badly organized and poorly attended. In comparison, Democratic Russia staged two exceptionally well-organized mass rallies in the center of Moscow, both of them much closer to the election date than Patriotic Bloc's rally. On February 4, Democratic Russia brought out 200,000 people to Manezh Square, just outside the Kremlin walls, and on February 25, despite stern warnings from the authorities, it gathered a smaller, but nevertheless significant crowd on the Sadovaya Ring in downtown Moscow.

More important than the failure to organize mass rallies was the Patriotic Bloc's failure to show a presence on the streets. Timothy Colton, who was in Moscow during the final stages of the electoral campaign, gives the following description of the bloc's activities:

Backers [of the Patriotic Bloc] put together some outdoor pep talks the weekend of the election, but otherwise mustered little presence on the streets, giving out almost no handbills or posters . . . Here and there, zealots who may or may not have been leagued with the bloc pasted up placards alluding to perfidious ties between Democratic Russia and the three planetary bogies of "international Zionism," the big banks, and the CIA. "If we do not stop them," one poster blared, "Russia may share the sad destiny of Poland, Panama, and Palestine."[48]

In addition to poor campaigning, the unattractiveness of the Russian nationalist program was one of the major reasons for the bloc's resounding defeat in the March 1990 election. Residents of Moscow and other major Russian cities rejected the bloc's pro-communist, antimarket, and antidemocratic vision. The ideology of Democratic Russia, which combined a decisive rejection of communism and a strong commitment to democratic and market institutions with such nationalist ideas as Russia's political and economic sovereignty, had significantly greater electoral appeal. In fact, the 1990 election established a pattern that reappeared in all subsequent elections and referenda: the weakness of communist and nationalist candidates, parties, and causes in major Russian cities.

The bloc nominated 79 candidates to the 65 Moscow seats in the RSFSR Supreme Soviet and 146 candidates to the 498 seats in the Moscow City Soviet. A vast majority of the most prominent Moscow-based Russian nationalist intellectuals and United Workers' Front leaders were on the ballot. In the first round of balloting on March 4, 65 of the bloc's candidates to the RSFSR Supreme Soviet were soundly defeated, and only 14 mustered enough votes to qualify for the second round. In the runoffs held on March 18, only 2 of the remaining 14 candidates were elected to the RSFSR Supreme Soviet.

The Patriotic Bloc hardly fared better in the election to the Moscow City Soviet. None of its 146 candidates was elected in the first round, and only 32 received enough votes to qualify for the second round, in which 12 bloc members were elected to the Moscow City Soviet.

The full extent of the Patriotic Bloc's defeat becomes clear when compared to the scope of Democratic Russia's victory. Democratic Russia candidates won 56 seats in the RSFSR Supreme Soviet and 288 in the Moscow City Soviet. The bloc's defeat in Moscow came hand in hand with its defeat in Leningrad, Russia's second biggest city. Here, the candidates of the democratic alliance won 25 of 34 seats in the RSFSR Congress of People's Deputies and 227 of 400 seats in the Leningrad City Soviet. In contrast, the local Russian nationalist-orthodox communist electoral alliance, Rossiya, won no seats in Congress of People's Deputies and only approximately 13 seats in the Leningrad City Soviet, despite strong support of the local party organization. Finally, Russian nationalist alliances in other major Russian cities failed to get their candidates elected to the RSFSR Supreme Soviet or to gain a substantial number of seats in the city and regional legislatures.[49]

Reaction to the Election Results

Members of the Patriotic Bloc were shocked by the outcome of the elections and refused to believe that the defeat was a consequence of a faulty strategy or their ideological message. In the March 16 issue of *Moskovsky literator,* its chief editor, Nikolai Doroshenko, defeated in his bid for a seat in the RSFSR Congress of People's Deputies, asserted that Democratic Russia's victory was the result of a conspiracy orchestrated by supporters of perestroika in the party apparat who had given the democrats control of the print and electronic media and allowed gross violations of the election laws. In its March 16, 23, and 30 and April 20 issues, *Literaturnaya Rossiya* printed a column entitled "Grimaces of Democracy" *(Grimasy demokratii),* which consisted of letters written by bloc candidates and activists recounting gross campaign violations by Democratic Russia and demands for the annulment of the election results.[50]

The first opportunity to discuss the outcome of the elections publicly was at the plenary meeting of the Governing Board of the RSFSR Writers' Union, which took place on March 19 and 20. This discussion revealed that the defeat had created a split within the Russian nationalist alliance. The majority of the speakers effectively shared Doroshenko's view and blamed the bloc's defeat on perestroika's supporters in the Soviet leadership, democratic control of the mass media, and gross violations of the campaign laws. This view was most clearly articulated by Anatoly Salutsky and Vera Bryusova, Patriotic Bloc candidates to the RSFSR Supreme Soviet who were defeated by Democratic Russia candidates.

One of the most important implications of Salutsky's and Bryusova's argument was the need to continue unqualified support of conservative forces within the political establishment. This reasoning, however, was boldly challenged by Vladimir Bondarenko, who was also defeated by a Democratic Russia candidate. He blamed the electoral defeat not on the democrats' manipulation of the media and the electoral system, but on the strategy chosen by the Russian nationalist alliance. Bondarenko declared that the bloc's candidates were resoundingly defeated because of the Patriotic Bloc's decision to support the party apparat. That the leaders of the Russian nationalist intelligentsia, he asserted, had sincerely thought that the party apparat would further the Russian nationalist cause demonstrated how out of touch with reality they were. In reality, support from the party apparat had tainted the alliance and resulted in the loss of popular support. Moreover, the apparat did not deserve Russian nationalist support because it had betrayed the movement at every opportunity. The continuation of the alliance with the party apparat, Bondarenko concluded, would completely destroy the Russian nationalist alliance as a significant political force.[51]

Bondarenko's proposal to divorce the bloc from the conservative forces within the political establishment remained a minority view, however, held by only a few of the participants at the plenary meeting. In fact, Russian nationalist politics in the aftermath of the elections aimed at strengthening the linkage with the antireformist forces within the Soviet political establishment, in general, and the CPSU, in particular. In pursuing these policies, Russian nationalist intellectuals in effect admitted their failure to emerge as a major independent political player. Instead, they began exclusively pinning their hopes on the ability of the conservative elements within the Soviet political elite to put an end to the democratization process and preserve the empire. Russian nationalist efforts between spring 1990 and summer 1991 were almost exclusively directed at convincing the conservatives within the political elite to take decisive action against Gorbachev and Yeltsin.[52]

This goal was clearly evident in a major campaign initiated by Russian nationalist intellectuals to convince the CPSU to put an end to the policies of glasnost. This campaign began with the publication in *Literaturnaya Rossiya* and *Moskovsky literator* of an open letter signed by seventy-four prominent Russian nationalist intellectuals, including Bondarev, Kozhinov, Prokhanov, Rasputin, and Shafarevich, and entitled "Letter of the Russian Writers" *(Pismo pisatelei Rossii).*[53]

The "Letter of Seventy-four," as the document came to be known, was addressed not to the Russian people but to the Supreme Soviets of the USSR and the RSFSR and to the Central Committee of the CPSU—the conservative members of these institutions—and constituted a Russian nationalist call for action against Gorbachev. The "Letter" forcefully reiterated the Russian nationalist indictment of perestroika as a set of policies that had led to the loss of Eastern Europe and the reunification of Germany and had undermined the military might of the Soviet Union. The passages that were deleted from the *Literaturnaya Rossiya* version of the "Letter," but were published in a later rendition openly called for the defense of Russia "from the absolute power of political adventurers [Gorbachev] who are rushing to turn Russia into a [Western] colony and a kingdom of the newest totalitarianism, flooded with our blood."[54]

Most of the "Letter" was unprecedented in its virulent attack on Jews, party reformers, and perestroika supporters within the press and electronic media. They were accused of having organized a campaign of moral terror against the Russian people. The "Letter" "exposed" Aleksandr Yakovlev as the architect of this anti-Russian campaign.[55] Finally, it demanded that the Soviet leadership "put an end to the anti-Russian ideological campaign in the press, radio and television . . . ; ban immediately all forms of Russia-hating on the territory of Russia and other Soviet Socialist republics . . . ; [and] carry out a just redistribution in favor of Russia of the printed means of mass information."

The "Letter" claimed that a redistribution of the press was necessary in order to correct a situation in which Russia-hating liberal-reformers controlled newspapers and journals with a total circulation of 60 million copies, while the press of the patriotic forces had a total circulation of only 1.5 million copies.

The March 1990 meeting of the RSFSR Writers' Union Governing Board adopted a resolution expressing its support for the contents of the "Letter" and called on the Russian republic newspapers and journals to reprint it. This resolution was the signal for the start of an aggressive public campaign to pressure Gorbachev to retreat from glasnost by removing Yakovlev from his post and handing over to the Russian nationalists control of several large-circulation newspapers and journals. This campaign was largely carried out on the pages of Russian nationalist publications. *Nash sovremennik, Molodaya gvardiya, Moskva,* and several provincial literary journals reprinted the "Letter," making it the only document in the Gorbachev era to appear in all of these journals. Moreover, between March and June 1990, every issue of *Literaturnaya Rossiya* contained a column, entitled "In Support of the 'Letter of the Russian Writers'" (*V podderzhku 'Pisma pisatelei Rossii'*), in which individuals, Russian nationalist organizations, the United Workers' Front, and branches of the Russian Republic Writers' Union from all parts of the RSFSR declared their support for the content of the "Letter."[56]

The campaign inspired by the letter fell short of its goals. The glasnost policies were not reversed, and the mass media continued, with increased aggressiveness, to promote the reforms. Russian nationalists had high hopes that the conservative party apparat in the provinces would support their campaign by reprinting the "Letter" in regional newspapers, however, the majority of the regional party secretaries were still hesitant to challenge Gorbachev openly. As a result, only the party newspapers in the towns of Kaluga and Smolensk reprinted the "Letter."[57]

Moreover, Gorbachev successfully deprived the Russian nationalist drive of its two most eloquent spokesmen. On March 24, he appointed Rasputin and the United Workers' Front leader Yarin to serve on the newly created Presidential Council, together with Yakovlev, the "Letter's" main target of criticism. The Presidential Council never became a fully functioning institution with real power and was abolished within a year, but during its existence, it effectively silenced Rasputin and Yarin and removed them from active politics. Without effective leadership and the support of provincial Russian party organizations, *Literaturnaya Rossiya* called off the campaign in mid-June 1990.

Russian Nationalists and the Congress of People's Deputies of the RSFSR

The second goal of the Russian nationalists in the aftermath of the spring 1990 elections was to support antireform forces within the Soviet political establishment in their struggle against Gorbachev. Indeed, the defeat of the Russian nationalist alliance in the spring 1990 elections only strengthened the determination of the majority of its members to help party conservatives put an end to perestroika. In the spring of 1990, two major battles faced the party conservatives: one with the Yeltsin-led liberal-reformist forces for control over the Russian government in the forthcoming Congress of People's Deputies of RSFSR and the other with Gorbachev and party reformers over the question of the formation of the Russian Communist Party (RCP).

Deep disdain for democratic politics, the crushing electoral defeat, and a belief that real power still lay with the central government and the CPSU were the primary reasons that the Russian nationalists virtually ignored any preparations for the convocation of the RSFSR Congress of People's Deputies. This also explains why they did not stage a frontal assault on Yeltsin in order to discredit him as a candidate for the position of chairman of the RSFSR Supreme Soviet. Before the Congress convened, only one attack on Yeltsin appeared in Russian nationalist publications.[58]

The Russian nationalist response to events in the Congress of People's Deputies of the RSFSR was highly predictable. A *Literaturnaya Rossiya* correspondent at the Congress, encouraged by Yeltsin's temporary inability to master the majority needed to secure election to the position of chairman of the RSFSR Supreme Soviet, entitled his report, *There Is Still Hope (Poka est nadezhda)*. Writing in *Moskovsky literator*, Mikhail Lobanov called on participants of the congress to resist the pressure exerted by Democratic Russia deputies to hand them power. Democratic Russia's victory at the Congress, he warned, would lead to the partition of Russia and its transformation into a colony of transnational corporations. Vasily Belov issued a similar warning in *Literaturnaya Rossiya*. Yeltsin and other leaders of Democratic Russia, he asserted, were "ready to sell everything for dollars, from Sakhalin Island to the last basket of cloudberries and cranberries."[59]

After Yeltsin was elected chairman of the RSFSR Supreme Soviet, Russian nationalists could not contain their deep disappointment. In an open letter to the deputies of the Russian parliament, the Secretariat of the RSFSR Writers' Union proclaimed that "Russia does not need . . . power-hungry leaders with scandalous reputations [Yeltsin], but leaders who are strong, wise, and reliable and who have a deep understanding of the tragedy of their own people."[60]

Russian Nationalists and the Formation of the Russian Communist Party

Russian nationalists showed relatively little interest in the fate of the Russian government, but their interest in developments within the CPSU was enormous. In fact, in the four months following the elections, most of their efforts focused on promoting the United Workers' Front initiative to create the Russian Communist Party as a conservative alternative to Gorbachev's CPSU and Yeltsin's Russian government. In fact, at least since 1987, Russian nationalist intellectuals had been openly calling for the creation of a Russian Communist Party that would embrace Russian nationalist ideas and causes.

The initiative to create an antireform Russian Communist Party as an ideological and institutional alternative to Gorbachev's CPSU originated at the Second Congress of the United Workers' Front in January 1990. On February 7, leaders of the Leningrad United Workers' Front, with the active support of the Leningrad party organization, created a committee to organize the Russian Communist Party (RCP) on the basis of the United Workers' Front platform. This committee called on party organizations throughout the republic to send their delegates to an "Action Congress," to be held on April 21 and 22, in order to lay the organizational and ideological foundations for the RCP.

On March 20, *Leningradskaya pravda* published a draft of the RCP program, which proclaimed that creation of the party was the only way to prevent the CPSU's degeneration into a social democratic party and the restoration of capitalism.[61] Publication of the draft coincided with the March plenary meeting of the Governing Board of the RSFSR Writers' Union, where Russian nationalist intellectuals expressed their enthusiastic support for the initiative to form the RCP. The statement issued at the end of the plenum solemnly proclaimed that "the writers of Russia support the formation of an independent Russian Communist Party." Following the meeting, Russian nationalists began promoting the idea of creating the RCP as the institutional stronghold of opposition to Gorbachev's reform and expressed confidence that the new party would embrace their main ideas.[62]

Despite the fact that the Action Congress was merely a United Workers' Front–organized gathering, hardly reflective of the views prevailing among CPSU members, it was used by Ligachev and other conservatives in the political elite to increase pressure on Gorbachev to agree to the formation of the RCP at the June conference of the Russian Republic delegates to the Twenty-eighth Congress of the CPSU.[63]

Although the June conference did not adopt the program of the Action Congress, its results nevertheless fulfilled most of the expectations of members of the Russian nationalist alliance. The conference was completely dominated by the opponents of perestroika who voted to reconstitute the meeting as the constituent congress of the RCP. More important, Ivan Polozkov, the first secretary of the Krasnodar regional party organization and one of the leaders of the orthodox communist wing of the CPSU, was elected as the RCP's first secretary, effectively guarantee the anti-perestroika orientation of the RCP.

Nationalization of the Conservative Wing of the Political Elite

Shortly after his election as the RCP's first secretary, Polozkov granted an interview to Russian nationalist journalist Anatoly Salutsky. Polozkov presented himself as a politician who shared Russian nationalist views on many of the key issues on the political agenda. In particular, he proposed an alliance between the RCP and the Russian Orthodox Church, the party's "natural ally in the struggle to enforce morality and prevent interethnic conflict."[64] Polozkov's comment was the first time this view was voiced by a high-ranking communist official.

At first glance, the fact that an orthodox communist, Polozkov, was openly supportive of a major argument of the Russian nationalist intellectuals was puzzling in the light of the fact that their political influence was progressively fading. This was a consequence of both the the electoral failures of Russian nationalist candidates and the decline in the importance of intellectuals in Soviet politics in general. By mid-1990, political struggles in the Soviet and Russian parliaments had become the center of politics, progressively relegating intellectuals to political oblivion. Subsequently, the general public began losing its interest in intellectual politics, and this manifested itself in a sharp decline in the circulation of the thick journals of all political persuasions in 1991. Between 1990 and 1991, the combined circulation of *Nash sovremennik, Molodaya gvardiya,* and *Moskva* declined by 48 percent. Russian nationalists could console themselves only with the fact that the decline in the circulation of the pro-perestroika thick journals was even steeper.[65]

Polozkov's statement was a clear sign that the conservative forces within the Soviet political elite had finally concluded that the only way to retain power in the face of a growing anticommunist tide was to replace orthodox communist ideology with Russian nationalism and transform the Communist party in the process. This transformation had several major manifestations. The most serious attempt to revise official ideology into a nationalist creed was associated with the Experimental Creative Center, a think tank headed by Russian nationalist theater director and the Patriotic Bloc's candidate in the March 1990 Russian parliamentary election, Sergei Kurginyan. The center was established by the USSR Council of Ministers, and its activities were actively supported by the Moscow City party organization.[66]

The first major work by Kurginyan's center was a ninety-page book, entitled *Post-Perestroika (Postperestroika),* which appeared in late fall 1990. *Post-Perestroika* constituted a major effort to transform official communist ideology into a nationalist creed capable of providing a new justification for the rejection of market-oriented reforms and the preservation of the Soviet state. The book charged that the official Marxist-Leninist ideology was incapable of providing solutions to the country's current problems and must be discarded by the party. The new ideology had to be based on Russia's cultural and historical traditions. The party could easily accept these traditions as its own because they shared one fundamental principle with communist ideology: their collectivistic nature.

Moreover, because of their collectivistic nature, these traditions were incompatible with the individualistic traditions and institutions that provided the basis of the market economy that reformers were trying to impose on Russia. Thus, "to weave into our social fabric tens of thousands of social and economic institutions which insure the effectiveness of a contemporary market [economy] without destroying this [social] fabric is impossible." The market economy could be established in Russia only through the use of force by criminal elements in society, who would be the main beneficiaries of the economic reforms.

The authors of *Post-Perestroika* in fact claimed that organized crime was the force behind the rising nationalist movements in the non-Russian republics, though it hid behind nationalist slogans its true intention of seizing power and mercilessly exploiting the local population. By portraying the liberal-reformers in Russia and nationalist movements in the non-Russian republics as mere tools of criminal elements, Kurginyan and his colleagues attempted to discredit the anticommunist forces and justify their suppression in the future.[67]

The think tank's second major work was its draft proposal of a new platform for the CPSU. Published in the Moscow City party organization newspaper, *Moskovskaya pravda,* in late July 1991, the draft further developed some of the major themes of *Post-Perestroika*. It explicitly called for abandoning the class approach as the fundamental ideological principle of the party.

The world, according to this document, is divided not into antagonist classes but into individualist and collectivist civilizations. The most important social and economic institution of the individualist civilization is its highly developed market economy. In contrast, the collectivist civilization is traditionalist in nature, emphasizing spirituality and limiting the consumption of its members in order to achieve higher social goals.

Russians belong to a collectivist civilization. Bringing into Russia Western political, social, and economic institutions in effect constitutes an effort to impose on the nation the institutions and values of the individualistic civilization—a goal unattainable without major social and political upheavals, including the destruction of the Russian state itself. The CPSU should not allow itself to become the party that aids the development of Western political, social, and economic institutions on Russian soil. Instead, it should defend Russia's collectivistic civilization and its political, social, economic, and cultural institutions. Since the Orthodox Church was one of the main institutions of Russian civilization, the party must treat it as its "trusted ally" in its struggle to prevent the Westernization of Russia.[68]

Post-Perestroika and the draft proposal of the CPSU platform clearly showed the new direction in the ideological evolution of the conservative wing of the CPSU. Polozkov's proposed alliance between the party and the Orthodox Church was grounded in Kurginyan's group theorizing. The fact that a copy of *Post-Perestroika* was found on the desk of the KGB chief and one of the main organizers of the August coup, Vladimir Kryuchkov, suggests that if the coup had succeeded, Kurginyan's ideas could have become the basis of a new state ideology.[69]

While Kurginyan was developing the ideological justification for the transformation of the CPSU into a party with a Russian nationalist orientation, two prominent leaders of the conservative wing of the party were creating the organizational framework for just such a transformation. One effort is associated with Lieutenant-General Boris Tarasov, a chief political officer of the Volga-Urals military district and a deputy in the RSFSR Congress of People's Deputies. In December 1990, Tarasov organized the Fatherland (*Otchizna*) faction in the Russian parliament and became its leader. The 139-member faction included Polozkov, as well as eleven first and second regional party secretaries; thirteen chairmen and deputy chairmen of regional governments (Ispolkoms); five senior KGB officials, including first deputy chairman of the agency Geny Ageev; twenty-one generals and admirals, including deputy ministers of defense Colonel-General Vladislav Achalov and General of the Army Viktor Ermakov; nineteen managers of major industrial enterprises; and fourteen heads of collective and state farms.[70] In short, the Fatherland faction was representative of the traditional Soviet political elite.

Tarasov's goal was to transform the parliamentary faction into a full-fledged political movement with a Russian nationalist orientation. In June 1991, the Fatherland faction organized a conference that laid the organizational and ideological foundations of the All-Russian Patriotic Movement, the "Fatherland" (*Vserossiiskoe patrioticheskoe dvizhenie "Otchizna"*). Communist rhetoric was completely absent from Fatherland's programmatic documents. Instead, these documents bear a close resemblance to a variety of Russian nationalist programs articulated since 1988. Thus, Fatherland declared its main goals to be the preservation of the USSR; the waging of a relentless struggle against nationalist movements in the non-Russian republics and the protection of the rights and freedoms of ethnic Russians in these republics; the strengthening of the military and the military-industrial complex; an increase in the prestige of the armed forces in Russian society, in general, and among the youth, in particular; the protection of Russian culture from the invasion of Western mass culture, which cultivates "moral degradation, pornography, and violence"; and the strengthening of the family and a declation of war on alcoholism.[71]

Tarasov's plans to transfom Fatherland into a mass political movement failed. By the time of the August 1991 coup, in which some of Fatherland's members took an active part, only the Moscow branch of the movement had been set up. The failure of the coup led to a purge of the leading members of Fatherland from their high state posts and the collapse of the movement.

The most important effort to transform the Communist party into a nationalist movement was associated with a Politburo member and secretary for ideology of the RCP, Gennady Zyuganov. Coming out of the propaganda Department of the CPSU's Central Committee, the institution that implemented inclusionary politics and cultivated ties with Russian nationalist intellectuals for decades, Zyuganov was a firm believer that Russian communists could retain power only if they adopted a Russian nationalist ideology. He was inspired by the events in Serbia, where the ruling party became the only Communist party in Eastern Europe to stay in power by adopting an unabashedly nationalist platform.

In December 1990, Zyuganov attended the Seventh Congress of the RSFSR Writers' Union, where for the first time he openly provided a rationale for the ideological transformation of the RCP. The country, he declared, needed a new political ideology as well as a new institutional framework with a nationalist orientation that could unify all the opponents of reform.[72]

Zyuganov envisioned the RCP to be the organizational basis of this new political movement imbued with nationalist ideology. In February 1991, he organized a large conference, appropriately entitled "For a Great, United Russia!" (*Za velikuyu, edinuyu Rossiyu*), in which, in addition to the RCP, twenty-six Russian nationalist organizations took part. To make the conference authoritative, Polozkov was invited to give the keynote address.[73]

The meeting's main accomplishment was the creation of the Coordinating Council of the National-Patriotic Movements of Russia (*Koordinatsionny sovet narodno-patrioticheskikh dvizhenii Rossii*), an umbrella organization of the institutional participants in the conference, with radical

Russian nationalist intellectual Eduard Volodin as its chair. The council's chief role was to prepare the ideological and organizational transformation of the RCP from a Soviet-era bureaucratic structure to an active political movement guided by Russian nationalist ideology.[74]

In early May 1991, Volodin published a programmatic essay in which he openly asserted that adopting a nationalist ideology was "the last hope of the Communist party to remain a force which shapes public life." He went on to propose developing a political action program, guided by Russian nationalist ideology for the emerging mass political movement. The key element of this program was removal of Gorbachev and Yeltsin from power.[75]

On July 23, 1991, the ideological manifesto of this movement, entitled "Word to the People" (Slovo k narodu), was published in Sovetskaya Rossiya. This document, of which Zyuganov and Prokhanov were initiators, was probably the harshest public condemnation of Gorbachev's reforms issued jointly by prominent Russian nationalist intellectuals and high-ranking members of the Soviet political establishment, as well as a call for Russians from all walks of life to unify into a patriotic movement to preserve the empire.[76] On August 16, three days before the abortive coup attempt, Sovetskaya Rossiya printed a follow-up to the manifesto that reiterated its main points and announced the creation of a political movement aimed at realizing the political goals stated in the manifesto. It is not difficult to imagine that the new movement would have been a revamped RCP with a new name and a new, more attractive ideology. As Volodin revealed in an article in Sovetskaya Rossiya, they planned to launch this new movement in the fall of 1991.[77] The coup, however, derailed their plans to create the movement and thus prevented a repeat of the Serbian model in Russia. The idea of a Communist party–based Russian nationalist movement would have to wait another five years, when it was realized in the Bloc of National-Patriotic Forces of Russia, the organizational backbone of Zyuganov's 1996 Russian presidential election bid.

The Zhirinovsky Alternative

Zhirinovsky provided a distinctly different alternative to the attempts by Russian nationalist intellectuals and the conservative members of the Soviet political elite to transform the RCP into a Russian nationalist movement. Neither a prominent Russian nationalist intellectual nor a member of the Soviet political elite, Zhirinovsky had a sense of the mood prevailing in Russian society at large. Although he shared the core radical nationalist commitment to a strong authoritarian and imperial state, he decided to cut the tie between Russian nationalism and the CPSU that had developed during the perestroika years. In his 1991 presidential bid, he declared his Liberal-Democratic Party of the USSR, a tiny organization at the time, to be anticommunist in its orientation. Moreover, he gladly accepted the principle of a market economy and electoral competition. To this set of ideas he added a populist appeal promising strong measures to restore law and order and to lower the prices of alcohol in state stores.[78]

This combination of nationalism and populism was an enormous success, even in 1991: Zhirinovsky received 6.2 million votes (7.8 percent of the vote), finishing third after Yeltsin and Nikolai Ryzhkov, the former prime minister of the USSR and the official candidate of the RCP. Moreover, he did very well in Siberia, the Far East, and the south of Russia, receiving in those regions between 10 and 13 percent of the vote. While Russian voters found Zhirinovsky's ideas relatively appealing, they decisively rejected the platform of the orthodox communists. General Albert Makashov and his vice-presidential running mate, one of the leaders of the United Workers' Front, Aleksei Sergeev, campaigned on an aggressive orthodox communist platform and received a mere 3.7 percent of the vote.

Zhirinovsky intended to use his electoral success to build a powerful nationalist party. He even expressed his readiness to cooperate with the movement that Zyuganov and Volodin were organizing, but the August coup interrupted these plans. Zhirinovsky would be able to resume building his party only on the eve of the 1993 Russia parliamentary election.

On August 23, 1991, two days after the collapse of the coup attempt, which virtually all Russian nationalists, including Zhirinovsky, explicitly or implicitly endorsed, Yeltsin suspended the activities of the CPSU and the RCP on the territory of the Russian Federation. On November 6, a day before the seventy-fourth anniversary of the October Revolution, Yeltsin issued a decree permanently banning both parties. On December 12, the Supreme Soviet of the Russian Republic voted 188 to 6 to ratify the Belovezh Forest Accords, which put an end to the existence of the USSR. At midnight on December 25, 1991, the Soviet flag was lowered from the flagpole of the Kremlin Palace, replaced by the white, blue, and red banner of Democratic Russia, now the official flag of the Russian Federation, symbolizing the end of the Soviet state.

Along with the CPSU and RCP, Russian nationalists were the main losers. They failed to achieve their main goal—to preserve the authoritarian empire. For the first time in years, the Russian political elite consisted almost exclusively of their sworn enemies. In the new postcommunist world, Russian nationalists were entirely on their own. How they adjusted to this new reality and how they were able to make a remarkable political comeback is the story for another book.

Epilogue: Russian Nationalism in Postcommunist Russia

On March 15, 1996, the State Duma, the lower house of the Russian parliament, abrogated the December 12, 1991, decision of its predecessor, the Supreme Soviet of the Russian Republic, to ratify the Belovezh Forest Accords by an overwhelming majority of 250 to 98. In a concurrent decision, it voted 252 to 33 to recognize as legally binding the results of the March 17, 1991, referendum in which 70 percent of Russian voters supported preservation of the USSR. These two votes constituted an unambiguous sign that in the five years since the dismantling of the USSR, the Russian political elite strongly supported the restoration of the lost empire.

In the June–July 1996 presidential election, the chairman of the reconstituted Communist Party of the Russian Federation (CPRF), Gennady Zyuganov, attempted to unseat Yeltsin. Zyuganov did not campaign as the leader of CPRF but as the candidate of the communist-nationalist alliance, the Bloc of National-Patriotic Forces of Russia *(Blok narodno-patrioticheskikh sil Rossii)*. Its platform elaborated in great detail the key ideas that Russian nationalists had been articulating for the past thirty years. It declared the peasantry to be the most important pillar of the Russian state and the embodiment of the spiritual and moral values of the Russian nation—even though the peasantry constitutes only 23 percent of Russia's population and is its most backward social group. The program contained familiar Russian nationalist rhetoric about the ongoing Western assault on the social, moral, and cultural traditions of the Russian nation and about Western attempts to impose its values of greed, violence, license, and selfishness on Russia. It accused Yeltsin of destroying the USSR and abandoning 25 million ethnic Russians in the former Soviet republics. The platform promised to restore the territorial integrity of the former Soviet state, regain its former superpower status, recreate a strong military, and abrogate international treaties that undermined Russian national interests.

Zyuganov failed to unseat Yeltsin, but he received 40.2 percent of the vote in the second round of the Russian presidential election, a clear indication of strong popular support. Zyuganov's success in the election was no accident but only the latest in a series of electoral successes of parties that, in one form or another, promoted Russian nationalist ideas articulated well before the collapse of the communist regime. In the December 1993 parliamentary election, communist and nationalist parties received 44 percent of the vote, and in the December 1995 parliamentary election, they increased their share to 53 percent.

Yeltsin's victory in the 1996 presidential election was not a decisive repudiation of Russian nationalist ideas. In fact, since 1992, Yeltsin's government has adopted some of the key Russian nationalist positions as its own. Since 1992, the so-called Kozyrev's doctrine had openly declared Russia's right to protect ethnic Russians in the former Soviet republics. In December 1994, Yeltsin ordered Russian troops to suppress the Chechen secession and received strong Russian nationalist support. In the postcommunist era, he often spoke about the reintegration of the former Soviet territory, and in 1996, this rhetoric became an integral part of his electoral campaign. Thus, on March 29, he signed an agreement with the presidents of Belarus, Kazakhstan, and Kirgyzstan to establish a customs union between these republics and the Russian Federation. Four days later, he signed a treaty with Belarus that committed Russia to political and economic integration with the former Soviet republic.

At the same time, the liberal-democratic parties, which had articulated a clear antinationalist vision, became increasingly unpopular at the polls. In the December 1993 parliamentary election, four liberal-democratic parties received a 34 percent of the vote; just two years later, eleven liberal parties received a scant 17 percent of the vote. Russia's Democratic Choice, the main liberal party and the heir to the Democratic Russia movement, which had received nearly 16 percent of the vote in 1993, was reduced to a mere 4 percent of the vote in 1995. In the 1996 presidential election, Grigory Yavlinsky, the sole liberal-democratic candidate on the ballot, received only 7 percent of the vote.

The Duma resolutions, the parliamentary and presidential election results, and Yeltsin's political decisions clearly reflected a political reality in which many key Russian nationalist ideas struck deep roots among Russian political elite and society in general, while liberal-democratic ideas, so popular at end of the Soviet period, became increasingly unpopular.

At the end of 1991, this trend could hardly have been predicted. The August 1991 coup had greatly discredited the Russian nationalist cause, and only six Russian Supreme Soviet deputies dared to vote against the Belavezh Forest Accords in December 1991—a clear reflection of the lack in popularity of Russian nationalist ideas.

The neoliberal economic reform that the Yeltsin government initiated in 1992 is commonly blamed for the rise in popularity of Russian nationalist ideas and the concurrent decline of support for liberal-reformist ideas, parties, and candidates. But I see the rise in popularity of Russian nationalist parties, candidates, and causes not simply as a consequence of elite and mass public disaffection with the neoliberal economic reforms. If this were the case, the liberal Yabloko party, whose leader, Gregory Yavlinsky, opposed "shock therapy" from the beginning, should have fared much better than a 7 percent share of the vote in the December 1995 parliamentary and June 1996 presidential elections.

Rather, the roots of the rise in popularity of Russian nationalist ideas, parties, and candidates lie much deeper, based in the inability of the liberal-democratic elite to develop an ideology of liberal nationalism that could legitimize the democratic form of government, a market economy, and the nonimperial borders of the Russian state.[1]

Schöpflin points out that in postcommunist societies, "civic institutions and the identities derived from them are too weak to fill the public sphere, with the result that ethnic nationhood is called upon to decide issues of power."[2] Adopting democratic conceptions of membership, identity, and boundaries of the nation is as crucial to democratic consolidation as the formation of a market economy and the creation of a multiparty system. In postcommunist societies, however, the nationalist movements that often control the debate on the issue of national identity and national boundaries do not necessarily advance a democratic notion of membership, identity, and boundaries of the nation. Moreover, as Kolankiewicz notes, liberal ideas that exclusively focus on the construction of capitalism have little mobilizational power in postcommunist societies because "it is difficult enough to mobilize society on the promise of greater inequality let alone admit that it will be inherently unjust and will consign one-third of its citizens to social redundancy."[3] The only way to do so is to ground the transition to a market economy in the liberal-nationalist concept of identity, which, indeed, was done in Eastern Europe and the Baltics. Adopting a democratic conception of membership, identity, and the boundaries of the nation is as crucial to democratic consolidation as is the formation of a market economy and the creation of a multiparty system.

This issue was the Achilles heel of the Russian liberal-democratic movement. It adopted a key philosophical underpinning of Western liberalism that viewed society as a collection of individuals pursuing their own economic interests. In actual politics, however, this philosophical base resulted in a failure of liberal democrats to realize the importance of issues related to nation building and viewed the overthrow of communism and the rapid creation of a market economy as the panacea for all of Russia's ills. Liberal-democrats worked feverishly to design blueprints for economic reform, while largely avoiding such issues as who is Russian or whether Russia should remain at the center of an empire, a multiethnic federation, or become a unitary state. Those few, like Andrei Sakharov and Galina Starovoitova, who did think and write on these issues, did not venture beyond the advocacy of radical decentralization and the sovereignization of the USSR and Russia.[4] Democratic Russia's opposition to Gorbachev during the March 1991 referendum on the preservation of the Union was both a reflection of Sakharov and Starovoitova's ideas and a desire to embarrass Gorbachev and the CPSU. Moreover, the crucial decision in the fall of 1991, by such prominent liberals as Egor Gaidar, to push for the dismantling of the USSR was not grounded in any well-thought-out conception of Russian nationhood, but was merely a consequence of their determination to carry out radical economic reforms with the least possible opposition from other Soviet republics.

Before the end of communism, Yeltsin was no different from other leaders of the anticommunist camp. He never developed a coherent position on the subject of the nature of Russian nationhood or statehood. His famous 1990 statement that the republics within Russia should grab as much sovereignty as they could swallow was not dictated by any clear view of the issues involved, but was a tactical maneuver in his power struggle with Gorbachev. The dismantling of the USSR in December 1991 was driven by an attempt to remove Gorbachev from the political arena rather than a desire to dismantle the empire and create a Russian nation-state.

As economic reform failed to live up to expectations, republics within Russia began either to secede, like Chechnya, or to threaten to secede, like Tatarstan, and 25 million ethnic Russians found themselves often discriminated against and disenfranchised in newly independent states. The liberal-democrats had no conceptual and ideological tools capable of addressing this development.

Russian nationalists and communists, who effectively adopted Russian nationalist ideas on these issues, were quick to fill the void with their own agenda. Contrary to the liberal-democrats, the nationalists, while paying little attention to the issue of economic reform, spent enormous time and effort discussing the issues of membership, national identity, and state boundaries—issues at the center of Russian nationalist politics during the Gorbachev era. After the collapse of communism, their ideas spread virtually unopposed, allowing them to set the terms of the debate. These ideas, however, were neither democratic nor liberal; they preached restoration of the Soviet state and defined the Russian nation in ethnic rather than civic terms, which led them to demand that the Russian state intervene to defend ethnic Russians in the former Soviet republics.[5]

As the economic reforms unraveled, their ideas began to penetrate into the consciousness of the political elite and general public alike. A stream of prominent liberal–democrats, including Yury Vlasov, Mikhail Astafiev (the man who gave Democratic Russia its name), Iliya Konstantinov, and Viktor Aksyuchits, disappointed by the course of economic reform, began moving toward the nationalist platform on the nationality issue and subsequently joined the nationalist opposition. The same process occurred with Rutskoi and Khasbulatov, who during their "democratic" phase played a crucial role in destroying the USSR and the CPSU.

In December 1991, Ruslan Khasbulatov played a crucial role in the Russian Supreme Soviet vote to ratify the Belovezh Forest Accords. And before the coup, he had been one of the harshest critics of Russian nationalism within Yeltsin's entourage. By spring and summer 1993, however, Khasbulatov had effectively adopted virtually all the main Russian nationalist ideas, which he had so harshly criticized only two years before. He no longer defended the institution of the soviets on the grounds of the separation of power theory. Instead, he argued that they were traditional Russian representative institutions with roots in the medieval town meetings (*veche*) and land assemblies (*Zemskie sobory*), and that now they served as defenders of Russia against attempts by the West to transform it "into a colonial enclave region which performs the role of a mere supplier of strategic raw materials for the world economy and a dumping ground for [its] obsolete technologies." Moreover, he began denouncing the Belovezh Forest Accords as an anticonstitutional plot that had destroyed Russia as a great power and made pronouncements calling for the reconstitution of the USSR.[6]

Many members of the liberal-democratic elite who did not switch sides formally, such as Sergei Stankevich, began incorporating key Russian nationalist ideas about the nation into their thinking.[7] In 1992 and 1993, Yeltsin did nothing to articulate a new democratic conception of the Russian nation. Although he kept using the civic definition of Russian ethnicity, his rhetoric about the defense of the rights of ethnic Russians in the former Soviet republics legitimized the use of the nondemocratic ethnic definition of the Russian nation.

With Yeltsin largely absent from the debate, an elite consensus emerged on the inevitability of the future restoration of the USSR, the need for the aggressive protection of ethnic Russians in the former Soviet republics, and a determination to support the Serbian side in the unfolding crisis in the Balkans. In 1991, these views had been the exclusive domain of the Russian nationalist opposition to Gorbachev.

This elite consensus began dominating both the print and electronic media and inevitably infiltrated into the consciousness of the general public (especially outside major metropolitan centers), which, by the end of 1991, by and large had accepted the inevitability of the dismantling of the USSR, expressed little concern for Russians in the "near-abroad," and cared little about the plight of their Serbian brethren. A December 1995 study by Hough, Davidheiser, and Lehmann revealed that only 31 percent of the population supported the notion of an independent Ukraine, while 53 percent believed that the two countries should be united. The same study also revealed that 90 percent of Russians believed that their government should defend the rights of ethnic Russians in the former Soviet republics. The most striking of their findings was the rise in imperial notions of identity among Russians: in 1993, only 29 percent identified Soviet Union as their motherland, while 50 percent chose Russia; in 1995, 39 percent identified the USSR as their motherland, while the same percentage chose Russia.[8]

Gaidar, Chubais, and other leaders of the liberal-democrats had no alternative set of ideas to counteract this creeping hegemony of the nationalist position on these issues.[9] They remained convinced that the rational mind of *homo economicus* would ultimately prevail as economic reforms took root. However, this only bolstered the impression that the liberal-democrats were politicians who did not care about Russia and its "true" national interests. The failure of economic reform to improve the standard of living of the majority of Russians left the liberal-democrats with no issue they could call their own.

Zhirinovsky's electoral success in 1993 and the communists' success in 1995, combined with liberal-democratic defeats in both elections, the war in Chechnya, and attempts at unification with Belarus, were but natural consequences of the simplistic liberal-democratic belief that successful economic reform was the one and only foundation stone for stable democracy in Russia.[10] Losing control of the discourse on the issue of the nation proved to be a key turning point in the erosion of support for liberal-democratic politics and a rise in popularity of Russian nationalist ideas, a reality the 1996 Russian presidential elections did not change. The Russian nationalist movement's ability to impose its profoundly nondemocratic views concerning the identity and boundaries of the nation-state on the political elite became a major obstacle in the process of the consolidation of democracy.

Notes

For the citation of archival references, TsKhSD: Tsentr khraneniya sovre-mennoi dokumentatsii (Central Repository of Contemporary Documenta-tion, formerly the Archive of the Central Committee of the Communist Party of the Soviet Union), I follow a slightly modified form of standard citation from this archive: f. (fund), op. (registry), d. (file), and p. (page).

1. Russian Nationalists in Soviet Politics

1. On the primordial and the instrumentalist schools of thought as the main interpretive approaches to nationalism, see Crawford Young, "The Temple of Ethnicity," *World Politics,* vol. 35, no. 4 (July 1983), pp. 652–662.
2. For various articulations of the primordial approach, see John A. Armstrong, *Nation before Nationalism* (Chapel Hill: University of North Carolina Press, 1982); Walker Connor, *Ethnonationalism* (Princeton, N.J.: Princeton University Press, 1994); Clifford Geertz, *The Interpretation of Cultures* (New York: Basic Books, 1973), ch. 10; Donald L. Horowitz, *Ethnic Groups in Conflict* (Berkeley: University of California Press, 1985); Anthony D. Smith, *The Ethnic Origins of Nations* (Oxford: Blackwell, 1986).
3. Zbigniew Brzezinski, "Post-Communist Nationalism," *Foreign Affairs,* vol. 68, no. 5 (Winter 1989/1990), pp. 1, 6. For a political culture approach that emphasizes precommunist rather than communist political culture as a key factor in the emergence of nationalism in Eastern Europe and the former Soviet Union, see Shlomo Avineri, "The End of the Soviet Union and Return to History," in *Trials of Transition,* ed. Michael Keren and Gur Ofer (Boulder, Colo.: Westview Press, 1992), pp. 11–17. For other examples of the primordial explanation of the rise of nationalism in the former USSR, see Helénè Carrère d'Encausse, *The End of the Soviet Empire* (New York: Basic Books, 1993); Ghia Nodia, "Nationalism and Democracy," *Journal of Democracy,* vol. 3, no. 4

(October 1992), pp. 3–22; John A. Armstrong, "The Autonomy of Ethnic Identity: Historical Cleavages and Nationality Relations in the USSR," in *Thinking Theoretically about Soviet Nationalities,* ed. Alexander J. Motyl (New York: Columbia University Press, 1992), pp. 23–43; Anthony D. Smith, "Ethnic Identity and Territorial Nationalism in Comparative Perspective," in *Thinking Theoretically,* pp. 45–65.

4. Jack Snyder, "Nationalism and the Crisis of the Post-Soviet State," in *Ethnic Conflict and International Security,* ed. Michael E. Brown (Princeton, N.J.: Princeton University Press, 1993), pp. 79–102.

5. Paul R. Brass, *Ethnicity and Nationalism* (New Delhi: Sage, 1991), p. 16. For additional examples of the instrumentalist interpretation of nationalism, see Benedict Anderson, *Imagined Communities,* rev. ed. (London: Verso, 1991); Eric Hobsbawm, *Nations and Nationalism since 1780,* 2d ed. (Cambridge: Cambridge University Press, 1990); David D. Laitin, *Hegemony and Culture* (Chicago: University of Chicago Press, 1986); Crawford Young, *The Politics of Cultural Pluralism* (Madison: University of Wisconsin Press, 1976).

6. For examples of the institutional explanation of the rise of nationalism in Eastern Europe and the former USSR, see Rogers Brubaker, *Nationalism Reframed* (Cambridge: Cambridge University Press, 1996), ch. 2; Ronald Grigor Suny, *The Revenge of the Past* (Stanford, Calif.: Stanford University Press, 1993), ch. 3–4; Philip G. Roeder, "Soviet Federalism and Ethnic Mobilization," *World Politics,* vol. 43, no. 2 (January 1991), pp. 196–232; Katherine Verdery, "Nationalism and National Sentiment in Post-Socialist Romania," *Slavic Review,* vol. 52, no. 2 (Summer 1993), pp. 179–203; Victor Zaslavsky, "Nationalism and Democratic Transition in Postcommunist Societies," *Daedalus,* vol. 121, no. 2 (Spring 1992), pp. 97–121; Robert J. Kaiser, *The Geography of Nationalism in Russia and the USSR* (Princeton, N.J.: Princeton University Press, 1994).

7. Ronald Rogowski, "Causes and Varieties of Nationalism: A Rationalist Account," in *New Nationalisms of the Developed West,* ed. Eduard A. Tiryakian and Ronald Rogowski (Boston: Allan & Unwin, 1985), p. 87. For additional examples of the rational choice explanation of nationalism, see: David D. Laitin, *Language Repertoires and State Construction in Africa* (New York: Cambridge University Press, 1992); Michael Hechter, "Nationalism and Group Solidarity," *Ethnic and Racial Studies* (October 1987), pp. 415–426; Hudson Meadwell, "Ethnic Nationalism and Collective Choice Theory," *Comparative Political Studies,* vol. 22 (1989), pp. 139–154.

8. For rational choice interpretations of the rise of the nationalist movements in the former USSR, see David D. Laitin, "The Four Nationality Games and Soviet Politics," *Journal of Soviet Nationalities,* vol. 2, no. 1 (Spring 1991), pp. 1–37; David D. Laitin, "The National Uprisings in the Soviet Union,"

World Politics, vol. 44 (October 1991), pp. 139–177; Alexander J. Motyl, *Sovietology, Rationality, Nationality* (New York: Columbia University Press, 1990), ch. 12; Charles Furtado, Jr., and Michael Hechter, "The Emergence of Nationalist Politics in the USSR: A Comparison of Estonia and the Ukraine," in *Thinking Theoretically*, ch. 7.

9. Hans Kohn, *The Idea of Nationalism* (New York: Macmillan, 1944); Liah Greenfeld, *Nationalism* (Cambridge, Mass.: Harvard University Press, 1992); Ernst B. Haas, *Nationalism, Liberalism, and Progress*, vol. 1 (Ithaca, N.Y.: Cornell University Press, 1997).

10. Ibid. p. 3.

11. Connor, *Ethnonationalism*, p. 91.

12. Max Weber, *Economy and Society*, vol. 1 (Berkeley: University of California Press, 1972), p. 389; Ernest Gellner, *Nations and Nationalism* (Ithaca, N.Y.: Cornell University Press, 1983); Karl W. Deutsch, *Nationalism and Social Communication*, 2d ed. (Cambridge, Mass.: MIT Press, 1966); Anderson, *Imagined Communities*.

13. The quote is from Young, *Politics of Cultural Pluralism*, p. 71. The emphasis on the legitimizing principle as the core of the nationalist ideology is part of Gellner's definition of nationalism. However, as my subsequent discussion shows, I disagree with Gellner's argument that nationalist ideology "requires that ethnic boundaries should not cut across the political ones." See Gellner, *Nations and Nationalism*, p. 1.

14. Smith, *Ethnic Origins*, pp. 134–38; Greenfeld, *Nationalism*, pp. 10–11. The same argument is advanced in Rogers Brubaker, *Citizenship and Nationhood in France and Germany* (Cambridge, Mass.: Harvard University Press, 1992).

15. For a similar definition of the components of the nationalist ideologies, see Milton J. Esman, *Ethnic Politics* (Ithaca, N.Y.: Cornell University Press, 1994), p. 34.

16. Haas, for example, divides nationalist ideologies into seven types; see Haas, *Nationalism*, pp. 44–53.

17. Rogers Brubaker, "East European, Soviet, and Post-Soviet Nationalism," in *Research on Democracy and Society*, vol. 1, ed. Frederick D. Weil, Jeffrey Huffman, and Mary Gautier (Greenwich, Conn.: JAI Press, 1993), pp. 353–378. This typology represents a simplified variation on the threefold typology first presented by John Breuilly in *Nationalism and the State*, 2d ed. (Manchester: Manchester University Press, 1993), p. 9.

18. As Connor points out, of 132 existing states (a 1972 count), only 12 fit the definition "one nation—one state." See *Ethnonationalism*, p. 29.

19. On "official nationalism," see Anderson, *Imagined Communities*, ch. 6; Hobsbawm, *Nations and Nationalism*, ch. 3.

20. Making claims on behalf of the nation as a key feature of nationalist move-

ments is pointed out by Edward A. Tyrakian and Neil Nevitte, "Nationalism and Modernity," in *New Nationalisms of the Developed West*, pp. 67–68.

21. Mark R. Beissinger, "The Persisting Ambiguity of the Empire," *Post-Soviet Affairs*, vol. 11, no. 2 (April–June 1995), p. 162; Edward Allworth, "Ambiguities in Russian Group Identity and the Leadership of the RSFSR," in *Ethnic Russia in the USSR*, ed. Edward Allworth (New York: Pergamon Press, 1980), pp. 17–38.

22. Because of this ambiguity-created perception by the Russians that the USSR is the Russian nation-state, the desire of Russian nationalist groups and parties to preserve its territorial integrity should not disqualify them (as Motyl does) from being classified as "nationalist" on the grounds that true "Russian nationalists must actually want or be willing to countenance the dismemberment of the multinational Soviet state." This statement also suggests that Motyl recognizes only the polity-seeking type of nationalism, while denying the nation-shaping type. See Motyl, *Sovietology, Rationality, Nationality,* p. 163.

23. Beissinger, "Persisting Ambiguity," p. 162. The same point is made in Anatoly Khazanov, *After the USSR* (Madison: The University of Wisconsin Press, 1995), p. 12. For a comprehensive treatment of the ideology and policies of the official nationalism of the Soviet state up to the mid-1950s, see Frederick C. Barghoorn, *Soviet Russian Nationalism* (New York: Oxford University Press, 1956).

24. As Brubaker points out, the concept "Soviet nation" was not meant to replace the ethnic definition of the nation, which was institutionalized as a major legal category and the basis of individual identity, but rather was conceived as a supranational identity to describe the common ideological bonds between ethnically defined nations living on the territory of the USSR. See Brubaker, *Nationalism Reframed*, p. 28.

25. Roman Szporluk, "Dilemmas of Russian Nationalism," *Problems of Communism*, vol. 38, no. 4 (July–August 1989), pp. 15–35.

26. For a different fourfold typology, see John B. Dunlop, *The Rise of Russia and the Fall of the Soviet Empire* (Princeton, N.J.: Princeton University Press, 1993), especially ch. 4.

27. The first seven issues were extremely important during the political debates of the pre-perestroika period, even though some, such as attitudes toward Western political, social, and cultural values and anti-Semitism, continued to play an important role throughout the perestroika period as well. The two remaining categories, as their names suggest, deal with the period between 1985 and 1991.

28. These labels refer to the nondissident Russian nationalist intellectuals who are the subject of this book. Russian nationalist dissent and its politics falls out-

side the purview of this work. For an excellent study of Russian nationalist dissidents and their ideas, see John B. Dunlop, *The Faces of Contemporary Russian Nationalism* (Princeton, N.J.: Princeton University Press, 1983).

29. Katherine Verdery, *National Ideology under Socialism* (Berkeley: University of California Press, 1991), p. 3.

30. James C. Scott, *Domination and the Art of Resistance* (New Haven, Conn.: Yale University Press, 1990).

31. Miroslav Hroch, *Social Preconditions of National Revival in Europe* (Cambridge: Cambridge University Press, 1985), pp. 22–24.

32. Verdery, *National Ideology,* p. 85.

33. Albert O. Hirschman, *Exit, Voice, and Loyalty* (Cambridge, Mass.: Harvard University Press, 1970).

34. Kenneth Jowitt, "Inclusion and Mobilization in European Leninist Regimes," *World Politics,* vol. 28, no. 1 (October 1975), pp. 71, 79, 86.

35. Anatoly M. Khazanov, "Ethnic Nationalism in the Russian Federation," *Daedelus,* vol. 126, no. 3 (Summer 1997), p. 130.

2. The Emergence of Politics by Culture, 1953–1964

1. Teresa Rakowska-Harmstone, "The Dialectics of Nationalism in the USSR," *Problems of Communism,* vol. 23, no. 3 (May–June 1974), p. 1.

2. Ibid., p. 9; see also Teresa Rakowska-Harmstone, "Minority Nationalism Today: An Overview," in *The Last Empire,* ed. Robert Conquest (Stanford, Calif.: Hoover Institution Press, 1986), pp. 240–241.

3. Bohdan Krawchenko, *Social Change and National Consciousness in Twentieth Century Ukraine* (London: Macmillan, 1985), pp. 171–258. Isajiw advances a similar "socioeconomic" explanation for the emergence of Ukrainian nationalism. See Wsevolod Isajiw, "Urban Migration and Social Change in Contemporary Soviet Ukraine," *Canadian Slavonic Papers* (March 1980), pp. 56–66.

4. Victor Zaslavsky, *The Neo-Stalinist State* (Armonk, N.Y.: M. E. Sharpe, 1982), p. 126.

5. Alexander Motyl, *Will the Non-Russians Rebel?* (Ithaca, N.Y.: Cornell University Press, 1987), pp. 53–70, 124–138. The primacy of political factors is also emphasized by Alekseeva; see Ludmilla Alekseeva, *Soviet Dissent* (Middletown, Conn.: Wesleyan University Press, 1987), p. 7.

6. Among the political factors contributing to the rise of ethnic nationalism in the USSR, Suny especially points to the failure of Khrushchev's reforms and Brezhnev's inability to carry out reforms. See Ronald Grigor Suny, *The Making of the Georgian Nation,* 2d ed. (Bloomington: Indiana University Press, 1994), p. 308.

7. Walter D. Connor, *Socialism's Dilemmas* (New York: Columbia University Press, 1988), p. 44.

8. John B. Dunlop, *The Faces of Contemporary Russian Nationalism* (Princeton, N.J.: Princeton University Press, 1983), pp. 175–176.

9. The analysis of politics in the Khrushchev era in this chapter is based on George W. Breslauer, *Khrushchev and Brezhnev as Leaders* (London: Allen & Unwin, 1982), chaps. 2–7; Stephen F. Cohen, *Rethinking the Soviet Experience* (New York: Oxford University Press, 1985), chaps. 4–5; Jerry F. Hough and Merle Fainsod, *How the Soviet Union Is Governed* (Cambridge, Mass.: Harvard University Press, 1979), chap. 6; Karl Linden, *Khrushchev and the Soviet Leadership, 1957–1964* (Baltimore, Md.: Johns Hopkins University Press, 1966); Martin McCauley, ed., *Khrushchev and Khrushchevism* (Bloomington: Indiana University Press, 1987).

10. The concept was introduced in 1959 in a theory textbook entitled *Fundamentals of Marxism-Leninism (Osnovy Marksizma-Leninizma)*. On the history of the writing of this textbook, see Fyodor Burlatsky, "Posle Stalina," *Novy mir,* no. 10 (1988), pp. 167–173. On the concept of the "all-people's state" and its fate under Brezhnev, see Ronald J. Hill, "The 'All-People's State' and 'Developed Socialism,'" in *The State in Socialist Society,* ed. Neil Harding (Albany: State University of New York Press, 1984), pp. 104–128.

11. For an approach that reduces articulate members of social elites to the status of mere spokesmen of rival factions in the leadership, see Sidney Ploss, *Conflict and Decision-Making in Soviet Russia* (Princeton, N.J.: Princeton University Press, 1965). Ploss, for example, presents Valentin Ovechkin, the writer who in a series of essays in the 1950s and early 1960s, preached for radical agrarian reform, merely as Khrushchev's "spokesman among the literati." See Ibid, p. 51.

12. Between 1955 and 1957 alone, twenty-seven thick journals were created or revived, among them such important publications as *Yunost, Moskva, Neva, Druzhba narodov* and *Molodaya gvardiya.* "Revival" in this context means that the journal started to appear every month. The regular monthly appearance brought the journal to the attention of the reading public and guaranteed contributions by important writers and critics. *Molodaya gvardiya* and *Nash sovremennik,* two of the most important Russian nationalist thick journals of the Brezhnev era, became monthlies under Khrushchev: *Molodaya gvardiya* in 1956 and *Nash sovremennik* in 1964.

13. On the politics of *Novy mir* between 1953 and 1970, see Dina R. Spechler, *Permitted Dissent in the USSR* (New York: Praeger, 1982).

14. My explanation of Khrushchev's reasons for tolerating the publication of both Stalinist and anti-Stalinist views is influenced in part by Spechler's analysis of

why Khrushchev allowed the journal *Novy mir* to become the independent voice of the anti-Stalinist intelligentsia. See Ibid., pp. 249–265.

15. Cohen, *Rethinking*, p. 133.

16. Breslauer, *Khrushchev*, p. 12.

17. On Khrushchev's role in the publication of *Ivan Denisovich* and his subsequent use of the work in his de-Stalinization campaign, see Michael Scammel, *Solzhenitsyn* (New York: Norton, 1984), pp. 410–449.

18. This, in my view, was a real possibility. After all, Kochetov was dismissed as chief editor of *Literaturnaya gazeta* by Khrushchev in 1959 for opposing de-Stalinization. Moreover, *Novy mir*'s editors implicitly accused Kochetov of supporting Khrushchev's rivals during the antiparty group crisis and organizing a new faction in order to oppose Khrushchev's policies of de-Stalinization. See Spechler, *Permitted Dissent*, pp. 93, 115, 156.

19. Robert C. Tucker, *Politics as Leadership* (Columbia: University of Missouri Press, 1981), p. 7.

20. Linden, *Khrushchev*, p. 144; Spechler, *Permitted Dissent*, p. 155.

21. Anthony D. Smith, *Nationalism in the Twentieth Century* (New York: New York University Press, 1979), p. 158.

22. Anthony D. Smith, *Theories of Nationalism*, 2d ed. (New York: Holmes & Meier, 1985), p. 136.

23. Karl Mannheim, *Essays in the Sociology of Knowledge* (London: Routlage & Kegan Paul, 1952), pp. 286–287.

24. On the concept of the generational unit, see ibid., pp. 304–307.

25. I adopt, with some modification, Hough and Bahry' generational scheme. See Jerry F. Hough, *Soviet Leadership in Transition* (Washington, D.C.: Brookings Institution, 1980), and Donna Bahry, "Politics, Generations and, Change in the USSR," in *Politics, Work, and Daily Life in the USSR*, ed. James R. Millar (New York: Cambridge University Press, 1987), p. 74.

26. See the following examples: prominent Russian nationalist writer Vladimir Soloukhin (b. 1924) became nationally known in 1957 after the publication of his travelogue, "Vladimir's Country Roads"; the writer Vasily Belov (b. 1932) became widely known in 1966 after the appearance of his novel, *An Ordinary Thing*; the writer Anatoly Ivanov (b. 1928), chief editor of the journal *Molodaya gvardiya* since 1972, became widely known after his first story, "Alka's Songs," was published in 1956 and adapted for theater, radio, and television; film director and writer Vasily Shukshin (1929–1974) became famous after the 1963 publication of his first book and after his film received the Golden Lion award at the Venice Film Festival in 1964; the painter Ilya Glazunov (b. 1930) became a well-known artist in the aftermath of his first personal exhibit (in itself a highly prestigious event) in Moscow in 1957.

27. Volkov became known in the mid-1960s as a result of his ecological essays, and Solzhenitsyn was recognized in the aftermath of the publication of *One Day in the Life of Ivan Denisovich* (1962). Troepolsky became a well-known writer after the publication of his *Notes of the Agronomist* (1953–1956), and Zalygin gained renown in the wake of the publication of his novel, *By the Irtysh* (1964). Before they became writers, Troepolsky worked as an agronomist, and Zalygin taught earth sciences in the Siberian city of Omsk.

28. The social profile of Russian nationalists as being largely well-educated members of the postwar generation confirms the findings of the Soviet Interview Project. After a quantitative analysis of the responses of ex-Soviet citizens (mostly of Jewish origin) who immigrated to United States in the 1970s, Donna Bahry and Brian Silver came to the conclusion that belonging to the postwar and post-Stalin generations (born between 1941 and 1960) and having obtaining a better education heavily contributed to a greater readiness to challenge established policies and practices. See Brian D. Silver, "Political Beliefs of the Soviet Citizen: Sources of Support for Regime Norms," in *Politics, Work, and Daily Life,* pp. 100–141.

29. Moshe Lewin, *The Gorbachev Phenomenon* (Berkeley: University of California Press, 1988), p. 34.

30. Michael Ryan and Richard Prentice, *Social Trends in the Soviet Union from 1950* (London: Macmillan, 1987), p. 20.

31. According to a sociological study, the size of the Soviet working class grew from 23.9 million in 1940 to 80.9 million in 1983. The study attributes this growth mainly to peasant migration. The same study claims that more than 80 percent of former peasants had joined the working class. See *Sovetsky gorod, sotsialnaya struktura* (Moscow: Mysl, 1988), pp. 175, 183.

32. Lewin, *Gorbachev,* p. 34.

33. According to a Soviet study, up to 20 percent of recorded violations of labor discipline were committed by recent migrants from the countryside. The same study claims that as late as 1982, 18 percent of recent migrants to the cities lived in dormitories (versus 6 percent of those born in the city). See *Sovetsky gorod,* pp. 185–186.

34. For a fictionalized description of the daily life of first-generation workers, see Vitaly Syomin, "Semero v odnom dome," *Novy mir,* no. 6 (1965), pp. 62–144.

35. Moshe Lewin, *The Making of the Soviet System* (New York: Pantheon Books, 1985), pp. 303–304.

36. These theories, known as the psychological theories of nationalism, argue that the rise of nationalist movements in Europe and the Third World was a response of newly urbanized members of society to the loss of identity, alienation and anomie they experienced as a result of rapid industrialization and urbanization. See Manfred Halperin, *The Politics of Social Change in the Mid-*

dle East and North Africa (Princeton, N.J.: Princeton University Press, 1963); Samuel P. Huntington, *Political Order in Changing Societies* (New Haven, Conn.: Yale University Press, 1968); William Kornhauser, *The Politics of Mass Society* (Glencoe, Ill.: Free Press, 1959).

37. On the publication of Western literature in the Khrushchev era, see Maurice Friedberg, *A Decade of Euphoria* (Bloomington: Indiana University Press, 1977).

38. Quoted in Artemy Troitsky, *Back in the USSR* (Boston: Faber and Faber, 1988), p. 18.

39. Zhores A. Medvedev, *Soviet Agriculture* (New York: Norton, 1987), pp. 162–165.

40. Hough and Fainsod, *How the Soviet Union Is Governed*, p. 225.

41. Khrushchev's fascination with corn was a consequence of his belief that it was a "miracle" crop that could both solve the problem of animal feed and enrich the rather limited diet of Soviet citizens.

42. Medvedev, *Soviet Agriculture*, pp. 194–196.

43. Vasily Belov, "Remeslo otchzhdeniya," *Novy mir*, no. 6 (1988), p. 164.

44. I. V. Rusinov, "Agrarnaya politika KPSS v 50-e—pervoi polovine 60-kh godov: opyt i uroki," *Voprosy istorii KPSS*, no. 9 (1988), p. 43.

45. Ibid., Medvedev claims that the number of state farms grew from 5,099 in 1956 to 10,078 in 1964. See Medvedev, *Soviet Agriculture*, pp. 200, 319.

46. Alastair McAuley, *Economic Welfare in the Soviet Union* (Madison: University of Wisconsin Press, 1979), pp. 30–31.

47. Connor, *Socialism's Dilemmas*, p. 87.

48. Demitri B. Shimkin, "Current Characteristics and Problems of the Soviet Rural Population," in *Soviet Agricultural and Peasant Affairs*, ed. Roy D. Laird (Lawrence: University of Kansas Press, 1963), p. 89.

49. In 1952 and 1953, a group of thirty-seven leading Soviet physicians and members of their families were arrested on trumped-up charges of trying to kill Andrei Zhdanov and Aleksandr Shcherbakov, leading Soviet officials who died of natural causes in the late 1940s, as well as attempting to assassinate members of the Soviet high command. Most of the doctors were Jewish and their arrest was accompanied by an outburst of virulent anti-Semitic campaigning. The affair, known as the "doctors' plot," ended shortly after Stalin's death with the release and complete exoneration of the accused physicians. On the affair, see Gennady V. Kostyrchenko, *V plenu u krasnogo faraona* (Moscow: Mezhdunarodnye otnosheniya, 1994), chap. 6.

50. The denunciation of the Stalinist cult of Ivan the Terrible took place at a meeting of Soviet historians in May 1956. On this meeting, see M. D. Kurmacheva, "Ob otsenke deyatelnosti Ivana Groznogo," *Voprosy istorii*, no. 9 (1965), pp. 195–203.

51. *KPSS v rezolyutsiyakh i resheniyakh siezdov, konferentsiy i plenumov Ts.K.* (Moscow: Politizdat, 1972), 8:206.
52. Ibid., pp. 282–283.
53. Ibid., pp. 206, 212, 284–285.
54. On Khrushchev's antireligious campaign, see Dimitry V. Pospielovsky, *Soviet Anti-Religious Campaigns and Persecutions* (New York: St. Martin Press, 1988), pp. 121–144.
55. Timothy J. Colton, *Moscow* (Cambridge, Mass.: Harvard University Press, 1995), p. 554; Jane Ellis, *The Russian Orthodox Church* (Bloomington: Indiana University Press, 1986), pp. 14, 125.
56. Donald A. Lowrie and William C. Fletcher, "Khrushchev's Religious Policy," in *Aspects of Religion in the Soviet Union, 1917–1967,* ed. Richard H. Marshall, Jr. (Chicago: University of Chicago Press, 1971), pp. 143–144.
57. Ellis, *Russian Orthodox,* pp. 195–198.
58. Ibid., p. 184.
59. The only surviving building on Kalinin (now New Arbat) Avenue is the seventeenth-century Church of Simeon Stolpnik. In 1967, architect L. Antropov laid down in the bucket of a bulldozer to prevent the razing of the church. In the same year, the Politburo decided to preserve the building. The juxtaposition of a small ancient church standing next to a modern high-rise became a symbol of the senseless destruction of historic Moscow. On the affair, see Colton, *Moscow,* pp. 557–558.
60. Dunlop, *Faces,* p. 31; on the Khrushchev era efforts to prevent destruction of historic buildings, see Colton, *Moscow,* p. 554.
61. Vladimir Soloukhin embarked on a hiking trip in his native Vladimir province in 1956, while Aleksandr Solzhenitsyn started taking bicycle tours around Ryazan in 1958. Both writers played a major role in the birth of the Russian nationalist movement.
62. On the construction of the industrial plant by Lake Baikal as a major factor in the emergence of a Russian ecological movement, see Thane Gustafson, *Reform in Soviet Politics: Lessons of Recent Policies on Land and Water* (New York: Cambridge University Press, 1981), pp. 40–46; Marshall I. Goldman, *The Spoils of Progress: Environmental Pollution in the Soviet Union* (Cambridge, Mass.: MIT Press, 1972), pp. 183–185.
63. Gustafson, *Reform,* pp. 51–52.
64. Valentin Ovechkin, "Raionnye budni," *Novy mir,* no. 9 (1952), pp. 204–221.
65. Spechler, *Permitted Dissent,* p. 5.
66. On the village prose of the Khrushchev era, see also Deming Brown, *Soviet Russian Literature since Stalin* (Cambridge: Cambridge University Press, 1978), pp. 223–237.

67. Valentin Ovechkin, "V tom zhe raione," *Novy mir*, no. 3 (1954), pp. 8–49; Valentin Ovechkin, "Trudnaya vesna," *Novy mir*, nos. 3, 5, 9 (1956). On Ovechkin, see also Patricia Carden, "Reassessing Ovechkin," in *Russian and Slavic Literature*, ed. Richard Freeborn, R. R. Milner-Gulland, and Charles A. Ward (Columbus, Oh.: Slavica Publishers, 1976), pp. 407–424.

68. Gavriil Troepolsky, *Zapiski agronoma* (Moscow: Sovetsky pisatel, 1961). The first story in the "Notes of an Agronomist" series was published in *Novy mir* in August 1953.

69. Vladimir Tendryakov, "Padenie Ivana Chuprova," *Novy mir*, no. 11 (1953), pp. 104–134.

70. Efim Dorosh, "Derevensky dnevnik," in *Literaturnaya Moskva. Sbornik vtoroi* (Moscow: Khudozhestvennaya literatura, 1956), pp. 546–626.

71. Efim Dorosh, *Dozhd popolam s solntsem* (Moscow: Sovetsky pisatel, 1973), pp. 37–38, 97–98. On "A Village Diary," see also Gleb Zekulin, "Efim Dorosh," in *Russian and Slavic Literature*, pp. 425–448.

72. Aleksandr Yashin, "Rychagi," *Literaturnaya Moskva*, pp. 502–513. On the tremendous impact the story had on the Russian intelligentsia, see Grigory Svirsky, *Na lobnom meste* (London: Overseas Publications Interchange, 1979), pp. 144–152, 159–161. For Khrushchev's condemnation of "Levers," see Nikita Khrushchev, "Za tesnuyu svyaz literatury i iskusstva s zhizniyu naroda," *Novy mir*, no. 9 (1957), p. 16.

73. Yashin, "Rychagi," p. 504.

74. Fyodor Abramov, "Lyudi kolkhoznoi derevni v poslevoennoi proze," *Novy mir*, no. 4 (1954), pp. 210–231.

75. Fyodor Abramov, *Chem zhivem—kormimsya* (Leningrad: Sovetsky pisatel, 1986), pp. 45–91.

76. Ibid., pp. 78–80.

77. Igor Zolotussky, "Inache on ne mog," *Literaturnoe obozrenie*, no. 3 (1986), p. 24.

78. On the Soviet historical debate about Stalinism in the aftermath of the Twenty-second Party Congress, see Nancy Whittier Heer, *Politics and History in the Soviet Union* (Cambridge, Mass.: MIT Press, 1971), pp. 117–129, 135–173. On the treatment of Stalin in fiction, literary criticism, and memoirs, see Spechler, *Permitted Dissent*, pp. 137–160.

79. Sergei Zalygin, "Na Irtyshe," *Novy mir*, no. 2 (1964), pp. 3–80.

80. Aleksandr Yashin, "Vologodskaya svadba," *Novy mir*, no. 12 (1962), pp. 3–26. The work was harshly criticized in the Soviet press. See *Komsomolskaya pravda*, March 22, 1963.

81. Aleksandr Solzhenitsyn, "Matryonin dvor," *Novy mir*, no. 1 (1963), pp. 42–63. The Stalinist literary critic Sergovantsev accused both Solzhenitsyn and

Yashin of idealizing the patriarchal Russian peasantry and denying the achievements of collectivized agriculture. See Nikolai Sergovantsev, "Tragediya odinochestva i 'sploshnoi byt,'" *Oktyabr,* no. 4 (1963), pp. 201–207.

82. Viktor Likhonosov, "Bryanskie," *Novy mir,* no. 11 (1963), pp. 142–145.

83. On Rubtsov, see Richard Freeborn, "Nikolay Rubtsov: His Life and Lyricism," *Slavonic and East European Review,* vol. 65, no. 3 (July 1987), pp. 350–370.

84. Nikolai Rubtsov, "Ya budy skakat po kholmam zadremavshei Otchizny," "Zvezda polei," "Vzbegu na kholm i upadu v travu," *Oktyabr,* no. 8 (1964), pp. 130–132.

85. All these stories were reprinted in Vasily Shukshin, *Sobranie sochineny* (Moscow: Molodaya gvardiya, 1985), 2:6–18, 30–37, 90–108. Vsevolod Kochetov himself highly praised these early stories by Shukshin. See *Komsomolskaya pravda,* November 16, 1962.

86. Shukshin, *Sobranie,* pp. 98–108.

87. Between February 1963 and July 1970, *Novy mir* published twenty-two short stories by Shukshin. See Shukshin, *Sobranie,* pp. 108–152, 168–178, 233–245, 257–275, 285–306, 315–351, 360–379, 431–446, 455–480. For *Oktyabr*'s attack on Shukshin, see Larisa Kryachko, "Boi za dobrotu," *Oktyabr,* no. 3 (1965), pp. 174–184.

88. Vladimir Soloukhin, "Vladimirskie prosyolki," *Novy mir,* no. 9 (1957), pp. 82–141; no. 10 (1957), pp. 75–134.

89. Vladimir Chivilikhin, "Svetloe oko Sibiri," *Oktyabr,* no. 4 (1963), pp. 151–172.

3. The First Phase of Inclusionary Politics, 1965–1970

1. Alexander Yanov, *The Russian New Right* (Berkeley, Calif.: Institute for International Studies, 1978); Alexander Yanov, *The Russian Challenge and the Year 2000* (Oxford: Basil Blackwell, 1987).

2. John B. Dunlop, *The Faces of Contemporary Russian Nationalism* (Princeton, N.J.: Princeton University Press, 1983), p. 60.

3. Mikhail Gorbachev, *Memoirs* (London: Bantam Books, 1997), p. 173. On agriculture as the major policy concern of Brezhnev in the years 1965–1970, see George W. Breslauer, *Khrushchev and Brezhnev as Leaders* (Boston: Allen & Unwin, 1982), pp. 140–152, 187–191; Thane Gustafson, *Reform in Soviet Politics* (New York: Cambridge University Press, 1981), pp. 25–29.

4. *KPSS v rezolyutsiyakh i resheniyakh siezdov, konferentsyi i plenumov Ts.K.* (Moscow: Politizdat, 1972), 8:502–504, 508–510; Vladimir Treml, "Subsidies in Soviet Agriculture: Records and Prospects," in *Soviet Economy in the 1980's,* pt. 2 (Washington, D.C.: U.S. Government Printing Office, 1983),

p. 171; Linda J. Cook, *The Soviet Social Contract and Why It Failed* (Cambridge, Mass.: Harvard University Press, 1993), p. 59.

5. Zhores A. Medvedev, *Soviet Agriculture* (New York: Norton, 1987), p. 361.

6. Alastair McAuley, *Economic Welfare in the Soviet Union* (Madison: University of Wisconsin Press, 1979), pp. 31, 128, 271.

7. Breslauer, *Khrushchev and Brezhnev,* pp. 150–152; Gustafson, *Reform,* pp. 25–27.

8. Samuel P. Huntington, "Social and Institutional Dynamics of One-Party Systems," in *Authoritarian Politics in Modern Society,* ed. Samuel P. Huntington and Clement H. Moore (New York: Basic Books, 1970), pp. 26–27.

9. Thomas F. Remington, *The Truth of Authority* (Pittsburgh: University of Pittsburgh Press, 1988), p. 25.

10. Huntington, "Social and Institutional Dynamics," pp. 26–27.

11. On these efforts to rehabilitate Stalinism, see Stephen F. Cohen, *Rethinking the Soviet Experience* (New York: Oxford University Press, 1985), pp. 117–121; Roy A. Medvedev, *On Stalin and Stalinism* (Oxford: Oxford University Press, 1979), pp. 177–181; Dina R. Spechler, *Permitted Dissent in the USSR* (New York: Praeger, 1982), pp. 213–218; Michel Tatu, *Power in the Kremlin* (New York: Viking Press, 1968), pp. 474–493.

12. *Vernye podvigu ottsov. Materialy VIII plenuma Ts.K. VLKSM* (Moscow: Molodaya gvardiya, 1966), pp. 18–19, 42–43, 54–56, 74, 102, 107–108, 127–131, 182–184.

13. Ibid., pp. 190, 194–195, 200–204. Similar, although slightly toned down views were expressed at the Fifteenth Congress of the Komsomol in May 1966. See *XV Siezd Vsesoyuznogo Leninskogo Kommunisticheskogo Soyuza Molodezhi. Stenograficheskly otchet* (Moscow: Molodaya gvardiya, 1966), esp. pp. 90, 350–354, 565–570.

14. *Politichesky dnevnik* (Amsterdam: Fond imeni Gertsena, 1972), 1:123–124.

15. The Cultural Department of the Central Committee was created in September 1955 as a result of a split of the Science and Culture Department. In December 1962, the Cultural Department was abolished as a part of the late Khrushchev-era reorganization of the party apparat. In May 1965, the Cultural Department was reestablished and continued to exist until the collapse of the CPSU in 1991. The Cultural Department had four main sections—literature, art, theater, and cinematography—which made it a powerful player in shaping the direction of Soviet cultural life.

16. The Propaganda Department had sections that supervised literature, publishing houses, newspapers and journals, radio, and television, as well as a section that supervised various cultural institutions and mass media within the union republics, including the RSFSR. All these sections allowed the Propaganda

Department to exercise effective control over Soviet cultural life. For the structure of the Propaganda Department, see Jerry F. Hough and Merle Fainsod, *How the Soviet Union Is Governed* (Cambridge, Mass.: Harvard University Press, 1979), p. 421.

17. *Politichesky dnevnik* (Amsterdam: Fond imeni Gertsena, 1975), 2:702. Stepakov became a full member of the Central Committee at the Twenty-third Party Congress (March–April 1966). Shortly after the congress (May 1966), he was promoted from acting head of the Propaganda Department to permanent head.

18. Andrei Sinyavsky, "Pamflet ili paskvil?" *Novy mir*, no. 12 (1964), pp. 228–233.

19. Spechler, *Permitted Dissent*, p. 217.

20. Stephen F. Cohen, ed., *An End to Silence* (New York: Norton, 1982), pp. 177–179.

21. See, for example, Oleg Mikhailov, "Rodina i literatura," *Volga*, no. 11 (1967), pp. 159–174; Pavel Glinkin, "Pafos vremeni," *Volga*, no. 8 (1968), pp. 124–137; Viktor Petelin, "Rossiya—lyubov moya," *Volga*, no. 3 (1969), pp. 156–182.

22. For publications in *Moskva* of the above-mentioned writers and critics, see Fyodor Abramov, "Materinskoe serdtse," *Moskva*, no. 9 (1970), pp. 120–124; Aleksandr Baigushev, "Ne poteryat cheloveka," *Moskva*, no. 3 (1969), pp. 189–193; Pavel Glinkin, "Rubezhi i pozitsii," *Moskva*, no. 7 (1969), pp. 207–213; Sergei Krutilin, "Staraya skvorechnya," *Moskva*, no. 10 (1970), pp. 9–64; Anatoly Lanshchikov, "Ot literaturnykh fiktsii k literature deistvitel-nosti," *Moskva*, no. 3 (1969), pp. 206–216; Vladimir Soloukhin, "Chernye doski," *Moskva*, no. 1 (1969), pp. 129–187; Vladimir Soloukhin, "Osennie listiya," *Moskva*, no. 10 (1970), pp. 125–144; Vladimir Tendryakov, "Konchina," *Moskva*, no. 3 (1968), pp. 3–138; Aleksandr Yashin, "Dva rasskaza," *Moskva*, no. 8 (1968), pp. 55–63; Sergei Zalygin, "Moi poet," *Moskva*, no. 5 (1969), pp. 88–131; selected poems of Olga Fokina and Nikolai Tryapkin were published in *Moskva*, nos. 8 and 9 (1970), pp. 88–89 and 69–70.

23. In his memoirs, Vikulov writes that he was strongly recommended for the position of *Nash sovremennik*'s chief editor by the head of RSFSR Writers' Union, Leonid Sobolev. See Sergei Vikulov, "Chto napisano perom," *Nash sovremennik*, no. 9 (1996), pp. 4–5. Although he was not formally a member of the CPSU, Sobolev was one of the most conservative figures in the Soviet cultural establishment. By appointing Vikulov, a poet with close connections to the village prose writers, Sobolev sought to break up the *Novy mir* coalition of liberal-reformers and village prose writers.

24. Viktor Astafiev, "Yashka-los," *Nash sovremennik*, no. 12 (1968), pp. 18–25; Vasily Belov, "Mozdoksky bazar," *Nash sovremennik*, no. 6 (1969), pp. 48–56; Leonid Frolov, "Glukhaya izba," *Nash sovremennik*, no. 7 (1969), pp. 31–37;

Viktor Likhonosov, "Lyublyu tebya svetlo," *Nash sovremennik*, no. 9 (1969), pp. 11–44; Evgeny Nosov, "I uplyvayut parakhody i ostayutsya berega," *Nash sovremennik*, no. 6 (1970), pp. 6–43; Valentin Rasputin, "Posledny srok," Nash sovremennik, no. 7 (1970), pp. 3–53, and no. 8 (1970), pp. 8–54; Anatoly Tkachenko, "Rasskaty," *Nash sovremennik*, no. 4 (1970), pp. 56–83; the poetry of Nikolai Rubtsov and Olga Fokina appeared in *Nash sovremennik*, no. 11 (1968), pp. 54–57; no. 12 (1968), pp. 13–17; no. 3 (1969), pp. 3–6; no. 1 (1970), pp. 69–70; no. 3 (1970), pp. 3–5; no. 11 (1970), pp. 51–55.

25. See, for example, Viktor Chalmaev, "Ogon v odezhde slova," *Nash sovremennik*, no. 5 (1969), pp. 110–119; Stanislav Kunyaev, "Esli dushu vylyubit do dna," *Nash sovremennik*, no. 10 (1970), pp. 107–113; Oleg Mikhailov, "V chas muzhestva," *Nash sovremennik*, no. 4 (1969), pp. 106–114; Mikhail Lobanov, "Dostoyanie narodnoe," *Nash sovremennik*, no. 2 (1969), pp. 99–101; Sergei Semanov, "Vtoruyu tysyachy let," *Nash sovremennik*, no. 5 (1970), pp. 108–113.

26. *Nash sovremennik* continued with a circulation of 60,000 copies until January 1969. At that time, the number of copies printed was increased to 70,000. It rose to 100,000 copies in March 1969 and reached 145,000 in May 1969.

27. A. Korobov, P. Revyakin, V. Tydman, and N. Chetunova, "Kak dalshe stroit Moskvu?" *Moskva*, no. 3 (1962), pp. 147–160; "Eshche raz po povodu izlishestv v stroitelstve i arkhitekture," *Pravda*, May 10, 1962; "Protiv vrednoi putanitsy v voprosakh gradostroitelstva," *Pravda*, May 11, 1962. The May 11 essay was signed by twenty-one prominent Moscow architects, including three former chief architects of the city of Moscow. For a detailed analysis of the 1962 controversy, see Colton, *Moscow*, pp. 419–421.

28. The December 2, 1965 TASS statement is cited by Dimitri Pospielovsky, "The Resurgence of Russian Nationalism in Samizdat," *Survey*, vol. 19, no. 1 (Winter 1973), p. 52. According to Colton, Rodina founders were students of the Mendeleev Chemical Technology Institute who worked as volunteers on a restoration project carried out by a veteran Russian restorer Pyotr Baranovsky. See *Ibid*, pp. 406–407.

29. *Vernye podvigu ottsov*, p. 154. This source also mentions the existence of Rodina clubs outside Moscow.

30. Sergei Konnenkov, Pavel Korin, and Leonid Leonov, "Beregite svyatynyu nashu!" *Molodaya gvardiya*, no. 5 (1965), pp. 216–219.

31. According to the authors of the letter, twenty-six out of twenty-nine Moscow city representatives on VOOPIK's organizing committee were senior officials in various bureaucratic agencies. See "Ne ochen udachnoe nachalo," *Literaturnaya gazeta*, October 30, 1965.

32. The writer Pyotr Dudochkin clearly articulated this anger in his speech at a

conference of VOOPIK's Kalinin chapter in March 1968. See Dunlop, *Faces,* pp. 69–70.

33. See Sergei Vysotsky, "Kizhi, oktyabr," *Molodaya gvardiya,* no. 7 (1965), pp. 267–280. Printing a selection from readers' responses to a publication was typically a sign of its great resonance. For reactions to the "Letter of Three," see "V podderzhku i v zashchity," *Molodaya gvardiya,* no. 11 (1965), pp. 301–303.

34. Vladislav Shoshin, "Grekhi sodeyannye tut," *Molodaya gvardiya,* no. 1 (1966), pp. 294–301.

35. Dmitry Balashev, "Stroim ne v chistom pole," *Molodaya gvardiya,* no. 9 (1966), pp. 292–295.

36. Dmitry Balashev, "S chuzhogo plecha—sebe dorozhe," *Molodaya gvardiya,* no. 4 (1966), pp. 309–316. For a similar use of the column to rehabilitate the Orthodox Church and criticize Soviet city planning, see "Tysyacheletnie korni russkoi kultury," *Molodaya gvardiya,* no. 9 (1968), pp. 248–258.

37. Iliya Glazunov, "Doroga k tebe," *Molodaya gvardiya,* nos. 10, 12 (1965); 2, 6 (1966).

38. The *Letters* were harshly criticized on the pages of the newspaper *Vechernyaya Moskva;* see G. Morgunov, I. Grigoriev, and G. Maslennikov, "Net, ne prav pisatel Soloukhin," *Vechernyaya Moskva,* December 16, 1966. In 1967, *Molodaya gvardiya* published a selection of letters mostly supporting Soloukhin's position with his own preface. See "Po povodu 'Pisem iz Russkogo muzeya,'" *Molodaya gvardiya,* no. 4 (1967), pp. 278–294.

39. Vladimir Soloukhin, "Pisma iz Russkogo muzeya," *Molodaya gvardiya,* no. 9 (1966), pp. 242–243.

40. Ibid., pp. 248–249, 260–270; *Molodaya gvardiya,* no. 10 (1966), pp. 256–265.

41. The basis for this theory is a statement by Lenin in "Critical Remarks on the National Question". See Robert C. Tucker, ed., *The Lenin Anthology* (New York: Norton, 1975), p. 654.

42. This section is based on interviews conducted in September and October 1989 with such prominent members of this group as Oleg Mikhailov and Anatoly Lanshchikov, as well as with the liberal nationalist literary critic Lev Anninsky, a Moscow University classmate of many future leading contributors to *Molodaya gvardiya.*

43. For a thinly veiled presentation of this argument, see Yury Ivanov, "Ekho russkogo naroda," *Molodaya gvardiya,* no. 6 (1969), pp. 286–294; Yury Ivanov, "Vyrazitel narodnoi mysli," *Molodaya gvardiya,* no. 12 (1969), pp. 290–293.

44. Pavel Glinkin, "Zemlya i asfalt," *Molodaya gvardiya,* no. 9 (1967), pp. 240–255.

45. Mikhail Lobanov, "Chtoby pobedilo zhivoe," *Molodaya gvardiya,* no. 12 (1965), esp. pp. 280–285, 287; Mikhail Lobanov, "Vnutrenny i vneshny

chelovek," *Molodaya gvardiya*, no. 5 (1966), esp. pp. 287–288; Mikhail Lobanov, "Lichnost istinnaya i mnimaya," *Molodaya gvardiya*, no. 8 (1966), esp. pp. 282, 289–293; Mikhail Lobanov, "Zhiznennost slova," *Molodaya gvardiya*, no. 9 (1967), esp. pp. 258, 261, 263–264.

46. Mikhail Lobanov, "Prosveshchennoe meshchanstvo," *Molodaya gvardiya*, no. 4 (1968), pp. 294–306.

47. Ibid., pp. 303–305.

48. Viktor Chalmaev, "Filosofiya patriotizma," *Molodaya gvardiya*, no. 10 (1967), p. 274.

49. Ibid., pp. 277–278, 284, 288.

50. Viktor Chalmaev, "Velikie iskaniya," *Molodaya gvardiya*, no. 3 (1968), p. 273.

51. Ibid., p. 294.

52. Viktor Chalmaev, "Neibezhnost," *Molodaya gvardiya*, no. 9 (1968), p. 269.

53. Ibid., pp. 263, 267, 271–274, 276.

54. Ibid., pp. 265–267.

55. Ibid., pp. 275, 280–286.

56. Sergei Zalygin, *Sobesedovaniya* (Moscow: Molodaya gvardiya, 1982), p. 13.

57. For a detailed analysis of the political ideas of the liberal and conservative village prose written during this period, see Yitzhak M. Brudny, "Russian Nationalist Intellectuals and the Soviet State, the Rise and Fall of the Politics of Inclusion, 1953–1990" (Ph.D. dissertation, Princeton University, 1992), pp. 138–165.

58. Boris Mozhaev, "Iz zhizni Fyodora Kuzkina," *Novy mir*, no. 7 (1966), pp. 42–118. *Alive*, the original title of the novel, was changed by Tvardovsky to *From the Life of Fyodor Kuzkin* because of censorship considerations. In the 1970s, Mozhaev restored the original title of the novel. Also in response to censors, Mozhaev changed the time of the event from the 1960s to the mid-1950s.

59. For obvious reasons, the party ideological establishment disliked the novel intensely. Mozhaev could not reprint the novel for seven years, and the stage production of the novel at the Taganka Theater in Moscow was banned on the eve of its premiere in 1968. The play finally premiered in the Taganka Theater on February 23, 1989.

60. Vasily Belov, "Privychnoe delo," *Sever*, no. 1 (1966), pp. 7–130. A glowing review of the novel by Efim Dorosh in *Novy mir* helped to establish the novel's status as one of the most important works of the village prose. See Efim Dorosh, "Ivan Afrikanovich," *Novy mir*, no. 8 (1966), pp. 257–261.

61. Viktor Kamyanov, "Ne dobrotoi edinoi," *Literaturnaya gazeta*, November 22, 1967.

62. Fyodor Levin, "Osnavana li trevoga," *Literaturnaya gazeta*, January 17, 1968.

63. Vadim Kozhinov, "Tsennosti istinnye i mnimye," *Literaturnaya gazeta*, January 30, 1968.

64. Vladimir Gusev, "O proze, derevne, i tselnykh lyudyakh," *Literaturnaya gazeta*, February 14, 1968.

65. Aleksandr Yanov, "Esli zaglyanut v buduyushchee," *Literaturnaya gazeta*, February 28, 1968.

66. Vladimir Voronov, "Eshche raz o tsennostyakh istinnykh i mnimykh," *Literaturnaya gazeta*, March 13, 1968; Vladimir Voronov, "Zaklinaniya dukhov," *Yunost*, no. 2 (1968), pp. 96–99.

67. Vladimir Borshchugov, "V zashchity istorizma," *Literaturnaya gazeta*, July 17, 1968; Vadim Kovsky, "Ob intellektualizme, meshchanstve i chuvstve vremeni," *Literaturnaya gazeta*, October 23, 1968.

68. Yury Surovtsvev, "Pridumannaya 'neizbezhnost,'" *Literaturnaya Rossiya*, November 7, 1968; Fyodor Chapchakhov, "Zashchita 'istokov' ili propoved nadklassovti?" *Literaturnaya gazeta*, November 27, 1968; Pyotr Strokov, "O narode 'Savrasushke,' o 'zagadkakh' russkogo kharaktera i iskaniyakh 'pri svete sovesti,'" *Oktyabr*, no. 12 (1968), pp. 190–199; Igor Motyashov, "Otvetstvennost khudozhnika," *Voprosy literatury*, no. 12 (1968), esp. 26–32; Aleksandr Metchenko, "Sovremennoe i vechnoe," *Moskva*, no. 1 (1969), pp. 3–32.

69. For a defense of the essays by the editors of *Molodaya gvardiya*, see "Sobralis kritiki," *Molodaya gvardiya*, no. 3 (1969), pp. 319–320. For Lobanov's own defense of his position, see Mikhail Lobanov, "'Intellektualism' i 'nadobnost v ponyatiakh,'" *Literaturnaya gazeta*, November 27, 1968. For the radical nationalist defense of Lobanov and Chalmaev, see Vladimir Bushin, "Vpredi progressa," *Literaturnaya gazeta*, December 25, 1968; Anatoly Lanshchikov, "Ostorozhno—kontseptsiya!" *Molodaya gvardiya*, no. 2 (1969), pp. 275–297.

70. For the text of the decree, see: TsKhSD f. 4, op. 19, d. 131, pp. 2–6. Despite the fact that the decree was marked "top secret," its existence was common knowledge to many members of Soviet intellectual elite. As the decree stipulated, its content was provided to the heads of cultural institutions, including literary journals. It was regularly invoked by Glavlit, the state censorship agency in its efforts to force the editors of Russian literary journals to censor submitted manuscripts more rigorously.

71. *Politichesky dnevnik*, 1:508–509.

72. Ibid., pp. 494–508. In the mid-1970s, Feliks Kuznetsov was appointed secretary of the Moscow Writers' Union, a position he relinquished only in 1987. After his co-optation into the Soviet cultural establishment, Kuznetsov abandoned his liberal-reformist ideas.

73. Igor Dedkov, "Stranitsy derevenskoi zhizni," *Novy mir*, no. 3 (1969), pp. 231–246.

74. Aleksandr Dementiev, "O traditsiyakh i narodnosti," *Novy mir*, no. 4 (1969), pp. 215–235.

75. "Protiv chego vystypaet 'Novy mir'?" *Ogonyok*, no. 30 (1969), pp. 26–29. In the Gorbachev era, the "Letter" was reprinted in *Nash sovremennik* as part of the Russian nationalist struggle against the liberal-reformist intelligentsia which viewed itself as continuing the *Novy mir* tradition. See *Nash sovremennik*, no. 1 (1989), pp. 175–179.

76. "Ot redaktsii," *Novy mir*, no. 7 (1969), pp. 285–286.

77. V. Ivanov, "Natsionalnyi kharakter i literatura," *Literaturnaya gazeta*, May 6, 1969. For additional criticism of *Molodaya gvardiya* nationalists during the discussion, see Z. Kedrina, "Obrashchayas k istokam," *Literaturnaya gazeta*, June 18, 1969; A. Ponomarev, "Uvy ne obmolvka," *Literaturnaya gazeta*, July 2, 1969.

78. Vadim Kozhinov, "Natsionalnaya literatura: proshsloe ili budushchee?" *Literaturnaya gazeta*, July 23, 1969.

79. The 1969 *Voprosy literatury* debate was, in fact, a culmination of the debate over the Slavophile legacy that had begun in 1966. See A. Galaktionov and P. Nikandrov, "Slavyanofilstvo, ego natsionalnye istoki i mesto v istorii russkoi mysli," *Voprosy filosofii*, no. 6 (1966), pp. 120–130 (an attempt to rehabilitate the Slavophile legacy); V. Malinin, "O sotsialnykh i teoreticheskikh istokakh slavyanofilstva," *Filosofskie nauki*, no. 1 (1967), pp. 77–85 (criticism of the Galaktionov and Nikandrov arguments); Vadim Kozhinov, "K metodologii istorii russkoi literatury," *Voprosy literatury*, no. 5 (1968), pp. 60–82 (defense of the Slavophile legacy); and Aleksandr Dementiev, "Somnitelnaya metodologiya," *Voprosy literatury*, 12 (1968), pp. 69–90 (criticism of Kozhinov's views). On the 1969 *Voprosy literatury* debate, see also Dunlop, *Faces*, pp. 205–207.

80. Aleksandr Yanov, "Zagadka slavyanofilskoi kritiki," *Voprosy literatury*, no. 5 (1969), pp. 91–116; Aleksandr Yanov, "Otvet opponentam," *Voprosy literatury*, no. 12 (1969), pp. 85–101.

81. Boris Egorov, "Problema, kotoruyu neobkhodimo reshit," *Voprosy literatury*, no. 5 (1969), pp. 128–135; Leonid Frizman, "Za nauchnuyu obiektivnost," *Voprosy literatury*, no. 7 (1969), pp. 138–152; Evgeny Maimin, "Nuzhny konkretnye issledovadiya," *Voprosy literatury*, no. 10 (1969), pp. 103–113; Sergei Dmitriev, "Podkhod dolzhen byt konkretno-istorichesky," *Voprosy literatury*, no. 12 (1969), pp. 73–84.

82. Sergei Pokrovsky, "Mnimaya zagadka," *Voprosy literatury*, no. 5 (1969), pp. 117–128; Aleksandr Dementiev, "'Kontseptsiya,' 'konstruktsiya' i 'model,'" *Voprosy literatury*, no. 7 (1969), pp. 116–129; Vasily Kuleshov, "Slavyanofilstvo kak ono est," *Voprosy literatury*, no. 10 (1969), pp. 131–144; Sergei Mashinsky, "Slavyanofilstvo i ego istolkovateli (Nekotorye itogi diskussii)," *Voprosy literatury*, no. 12 (1969), pp. 102–140.

83. Anatoly Ivanov, "Otritsatelnoe dostoinstvo," *Voprosy literatury*, no. 7 (1969),

pp. 129–138; Vadim Kozhinov, "O glavnom v nasledii slavyanofilov," *Voprosy literatury*, no. 10 (1969), pp. 113–131.

84. Yury Barabash, "O narodnosti literatury," *Kommunist*, no. 8 (1969), esp. pp. 47, 53–54.

85. Chalmaev was also expelled from the CPSU. The excuse for the expulsion was his failure to pay party dues from his royalties.

86. According to Spechler, the immediate causes of the purge of *Novy mir* were the publication of Tvardovsky's anti-Stalinist poem, "By Right of Memory," in the West, his continuing association with Solzhenitsyn, and the defection to the West of writer Anatoly Kuznetsov, one of the most prominent contributors to the journal. See Spechler, *Permitted Dissent*, pp. 213–230.

87. *Politichesky dnevnik*, 1:658. According to Arbatov, Stepakov was removed from his position when close associates of Aleksandr Shelepin, one of Brezhnev's chief political rivals in the late 1960s, were purged from the party apparat. See Georgy Arbatov, *Zatyanuvsheesya vyzdorovlenie* (Moscow: Mezhdunarodnye otnosheniya, 1991), p. 155.

88. Ivan Shevtsov, *Vo imya ottsa i syna* (Moscow: Moskovsky rabochy, 1970). On the ideological message of the novel, see Dunlop, *Faces*, pp. 266–267; Alexander Yanov, *Détente after Brezhnev* (Berkeley, Calif.: Institute for International Studies, 1977), pp. 51–55.

89. Igor Kobzev, "Skvoz kriticheskiy tuman," *Sovetskaya Rossiya*, April 24, 1970.

90. The *Sovetskaya Rossiya* affair is well documented in the party archives. See TsKhSD f. 5, op. 62, d. 39, pp. 135, 174.

91. Sergei Semanov, "O tsennostyakh otnositelnykh i vechnykh," *Molodaya gvardiya*, no. 8 (1970), pp. 308–320.

92. Semanov's essay also provoked the sharp reaction of the liberal-reformist intelligentsia. Feliks Kuznetsov submitted his reply to *Novy mir*, while Raisa Lert wrote to the journal *Voprosy istorii*. Neither of these essays was published at the time. Lert's essay was eventually published by Roy Medvedev in samizdat. See Raisa Lert, "Traktat o prelestyakh knuta," in *Politichesky dnevnik*, 2:713–738.

93. Yanov, *Russian Challenge*, pp. 118–120. The existence of this meeting was confirmed to me by one of the Russian nationalist contributors to *Molodaya gvardiya* of the 1960s. It is quite possible that Melentiev's dismissal was linked to the ongoing purge of the Central Committee apparatus of political protégés of Aleksandr Shelepin. Like many of Shelepin's protégés, Melentiev came to the Central Committee apparatus from the Central Committee of the Komsomol in the mid-1960s, at the peak of Shelepin's power.

94. V. Ivanov, "Sotsializm i kulturnoe nasledie," *Kommunist*, no. 17 (1970), pp. 89–100.

95. TsKhSD f. 5, op. 62, d. 84, pp. 210–211.

96. Roy Medvedev, "The Death of the 'Chief Ideologue,'" *New Left Review*, no. 136 (November–December 1982), p. 64; Vikulov, "Chto napisano," p. 6; Mikhail Lobanov, "Posleslovie," *Nash sovremennik*, no. 4 (1988), pp. 158–159. Medvedev and Lobanov claim that *Molodaya gvardiya*'s publications were discussed at the Politburo meeting. Judging by other decisions of this type, it seems that Vikulov is correct in claiming that the decision was made at the Central Committee Secretariat level. *Political Diary* reports that Brezhnev's position in the debate was decisive; see *Politichesky dnevnik*, 2:701.

4. The Rise and Fall of Inclusionary Politics, 1971–1985

1. "Ob oshibochnykh otsenkakh religii i ateizma v nekotorykh proizvedeniyakh literatury i iskusstva," TsKhSD f. 5, op. 63, d. 143, pp. 2–18.
2. Aleksandr Yakovlev, "XXIV siezd K.P.S.S.: problemy ideino-vospitatelnoi raboty," *Kommunist*, no. 10 (1971), pp. 40–56.
3. TsKhSD f. 5, op. 63, d. 143, pp. 120–126.
4. *K.P.S.S. v rezoluytsiyakh i resheniyakh siezdov, konferentsiy i plenumov Ts.K.* (Moscow: Politizdat, 1978), 11:29–33.
5. Valentin Oskotsky, "Kontrasty kriticheskoi mysli," *Literaturnaya gazeta*, January 26, 1972. The target of Oskotsky's attack were essays by two prominent radical nationalists, Viktor Chalmaev and Oleg Mikhailov, published in *Nash sovremennik* in 1971. On the meeting of the Governing Board of the USSR Writers' Union, see Dirk Krechmar, *Politika i kultura pri Brezhneve, Andropove, i Chernenko, 1970–1985* (Moscow: AIRO-XX, 1997), pp. 50-54.
6. Radical nationalist literary historian Dmitry Zhukov, one of the leading contributors to *Molodaya gvardiya* in the late 1960s, claimed that in 1972, Yakovlev's office banned publication of his biography of the seventeenth-century leader of Russian Old Believers, Archipriest Avvakum. The ban was lifted in 1973, after Yakovlev was sent into "political exile" as Soviet ambassador to Canada. See *Literaturnaya Rossiya*, March 30, 1990.
7. Anatoly N. Ivanov, chief editor of *Molodaya gvardiya* and a leading member of the Soviet cultural establishment, should not to be confused with Anatoly M. Ivanov (also known as Ivanov-Skuratov), a participant in the 1969 debate on the Slavophile legacy and a prominent dissident nationalist of the 1970s.
8. Among the institute's fellows were such well-known reform-minded social scientists as sociologists Boris Grushin, Yury Levada, and Vladimir Shubkin; the economist Gennady Lisichkin; and political scientists Len Karpinsky and Fyodor Burlatsky. On the institute and its politics, see Vladimir Shlapentokh, *The Politics of Sociology in the Soviet Union* (Boulder, Colo.: Westview Press, 1987), pp. 36–47.

9. Roman Solchanyk, "Ukraine, Belorussia, and Moldavia: Imperial Integration, Russification, and the Struggle for National Survival," in *The Nationalities Factor in Soviet Politics and Society*, ed. Lubomir Hajda and Mark Beissenger (Boulder, Colo.: Westview Press, 1990), pp. 177–178; Ronald Grigor Suny, *The Making of the Georgian Nation*, 2d ed. (Bloomington: Indiana University Press, 1994), p. 306.

10. The KGB allowed Osipov to continue to produce *Veche* despite the fact that the Glavlit report on the first four issues of the journal, prepared at the KGB's own request, was very critical of *Veche*. Dated August 9, 1972, the report claims that the journal presented a distorted picture of Soviet society and was harshly critical of official policies on ethnic relations and religion. More important, Glavlit found that the journal could be considered threatening to the regime by cultivating among its readers religious fanatism and intolerence toward non-Russians. For the Glavlit document see *Istoriya sovetskoi politicheskoi tsensury* (Moscow: ROSSPEN, 1997), pp. 585–587. On Osipov and the journal *Veche*, see John B. Dunlop, *The Faces of Contemporary Russian Nationalism* (Princeton, N.J.: Princeton University Press, 1983), pp. 44–46, 79–85, 143–145, 149–153, 159–161, 203–205, 212–214, 229–233, 296–308, 327–344.

11. Aleksandr Yakovlev, "Ob osveshchenii na stranitsakh zhurnala 'Kommunist' ideino-teoreticheskikh problem vydvinutykh XXIV siezdom KPSS," TsKhSD f. 5, op. 64, d. 71, pp. 232–240. Although Yakovlev was the author of the memorandum, it was not presented as his personal note but rather as a document of the Propaganda Department, probably done to add political weight to the memorandum's content.

12. Aleksandr Yakovlev, "Protiv antiistorizma," *Literaturnaya gazeta*, November 15, 1972.

13. In fact, the only written response appeared in samizdat; *Veche* no. 7 (February 1973) contained a harsh attack on Yakovlev's essay, written by Osipov, see "Borba s tak nazyvaemym russofilstvom, ili put gosudarstvennogo samoubiystva," reprinted in Vladimir Osipov, *Tri otnosheniya k rodine* (Frankfurt: Posev, 1978) pp. 112–147.

14. According to Arbatov, the person who brought Yakovlev's essay to Brezhnev's attention was Brezhnev's assistant, Viktor Golikov, a person with conservative political views. See Georgy A. Arbatov, *Zatyanuvsheesya vyzdorolenie* (Moscow: Mezhdunarodnye otnosheniya, 1991), pp. 126, 155. It is likely that Golikov was a major supporter of inclusionary politics in the party apparat and used his direct access to Brezhnev to discredit Yakovlev. To strengthen his case against Yakovlev, Golikov might have mentioned to Brezhnev that Yakovlev was regarded as a protégé of his former political rival, Aleksandr Shelepin. According to Vadim Medvedev, Yakovlev's deputy in the Propaganda

Department in the early 1970s, the fact that Yakovlev was perceived to be Shelepin's protégé played a crucial role in the decision to dismiss him from his Central Committee post. See Vadim Medvedev, *V komande Gorbacheva* (Moscow: Bylina, 1994), p. 20.

15. Ligachev tells in his memoirs that one of the authors of such letters was the Nobel Prize laureate Mikhail Sholokhov, see Egor Ligachev, *Zagadka Gorbacheva* (Novosibirsk: Interbook, 1992), p. 91. Anatoly Lanshchikov is my source of information about the ban on the publication of works by Russian nationalist authors criticized by Yakovlev. The interview was conducted in Moscow in September 1989. Recently, one such letter, addressed to the Central Committee, was discovered in Kochetov's archive. This letter is anonymous (signed "Russian patriots"), but judging by its radical nationalist, rather than orthodox communist, content Kochetov was not its author. See *Istochnik*, no. 4 (1996), pp. 73–77.

16. Among former senior officials of the Central Committee, there is no agreement on whether Yakovlev acted on his own or cleared his publication with his superiors, as he was obliged to do. According to Georgy Smirnov, Yakovlev's deputy at the Propaganda Department at that time, the publication of "Against Anti-Historicism" was done on Yakovlev's own initiative, without consulting with senior officials of the Propaganda Department and without clearing it with his immediate superior, the party secretary in charge of ideology, Pyotr Demichev. This account is contradicted by Anatoly Chernyaev, a senior official of the International Department during this period, who claims that the publication of the essay was cleared in advance with Demichev. However, at the Central Committee Secretariat meeting that discussed Yakovlev's essay, Demichev, knowing of Brezhnev and Suslov's negative reaction to "Against Anti-Historicism," claimed that he knew nothing about it. In his own recollection of the affair, Yakovlev admits that at the Secretariat meeting he was accused of not clearing the essay with his superiors. However, he does not reveal whether their accusation was true or not. From all accounts, the publication of the essay was not cleared at the Secretariat level. See Georgy L. Smirnov, *Uroki minuvshego* (Moscow: ROSSPEN, 1997), pp. 127–128; Anatoly S. Chernyaev, *Moya zhizn i moe vremya* (Moskva: Mezhdunarodnye otnosheniya, 1995), p. 297; Aleksandr Yakovlev, "Politika interesna v perekhodnye veemena," *Komsomolskaya pravda*, June 5, 1990.

17. Information about these meetings was given to me by Anatoly Lanshchikov and Oleg Mikhailov in Moscow in September 1989.

18. TsKhSD f. 5, op. 64, d. 87, pp. 61–89. Egorov did not fail to mention the publication of the essay "Socialism and Cultural Heritage" by "V. Ivanov" in the November 1970 issue of the journal, without revealing, however, the real name of its author. For discussion of the "Ivanov" essay, see Chapter 3.

19. On the importance of the April 1973 plenum of the Central Committee, see Chernyaev, *Moya zhizn,* pp. 292–296.

20. In his memoirs, Georgy Smirnov calls this personnel overhaul a "rout of the [entire] leadership of the ideological sector." See Smirnov, *Uroki minuvshego,* p. 126.

21. In his 1990 recollection of the affair, Yakovlev claimed that he offered to leave the Central Committee apparatus for a position in academia. After Yakovlev and his superiors failed to agree on a suitable academic position, Yakovlev asked to be appointed ambassador to an English-speaking country and mentioned Canada as a desirable post. This request was granted immediately. See Yakovlev, "Politika intersna."

22. Tyazhelnikov was Komsomol's first secretary between 1968 and 1977.

23. In the 1970s, Russian nationalist intellectuals invoked the "Against Anti-Historicism" incident every time they perceived unfair criticism by members of the party apparat. An example of such an invocation is a recently published letter by radical nationalist literary critic Viktor Petelin to Mikhail Zimyanin, dated August 2, 1976. In the letter, Petelin complains that heavy censorship of his recent book demonstrates that despite Yakovlev's punishment for his anti-nationalist views, his ideas continue to prevail among officials within the party ideological establishment. See *Istochnik,* no. 1 (1997), pp. 88–89.

24. In his memoirs, Chernyaev reaches the same conclusion: Chernyaev, *Moya zhizn,* p. 394.

25. *Natsionalnaya politika Rossii* (Moscow: Russky mir, 1997), p. 343; Chernyaev, *Moya zhizn,* pp. 331–332.

26. On Khudenko and the "link" reform, see Alexander Yanov, *The Drama of the Soviet 1960's* (Berkeley, Calif.: Institute for International Studies, 1984), pp. 23–38, 60–70, 116–122; *Obratnogo khoda net* (Moscow: Politizdat, 1989), pp. 506–523.

27. Linda J. Cook, *The Soviet Social Contract and Why It Failed* (Cambridge, Mass.: Harvard University Press, 1993), p. 59. Thane Gustafson, *Reform in Soviet Politics* (Cambridge: Cambridge University Press, 1981), pp. 25–29; George W. Breslauer, *Khrushchev and Brezhnev as Leaders* (Boston: George Allen & Unwin, 1982), pp. 204–206.

28. *KPSS v rezoluytsiakh,* pp. 355–371. On this project and its fate, see Zhores A. Medvedev, *Soviet Agriculture* (New York: W. W. Norton, 1987), pp. 400–406.

29. The idea of using village prose writers to manipulate public opinion in support of high budgetary allocations to agriculture probably originated with Brezhnev's assistant on agricultural matters, Viktor Golikov. Golikov, as his behavior in the "Against Anti-Historicism" affair shows, was also a supporter of inclusionary politics within the party apparat.

30. Zalygin was awarded the State Prize in 1968 for his novel *The Salt Valley*

(*Solyonnaya Pad*), which describes the Siberian countryside during the Civil War years.

31. John Garrard and Carol Garrard, *Inside the Soviet Writers' Union* (New York: Free Press, 1990), p. 129.

32. If one calculates the growth of *Nash sovremennik*'s circulation from its October 1968 issue (the first issue edited by Sergei Vikulov) to the December 1982 issue, then the figure is even more striking: a 450 percent increase (from 60,000 copies to 336,000 copies). *Molodaya gvardiya*'s figures for the same period are also very impressive; its circulation rose by 296 percent (from 220,000 copies to 870,000 copies).

33. TsKhSD f. 89, op. 37, d. 16, pp. 1–2.

34. This information is taken from Iliya Glazunov, *Vystavka proizvedeny narodnogo khudozhika RSFSR Iliyi Glazunova* (Moscow: Izobrazitelnoe iskusstvo, 1979); Sergei Vysotsky's introductory essay in *Iliya Glazunov. Albom* (Moscow: Izobrazitelnoe iskusstvo, 1986), pp. 5–40.

35. Both exhibits provoked many glowing reviews in major Russian nationalist thick journals; see Oleg Volkov, "Ya uvidel Rossiyu," *Nash sovremennik,* no. 3 (1979), pp. 174–183; Sergei Borovikov, "Otzyvchevost," *Volga,* no. 9 (1979), pp. 159–164. The book of viewers' comments from the exhibits was published in the West under the title *Khudozhnik i Rossiya* (Düsseldorf: Grad Kitezh, 1980).

36. In 1985, Shilov was awarded the title of People's Artist of the USSR. The information on Shilov is taken from the catalog of Shilov's 1989 Moscow personal exhibition: *Narodny khudozhik SSSR Aleksandr Shilov. Katalog* (Moscow: Izobrazitelnoe iskusstvo, 1989), p. 4.

37. *Yury Mikhailovich Raksha. Zhivopis, grafika, kino, statii* (Moscow: Gosznak, 1987), pp. 188–190.

38. In comparison, in the same list there were only five writers clearly identified with liberal-reformist causes (Chingiz Aitmatov, Vasil Bykov, Yury Nagibin, Konstantin Simonov, and Yury Trifonov). On the list of the twenty-four runners-up are an additional three Russian nationalist writers (Mikhail Alekseev, Gavriil Troepolsky, and Sergei Zalygin) and four liberal-reformers (Daniil Granin, Fazil Iskander, Veniamin Kaverin, and Anatoly Rybakov). See Klaus Mehnert, *Russians and their Favorite Books* (Stanford, Calif.: Hoover Institution Press, 1983), pp. 32–34.

39. *Literaturnaya gazeta,* January 14, 1987.

40. TsKhSD f. 5, op. 73, d. 422, pp. 5–11.

41. *Chetverty siezd pisatelei RSFSR. Stenograficheskyy otchet* (Moscow: Sovremennik, 1977), pp. 90–97, 126–131. See also Bondarev's speech at the Sixth Congress of the USSR Writers Union: *Literaturnaya gazeta,* June 23, 1976.

42. TsKhSD f. 89, op. 16, d. 16, pp. 1–2.

43. Ibid., f. 5, op. 25, d. 96, pp. 10–14. In addition to Zimyanin himself, the original panel members were: candidate member of the Politburo and chairman of the RSFSR Council of Ministers, Mikhail Solomentsev; candidate member of the Politburo and minister of culture of the USSR, Pyotr Demichev; heads of the Propaganda, Culture, and Science departments of the Central Committee, Evgeny Tyazhelnikov, Vasily Shauro, and Sergei Trapeznikov; and head of the USSR Writers' Union, Georgy Markov. Later, Solomentsev and Trapeznikov were dropped from the panel and replaced by Central Committee secretary and head of the Party Organization Department, Ivan Kapitonov, and deputy prime minister of the RSFSR and head of the All-Russian Society for the Preservation of Historical and Cultural Monuments (VOOPIK), Vyacheslav Kochemasov.

44. TsKhSD f. 89, op. 16, d. 16, pp. 1–17. A note in the archival file states that on June 26, 1978, the Central Committee Secretariat heard the panel's report and unanimously accepted its recommendations.

45. To prove that ethnic Russians dominate Russian cultural life, the report cites data on the ethnic composition of contributors to *Novy mir* and *Oktyabr* between 1976 and 1978. The data reveal that ethnic Russians constituted 62 percent of *Novy mir*'s authors and 70 percent of *Oktyabr*'s authors. Jews, on the other hand, constituted only 17 percent *Novy mir*'s writers and 6 percent of *Oktyabr*'s contributors.

46. Vl. Gakov and N. Mikhailovskaya, "Ostorozhno s istoriei," *Kommunist*, no. 8 (1979), pp. 126–128.

47. After publishing Aleksandr Yakovlev's essay in its November 15, 1972 issue, *Literaturnaya gazeta* avoided printing frontal attacks on Russian nationalist intellectuals. This began to change in 1978 when the newspaper, apparently in an attempt to renew the debate on the politics of inclusion, published two editorials attacking Russian nationalist writers. See *Literaturnaya gazeta*, June 19, October 25, 1978.

48. "O proshlom dlya budushchego," *Literaturnaya gazeta*, July 4, 1979.

49. Valentin Pikul, "U poslednei cherty," *Nash sovremennik*, nos. 4–7 (1979). The novel was originally entitled *The Force of Evil (Nechistaya sila)*. In 1974, Pikul submitted the novel under its original title to Lenizdat, a major Leningrad publishing house. The manuscript languished at Lenizdat for several years as a consequence of highly negative reviews from historians, until *Nash sovremennik* decided to publish a censored version of the novel in 1979. The novel's full version appeared under its original title only in 1989. See Valentin Pikul, *Nechistaya sila* (Voronezh: Nechernozyomnoe knizhnoe izdatelstvo, 1989).

50. Sergei Vikulov, "Chto napisano perom," *Nash sovremennik*, no. 10 (1996), p. 19.

51. Krechmar, *Politika i kultura,* pp. 101–102.

52. TsKhSD f. 5, op. 76, d. 282, pp. 5–13.

53. Ibid., pp. 1–3. According to Vikulov's account of the meeting, it was attended by Zimyanin, Shauro, and Shauro's deputy Belyaev. In his criticism of the novel, Zimyanin essentially repeated all the main points of Mirsky's letter. However, as Tyazhelnikov and Shauro had recommended, Zimyanin did not order *Nash sovremennik* to shelve the novel but merely ordered Belyaev to soften its blatantly anti-Semitic edge. See Vikulov, "Chto napisano," pp. 18–20.

54. Irina Pushkareva, "Kogda utracheno chuvstvo mery," *Literaturnaya Rossiya,* July 27, 1979. In 1974, Pushkareva reviewed Pikul's novel at the request of Lenizdat and recommended against its publication.

55. Valentin Oskotsky, "Vospitanie istoriei," *Pravda,* October 8, 1979.

56. *Literaturnaya Rossiya,* October 12, 1979. For Vikulov's account of the meeting of the Secretariat of the RSFSR Writers' Union, see Vikulov, "Chto napisano," pp. 22–24.

57. Vikulov, "Chto napisano," p. 25. Vikulov was present at the conference and claims that the audience clearly understood the target of Suslov's remarks.

58. "Narod, revolyutsia, istoriya," *Kommunist,* no. 15 (1979), pp. 10–21.

59. "Kritika: svoevolie i svoeobrazie," *Literaturnaya gazeta,* December 5, 1979; D. Angeliev, "Na novoi derevenskoi ulitse," *Literaturnaya gazeta,* December 19, 1979.

60. Yury Surovtsev, "Polemicheskie marginalii," *Voprosy literatury,* no. 12 (1979), pp. 146–188; *Literaturnaya gazeta,* February 13, 1980.

61. TsKhSD f. 5, op. 76, d. 282, pp. 16–20.

62. The information on the freezing of subscriptions to *Nash sovremennik* as a consequence of the publication of Pikul's novel was given to me by Sergei Vikulov during an interview in Moscow in September 1989.

63. The main reason for Ganichev's dismissal was personal behavior incompatible with his high post. Ganichev was accused of frequenting a bathhouse, where he engaged in orgies, drinking binges, and of making statements that he would be the next chief ideologue of the Komsomol. However, the report, signed by the deputy head of the Party Organization Department, Nikolai Petrovichev, also mentioned Ganichev's well-known Russian nationalist convictions as an additional reason. This suggests that the party apparat was no longer willing to tolerate prominent Russian nationalist intellectuals in its ranks. At the same time, Ganichev was allowed to remain a prominent member of the Soviet literary establishment. Shortly after his dismissal, he was appointed chief editor of *Roman-gazeta.* For the party file dealing with Ganichev's dismissal, see TsKhSD f. 5, op. 77, d. 69, pp. 15–21.

64. Timothy J. Colton, *The Dilemma of Reform in Soviet Politics,* rev. ed. (New

York: Council on Foreign Relations, 1986), pp. 47–50. On the same issue, see Valerie Bunce, "The Political Economy of the Brezhnev Era," *British Journal of Political Science*, vol. 13, no. 4 (April 1983), pp. 129–158; Peter Hauslohner, "Gorbachev's Social Contract," *Soviet Economy*, vol. 3, no. 1 (January–March 1987), pp. 54–89.

65. On the struggles within the party apparat over the 1982 Food Program, see Mikhail Gorbachev, *Memoirs* (London: Bantam Books, 1997), pp. 148–156, 162–167.

66. Significant criticism of Russian nationalism during the Kulikovo anniversary appeared only in the antireligious publications *Nauka i religiya* and *Voprosy nauchnogo ateizma*. Written by Aleksandr Shamaro, hardly an important member of the Soviet cultural establishment, the criticism was limited to Russian nationalist attempts to glorify the role of the Russian Orthodox Church in Russian history and did not provoke party action. See Aleksandr Shamaro, "Kak ustayala Rus," *Nauka i religiya*, no. 7 (1980), pp. 18–28, no. 8 (1980), pp. 15–25; Aleksandr Shamaro, "Kulikovskaya bitva. Dmitry Donskoi i Sergei Radonezhsky," *Voprosy nauchnogo ateizma*, vol. 25 (1980), pp. 36–61. *Literaturnaya gazeta* did not criticize Russian nationalism openly during the anniversary celebrations, but it found an indirect way of doing so. The lead article in its anniversary issue was written not by a Russian nationalist but by Yury Trifonov, a leading representative of the liberal-reformist intelligentsia. Trifonov used the occasion to attack the radical nationalists who were longing for the "order" of the Stalin era. See Yury Trifonov, "Slavim cherez shest vekov," *Literaturnaya gazeta*, September 3, 1980.

67. On Russian nationalist intellectuals in the years 1981–1982, see also John B. Dunlop, *The New Russian Nationalism* (New York: Praeger, 1985), chaps. 1–2.

68. Vladimir Soloukhin, "Kamushki na ladoni," *Nash sovremennik*, no. 3 (1981), p. 39.

69. Zulfiya Tazhurizina and Kirill Nikonov, "Chto takoe starchestvo," *Nauka i religiya*, no. 4 (1981), pp. 38–41; no. 5 (1981), pp. 24–27; no. 6 (1981), pp. 34–37; Yury Surovtsev, "Polemicheskie marginalii," *Znamya*, no. 9 (1981), pp. 221–236; *Literaturnaya gazeta*, October 21, 1981.

70. *Istochnik*, no. 6 (1994), pp. 108–111; no. 2 (1996), pp. 86–87.

71. Vadim Kozhinov, "I nazovyet menya vsyak sushchy v nei yazyk," *Nash sovremennik*, no. 11 (1981), pp. 153–176.

72. Vladimir Krupin, "Sorokovoi den," *Nash sovremennik*, no. 11 (1981), pp. 72–117. According to Vikulov, the novel was strongly recommended for publication by Belov and Rasputin. Both writers threatened to quit the *Nash sovremennik* editorial board if the journal was too timid to publish *The Fortieth Day*. See Sergei Vikulov, "Chto napisano perom," *Nash sovremennik*, no. 11 (1996), p. 19.

73. On the December 1981 meeting of the Secretariat of the RSFSR Writers' Union, see Vikulov, "Chto napisano perom," pp. 21–23.

74. The five new board members were the novelist and former chief editor of the journal *Volga*, Nikolai Shundik; the poet Aleksei Shitikov; the literary critics Sergei Zhuravlev and Vladimir Korobov; and the historian Apollon Kuzmin. Kuzmin soon emerged as the most outspoken Russian nationalist critic of Surovtsev, Oskotsky, and other opponents of the politics of inclusion in the Soviet cultural establishment.

75. Feliks Kuznetsov, "Dolgovremennaya programma deitsvii," *Sovetskaya kultura*, January 22, 1982; "Pochta zhurnala," *Kommunist*, no. 2 (1982), pp. 127–128.

76. Vasily Kuleshov, "Tochnost kriteriev," *Pravda*, February 1, 1982. On February 2, 1982, at the meeting of the committee for literary criticism of the USSR Writers' Union, Kuleshov's arguments were repeated by several leading members of the Soviet literary establishment. See Krechmar, *Literatura i politika*, pp. 739–740.

77. Yury Surovtsev, "V stile ekstaza," *Znamya*, no. 3 (1982), pp. 202–224.

78. Information on the April 1982 meeting, as well as the reasons for the overhaul of the journal's editorial board in December 1981, is contained in the memorandum sent to Zimyanin by Tyazhelnikov and Shauro on June 10, 1982; see TsKhSD f. 5, op. 88, d. 133, pp. 11–17.

79. "Pochta zhurnala," *Kommunist*, no. 8 (1982), p. 128. *Nash sovremennik* did not rush to reprint this letter in its own pages. It did so only in its October 1982 issue. See "Ot redaktsii," *Nash sovremennik*, no. 10 (1982), p. 176.

80. TsKhSD f. 5, op. 88, d. 133, pp. 3–10.

81. "O tvorcheskikh svyazyakh literaturno-khudozhestvennykh zhurnalov s praktikoi kommunisticheskogo stroitelstva," *Spravochnik partiinogo rabotnika*, vol. 23 (1983), pp. 456–459. According to Mozhaev, during the discussion of the draft of the July 1982 resolution between senior party officials, including Andropov, and leaders of the USSR Writers' Union, which took place several days before its publication, Shauro and Zimyanin attempted to shield *Nash sovremennik* from being explicitly mentioned in the decree. Instead, they insisted on mentioning the liberal-reformist journal *Druzhba narodov* for committing a grave ideological error in publishing Yury Trifonov's antiStalinist novel *The Old Man* (Starik) and Mozhaev's novel *One and a Half Square Meter* (Poltora kvadratnykh metra) which contained a s sharp criticism of the abusive behavior of Soviet bureaucrats. Andropov, however, refused such a demand. In the end neither *Nash sovremennik* nor *Druzhba narodov* were mentioned in the July 1982 decree. Interview with Boris Mozhaev, September 1989.

82. Yury Surovtsev, "Vospitanie slovom," *Pravda*, August 17, 1982. Kuzmin's April

1982 essay was also sharply criticized by Yury Lukin, head of the Department of Socialist Culture at the Academy of Social Sciences of the Central Committee of the CPSU. In the memorandum sent in late September 1982 to the Propaganda Department and forwarded to Zimyanin, Lukin harshly criticized Kuzmin for his idealization of Slavophile and pan-Slavic thinkers and for his attacks on Valentin Oskotsky, a prominent literary critic and a staunch opponent of Russian nationalism. See TsKhSD f. 5, op. 58, d. 67, pp. 67–73.

83. Ibid., op. 88, d. 133, pp. 18–20.

84. Ibid., p. 41.

85. *Pravda,* November 7, 1982.

86. Smirnov, *Uroki minuvshego,* p. 141. According to Gorbachev, at the November 22, 1982 plenum of the Central Committee, Andropov announced his intention to carry out significant personnel changes in the party ideological establishment. See Gorbachev, *Memoirs,* p. 182.

87. Mikhail Lobanov, "Osvobozhdenie," *Volga,* no. 10 (1982), pp. 146–164. In the same month, another essay by Lobanov was published in the journal *Oktyabr.* It was a review of Vasily Belov's anticollectivization novel, *On the Eve (Kanuny).* Here Lobanov articulated in a more restrained manner the ideas he aggressively put forward in the *Volga* essay. Probably for this reason, the *Oktyabr* essay was not mentioned in the ensuing attacks on Lobanov; see Mikhail Lobanov, "Muzhestvo talanta," *Oktyabr,* no. 10 (1982), pp. 179–186.

88. Andropov revealed his personal involvement in the *Volga* affair in a conversation with the head of the USSR Writers' Union, Georgy Markov. See Krechmar, *Politika i kultura,* p. 162.

89. As a compromise with the supporters of inclusion in the party apparat the circulation of *Druzhba Naradov* was also cut by 33 percent. The circulation numbers of *Molodaya gvardiya* and *Moskva,* two other Moscow Russian nationalist thick journals, were unaffected. The circulation of *Volga* was also not affected, probably because it was already small (35,000 copies).

90. Pyotr Nikolaev, "Osvobozhdenie ot chego?" *Literaturnaya gazeta,* January 1, 1983; Valentin Oskotsky, "Literaturnye igrishcha, ili totalny nigilism," *Literaturnaya Rossiya,* January 21, 1983; "Dnevnik LG," *Literaturuaya gazeta,* February 9, 1993.

91. A summary of the February 8 meeting appeared in *Literaturnaya Rossiya* in its February 23 issue. The complete transcript of the meeting was published in 1990. See *Kuban,* no. 10 (1990), pp. 6-14.

92. "Otrazhat narodnye sudby," *Volga,* no. 3 (1983), p. 110.

93. A short account of the meeting appeared in *Literaturnaya gazeta.* See "Vremya trebuet," *Literaturnaya gazeta,* January 26, 1983. For a detailed account of the meeting, see Krechmar, *Politika i kultura,* pp. 159-161.

94. Yury Surovtsev, "Diktuet zhizn," *Pravda*, February 13, 1983. For an additional manifestation of pressure to take action against Russian nationalist intellectuals, see Yury Lukin, "Iskusstvo i politicheskaya kultura lichnosti," *Sovetskaya kultura*, April 16, 1983.

95. Konstantin Chernenko, "Aktualnye voprosy ideologicheskoi, massovo-politicheskoi raboty partii," *Kommunist*, no. 9 (1983), p. 28.

96. "Aktualnye voprosy ideologicheskoi, massovo-politicheskoi raboty partii. Postonovlenie Plenuma Tsk KPSS, 15-go iunya 1983 goda," *Kommunist*, no. 9 (1983), p. 44.

97. In his memoirs, a former head of the KGB and one of the leaders of the August 1991 coup, Vladimir Kryuchkov, claims that Andropov deeply mistrusted Yakovlev and implied that he had nothing to do with Yakovlev's return from Canada. This evidence is not corroborated by any other sources. Ligachev, the head of the Party Organization Department of the Central Committee throughout most of the Andropov era, would have known about Andropov's negative views of Yakovlev if they indeed existed. Yet his memoirs, which are otherwise full of invectives against Yakovlev, are conspicuously silent on this issue. Finally, Aleksandrov-Agentov, an assistant for international affairs to both Brezhnev and Andropov, who by his own admission actively lobbied for Yakovlev's return, claims in his memoirs that Andropov merely opposed Yakovlev's return to a post within the Central Committee apparat. See Vladimir Kryuchkov, *Lichnoe delo* (Moscow: Olimp, 1996), 1:293; Aleksei M. Aleksandrov-Agentov, *Ot Kollontai do Gorbacheva* (Moscow: Mezhdunarodnye otnosheniya, 1994), p. 276.

98. Andropov's base of support in the intellectual community remained a small group of reform-oriented party intellectuals whose leading figures were Fyodor Burlatsky, Aleksandr Bovin, Evgeny Primakov, and Georgy Arbatov. However, as Arbatov points out in his memoirs, his and Bovin's relationship with Andropov became strained in late 1982 and early 1983. See Arbatov, *Zatyanuvsheesya vyzdorovlenie*, pp. 324–328.

99. For a different interpretation of the same period, see Dunlop, *The New Russian Nationalism*, pp. 26–35.

100. For the full list of deputies of the USSR Supreme Soviet, see *Pravda*, March, 7, 1984.

101. The complete honors' list appeared in *Literaturnaya gazeta*, November 21, 1984. Bondarev and Soloukhin were absent from the list due to the fact that they received state honors earlier that year. Honoring their sixtieth birthdays, the party awarded Bondarev the Order of the Hero of Socialist Labor and Soloukhin, the less prestigious Order of the Red Banner of Labor. See *Pravda*, March 15, 1984; *Literaturnaya Rossiya*, June 15, 1984.

102. Valentin Oskotsky, "V borbe s antiistorizmom," *Pravda*, May 6, 1984.

103. Apollon Kuzmin, "V prodolzhenii vazhnogo razgovora," *Nash sovremennik*, no. 3 (1985), pp. 182–190.

5. What Went Wrong with the Politics of Inclusion?

1. TsKhSD f. 5, op. 88, d. 133, pp. 3–10.
2. Ibid., op. 73, d. 422, pp. 5–11. *The Queen Fish* and *Farewell to Matyora* and the debate they provoked are analyzed in Chapter 6.
3. In 1990, Abramov's widow recounted the history of Abramov's relationship with the censors and published excerpts from censored passages. See Lybov Krutikova, "Fyodor Abramov i tsenzura," *Moskva*, no. 10 (1990), pp. 176–196.
4. TsKhSD f. 5, op. 88, d. 133, pp. 18–20.
5. The censored parts of Belov's novel appeared in 1972 and 1976. The full version of the novel was published only during the Gorbachev era. See Vasily Belov, *Kanuny* (Moscow: Molodaya gvardiya, 1988). The "Harmony" chapter, entitled "Inseparable Pair" *(Nerazluchnaya para)*, was scheduled for publication in the January 1981 issue of *Nash sovremennik* before it was removed by the censors. See TsKhSD f. 5, op. 88, d. 133, pp. 3–10.
6. Mikhail Alekseev, "Drachuny," *Nash sovremennik*, nos. 6–7, 9 (1981); "Ekho. Iz pisem Mikhaily Alekseevy," *Literaturnoe obozrenie*, no. 12 (1988), pp. 76–79. The incident regarding the publication of "Pranksters" was reported by Romanov in his 1982 report to the Central Committee. See TsKhSD f. 5, op. 88, d. 133, pp. 3–10.
7. According to Mozhaev, the first volume of *The Country Folk* appeared in 1976, thanks to Valentin Sorokin's (the radical nationalist chief editor of the Sovremennik publishing house at the time) ability to convince officials in the Propaganda and Cultural departments of the Central Committee that the novel did not challenge the official dogma of collectivization as a great historic achievement (interviews with Mozhaev, Moscow, September 1989, June 1990). In his memoirs, Vikulov claims that Mozhaev attempted to convince him to publish the second volume of the novel in the early 1980s, but he declined, fearing that publication of the novel at a time when the journal was already under heavy fire would lead to a crackdown on *Nash sovremennik*. To protect the journal, Vikulov asked the head of the USSR Writers' Union, Georgy Markov, for permission to publish the novel. Markov passed this request on to Shauro, who ordered the manuscript returned to Mozhaev with a stern warning not to attempt to publish it in the USSR or abroad. See Sergei Vikulov, "Chto napisano perom," *Nash sovremennik*, no. 11 (1996), pp. 34–35. It is rather ironic that Mozhaev failed to publish the second volume of *The Country Folk* under Brezhnev since its appearance in the January through March 1987 issues of the thick journal *Don* became a major event in

the early Gorbachev era. In 1989, Mozhaev was awarded the USSR State Prize for the novel.

8. Dirk Krechmar, *Politika i kultura pri Brezhneve, Andropove i Chernenko, 1970–1975*, (Moscow: Airo-XX, 1997), p. 143.

9. Mikhail Lobanov, "Osvobozhdenie," *Volga*, no. 10 (1982), pp. 146–164.

10. *Khudozhnik i Rossiya* (Düsseldorf: Grad Kitezh, 1980), p. 153.

11. Such an attempt was made by the radical nationalist literary critic Anatoly Lanshchikov. In the mid-1970s, he tried to revive the 1969 *Voprosy literatury* debate on the Slavophile legacy. The essay he wrote as a response to views expressed during the 1960s debate, however, did not pass the censors. It was finally published in late 1988, with a preface explaining the history of the debate. See Anatoly Lanshchikov, "Voprosy istorii—voprosy sovremennosti," *Moskva*, no. 10 (1988), pp. 175–187. In 1981, the conservative nationalist literary critic Ivan Rogashchenkov attempted to start a new discussion on the Slavophile legacy in the journal *Literaturnoe obozrenie*. His emotional defense of the Slavophiles was criticized by the journal's chief editor, Leonard Lavlinsky, and debate was abruptly concluded. See Ivan Rogashchenkov, "Uvazhenie k naslediyu," *Literaturnoe obozrenie*, no. 7 (1981), pp. 6–7; Leonard Lavlinsky, "O novizne istinnoi i mnimoi," *Literaturnoe obozrenie*, no. 7 (1981), pp. 14–16.

12. After the first Soviet monograph on the Slavophiles appeared in 1972, scholarly works analyzing their philosophical and literary views and political activities were regularly published. See Yury Yankovsky, *Iz istorii russkoi obshchestvenno-literaturnoi mysli XIX stoletiya* (Kiev: Izdatelstvo Kievskogo gosudarstvennogo pedagogicheskogo institutta, 1972); Vasily Kuleshov, *Slavyanofily i russkaya literatura* (Moscow: Khudozhestvennaya literatura, 1976); *Literaturnye vzglyady i tvorchestvo slavyanofilov* (Moscow: Nauka, 1978); Nikolai Tsimbaev, *I. S. Aksakov v obshestvennoi zhizni poreformennoi Rossii* (Moscow: Izdatelstvo Moskovskogo universiteta, 1978); Yury Yankovsky, *Patriarkhalno-dvoryanskaya utopiya* (Moscow: Khudozhestvennaya literatura, 1981); Evgeniya Dudzinskaya, *Slavyanofily v obshchestvennoi borbe* (Moscow: Mysl, 1983); Vyacheslav Koshelev, *Esteticheskie i literaturnye vozzreniya russkikh slavyanofilov* (Moscow: Nauka, 1984).

13. For publications in the "For Lovers of Russian Letters" series, see Konstantin Aksakov and Ivan Aksakov, *Literaturnaya kritika* (Moscow: Sovremennik, 1981); Nikolai Karamzin, *Izbrannye statii i pisma* (Moscow: Sovremennik, 1982); Ivan Kireevsky, *Izbrannye statii* (Moscow: Sovremennik, 1984); for publications by Iskusstvo publishing house, see Ivan Kireevsky, *Kritika i estetika* (Moscow: Iskusstvo, 1979); *Russkaya estetika i kritika 40–50-kh godov XIX veka* (Moscow: Iskusstvo, 1982).

14. See, for example, Vsevolod Sakharov, "Vorzvrashchenie Ivana Kireevskogo,"

Nash sovremennik, no. 6 (1981), pp. 188–191; Apollon Kuzmin, "U istokov russkogo liberalizma," *Molodaya gvardiya,* no. 10 (1984), pp. 267–272.

15. See, for example, Vladimir Krupin, "Nabolevshee," *Literaturnaya gazeta,* October 3, 1979; Valentin Rasputin, "Prezhde vsego vospitanie chuvst," *Literaturnaya gazeta,* March 26, 1980; Semyon Shurtakov, "Ne tolko sozdanie velikogo pisatelya no i podvig velikogo cheloveka," *Literaturnaya gazeta,* July 6, 1984.

16. For a sample of these ecological writings, see Pyotr Dudochkin, "Zlo ili blago," *Volga,* no. 3 (1975), pp. 155–162; Aleksandr Malyshev, "Povestvovanie o reke," *Volga,* no. 2 (1979), pp. 91–112; no. 8 (1979), 123–163; Oleg Volkov, "Vologodskaya poezdka," *Sever,* no. 12 (1977), pp. 87–96; Viktor Astafiev, "Tsar-ryba," *Nash sovremennik,* nos. 4–6 (1976); Valentin Rasputin, "Proshchanie s Matyoroi," *Nash sovremennik,* nos. 10–11 (1976). See also the *Literaturnaya gazeta*-sponsored roundtable discussion on ecological issues with the participation of Dudochkin, Volkov, and Chivilikhin: "I khram i masterskaya," *Literaturnaya gazeta,* April 5, 1978.

17. Sergei Zalygin, "Komissiya," *Nash Sovremennik,* nos. 9–11 (1975). For *Nash Sovremennik*'s ecological essays, see Nikolai Reimers, "I khram, i masterskaya," *Nash sovremennik,* no. 9 (1973), pp. 137–149; Feliks Shtilmark, "Nashi kedrovye lesa," *Nash sovremennik,* no. 9 (1975), pp. 160–172; Boris Ryabinin, "Chelovek ostanovis!" *Nash sovremennik,* no. 8 (1976), pp. 189–191; Nikolai Priyma, "Liki prirody i litsa lyudei," *Nash sovremennik,* no. 2 (1977), pp. 186–188; Oleg Volkov, "Preemstvennost zhizni," *Nash sovremennik,* no. 3 (1978), pp. 150–156; Aleksandr Kabakov, "Prishel novy direktor," *Nash sovremennik,* no. 5 (1978), pp. 150–156; Vladimir Melnikov, "Trudnaya sudba ozera Nero," *Nash sovremennik,* no. 12 (1979), pp. 101–139.

18. Vladimir Soloukhin, "Trava," *Nauka i zhizn,* nos. 9–11 (1972). For the text of the Central Committee report, see TsKhSD f. 5, op. 64, d. 87, pp. 54–55.

19. *KPSS v rezolyutsiyakh* (Moscow: Politizdat, 1978), 11:210–236; *KPSS v rezolyutsiyakh* (Moscow: Politizdat, 1981), 13:281–297. The budgetary allocation for environmental protection is taken from Charles E. Ziegler, *Environmental Policy in the USSR* (Amherst, Mass.: University of Massachusetts Press, 1987), p. 61.

20. By the late 1980s, the environmental situation in the Soviet Union was viewed by Soviet scientists as catastrophic. See Aleksei Yablokov, "Ekologicheskoe nevezhestvo i ekologichesky avantyurizm. Zavaly na puti perestroiki," in *Inogo ne dano* (Moscow: Progress, 1988), pp. 238–253.

21. Oleg Volkov, "Nad Baikalom net perimen," *Pravda,* December 3, 1977. Rasputin's essays in defense of Lake Baikal were reprinted in Valentin Rasputin, *Chto v slove, chto za slovom?* (Irkutsk: Vostochno-sibirskoe knizhnoe izdatelstvo, 1987), pp. 92–100.

22. *KPSS v rezolyutsiyakh,* 13:302–307.
23. A. Bratsev, "Naiti optimalny variant," *Sever,* no. 3 (1978), pp. 77–83; G. Biske, "Sokhranit Onego," *Sever,* no. 3 (1978), pp. 83–88. In 1981, Yury Bondarev attacked the project in his speech at the Seventh Congress of the USSR Writers' Union. See *Sedmoi siezd pisatelei SSSR. Stenograficheskyy otchet* (Moscow: Sovetsky pisatel, 1983), p. 37.
24. *Pravda,* October 24, 1984.
25. Fatei Shipunov, "Dokuchaevskie 'bastiony,'" *Nash sovremennik,* no. 2 (1985), pp. 136–163.
26. Mikhail Alpatov, "Vospitanie chuvstv," *Pamyatniki otechestva* (Moscow: Sovremennik, 1972), p. 120. For a sample of Russian nationalist writings in the 1970s on preservation-related issues, see V. S. Banige, M. I. Milchik, and Yu. S. Ushakov, "Kakoi zhe byt Vologde?" *Sever,* no. 3 (1972), pp. 106–111; Sergei Semanov, "Moskva stroilas ne srazu," *Moskva,* no. 7 (1974), pp. 172–187; Dmitry Zhukov, "Kto vosstanovit pamyatnik," *Literaturnaya Rossiya,* January 20, 1978.
27. Colton, *Moscow,* pp. 555, 558.
28. Sergei Dmitriev, "Zhivotvornaya sila," *Volga,* no. 7 (1983), p. 162.
29. Mikhail Solomentsev, "Nasha istoriya—nasha gordost," *Literaturnaya gazeta,* June 21, 1978. Solomentsev's argument that in the 1970s VOOPIK's view was taken into consideration on the projects that affected the status of historic monuments was corroborated in 1991 by Viktor Grishin, the head of the Moscow party organization between 1967 and 1985. See Colton, *Moscow,* p. 559.
30. Dmitry Zhukov, "Aisty na ruinakh," *Literaturnaya gazeta,* September 13, 1978. Zhukov's argument that restoration usually led to the destruction of the "restored" object was corroborated in the Gorbachev era. In his memoirs, Russian nationalist art historian and VOOPIK activist Vladimir Desyatnikov tells of a very expensive restoration project in Yaroslavl that resulted in irrecoverable damage to the city's ancient churches. The indignation of the Russian nationalist intelligentsia was so strong that two restorers were put on trial, although they received very light sentences. See Vladimir Desyatnikov, "Monolog," *Molodaya gvardiya,* no. 9 (1988), pp. 248–249.
31. Vladimir Soloukhin, "Bolshoe Shakhmanovo," *Moskva,* no. 1 (1979), pp. 196–206; no. 2 (1979), pp. 183–200. This essay was the third in the series of Soloukhin's essays about the lack of preservation of sites associated with great Russian writers; for the previous essays, see Vladimir Soloukhin, "Poseshchenie Zvanki," *Moskva,* no. 7 (1975), pp. 187–202; Vladimir Soloukhin, "Aksakovskie mesta," *Moskva,* no. 8 (1976), pp. 180–201.
32. Ivan Belokon, "Pamyat i krasota," *Moskva,* no. 7 (1979), pp. 150–173; Dmitry Likhachev, "Ekologiya kultury," *Moskva,* no. 7 (1979), pp. 173–179.
33. Colton, *Moscow,* pp. 559–561; the quote is from pp. 559–560.

34. Oleg Volkov, *Pogruzhenie vo tmy* (Paris: Atheneum, 1987), p. 439.

35. This lack of a regular publication was an important source of discontent for the Russian nationalist intelligentsia beginning in the late 1960s. Pyotr Dudochkin expressed this discontent at the April 1968 conference of the Kalinin chapter of VOOPIK. For excerpts of his speech, see Dunlop, *Faces*, p. 70.

36. The files of the Propaganda Department of the Central Committee contain two letters by Kochemasov, dated September 30, 1970, and February 21, 1972, indicating that between 1968 and 1972, VOOPIK made three requests to allow publication of a mass circulation monthly or bi-monthly journal. Each of these requests was turned down. See TsKhSD f. 5, op. 62, d. 46, p. 231; f. 5, op. 64, d. 86, pp. 23–24.

37. The four *Pamyatniki Otechestva* collections appeared in 1972, 1975, 1977, and 1979, respectively.

38. *Literaturnaya gazeta*, April 4, 1979. Between 1980 and 1984 nine issues of the Almanac were published.

39. Vladimir Soloukhin, "Vremya sobirat kamni," *Moskva*, no. 2 (1980), pp. 186–212.

40. Vyacheslav Orfinsky, "Mozhno li spasti pamyatniki russkogo severa?" *Sever*, no. 7 (1981), pp. 92–103; no. 1 (1982), pp. 101–107.

41. Vladimir Soloukhin, "Prodolzhenie vremeni *Nash sovremennik*, no. 1 (1982), p. 19. The book Soloukhin is referring to is *Vremya sobirat kamni* (Moscow: Sovremennik, 1980).

42. Dmitry Likhachev, "Pamyat istorii svyachshena," *Ogonyok*, no. 29 (1982), pp. 18–20. The survey of readers' letters, as well as the subsequent government efforts to respond to Likhachev's criticism, was published by the magazine in February 1983. See *Ogonyok*, no. 7 (1983), pp. 19–20.

43. TsKhSD f. 5, op. 88, d. 141, pp. 6–10.

44. *KPSS v rezolyutsiyakh* (Moscow: Politizdat, 1982), 14:322–333.

45. As Zhores Medvedev points out, fewer than fifty peasants lived in more than half of the 142,000 villages located in the non-Black Earth Zone. See Zhores A. Medvedev, *Soviet Agriculture* (New York: W. W. Norton, 1987), p. 402.

46. This policy apparently was already practiced in some regions in the late 1960s since it drew fire from Boris Mozhaev in 1968. See Boris Mozhaev, *Nado li vspominat staroe?* (Moscow: Moskovsky rabochy, 1988), pp. 141–148.

47. In his January 20, 1977 report to the Central Committee, the head of Glavlit, Pavel Romanov, noted that because of the harsh criticism of the party's policy of declaring villages as "having no future," his agency had to censor heavily Ivan Filonenko's essay, "The Birch Trees," which appeared in the May 1976 issue of *Nash sovremennik*. See TsKhSD f. 5, op. 73, d. 422, pp. 5–11.

48. See, for example, Vyacheslav Orfinsky, "Mozhno li spasti pamyatniki russkogo

severa?" *Sever*, no. 7 (1981), pp. 97–99. For Gorbachev-era publications on the subject, see Vasily Belov, *Razdumiya na rodine* (Moscow: Sovremennik, 1986), pp. 78–79; Vasily Belov, "Remeslo otchuzhdeniya," *Novy mir*, no. 6 (1988), pp. 161–162; Rasputin, *Chto v slove*, pp. 169–170.

49. See, for example, Olga Fokina, "Staraya derevnya," *Nash sovremennik*, no. 2 (1975), p. 91; Olga Fokina, "Zaboty," *Nash sovremennik*, no. 3 (1985), p. 120; Oleg Poskrebyshev, "Na meste derevni," *Nash sovremennik*, no. 4 (1976), p. 116; Vasily Roslyakov, "Za rekoi v derevne," *Nash sovremennik*, no. 7 (1976), pp. 100–146; *Shestoi siezd pisatelei SSSR. Stenografichesky otchet* (Moscow: Sovetsky pisatel, 1978), pp. 95–96.

50. *KPSS v rezolyutsiyakh*, 13:371–374.

51. Fyodor Abramov, *Chem zhivem-kormimsya* (Leningrad: Sovetsky pisatel, 1986), pp. 98–174.

52. Viktor Perevedentsev, "Dlya vsekh i dlya kazhdodo," *Nash sovremennik*, no. 1 (1974), pp. 139–151; Viktor Perevedentsev, "Izmerenie peremen," *Nash sovremennik*, no. 3 (1974), pp. 135–151. Aware of the Russian nationalist sensitivity to the issue, the censors banned the publication of a later essay by Perevedentsev on the causes of depopulation of the countryside. The essay was scheduled for publication in the January 1977 issue of *Nash sovremennik*. See TsKhSD f. 5 op. 73, d. 422, pp. 5–11.

53. Viktor Perevedentsev, "Rastem ot goda k gody my," *Literaturnaya gazeta*, October 30, 1979. My own analysis of twelve major oblasts of the Non-Black Earth Zone shows a decline in their rural population by 24.4 percent in the years 1971–1981.

54. Fyodor Abramov, *Dela Rosiiskie* (Moscow: Molodaya gvardiya, 1987), p. 131.

55. *Vedomosti Verkhovnogo Soveta RSFSR*, no. 25 (1972), p. 639. On March 1, 1974, the RSFSR Supreme Soviet issued a new decree, "On the Forced Treatment of Alcoholics." See *Vedomosti Verkhovnogo Soveta RSFSR*, no. 10 (1974), p. 287.

56. Vladimir G. Treml, *Alcohol in the USSR* (Durham, N.C.: Duke University Press, 1982), p. 16.

57. Belov, *Razdumiya*, pp. 95–95, 135–141; *Shestoi siezd pisatelei SSSR*, p. 117; Sergei Vikulov, "Pervye vyorsty," *Nash sovremennik*, no. 12 (1978), p. 72; Astafiev, *Tsar-ryba*.

58. Nikolai Mashovets, "O trezvosti," *Nash sovremennik*, no. 6 (1981), pp. 163–172; Pyotr Dudochkin, "Trezvost—norma zhizni," *Nash sovremennik*, no. 8 (1981), pp. 134–145; "Trezvost—norma zhizni," *Nash sovremennik*, no. 11 (1981), pp. 144–151. In 1982, the censors began to crack down on *Nash sovremennik*'s antialcoholism campaign. Thus, they banned the journal from publishing in its November 1982 issue a poem by Aleksandr Shcherbakov entitled "By the District Bathhouse" *(U raionnoi bani)*. The poem portrayed

alcoholism as the most salient feature of village life. See TsKhSD f. 5, op. 88, d. 133, pp. 18–20.

59. Viktor Perevedentsev, "Plachu dolgi, dayu vzaimy," *Nash sovremennik*, no. 7 (1973), pp. 129–148; Viktor Perevedentsev, "Semiya: vchera, segodnya, zavtra," *Nash sovremennik*, no. 6 (1975), pp. 118–131; Viktor Perevedentsev, "Naselenie: prognoz i realnost," *Nash sovremennik*, no. 11 (1975), pp. 122–133.

60. Vasily Belov, "Svidaniya po utram," *Nash sovremennik*, no. 1 (1977), pp. 94–101. In nonfictional form, Belov articulated these ideas for the first time in his 1974 essay entitled "Reading Letters" *(Chitaya pisma)*. See Belov, *Razdumiya*, pp. 210–214.

61. Belov, *Razdumiya*, pp. 103–126.

62. Fyodor Abramov, *Dom* (Leningrad: Sovetsky pisatel, 1980); Vladimir Krupin, "Sorokovoi den," *Nash sovremennik*, no. 11 (1981), pp. 72–117.

63. Ivan Vasiliev, "Zemlya moikh ottsov," *Nash sovremennik*, no. 6 (1979), pp. 127–134; Ivan Vasiliev, "Zhivaya niva," *Nash sovremennik*, no. 6 (1980), pp. 115–135; Ivan Vasiliev, "V verkhoviyakh Lovati i Velikoi," *Nash sovremennik*, no. 4 (1981), pp. 95–153; Ivan Vasiliev, "Zemlya Russkaya," *Nash sovremennik*, no. 12 (1981), pp. 18–73. In 1982, the censors had had enough of Vasiliev's negative portrayals of the contemporary Russian village. They banned his essay, "The Rural World" *(Selsky mir)*, which was scheduled to be published in the September 1982 issue of *Nash sovremennik*. The essay ultimately appeared in the November 1982 issue under a different title and in a highly edited form. See Ivan Vasiliev, "Pisma iz derevni," *Nash sovremennik*, no. 11 (1982), pp. 89–142. For the censor's report on Vasiliev's essay, see TsKhSD f. 5, op. 88, d. 133, pp. 18–20.

64. Russian nationalist intellectuals could learn about this trend from *Literaturnaya gazeta*. In his 1979 essay analyzing the census results, Perevedentsev wrote about the "significant rise in the share of the Southern republics in the Soviet Union's population. The population of the six republics . . . grew in nine years [1970–1979] from 27.4 million [in 1971] to 34.5 millions [in 1979]." See *Literaturnaya gazeta*, October 30, 1979.

65. Boris Sporov, "Vzaimosvyaz," *Nash sovremennik*, no. 9 (1981), pp. 172–181.

66. Galina Litvinova, *Pravo i demograficheskie protsessy v SSSR* (Moscow: Nauka, 1981).

67. Ibid., pp. 63–64, 176, 181–182. In the Gorbachev era, Litvinova elaborated her main argument. See Galina Litvinova, *Svet i teni progressa* (Moscow: Sovetskaya Rossiya, 1989).

68. David K. Shipler, *Russia: Broken Idols, Solemn Dreams* (New York: Penguin Books, 1983), p. 347.

69. In the Gorbachev era, Soviet sociologists began to quantify the degree of

penetration of Western influences. Vladimir Shlapentokh reports that according to a poll taken in 1987 in four large cities in the Soviet Union, "one-third of all teenagers openly declared that 'imitation of the West' was one of their main values. Fifty-eight percent of the same teenagers were not ashamed to say that obtaining Western goods was among their life goals. Rock music was admired by sixty-seven percent of the young people." Vladimir Shlapentokh, *Public and Private Life of the Soviet People* (New York: Oxford University Press, 1989), p. 142.

70. Artemy Troitsky, *Back in the USSR* (Boston: Faber and Faber, 1988), p. 61.
71. Yury Bondarev, *Bereg. Vybor. Igra* (Moscow: Sovetsky pisatel, 1988), esp. pp. 25–32, 56–59, 239–240, 254–260, 266–273, 288, 640–643, 697–699.
72. Sporov, "Vzaimosvyaz," p. 176.
73. Krechmar, *Politika i kultura*, pp. 185–186.
74. Abramov, *Chem zhivem*, p. 97; Vladimir Soloukhin, "New York. Diskoteka," *Nash sovremennik*, no. 1 (1982), pp. 33–42; Viktor Astafiev, Maksimilian Vysotsky, Evgeny Oleinikov, Leonid Samoilov, Nikolai Silvestrov, and Roman Solntsev, "Ragu iz sinei ptitsy." *Komsomolskaya pravda*, April 11, 1982. For a similar criticism of Soviet rock music, see Mikhail Melnikov, "Zaboty devyatoi muzy," *Nash sovremennik*, no. 12 (1980), pp. 157–165; Stanislav Kunyaev, "Chto tebe poyut," *Nash Sovremennik*, no. 7 (1984), pp. 171–182.
75. Belov, *Razdumiya*, pp. 120–124, 178–181, 208–210.

6. What Is Russia, and Where Should It Go?

1. In the late 1980s, Soviet intellectuals themselves acknowledged the importance of these debates. See Boris Kagarlitsky, *The Thinking Reed* (London: Verso, 1988), pp. 261–314.
2. Vladimir Lichutin was the most prolific writer among the three. Between 1972 and 1983, he wrote eleven novels, almost all of them about the traditional peasantry of northern Russia.
3. There is no comprehensive analysis of the development of village prose in the 1970s. Perhaps the best available work, although it focuses almost exclusively on works published between 1976 and 1979, is Mikhail Agursky, *The New Russian Literature*, Research Paper no. 40 (Jerusalem: Soviet and East European Research Centre, Hebrew University of Jerusalem, 1980).
4. Fyodor Abramov, *Dela Rossiskie* (Moscow: Molodaya gvardiya, 1987), pp. 115–167; Vasily Shukshin, *Sobraniye sochineny* (Moscow: Molodaya gvardiya, 1985), 3:146–153.
5. Valentin Rasputin, "Prezhde vsego vospitanie chuvstv," *Literaturnaya gazeta*, March 26, 1980.
6. The best example of this highly idealized portrayal of the traditional peas-

antry, combined with harsh criticism of contemporary urban lifestyle culture and morality, is Vasily Belov's nonfictional work *Harmony (Lad)*, a collection of essays on the traditional peasant way of life, customs, crafts, and morals. See Vasily Belov, "Lad," *Nash sovremennik*, nos. 10, 12 (1979); no. 3 (1980); nos. 1, 5, 6–7 (1981).

7. Shukshin's question appeared as the concluding statement of his nonfictional story "Denunciation" *(Klyauza)*. See Shukshin, *Sobranie*, p. 220.

8. Evgeny Nosov, "Usvyatskie shlemonostsy," *Nash sovremennik*, nos. 4–5 (1977).

9. Ekaterina Starikova, "Sotsiologichesky aspekt sovremennoi 'derevenskoi prozy,'" *Voprosy literatury*, no. 7 (1972), pp. 11–35.

10. Shamil Galimov, "Khudozhestvennost, sotsiologiya, zhizn," *Voprosy literatury*, no. 3 (1973), pp. 46–56.

11. Semyon Shurtakov, "Zhivoi chelovek, a ne obshchie tsifry," *Voprosy literatury*, no. 3 (1973), pp. 62–71.

12. Yury Galkin, "Derevnya—literaturnaya i podlinnaya," *Voprosy literatury*, no. 3 (1973), pp. 56–62. By the mid-1980s, Galkin abandoned his liberal village prose position and moved to the conservative wing of the school. During the Gorbachev era, he, like the rest of the conservative village prose, became an opponent of radical political and economic reform.

13. Leonid Ivanov, "Videt segodnyashchy den," *Voprosy literatury*, no. 3 (1973), pp. 71–78.

14. Prokhanov's view that the Russian nationalists must make their ideology appealing to the urban intelligentsia was to a large degree shared by Bondarev. In an essay he published in *Literaturnaya gazeta* two months before the newspaper officially launched its discussion of village prose, he asserted that Russian nationalist intellectuals must come to terms with the fact that the Russian nation had forever lost its peasant nature and that Russian nationalists should eliminate antiurbanism from their ideology. See Yury Bondarev, "Rabotat, rabotat, rabotat," *Literaturnaya gazeta*, June 20, 1979.

15. Aleksandr Prokhanov, "Metafora sovremennosti," *Literaturnaya gazeta*, September 12, 1979.

16. Vladimir Krupin, "Nabolevshee," *Literaturnaya gazeta*, October 3, 1979.

17. Boris Anashenkov, "Kak zerkalo NTR," *Literaturnaya gazeta*, October 17, 1979.

18. Boris Mozhaev, "Gde dyshit dukh?" *Literaturnaya gazeta*, October 31, 1979.

19. Vladimir Bondarenko, "V novuyu derevnyu—na staroi telege?" *Literaturnaya gazeta*, December 5, 1979.

20. Valentin Kurbatov, "Vsemu svoi chas," *Literaturnaya gazeta*, December 5, 1979.

21. Abramov's impressionistic conclusions were fully supported by Western re-

search on Soviet agriculture. Vladimir Treml estimates that although Soviet agricultural subsidies rose from about 17 billion rubles in 1970 to 37 billion in 1980, there was no commensurate increase in agricultural productivity. See Vladimir G. Treml, "Subsidies in Soviet Agriculture: Records and Prospects," *Soviet Economy in the 1980's: Problems and Prospects*, pt. 2 (1982), Joint Economic Committee, Congress of the United States (Washington, D.C.: U.S. Government Printing Office, 1983), pp. 171–165.

22. Fyodor Abramov, *Dom* (Leningrad: Sovetsky pisatel, 1980); Fyodor Abramov, *Chem zhivem—kormimsya* (Leningrad: Sovetsky pisatel, 1985), pp. 91–98. For entries from Abramov's diary that shed light on background events and the reactions of local peasants to the letter, see Lyubov Krutikova-Abramova, *Dom na Verkole* (Leningrad: Sovetsky pisatel, 1988), pp. 243–262.

23. Boris Mozhaev, *Nado li vspominat staroe?* (Moscow: Moskovsky rabochy, 1988), pp. 134–141, 148–229, 241–248.

24. Ibid., pp. 248–265. The information that Abramov requested Mozhaev's public endorsement of the letter came out during interviews with Boris Mozhaev in September 1989 and June 1990.

25. Fyodor Abramov, "O khlebe nasushchem i khlebe dukhovnom," *Leningradskaya pravda*, June 26, 1976.

26. Fyodor Abramov, "Dom i ego khozyaeva," *Literaturnaya gazeta*, March 22, 1978.

27. Boris Ekimov, "Kholyushino podvoriye," *Nash sovremennik*, no. 3 (1979), pp. 33–60.

28. Boris Anashenkov, "Ekho negeroicheskogo bytiya," *Literaturnoe obozrenie*, no. 7 (1980), pp. 38–42.

29. Gennady Lisichkin, "V podderzhky Mitki—kholyushenskogo opponenta," *Literaturnoe obozrenie*, no. 7 (1980), pp. 43–46.

30. Anatoly Strelyany, "Nazhivnoe delo," *Literaturnoe obozrenie*, no. 1 (1981), pp. 22–27.

31. Vyacheslav Palman, "Uzh esli Mitka zadumalsya," *Literaturnoe obozrenie*, no. 7 (1981), pp. 25–28; A. Obertynsky, "Chto mogut dengi," *Literaturnoe obozrenie*, no. 7 (1981), pp. 28–32.

32. Vsevolod Surganov, "Vozvrachenie k azbuke," *Literaturnoe obozrenie*, no. 9 (1981), pp. 26–31.

33. Abramov, *Chem zhivem*, pp. 221–223.

34. On Soviet writers' views of science and scientific progress in the post-Stalin era, see Rosalind J. Marsh, *Soviet Fiction since Stalin* (London: Croom Helm, 1986).

35. Viktor Astafiev, "Tsar-ryba," *Nash sovremennik*, nos. 4–6 (1976).

36. "O krasote prirody, o krasote cheloveka," *Literaturnoe obozrenie*, no. 10 (1976), pp. 50–57.

37. Kozhinov's essay may have been written as a response to Suslov's speech, published in *Pravda* on March 18, 1976. In this speech, Suslov stated that "the contemporary scientific and technological revolution opens up before society unseen possibilities in using science for mastering and protecting the forces of nature and solving social problems . . . and at the same time acts as material preparation for communist civilization."

38. Vadim Kozhinov, "Avtoritet istorii," *Literaturnoe obozrenie,* no. 3 (1977), pp. 63–67.

39. Valentin Rasputin, *Povesti* (Moscow: Sovetskaya Rossiya, 1986), p. 292. The novel was extremely popular and in 1982 its movie adaptation, titled *Farewell,* was produced by the distinguished Soviet movie directors Larissa Shepitko and Elem Klimov.

40. Evgeny Sidorov, "Preodolevaya zabvenie," *Literaturnaya gazeta,* January 26, 1977. Under Yeltsin, Sidorov would become Russia's minister of culture.

41. Oleg Salynsky, "Dom i dorogi," *Voprosy literatury,* no. 2 (1977), pp. 4–34.

42. Valentin Oskotsky, "Ne slishkom li dolgoe eto molchanie?" *Voprosy literatury,* no. 2 (1977), pp. 34–49.

43. Ekaterina Starikova, "Obratimsya k zhizni," *Voprosy literatury,* no. 2 (1977), pp. 72–81. Starikova elaborated her position on Rasputin in a long review essay dedicated to Rasputin's prose. See Ekaterina Starikova, "Zhit i pomnit," *Novy mir,* no. 11 (1977), pp. 236–248.

44. Yury Seleznev, "Zemlya ili territoriya?" *Voprosy literatury,* no. 2 (1977), pp. 49–63; Aleksandr Ovcharenko, "Vernost svoei probleme," *Voprosy litera-tury,* no. 2 (1977), pp. 63–72.

45. Boris Pankin, "Rodniki tvorchestva. O povestyakh V. Rasputina," *Pravda,* July 25, 1977. In 1978, Pankin elaborated his position in a review essay dedicated to the novel: Boris Pankin, "Proshchanie i vstrecha s Matyoroi," *Druzhba narodov,* no. 2 (1978), esp. pp. 246–247.

46. Anatoly Ananiev, "Gody bez voiny," *Novy mir,* no. 2 (1979), p. 153.

47. Nikolai Yanovsky, "Zaboty i trevogi Valentina Rasputina," *Sever,* no. 2 (1979), pp. 106–116.

48. Nina Podzorova, "Ravnozvuchie," *Nash sovremennik,* no. 10 (1978), pp. 180–186.

49. A full transcript of the discussion was published only in 1990. See "Klassika i my," *Moskva,* no. 1 (1990), pp. 183–200; no. 2 (1990), pp. 169–181; no. 3 (1990), pp. 186–196.

50. Olzhas Suleimenov, *Az i Ya* (Alma-Ata: Izdatelstvo "Zhazushi," 1975). The fact that 60,000 copies of the book were printed, a large number for a work of nonfiction published outside Moscow or Leningrad, suggests that neither the editors nor the censors viewed the book as problematic.

51. Suleimenov did not hesitate to repeat his charge in an interview he gave to

Komsomolskaya pravda soon after the publication of his book. It was probably this interview that attracted the attention of Russian nationalist intellectuals. See Olzhas Suleimenov, "Ot mifa k istine," *Komsomolskaya pravda,* October 9, 1975.

52. On these theories, see Lowell Tillett, *The Great Friendship* (Chapel Hill: University of North Carolina Press, 1969), chap. 16.

53. Apollon Kuzmin, "'Tochka v kruge,' iz kotoroi vyrastaet repei," *Molodaya gvardiya,* no. 12 (1975), pp. 270–280; L. Dmitriev, O. Tvorogov, "'Slovo o polku Igoreve' v interpretatsii O. Suleimenova," *Russkaya literatura,* no. 1 (1976), pp. 251–258.

54. Olzhas Suleimenov, "Posleslovie k opalnoi knige," *Literaturnaya gazeta,* July 18, 1990. A shortened version of the proceedings of the meeting at the USSR Academy of Sciences was published in the September 1976 issue of *Voprosy istorii.* See "Obsuzhdenie knigi Olzhasa Suleimenova," *Voprosy istorii,* no. 9 (1976), pp. 147–154. In the essay, published in the June 1976 issue of the Leningrad thick journal *Zvezda,* Likhachev reiterated the main arguments he made at the Academy of Sciences meeting. See Dmitry Likhachev, "Gipotezy ili fantazii v istolkovanii temnykh mest 'Slova o polku Igoreve,'" *Zvezda,* no. 6 (1976), pp. 203–210.

55. Yury Seleznev, "Mify i istiny," *Moskva,* no. 3 (1976), pp. 202–208.

56. Olzhas Suleimenov, *Esse, publitsistika. stikhi, poemy, Az i Ya* (Alma-Ata: Izdatelstvo "Zhalyn," 1990).

57. The "Flaming Revolutionaries" series was launched by Politicheskaya literatura publishing house in 1968; by 1977, over sixty biographies had been published, each with an initial run of 200,000 copies. For some of the most important books in the "Flaming Revolutionaries" series, see Bulat Okudzhava, *Glotok svobody* (Moscow: Politizdat, 1971); Vladimir Voinovich, *Stepen doveriya* (Moscow: Politizdat, 1972); Yury Trifonov, *Neterpenie* (Moscow: Politizdat, 1973); Vasily Aksenov, *Lyubov k elektrichestvu* (Moscow: Politizdat, 1974); Anatoly Gladilin, *Sny Shlissenburgskoi kreposti* (Moscow: Politizdat, 1974); Yury Davydov, *Zaveshchayu vam bratiya* (Moscow: Politizdat, 1975); Kamil Ikramov, *Vse vozmozhnoe schastie* (Moscow: Politizdat, 1979); Natan Eidelman, *Bolshoi Zhanno* (Moscow: Politizdat, 1982).

58. Semanov made this statement during a roundtable discussion with eight other Russian nationalist contributors to the series. See "Velikie biografii," *Ogonyok,* no. 28 (1980), pp. 22–24.

59. The "Lives of Remarkable People" series was published by the Molodaya gvardiya publishing house; 150,000 copies of each book in the series was printed. For some of the most important Russian nationalist books in the series, see Sergei Semanov, *Makorov* (Moscow: Molodaya gvardiya, 1972); Yury Loshchits, *Skovoroda* (Moscow: Molodaya gvardiya, 1972); Oleg Mik-

hailov, *Suvorov* (Moscow: Molodaya gvardiya, 1973); Oleg Mikhailov, *Derzhavin* (Moscow: Molodaya gvardiya, 1977); Viktor Petelin, *Aleksei Tolstoi* (Moscow: Molodaya gvardiya, 1978); Viktor Chalmaev, *Malyshev* (Moscow: Molodaya gvardiya, 1979); Sergei Semanov, *Brusilov* (Moscow: Molodaya gvardiya, 1980); Yury Seleznev, *Dostoevsky* (Moscow: Molodaya gvardiya, 1981); Dmitry Zhukov, *Aleksei Konstantinovich Tolstoi* (Moscow: Molodaya gvardiya, 1982).

60. See, for example, reviews of the books from the "Lives" series that appeared between 1980 and 1982 alone: Anatoly Znamensky, "Na sluzhbe otechestva," *Nash sovremennik*, no. 3 (1981), pp. 187–189; Mikhail Antonov, "Nravstvenny zavet Andreiya Rubleva," *Volga*, no. 5 (1982), pp. 143–147; Nikolai Kuzin, "Bessmertny syn otechestva," *Sever*, no. 10 (1981), pp. 126–128.

61. Yury Loshchits, *Goncharov* (Moscow: Molodaya gvardiya, 1977); Mikhail Lobonov, *Ostrovsky* (Moscow: Molodaya gvardiya, 1979); Igor Zolotussky, *Gogol* (Moscow: Molodaya gvardiya, 1979).

62. "Narod, revolyutsia, istoriya," *Kommunist*, no. 15 (1979), pp. 10–21; Vasily Kuleshov, "A bylo li 'temnoe tsarstvo'?" *Literaturnaya gazeta*, March 19, 1980.

63. Vsevolod Sakharov, "Logika kultury i sudba talanta," *Voprosy literatury*, no. 9 (1980), pp. 182–191; Nikolai Skatov, "Dvizhenie vpered," *Voprosy literatury*, no. 9 (1980), pp. 199–203; Yury Seleznev, "Sluzhit svoemy vremeni i narodu," *Voprosy literatury*, no. 9 (1980), pp. 234–244.

64. Aleksandr Dementiev, "Kogda nado zashchishchat khrestomatiinye istiny," *Voprosy literatury*, no. 9 (1980), pp. 204–216.

65. Vladimir Zhdanov, "A kak byt s istoricheskoi pravdoi?" *Voprosy literatury*, no. 9 (1980), pp. 191–199; Arkady Anastasiev, "Osparivaya Ostrovskogo," *Voprosy literatury*, no. 9 (1980), pp. 217–225; Pavlo Movchan, "Ataka stilem," *Voprosy literatury*, no. 9 (1980), pp. 225–234; Igor Dzeverin, "Neskolko soobshcheny obshchego kharaktera," *Voprosy literatury*, no. 9 (1980), pp. 245–249; "Ot redaktsii," *Voprosy literatury*, no. 9 (1980), pp. 249–251.

66. Feliks Kuznetsov, "Istina istorii," *Moskva*, no. 1 (1981), pp. 194–214; no. 7 (1984), pp. 178–190, no. 8 (1984), p. 182–197.

67. Georgy Berdnikov, "O partiinom otnoshenii k klassicheskomy naslediyu," *Znamya*, no. 8 (1982), pp. 214–232.

68. Valentin Rasputin, "Vechnoe pole," in *Mezh Nepryadvoi i Donom*, ed. Vladimir Krupin (Moscow: Sovremennik, 1980), p. 17.

69. The figure of 150 titles appears in V. Evsinkov and S. Komissarov, "Ispytanie istoriei," *Sibirskie ogni*, no. 2 (1986), p. 163. My own analysis of *Ezhegodnik knigi SSSR* reveals that in 1979–1980, nineteen books that directly referenced the Kulikovo anniversary in their titles were published in the Soviet Union. These books alone appeared in 1.7 million copies. If the figure given by

Evsenkov and Komissarov is correct, then the total number of books related to the anniversary could well be in the range of 5 to 10 million copies.

70. Vladimir Lebedev, "Iskuplenie," *Nash sovremennik*, nos. 8–9 (1980); Vladimir Vozovikov "Pole Kulikovo," *Molodaya gvardiya*, nos. 8–10 (1980); Boris Dedyukhin, "Chur menya," *Volga*, nos. 8–9 (1980); Yury Loshchits, *Dmitry Donskoi* (Moscow: Molodaya gvardiya, 1980). In its September 1980 issue, the journal *Volga* published an abridged version of chapters 10 and 11 of *Dmitry Donskoi* that contains extensive passages excluded by the censor from the book version. These passages depict Russia as a devoutly Christian nation. See Yury Loshchits, "Za drugi svoya," *Volga*, no. 9 (1980), pp. 144–145.

71. Arseny Gulyga, "Istoricheskoe soznanie i istorichesky roman," *Literaturnaya ucheba*, no. 4 (1980), pp. 147–148, 154.

72. Dmitry Likhachev, "Russkaya kultura i srazhenie na Kulikovom pole za Donom," *Zvezda*, no. 9 (1980), p. 3.

73. Gelian Prokhorov, "Kulturnoe svoeobrazie epokhi Kulikovskoi bitvy," *Trudy otdela drevnerusskoi literatury Instituta russkoi literatury AN SSSR* (1979), 34:3–17; Dmitry Likhachev, "Ozaryonnaya slovom," in *Mezh Nepryadvoi i Donom*, pp. 103–104; Gulyga, "Istoricheskoe soznanie," p. 147.

74. Boris Dedyukhin, "Chur menya," *Volga*, no. 8 (1980), pp. 83–84; Vladimir Vozovikov, "Pole Kulikovo," *Molodaya gvardiya*, no. 8 (1980), p. 67.

75. Apollon Kuzmin, "Prinyatie khristianstva na Rusi," *Voprosy nauchnogo ateizma*, vol. 25 (1980), pp. 7–35.

76. In 1988, during the celebrations marking the millennium of Christianity in Russia, Kuzmin again published his conception of paganism and Russian Orthodoxy: Apollon Kuzmin, *Padenie Peruna* (Moscow: Molodaya gvardiya, 1988). Another three prominent Russian nationalist proponents of the concept of paganism as the true religion of Russia are the historian Boris Rybakov, the novelist Pyotr Proskurin, and the poet Yury Kuznetsov. Rybakov presented his ideas in a two-volume study of paganism in Russia: *Yazychestvo drevnikh slavyan* (Moscow: Nauka, 1981) and *Yazychestvo Drevnei Rusi* (Moscow: Nauka, 1988). Proskurin advanced his own Russian nationalist vision, which combined an idealization of paganism with a justification of Stalinism, in such novels as *Fate* (*Sudba*, 1972), *Brink of Love* (*Porog lyubvi*, 1985), and *Abdication* (*Otrechenie*, 1987). For a collection of Kuznetsov's poems, which combine an exaltation of paganism with a call for the institutionalization of a powerful, authoritarian state, see Yury Kuznetsov, *Zolotaya gora* (Moscow: Sovetskaya Rossiya, 1989).

77. Vadim Kargalov, "Ratnaya slava Rossii," *Nash sovremennik*, no. 6 (1980), pp. 172–179; Vadim Kargalov, "Moskva i Kulikovskaya bitva," *Moskva*, no. 8 (1980), pp. 187–200; Vadim Kargalov, "Khudozhestvennaya letopis polya

Kulikova," *Molodaya gvardiya*, no. 9 (1980), pp. 297–310; Vadim Kargalov, "Ot Nepryavdy do Ugry," *Nash sovremennik*, no. 9 (1980), pp. 162–174.

78. Fyodor Nesterov, *Svyaz vremen* (Moscow: Molodaya gvardiya, 1980), p. 117. In 1981, Nesterov's book was awarded first prize by the Znanie Society for best nonfictional work of the year and was subsequently reprinted twice (1984, 1987), which indicates the popularity of his ideas among an important section of the Soviet political and intellectual elite.

79. Ibid., pp. 128–129, 142, 149, 205, 226.

80. Vladimir Chivilikhin, "Pamyat," *Nash sovremennik*, no. 9 (1980), pp. 6–7; Loshchits, *Dmitry Donskoi*, p. 61; Vladimir Lebedev, "Iskuplenie," *Nash sovremennik*, no. 9 (1980), pp. 88, 94, 148; Boris Dedyukhin, "Chur menya," *Volga*, no. 9 (1980), pp. 74, 80.

81. Rasputin, "Vechnoe pole," p. 18.

82. Nesterov, *Svyaz*, p. 11; Yury Seleznev, "Chtoby starye rasskazyvali, a molodye pomnili!" *Nash sovremennik*, no. 3 (1980), esp. pp. 178, 182–184.

83. Between 1970 and 1978, Gumilev elaborated his theory of the life cycle of nations in five essays that appeared in the journal *Priroda:* "Etnogenez i etnosfera," *Priroda*, no. 1 (1970), pp. 46–55; no. 2 (1970), pp. 43–50; "Etnogenez-prirodny protsess," *Priroda*, no. 2 (1971), pp. 80–82; "Izmeneniya klimata i migratsii kochevnikov," *Priroda*, no. 4 (1972), 44–52; "G. E. Grumm-Grzhimailo i rozhdenie nauki ob etnogeze," *Priroda*, no. 5 (1976), pp. 112–121; "Eshche raz ob etnose," *Priroda*, no. 12 (1978), pp. 97–105. These essays provoked sharp criticism by Soviet scholars specializing in ethnicity and ethnic studies. See Yulian Bromlei, "K voprosy o sushchnosti etnosa," *Priroda*, no. 2 (1970), pp. 51–55; Viktor Kozlov, "Chto zhe takoe etnos?" *Priroda*, no. 2 (1971), pp. 71–74; Viktor Kozlov, "O biologo-geograficheskoi kontseptsii etnicheskoi istorii," *Voprosy istorii*, no. 12 (1974), pp. 72–80; Abram Pershits and Vadim Pokshishevsky, "Ipostasi etnosa," *Priroda*, no. 12 (1978), pp. 106–113. For Gumilev's theory of Russian history, see Lev Gumilev, *Ot Rusi do Rossii* (Moscow: Di-Dik, 1997).

84. Although Gumilev was able to publish five books and over thirty major articles between the mid-1960s and early 1980, he paid a heavy price for his ideas. With the single exception of a 1977 publication in *Druzhba narodov*, no popular thick journal dared to publish his essays during the 1970s, forcing him to expound his ideas in small-circulation scholarly and semischolarly periodicals like *Vestnik Leningradskogo universiteta* and *Priroda*. Gumilev's books were published in a small number of copies and never reprinted; his most important work, *Ethnogenesis and the Earth's Biosphere (Etnogenez i biosfera zemli)*, was completed in 1974 but remained unpublished until 1989. In 1979, the manuscript of *Ethnogenesis* was deposited in the All-Union Institute of Scientific and Technical Information (VINITI), in Moscow where

about two thousand photocopies of it were made for scholars who requested it. He wrote five other monographs that elaborated the argument of *Ethnogenesis* and they also remained unpublished until 1989. In fact, as late as mid-1987, the Central Committee explicitly refused Gumilev's request to allow the publication of his books on the grounds that his theories were politically harmful. See *Istochnik*, no. 5 (1995), pp. 84–88.

85. Lev Gumilev, "Epokha Kulikovskoi bitvy," *Ogonyok*, no. 36 (1980), pp. 16–17; Lev Gumilev, "God rozhdeniya 1380," *Dekorotivnoe iskusstvo*, no. 12 (1980), pp. 34–37.

86. Gumilev, "God rozhdeniya," p. 37.

87. On the Eurasian movement, see Leonid Luks, "Die Ideologie der Eurasier in zeitgeschichtlichen Zusamenhang," *Jahrbücher für Geschichte Osteuropas*, vol. 34 (1986), pp. 374–395.

88. The radical nationalist novelist Dmitry Balashov was the most prominent popularizer in Soviet fiction of Gumilev's theory of Russian history. In the mid-1970s, he began writing a fictionalized history of the formation of the Russian state in the thirteenth and fourteenth centuries employing Gumilev's ideas. Between 1977 and 1991, Balashov published six novels on the subject that attracted significant attention and controversy: *Mladshy syn* (Petrozavodsk: Kareliya, 1977), *Veliky stol* (Petrozavodsk: Kareliya, 1980), *Bremya vlasti* (Petrozavodsk: Kareliya, 1982), *Simeon Gordy* (Petrozavodsk: Kareliya, 1984), *Veter vremeni* (Petrozavodsk: Kareliya, 1988), *Otrechenie* (Moscow: Sovremennik, 1991).

89. The full scope of Gumilev's theory and its implications became known only during the Gorbachev era. In fact, Gumilev was a major beneficiary of glasnost. Between 1989 and 1990 alone, four of his books, including *The Ethnogenesis and the Earth's Biosphere*, were published and reprinted countless of times: *Etnogenez i biosfera zemli* (Leningrad: Izdatelstvo LGU, 1989), *Drevnyaya Rus i Velikaya Step* (Moscow: Mysl, 1989), *Geografiya etnosa v istorichesky period* (Leningrad: Nauka, 1990) and, with Aleksandr Panchenko, *Chtoby svecha ne pogasla* (Leningrad: Sovetsky pisatel, 1990).

90. Yury Borodai, "Etnicheskie kontakty i okruzhayushchaya sreda," *Priroda*, no. 9 (1981), pp. 82–85. Under Gorbachev, Borodai applied this argument in challenging the suitability of a market economy to Russia: Yury Borodai, "Pochemu pravoslavnym ne goditsya protestansky kapitalism," *Nash sovremennik*, no. 10 (1990), pp. 3–16.

91. The November 11, 1981 resolution of the Presidium of the USSR Academy of Sciences was not published at the time, but it figures prominently in the 1987 report of the special commission of the USSR Academy of Sciences. The report, commisioned by the Propaganda and Science and Education departments of the Central Committee in order to provide recommendations re-

garding publication of Gumilev's oeuvre, was harshly critical of Gumilev's work. For this report, see *Istochnik,* no. 5 (1995), pp. 85–86.

92. Vadim Kozhinov, "I nazovyet menya vsyak sushchy v nei yazyk," *Nash sovremennik,* no. 11 (1981), pp. 153–176. Ten years later, Kozhinov repeated his views on the Asian orientation of Russia: Vadim Kozhinov, "Poiski budushchego," *Nash sovremennik,* no. 3 (1991), pp. 125–129.

7. The Zenith of Politics by Culture, 1985–1989

1. For different interpretations of the roots of perestroika, its aims, and its course, see Archie Brown, *The Gorbachev Factor* (Oxford: Oxford University Press, 1996); *The Soviet System: From Crisis to Collapse,* rev. ed., ed. Alexander Dallin and Gail W. Lapidus (Boulder, Colo.: Westview Press, 1995); Graeme Gill, *The Collapse of a Single-Party System* (Cambridge: Cambridge University Press, 1994); Jerry F. Hough, *Democratization and Revolution in the USSR, 1985–1991* (Washington, D.C.: Brookings Institution, 1997); Moshe Lewin, *The Gorbachev Phenomenon* (Berkeley: University of California Press, 1988); Philip G. Roeder, *Red Sunset* (Princeton, N.J.: Princeton University Press, 1993).

2. Vitaly Tretiyakov, *Gorbachev, Ligachev, Yeltsin. Politichiskie portrety na fone perestroiki* (Moscow: Muzei knigi A-Ya, 1990), p. 37.

3. On Russian nationalism under Gorbachev, see also: Yitzhak M. Brudny, "The Heralds of Opposition to *Perestroika,*" *Soviet Economy,* vol. 5, no. 2 (April–June 1989), pp. 162–200; Roman Szporluk, "Dilemmas of Russian Nationalism," *Problems of Communism,* vol. 38, no. 4 (July–August 1989), pp. 15–35; Walter Laqueur, *Black Hundred: Rise of Extreme Right in Russia* (New York: HarperCollins, 1993), chaps. 10–15; John B. Dunlop, *The Rise of Russia and the Fall of the Soviet Empire* (Princeton, N.J.: Princeton University Press, 1993), chap. 3.

4. On the river diversion project and the Russian nationalist campaign against it, see Nikolai N. Petro, "The Project of the Century: A Case Study of Russian Nationalist Dissent," *Studies in Comparative Communism,* vol. 20, nos. 3/4 (Autumn–Winter 1987), pp. 235–252; Robert G. Darst, Jr., "Environmentalism in the USSR: The Opposition to the River Diversion Projects," *Soviet Economy,* vol. 4, no. 3 (July–September 1988), pp. 223–252.

5. "Zemlya i khleb," *Nash sovremennik,* no. 7 (1985), pp. 115–152.

6. *Shestoi siezd pisatelei RSFSR. Stenografichesky otchet* (Moscow: Sovremennik, 1987), pp. 67–72, 117–122, 132–138, 146–149; *Vosmoi siezd pisatelei SSSR. Stenografichesky otchet* (Moscow: Sovetsky pisatel, 1988), pp. 31–36, 396–399, 402–403.

7. Sergei Yurenin, "Sergei Zalygin vo glave 'Novogo mira,'" *Radio Liberty Research Bulletin*, no. 147/86, p. 1.

8. In his memoirs, Gorbachev admits that strong public pressure played a major role in the cancellation of the river diversion project. Gorbachev does not reveal his position on the subject; however, elsewhere in the memoirs he condemns of the practice of flooding of millions of hectares of highly valuable agricultural land to build hydroelectric power stations. This statement suggests that Gorbachev as a former party secretary for agriculture probably opposed the project on the grounds that it would cause a large-scale flooding of the agricultural land; see Gorbachev, *Memoirs*, pp. 149, 264.

9. The first part of the novel appeared in *Druzhba narodov* in 1980 and 1982. On Zalygin's novel *After the Storm*, see Yitzhak M. Brudny, "Between Liberalism and Nationalism: The Case of Sergei Zalygin," *Studies in Comparative Communism*, vol. 21, nos. 3/4 (Autumn-Winter 1988), pp. 331–340.

10. For the main reviews of *After the Strom*, see Igor Dedkov, "Mysl neutomimaya," *Literaturnaya gazeta*, December 11, 1985; G. Orekhova, "Vremya posle buri," *Sovetskaya Rossiya*, December 24, 1985; Pyotr Nikolaev, "Utverzhdenie chelovechnosti," *Pravda*, May 30, 1986.

11. For a collection of Vasiliev's essays, see Ivan Vasiliev, *Izbrannye proizvedeniya*, vols. 1–2 (Moscow: Sovremennik, 1986).

12. Valentin Rasputin, "Pozhar," *Nash sovremennik*, no. 7 (1985), pp. 3–38; Viktor Astafiev, "Pechalny detektiv," *Oktyabr*, no. 1 (1986), pp. 8–141; Viktor Astafiev, "Mesto deistviya," *Nash sovremennik*, no. 5 (1986), pp. 100–140; Vasily Belov, "Vse vperedi," *Nash sovremennik*, no. 7 (1986), pp. 29–106, no. 8 (1986), pp. 59–110.

13. On the 1985 antialcohol policies, see Vladimir G. Treml, "A Noble Experiment? Gorbachev's Anti-Drinking Campaign," in *Soviet Society under Gorbachev*, ed. Maurice Friedberg and Heyward Isham (Armonk, N.Y.: Sharpe, 1987), pp. 52–75.

14. Mark Lyubomudrov, "Teatr nachinaetsya s Rodiny," *Nash sovremennik*, no. 6 (1985), pp. 163–178.

15. Apollon Kuzmin, "V prodolzhenii vazhnogo razgovora," *Nash Sovremennik*, no. 3 (1985), pp. 182–190; Apollon Kuzmin, "Otvety, porozhdayushchie voprosy," *Nash sovremennik*, no. 5 (1986), pp. 189–190.

16. Vadim Pigalev, "Chto oni ishchut u slavyanofilov?" *Nash sovremennik*, no. 10 (1986), pp. 156–162.

17. According to Hough, Yakovlev was in charge of culture, publishing, and the media, while Zimyanin supervised science and education. See Hough, *Democratization and Revolution*, p. 180.

18. Valery Legostaev, a former Ligachev assistant, argues in his memoirs that

Yakovlev was elected as a full member of the Politburo at the personal insistence of Gorbachev and despite strong conservative opposition in the Central Committee. See Valery Legostaev, "God 1987-i—peremena logiki," *Den*, no. 14 (1991), p. 2. The same January 1987 plenum of the Central Committee that elevated Yakovlev to Politburo membership also removed Mikhail Zimyanin from his post as the party secretary in charge of ideology. Thus, from January 1987 on, the party ideological establishment was free from senior officials who had played a major role in developing and implementing the inclusionary politics of the 1970s and early 1980s. On Yakovlev's politics between 1983 and 1989, see also Jonathan Harris, "The Public Politics of Aleksandr Nikolaevich Yakovlev, 1983–1989," *The Carl Beck Papers in Soviet and East European Studies*, no. 901 (Pittsburgh, Penn.: University of Pittsburgh Center for Russian and East European Studies, 1990).

19. The circulation of *Ogonyok* rose from 1.5 million copies in 1985 to 3.2 million copies in 1989; the circulation of *Znamya* grew from 175,000 copies in 1985 to 970,000 in 1989; the circulation of *Novy mir* increased from 425,000 in 1985 to 1.6 million copies. In comparison, in the same time period, the circulation of *Nash sovremennik* grew only by 25,000 copies; from 220,000 to 245,000.

20. Andrei Voznesensky, "A Poet's View of Glasnost," *Nation*, June 13, 1987, p. 811. On glasnost and its effects on Soviet cultural life, see Josephine Woll, "*Glasnost*' and Soviet Culture," *Problems of Communism*, vol. 38, no. 6 (November–December 1989), pp. 40–50.

21. For liberal-reformist criticism of Belov and Astafiev, see Vladimir Lakshin, "Po pravde govorya," *Izvestiya*, December 2–3, 1986; Andrei Malgin, "V poiskakh 'mirovogo zla,' *Voprosy literatury*, no. 9 (1987), pp. 132–164; Olga Kuchkina, "Strannaya literatura," *Pravda*, October 2, 1986; Nataliya Ivanova, "Ispytanie pravdoi," *Znamya*, no. 1 (1987), pp. 200–204. The Eidelman-Astafiev exchange was widely circulated in *samizdat* and was quickly published in the West. See *Vremya i my*, no. 93 (1986), pp. 192–200. The exchange was published in the Soviet Union in 1990.

22. This fence sitting was over by November 1987, when Belov and Rasputin joined Bondarev in condemning the cultural pluralism of the Gorbachev era. See Yury Bondarev, Vasily Belov, and Valentin Rasputin, "Legko li byt molodym?" *Pravda*, November 9, 1987. Astafiev's political position would not be consistent during the Gorbachev era. By 1990, his intense hatred of the CPSU led him to stop endorsing the positions of the anti-perestroika Russian nationalist alliance and to become Yeltsin's supporter. In 1991 (and again in 1996), he endorsed Yeltsin's candidacy for the presidency of Russia.

23. "Perestroika—volya, muzhestvo i otvetsvennost," *Literaturnaya Rossiya*, March 27, 1987.

24. Pyotr Proskurin, "Vechnoe pole," *Pravda*, April 26, 1987. For a position similar to that of Proskurin, see Anatoly Ivanov, "Dvizhenie vremeni, dvizhenie literatury," *Ogonyok*, no. 46 (1987), pp. 6–7; Vadim Baranov, "Vostorzhenno ili obiektivno," *Literaturnaya gazeta*, March 18, 1987.

25. *Literaturnaya gazeta*, May 6, 1987. See especially the speeches by Mikhail Alekseev, Sergei Alekseev, Yury Bondarev, Stanislav Kunyaev, Aleksandr Prokhanov, Yury Sergeev, Valentin Ustinov, Pyotr Proskurin, and Sergei Vikulov.

26. For an attack on rock music, see Yury Pisarev, "Nuzhna li nam rokovaya muzika?" *Molodaya gvardiya*, no. 7 (1987), pp. 273–278. For a criticism of modern dance and a demand for a return to the conservative dancing traditions of Stalin's time, see Aleksei Andreev, "Vospitanie krasotoi i agressivnost bezobraznogo," *Molodaya gvardiya*, no. 7 (1987), pp. 264–271. For an attack on Evtushenko, Voznesensky, and other liberal-reformist writers and critics, as well as on the policy of publishing the works of émigré writers, see Aleksandr Baigushev, "Preodolenie," *Molodaya gvardiya*, no. 4 (1987), pp. 227–253; no. 6 (1987), pp. 232–254; no. 12 (1987), pp. 229–251.

27. Vyacheslav Gorbachev, "Chto vperedi?" *Molodaya gvardiya*, no. 3 (1987), pp. 250–277; Vyacheslav Gorbachev, "Perestroika i nadstroika," *Molodaya gvardiya*, no. 7 (1987), pp. 220–247; Vyacheslav Gorbachev, "Prinyat k deistviyu," *Molodaya gvardiya*, no. 8 (1987), pp. 228–245.

28. *Ogonyok*, no. 30 (1987), pp. 26–27; Vladimir Petrov, "Kultura diskussii," *Pravda*, August 3, 1987; "V otvete za vremya," *Molodaya gvardiya*, no. 9 (1987), pp. 219–287.

29. Aleksandr Fomenko, "O samom glavnom," *Molodaya gvardiya*, no. 9 (1987), p. 280.

30. Vladimir Karpets, "Povorot k nravstvennosti," *Molodaya gvardiya*, no. 9 (1987), p. 243.

31. See, for example, Ekaterina Markova, "Otbleski golubogo ekrana," *Molodaya gvardiya*, no. 10 (1987), pp. 228–242; Anatoly Lisenkov and Yury Sergeev, "Kolovert bespamyatsva," *Molodaya gvardiya*, no. 10 (1987), pp. 256–270; Valery Khatyushin, "O novykh veyaniyakh v kritike," *Molodaya gvardiya*, no. 10 (1987), pp. 243–255; Anatoly Doronin, "O roke—bez prikras," *Molodaya gvardiya*, no. 12 (1987), pp. 213–228; Mikhail Antonov, "Idti svoim putem," *Molodaya gvardiya*, no. 1 (1988), pp. 195–200; Aleksandr Trukhin, "Sem raz otmer," *Molodaya gvardiya*, no. 1 (1988), pp. 217–225; Vladimir Bushin, "Esli znat i pomnit," *Molodaya gvardiya*, no. 2 (1988), pp. 269–279.

32. On Zalygin's editorial policies at *Novy mir* in 1987 and 1988, see Brudny, "Between Liberalism," pp. 338–340.

33. See, for example, Aleksandr Kazintsev, "Litsom k istorii: Prodolzhateli ili potrebiteli," *Nash sovremennik*, no. 11 (1986), pp. 166–175; Aleksandr Kazintsev, "Ochishchenie ili zloslovie?" *Nash sovremennik*, no. 2 (1988), pp. 186–

189; Vladimir Bushin, "S vysoty svoego kurgana," *Nash sovremennik,* no. 8 (1987), pp. 182–185; Mikhail Dunaev, "Rokovaya muzyka," *Nash sovremennik,* no. 1 (1988), pp. 157–168; no. 2 (1988), pp. 163–172.

34. Elida Dubrovina, "Ne otgoryat ryabinovye kisti," *Nash sovremennik,* no. 9 (1987), pp. 181–183; Vadim Kozhinov, "My menyaemsya?" *Nash sovremennik,* no. 10 (1987), pp. 164–65; Apollon Kuzmin, "Meli v eksterritorialnom potoke," *Nash sovremennik,* no. 9 (1987), p. 176.

35. Vasily Belov, "Prichiny yasny," *Sovetskaya Rossiya,* May 2, 1987. In the same article, Belov also asserted that drug addiction and alcoholism would not disappear until Russia was purged of discotheques and rock music, which in his opinion created a cultural environment highly conducive to alcoholism and drug use.

36. Fyodor Uglov, "Gladya pravde v glaza," *Nash sovremennik,* no. 7 (1987), pp. 150–157.

37. Boris Lapchenko, "Ne oboronyatsya—nastupat!" *Nash sovremennik,* no. 3 (1988), pp. 130–143; A. Kovalenin, "Trezvost—oruzhie perestroiki," *Nash sovremennik,* no. 3 (1988), pp. 143–145.

38. On Pamyat, see also Mark Deich and Leonid Zhuravlev, *"Pamyat" kak ona est* (Moscow: Tsunami, 1991). For documents of various Pamyat factions, see *Rossiya: Partii, Assotsiatsii, Soyzy, Kluby* (Moscow: RAU Press, 1992), 5:86–143.

39. *Rossiya: Partii,* pp. 88–91. This document is dated December 8, 1987.

40. The so-called *Protocols of the Elders of Zion* is a virulently anti-Semitic pamphlet produced in Russia in the first decade of twentieth century. It purportedly exposes the existence of a conspiracy between Jews and Free Masons to establish Jewish world domination. On the *Protocols* and their history, see Norman Cohn, *Warrant for Genocide* (New York: Harper & Row, 1967).

41. On the Union of Patriotic Organizations of the Urals and Siberia, see *Novye politicheskie partii i organizatsii Rossii* (Moscow: Postfactum, April 1991), p. 45. Albert Khavov, one of the leaders of the Union of Patriotic Organizations of the Urals and Siberia, clearly articulated his Pamyat-like political ideology in an essay that appeared in the Novosibirsk newspaper, *Sibirskaya gazeta:* Albert Khavov, "Chto takoe sionizm?" *Sibirskaya gazeta,* May 21–27, 1990.

42. *Veche,* no. 31 (1988), p. 231.

43. For criticism of Pamyat, see E. Lesoto, "V bespamyatstve," *Komsomolskaya pravda,* May 22, 1987; G. Alimov, R. Lynev, "Kuda uvodit 'Pamyat,'" *Izvestiya,* June 3, 1987; Pavel Gutiontov, "Podmena," *Izvestiya,* February 27, 1988; Anatoly Golovkov and Aleksei Pavlov, "O chem shumite vy," *Ogonyok,* no. 21 (1987), pp. 4–5; Andrei Cherkizov, "O podlennykh tsennostyakh i mnimykh vragakh," *Sovetskaya kultura,* June 18, 1987; Gennady Petrov, "Tak vy probivaetes k pravde?" *Sovetskaya kultura,* November 24, 1987.

44. Vadim Kozhinov, "My menyaemsya?" *Nash sovremennik,* no. 10 (1987), pp. 171–172. For a defense of Pamyat, see Apollon Kuzmin, "K kakomy khramy ishchem my dorogy," *Nash sovremennik,* no. 3 (1988), pp. 154–156.

45. Valentin Rasputin, "Zhertvovat soboyu dlya pravdy," *Nash sovremennik,* no. 1 (1988), p. 171. Views virtually identical to that of Pamyat were openly expressed in the Soviet media by Russian nationalist intellectuals who were not members of the organization. In the period from 1986 to 1988, the idea of a Judeo-Masonic conspiracy against Russia was a frequent theme in nationalist fiction, literary criticism, and the cinema. The movie *Lermontov,* which appeared on the Soviet screen in 1986, portrayed the death of the nineteenth-century Russian poet as being the result of a Judeo-Masonic conspiracy.

46. In 1989 and 1990, Pamyat attracted substantial attention from the pro-perestroika press, especially *Ogonyok,* by staging rallies in the centers of Moscow and Leningrad. The rallies protested the alleged control of the mass media (especially television) by pro-perestroika forces and picketed against democratic candidates during the electoral campaigns. See Andrei Chernov, "Deti Sharikova," *Ogonyok,* no. 3 (1989), pp. 30–31; K. Korneshov, "Etot sionist 'Nikon,'" *Sovetskaya kultura,* April 1, 1989; Vitaly Potemkin, "Antimiting ili dialog?" *Sovetskaya kultura,* May 13, 1989; Denis Gopelov, "Bogatyri slezayut s pechki," *Moskovsky komsomolets,* September 28, 1989; Pavel Gutiontov, "Opasnost sprava," *Ogonyok,* no. 10 (1990), pp. 19–20; Marina Katys, "Toska po Stalinu ili 'novy avangard marksizma," *Ogonyok,* no. 13 (1990), p. 26.

47. An estimate of two hundred Pamyat members in Moscow was provided by Major General of the KGB Aleksandr Karbainov. See "Do pervoi krovi?" *Moskovskie novosti,* February 18, 1990. An estimate of about four hundred members appears in a reference book on political parties and social movements in the RSFSR: *Novye politicheskie partii,* pp. 26–28. On the different Pamyat groups, see *Neformalnaya Rossiya* (Moscow: Sovetskaya Rossiya, 1990), pp. 60–63, 312–316.

48. Nina Andreeva, "Ne mogu postupitsya s printsipami," *Sovetskaya Rossiya,* March 13, 1988. In their memoirs, Vladimir Denisov, a senior editor of *Sovetskya Rossiya* at the time and the person who prepared Andreeva's essay for publication, and Vladimir Legostaev, a former Ligachev aide, revealed the full history of the affair and Ligachev's involvement in it. See Vladimir Denisov, "'Krestny otets' Niny Andreevoi," *Rodina,* no. 1 (1991), pp. 63–67; Valery Legostaev, "Nina Andreeva—izgoi pluralizma," *Den,* no. 16 (1991). According to Vadim Medvedev, the Politburo discussed Nina Andreeva's essay in two meetings on March 24 and 25, 1987. In these meetings, Gorbachev, Yakovlev, Shevardnadze, Ryzhkov, and Medvedev condemned the essay, while Chebrikov and Ligachev defended it. See Medvedev, *V komande Gorbacheva* pp. 68–71.

49. "Printsipy perestroiki: revolyutsionnost myshleniya i deistvy," *Pravda*, April 5, 1988. This essay was reprinted throughout the country, including in *Sovetskaya Rossiya*, which was even forced to publish letters protesting Andreeva's ideas as well as the editorial board's recantation that the March 13 publication was an ideological mistake. See "Partiya idet vo glave perestroiki," *Sovetskaya Rossiya*, April 15, 1988. According to Gorbachev, this essay was written by Aleksandr Yakovlev and Vadim Medvedev, with Gorbachev himself participating in the editing of the final text. See Gorbachev, *Memoirs*, p. 327.

50. Mikhail Malakhov, "Smysl nashei zhizni," *Molodaya gvardiya*, no. 4 (1988), pp. 257–275.

51. "Khochu vyskazat svoe mnenie," *Molodaya gvardiya*, no. 4 (1988), pp. 276–278; "Nesti lyudyam slovo dobroe, svetloe," *Molodaya gvardiya*, no. 5 (1988), pp. 265–279; "Podmena," *Molodaya gvardiya*, no. 6 (1988), pp. 250–264; "Kak nashe slovo otzovetsya," *Molodaya gvardiya*, no. 6 (1988), pp. 265–278.

52. Evgeny Chernykh, "Nastuplenie prodolzhaetsya," *Nash sovremennik*, no. 5 (1988), pp. 150–160.

53. Anatoly Ivanov, "Cherny khleb isskustva," *Nash sovremennik*, no. 5 (1988), pp. 171–179.

54. Vadim Kozhinov, "Pravda i istina," *Nash sovremennik*, no. 4 (1988), pp. 160–175.

55. Viktor Ivanov, "Sudny den," *Nash sovremennik*, nos. 4–6 (1988).

56. "Protiv podmen" *Nash sovremennik*, no. 5 (1988), pp. 189–190.

57. Ivan Shevtsov and Ivan Pstygo, "Vospitat patriota," *Molodaya gvardiya*, no. 7 (1988), pp. 221–230.

58. This "Letter" was printed almost six months later in the publication of the Irkutsk Writers' Union organization, *Literaturny Irkutsk*. The publication did not list the names of the signatories and was limited to a statement that it was signed by many leading cultural figures of Russia, including a significant number of members of the Irkutsk Writers' Union organization. See "Pismo sovetskom pravitelstvu," *Literaturny Irkutsk*, December 1988, pp. 4, 10.

59. The regional party secretaries who attacked glasnost were Boris Volodin (Rostov), Vladimir Kalashnikov (Volgograd), Fyodor Popov (Altai), Vladimir Melnikov (Komi), and Valentin Mesyats (Moscow oblast). See *XIX Vsesoyuznaya konferentsiya Kommunisticheskoi partii Sovetskogo Soyuza* (Moscow: Politizdat, 1988), 1:135–143, 149–151, 166–170, 223–228; 2:3–7, 20–23, 52–55, 82–88.

60. Ibid., 2:166–170.

61. For the Russian nationalist summer–early fall 1988 campaign for the imposition of the dry law, see A. Khukhry, A. Tarakanov, and I. Ivanov, "Tuman nad alkogolnoi propastiyu," *Nash sovremennik*, no. 8 (1988), pp. 92–97; "Dusha dorozhe kovsha," *Nash sovremennik*, no. 9 (1988), pp. 142–172.

62. On the exhibit, see Bill Keller, "Russians Mob Maverick Artist's Private Show," *New York Times*, July 30, 1988, p. 9. During the exhibition, *Sovetskaya kultura* published a long interview with Glazunov in which he explained the political message of his paintings. See *Sovetskaya kultura*, July 28, 1988. On Glazunov's art in the Gorbachev era, see John Simpson, "Perestroika and the Painter," *World Monitor*, December 1988, pp. 57–65.

63. "Povyshat sozitalenuyu rol pressy," *Zhurnalist*, no. 9 (1988), pp. 1–9.

64. An edited version of the minutes of the Ryazan meeting of the RSFSR Writers' Union Secretariat appeared almost a month later in *Literaturnaya Rossiya*. See "Nasha kultura i literatura v gody perestroiki," *Literaturnaya Rossiya*, October 28, 1988.

65. A. Kakovkin, "Propoveduya mudrost i krasoty," *Sovetskaya Rossiya*, October 13, 1988.

66. "Starye mify, novye strakhi," *Kommunist*, no. 17 (1988), pp. 23–26.

67. According to Kolosov, Bondarev first attempted to remove him from *Literaturnaya Rossiya* in 1987. He failed to do so at that time because of interference from the Central Committee and the USSR Writers' Union. See Mikhail Kolosov, "Otkrytoe pismo Yuriyu Bondarevu," *Ogonyok*, no. 1 (1989), pp. 8–9.

68. "Perestroika i publitsistika," *Literaturnaya Rossiya*, December 23, 1988, December 30, 1988.

69. Kolosov, "Otkrytoe pismo," pp. 8–9.

70. The Ideological Department of Central Committee was created in the aftermath of the Nineteenth Party Conference as a part of the reorganization of the party apparat. The new department absorbed functions previously performed by the Propaganda and Cultural departments. On the reform of the party apparat, see Graeme Gill, *The Collapse of the Single-Party System* (Cambridge: Cambridge University Press, 1995), pp. 72–74.

71. Mikhail Alekseev, Viktor Astafiev, Vasily Belov, Sergei Bondarchuk, Sergei Vikulov, Pyotr Proskurin, and Valentin Rasputin, "Pismo v 'Pravdu,'" *Pravda*, January 18, 1989.

72. This account of the election of Kosolov's successor is based on a story published in the newspaper *Moskovsky literator*: N. Serbovelikov, "Budut li vybory?!" *Moskovsky literator*, February 3, 1989. The announcement of Safonov's appointment appeared in the March 3, 1989, issue of *Moskovsky literator;* no date of the meeting was given. Possibly Egorov himself was the architect of this compromise. This could explain why in May 1989, a page-long interview with him, conducted by Safonov himself, appeared in *Literaturnaya Rossiya:* Vladimir Egorov, "S uchetom trebovany vremeni i traditsy narodov," *Literaturnaya Rossiya*, May 13, 1989.

73. "V otmosfere glasnosti," *Literaturnaya gazeta*, March 31, 1989.

74. Anatoly Zhukov, "Soedinit razorvannuyu tsep," *Literaturnaya Rossiya,* June 2, 1989.

75. Vasily Konotop, "V chiikh interesakh traktuyutsya nashi idealy i interesy?" *Molodaya gvardiya,* no. 10 (1988), pp. 230–244; Anatoly Zhitnukhin, "Sokhranyaya preemstvennost," *Molodaya gvardiya,* no. 10 (1988), pp. 23–33; Georgy Matveets, "Ne v nem odnom delo," *Molodaya gvardiya,* no. 12 (1988), pp. 240–244; Dmitry Mustafin, "Narod pomnit vse," *Molodaya gvardiya,* no. 3 (1989), pp. 234–236; Ivan Benediktov, "O Staline i Khrushcheve," *Molodaya gvardiya,* no. 4 (1989), pp. 12–67. Among these essays, that of the late Ivan Benediktov (d. 1983), minister of agriculture in the years 1938 to 1958 and later Soviet ambassador to India and Yugoslavia, clearly stands out. The essay is based on a series of interviews with Benediktov conducted in 1980–1981 but published only in April 1989. This was one of the most aggressive defenses of Stalinism published in the post-Stalin era. However, it was later claimed that the Benediktov essay was a fabrication. See Gennady Vychub, "Maket krasiv, a dalshe?" *Sovetskaya kultura,* December 8, 1989.

76. Benediktov, "O Staline," pp. 19–21, 62–64; Konotop, "V chiikh interesakh," pp. 237–243.

77. Anatoly Lanshchikov, "My vse glyadim v Napoleony," *Nash sovremennik,* no. 7 (1988), pp. 106–142; Vladimir Soloukhin, "Pochemu ya ne podpisalsya pod tem pismom," *Nash sovremennik,* no. 12 (1988), 189–196. The fact that Lanshchikov and Soloukhin were reiterating Solzhenitsyn's views was, in effect, the prologue to an open campaign by young Russian nationalist intellectuals staged in the spring 1989 to rehabilitate the political ideas of Solzhenitsyn and transform him into the spiritial leader of Russian nationalist opposition to perestroika. For examples of this campaign, see Vladimir Bondarenko, "Sterzhnevaya slovesnost," *Literaturnaya Rossiya,* May 26, 1989; Pyotr Palamarchuk, "Aleksandr Solzhenitsyn: putivoditel," *Kuban,* nos. 2–5 (1989); Aleksandr Kazintsev, "Novaya mifologiya," *Nash sovremennik,* no. 5 (1989), pp. 162–164.

78. Stanislav Kunyaev, "Razmyshleniya na starom Arbate," *Nash sovremennik,* no. 7 (1988), pp. 26–27; Stanislav Kunyaev, "Vse nachinalos s yarlykov," *Nash sovremennik,* no. 9 (1988), pp. 180–189.

79. Valery Khatyushin, "Dlya kogo osvobozhdayut piedestaly?" *Moskovsky literator,* March 31, 1989.

80. Vadim Kozhinov, "Samaya bolshaya opasnost," *Nash sovremennik,* no. 1 (1989), pp. 141–175.

81. Mikhail Antonov, an economist at IMEMO and a former Russian nationalist dissident, emerged in the first years of perestroika as the main spokesman of Russian nationalist opposition to radical economic reform. His August 1987 programmatic essay, published in the journal *Oktyabr,* contained an elaborate

criticism of both the command economy and proposals for its transformation. See Mikhail Antonov, "Tak chto zhe s nami proiskhodit?" *Oktyabr*, no. 8
(1987), pp. 3–66. For Antonov's early 1989 attacks on Bukharin and the proponents of radical economic reform, see Mikhail Antonov, "Nesush-
chestvuyushchie lyudi," *Nash sovremennik*, no. 2 (1989), pp. 125–150; Mikhail
Antonov, "Vremya ustraivat dom," *Moskva*, no. 3 (1989), pp. 146–167; Mikhail Antonov, "Speshim—kuda i zachem?" *Literaturnaya Rossiya*, March 31,
1989.

82. Kazintsev, "Novaya mifologiya," pp. 167–168.

83. The Russian nationalist linguist, Oleg Trubachev, was especially vocal in his
attacks on the poor knowledge of the Russian language in the non-Russian
areas. See Oleg Trubachev, "Slavyane. Yazyk i istoriya," *Pravda*, March 28,
1987; Oleg Trubachev, "Slavyane: yazyk i istoriya," *Druzhba narodov*, no. 5
(1988), pp. 243–249. For a complaint about the demographic decline of
ethnic Russians, see Evgeny Troitsky, "Russkaya sotsialisticheskaya natsiya,"
Molodaya gvardiya, no. 1 (1988), pp. 277–287. For a discussion of the language situation in Estonia, see Igor Teterin, "Realisty protiv ekstremistov,"
Molodaya gvardiya, no. 11 (1988), pp. 196–206; no. 12 (1988), pp. 218–237.

84. According to a *Literaturnaya Rossiya* report, this meeting was attended by
such prominent Russian nationalist scholars as the philosophers Eduard
Volodin and Arseny Gulyga, the mathematician Igor Shafarevich, the legal
scholar Galina Litvinova, the ethnographer and novelist Dmitry Balashov,
and the literary critic Vadim Kozhinov. See Yury Yushkin, "Obsuzhdayutsya
natsionalnye problemy," *Literaturnaya Rossiya*, January 6, 1989. For the statement drafted by the participants, see "Ukreplenie natsionalnogo mira vo imya
obnovleniya," *Literaturnaya Rossiya*, January 6, 1989. An essay by Shafarevich,
published in late March 1989, provides a vivid example of the Russian nationalist scholars' refusal to understand the causes of anti-Russian sentiment in
the non-Russian areas. In the essay, Shafarevich claimed that the grievances of
the national minorities had no real basis and were perpetuated because information about discrimination against the Russian nation had been suppressed
for decades. See Igor Shafarevich, "Natsiya i standartizirovannaya kultura,"
Literaturnaya Rossiya, March 31, 1989.

85. Apollon Kuzmin, "Kto vinovat i komu eto nuzhno?" *Nash sovremennik*, no. 1
(1989), pp. 191–192.

86. Bagaudtin Kaziev, "Tolcheya na puti k pravde," *Molodaya gvardiya*, no. 4
(1989), pp. 235–250.

87. This number is calculated on the basis of organizations listed in *Neformalnaya
Rossiya* (Moscow: Molodaya gvardiya, 1990). On the rise of political organiza-
tions during the perestroika era, see M. Steven Fish, *Democracy from Scratch*
(Princeton, N.J.: Princeton University Press, 1995), chap. 2; Michael Urban

with Vyacheslav Igrunov and Sergei Mitrokhin, *The Rebirth of Politics in Russia* (Cambridge: Cambridge University Press, 1997), chaps. 5–9.

88. The association's manifesto was published in *Moskovsky literator:* "Sozdano 'Tovarishchestvo russkikh khudozhnikov,'" *Moskovsky literator,* December 16, 1988. On the association, see also Boris Tsarev, "Siloi russkogo bratstva," *Literaturnaya Rossiya,* June 16, 1989; *Neformalnaya Rossiya,* pp. 339–340.

89. Mikhail Antonov, "Na pozitsiyakh sotsializma," *Moskovsky literator,* March 31, 1989; "Vozzvaniye soyuza dukhovnogo vozrozhdeniya otechestva," *Moskovsky literator,* March 31, 1989; On the Union, see also *Neformalnaya Rossiya,* pp. 333–334.

90. In an interview published in *Literaturnaya Rossiya* and later in an essay in *Molodaya gvardiya,* Apollon Kuzmin explained in detail the aims of Fatherland: Apollon Kuzmin, "Otechestvo—glavnaya tsennost," *Literaturnaya Rossiya,* June 23, 1989; Apollon Kuzmin, "Vysshaya tsennost—Otechestvo," *Molodaya gvardiya,* no. 10 (1989), pp. 4–11. On Otechestvo, see also *Neformalnaya Rossiya,* pp 311–312.

91. On the Public Committee to Save the Volga and the Committee Neva-Ladoga-Onega, see *Novye politicheskie partii,* pp. 23–24.

92. The program of the Christian Patriotic Union and some information about its first conference was published by the émigré Russian nationalist journal *Veche: Veche,* no. 32 (1988), pp. 205–214. On the later history of the organization, see *Novye politicheskie partii,* pp. 46, 49.

93. There are no reliable data on the membership of the Intermovements. One of the leaders of the Latvian Intermovement claimed a membership of 300,000, a figure that is highly exaggerated. On the Councils of Labor Collectives and the Intermovements, see *Izvestia TsK KPSS,* no. 3 (1991), pp. 100–102; no. 4 (1991), pp. 89, 91–92; no. 6 (1991), pp. 103–104; E. Govorushko, "Za konkurs idei," *Sovetskaya kultura,* January 17, 1989.

8. The Demise of Politics by Culture, 1989–1991

1. *Rossiya: Partii, Assotsiatsii, Soyuzy Kluby,* vol. 1, pt. II (Moscow: RAU Press, 1991), p. 193. On the Moscow Popular Front, see also Boris Kagarlitsky, *Farewell Perestroika* (London: Verso Press, 1990).

2. On the January 9, 1989, Pamyat attack on Korotich, see V. Chernov, "Deti Sharikova," *Ogonyok,* no. 3 (1989), pp. 30–31. On the election period Pamyat rallies, see Esther Fein, "Soviet Conservatives Try to Turn the Clock on Gorbachev's Policies," *New York Times,* February 27, 1989, p. A3.

3. In 1993, Lemeshev was elected to the State Duma from Zhirinovsky's Liberal Democratic Party of Russia list.

4. Bondarev's electoral campaign was covered in the Volgograd press, and an excerpt from his stump speech was reprinted in *Ogonyok;* see Yury Bondarev, "My zhivem v plyuralizme, chert vozmi," *Ogonyok,* no. 15 (1989), p. 13.

5. Although Belov did not have to campaign for election, in the months preceding the opening of the Congress, he made it very clear that opposition to perestroika policies would be high on his agenda as a parliament member. See Vasily Belov, "Ya khochu zashchishchat prava nashikh lyudei," *Pravda,* March 5, 1989. Rasputin's anti-perestroika position on the eve of the congress was fully articulated in two essays published in the newspaper *Sovetskaya kultura* in late May 1989: "Moe otkrytie Kitaya," *Sovetskaya kultura,* May 25, 1989; Valentin Rasputin, "Levaya, pravaya, gde storona?" *Sovetskaya kultura,* May 27, 1989.

6. For an excellent analysis of the 1989 elections and the parliament they created, see *Vesna 89,* ed. Vladimir Kolosov, Nikolai Petrov, and Leonid Smirnyagin (Moscow: Progress, 1990); Gilietto Chiesa with Douglas Taylor Northtrop, *Transition to Democracy* (Hanover, N.H.: University Press of New England, 1993).

7. *Pervy siezd narodnykh deputatov SSSR. Stenograficheskesy otchet* (Moscow: Izdanie Verkhovnogo Soveta SSSR, 1989), 2:53–59.

8. Ibid., pp. 453–460.

9. Ibid., pp. 339–444, 524–531..

10. Russian nationalists failed to replace the sixty-one-year-old chief editor of *Molodaya gvardiya,* Anatoly Ivanov. Although *Nash sovremennik* and *Moskva* were publications under the jurisdiction of the RSFSR Writers' Union, *Molodaya gvardiya* was the journal of the pro-perestroika Central Committee of the Komsomol. This made Ivanov's replacement with a younger and more innovative Russian nationalist intellectual an extremely difficult task, requiring the full cooperation of the chief editor. Ivanov refused to resign, thus squashing Russian nationalist hopes of broadening the journal's appeal.

11. Calculations are based on figures in *Izvestia TsK KPSS,* no. 1 (1990), pp. 89–90.

12. Mikhail Antonov, Vyacheslav Klykov, and Igor Shafarevich, "Pismo v sekretariat pravleniya Soyuza Pisatelei RSFSR," *Literaturnaya Rossiya,* August 4, 1989.

13. *Literaturnaya Rossiya,* December 8, 1989. For attacks on *Oktyabr* and its chief editor prior to the dismisal decision, see "Pisma na odnu temu," *Literaturnaya Rossiya,* September 15, 29, October 6, 1989; Pyotr Krasnov, "Svoboda i 'iskhodny proekt,'" *Literaturnaya Rossiya,* October 6, 1989.

14. "Snova o zhurnale 'Oktyabr,'" *Literaturnaya gazeta,* December 20, 1989.

15. In early January 1990, Sergei Mikhalkov, chairman of the RSFSR Writers'

Union, had to admit that the publication of the letter by Antonov, Klykov, and Shafarevich, and the subsequent attempt to remove Ananiev, had been a major error. See *Literaturnaya gazeta*, January 17, 1990.

16. The March 30, 1990, issue of *Literaturnaya Rossiya* reported that on March 24, 1990, Minister of Defense Dmitry Yazov and the head of the army's Main Political Administration, Aleksei Lizichev, met with a group of Russian nationalist intellectuals headed by Aleksandr Prokhanov. The same issue reported on a meeting (no date was given) between editors of and contributors to *Literaturnaya Rossiya* and soldiers of the Moscow garrison, in which Russian nationalist intellectuals promoted their sociopolitical ideas. The April 29, 1990, issue of *Literaturnaya Rossiya* reported on a meeting between prominent Russian nationalist novelist Anatoly Znamensky and the officers of the Chita garrison. See "Armiya i literatura," *Literaturnaya Rossiya*, March 30, 1990; "Vstrecha v TsDSA," *Literaturnaya Rossiya*, March 30, 1990; "Obsuzhdayutsya 'Krasnye dni,'" *Literaturnaya Rossiya*, April 29, 1990.

17. Boris Rybakov and Ivan Shevstov, "Batsilly dukhovnikh nedugov," *Sovetsky voin*, no. 11 (1987), pp. 42–43; Vasily Belov, "Lad zhizni i dushi," *Sovetsky voin*, no. 13 (1987), pp. 4–15; Vladimir Lichutin, "Drevo rodstva," *Sovetsky voin*, no. 18 (1987), pp. 46–47; Gennady Serebryakov, "Chuvstvo Rodiny," *Sovetsky voin*, no. 1 (1988), pp. 2–3; Valentin Sorokin and Grigory Samoilovich, "Istina ne khodit po krivoi," *Sovetsky voin*, no. 6 (1988), pp. 4–16; Mikhail Dunaev, "O roke vsereyoz," *Sovetsky voin*, no. 9 (1988), pp. 42–43; Yury Kuznetsov, "Proshu u Otchizny ne khleba," *Sovetsky voin*, no. 23 (1988), pp. 6–7; Pyotr Proskurin, "Protivostoyanie," *Sovetsky voin*, no. 5 (1989), pp. 76–78; Vladimir Leonov, "Tolko li izderzhki rosta?" *Sovetsky voin*, no. 6 (1989), pp. 66–68.

18. *Izvestiya TsK KPSS*, no. 1 (1990), p. 90. For a sample of the journal's publications during this period, see Anatoly Lanshchikov, "Pravo na iskrennost," *Sovetsky voin*, no. 12 (1989), pp. 26–27, 74–75; Valentin Rasputin, "Sovestlivost," *Sovetsky voin*, no. 13 (1989), pp. 69–71; Leonid Golovnev, "Kogo shchitat patriotom," *Sovetsky voin*, no. 14 (1989), p. 1; Leonid Golovnev, "Nas mnogo—derzhava odna," *Sovetsky voin*, no. 16 (1989), p. 1; V. Sosnitsky, "S kem ty, Tomas Matulyonis?" *Sovetsky voin*, no. 16 (1989), pp. 80–82.

19. In 1990, the circulation of *Kommunist voruzhennykh sil* was 260,000 copies; *Voenno-istorichesky zhurnal* published 210,000 copies.

20. A. Tambovsky, "V tu li storony letyat zhelezki?" *Kommunist voruzhennykh sil*, no. 2 (1989), pp. 90–95; Vladimir Bondarenko, "Chuvstvo Rodiny," *Kommunist voruzhennykh sil*, no. 4 (1989), pp. 89–96; A. Kozlov, "Rodinu zaochno ne zashchitit," *Kommunist voruzhennykh sil*, no. 7 (1989), pp. 85–86; Sergei Zhuravlev, "Chest Rossii—dorozhe zhizni," *Kommunist voruzhennykh sil*, no.

9 (1989), pp. 90–94; Vladimir Fomichev, "Rossiya: lyubov i bol moya," *Kommunist voruzhennykh sil*, no. 3 (1990), pp. 3–10.

21. Vladimir Bushin, "My ne raby. Raby nemy," *Voennoistorichesky zhurnal*, no. 11 (1989), pp. 3–11; no. 12 (1989), pp. 3–11; Karem Rash, "Armiya i kultura," *Voenno-istorichesky zhurnal*, no. 2 (1989), pp. 3–15; no. 3 (1989), pp. 3–11; no. 4 (1989), pp. 3–13; no. 5 (1989), pp. 3–11; no. 7 (1989), pp. 3–13; no. 8 (1989), pp. 3–13; no. 9 (1989), pp. 3–13.

22. Karem Rash, "Kuda my udem?" *Molodaya gvardiya*, no. 10 (1989), pp. 199–218; Karem Rash, "Armiya i kultura," *Nash sovremennik*, no. 5 (1990), pp. 99–113; Sergei Chervonopissky, "Ne dadim v obidu derzhavu," *Molodaya gvardiya*, no. 11 (1989), pp. 130–134; S. Ishchenko, "Armiya zashchishchaet nas, a kto zashchitit armiyu?" *Molodaya gvardiya*, no. 11 (1989), pp. 220–225; A. Efimov, "Zachem eto nado?" *Nash sovremennik*, no. 11 (1989), pp. 191–192.

23. A. Abramkin, "My dolzhny skazat pravdu," *Literaturnaya Rossiya*, May 12, 1989; V. Galaiko, "Po mneniyu voennogo," *Literaturnaya Rossiya*, June 30, 1989; Aleksandr Fomenko, "Predannaya armiya," *Literaturnaya Rossiya*, January, 26, 1990; Yu. Borisov and G. Samoleinko, "Voennye arsenaly: perespektivy i realnosti," *Literaturnaya Rossiya*, February 2, 1990; Aleksei Lizichev, "Meroi iskrennosti," *Literaturnaya Rossiya*, February 23, 1990; German Kirilenko, "Chto shchtat razumnym, a chto dostatochnym?" *Literaturnaya Rossiya*, March 23, 1990; S. Kulichkin, "Poruganie znamen," *Literaturnaya Rossiya*, April 13, 1990; Igor Rodionov, "Lish polnaya pravda mozhet ubedit," *Literaturnaya Rossiya*, April 20, 1990.

24. Yury Katasonov, "Armiya i demogogi," *Literaturnaya Rossiya*, April 27, 1990.

25. Aleksandr Prokhanov, "Dostatochnaya oborona," *Literaturnaya Rossiya*, April 6, 1990.

26. In addition to Kosolapov, the philosopher Mikhail Popov and the economists Aleksei Sergeev and Vladimir Yakushev were leaders of the Association for Scientific Communism.

27. On the United Workers' Front, see *Slovar novykh politicheskikh partii i organizatsii Rossii*, ed. Vladimir Pribylovsky (Moscow: Panorama, 1993), pp. 68–69; *Rossiya: Partii, Assotsiatsii, Soyzy, Kluby* (Moscow: RAU Press, 1992), 5:20–58.

28. For the text of the Leningrad program, see *Rossiya: Partii, Assotsiatsii*, pp. 24–26. The three principal drafters of the program were Viktor Dolgov, Vasily Elmeev, and Mikhail Popov. In the spring of 1991, they coauthored a book in which they fully elaborated their program: Viktor Dolgov, Vasily Elmeev, and Mikhail Popov, *Vybor novogo kursa* (Moscow: Mysl, 1991).

29. On Sergeev's appearance at the conference, see Vladimir Gurevich, "Chetverty variant," *Moskovskie novosti*, December 3, 1989.

30. Anatoly Salutsky, "Moskva, Kolonny zal," *Literaturnaya Rossiya*, December 8, 1989.

31. Anatoly Salutsky, "Na Petrogradskoi storone," *Literaturnaya Rossiya*, August 25, 1989.

32. Anatoly Salutsky and Aleksei Sergeev, "Zavtra ili pozavchera?" *Nash sovremennik*, no. 10 (1989), pp. 102–109; Georgy Kostin, "Tsel perestroiki—silnaya nezavisimaya derzhava," *Molodaya gvardiya*, no. 1 (1990), pp. 214–222; Sergei Nepobedimy, "Pora vozrozhdat Rossiyu," *Nash sovremennik*, no. 1 (1990), pp. 3–5; Aleksei Sergeev, "Entsiklopediya kriminalnoi burzhuazii," *Nash sovremennik*, no. 4 (1990), pp. 146–155; Galina Makeeva, "Novgorod s molotka," *Literaturnaya Rossiya*, November 11, 1989; V. Shabarov, "Tsena oshibok," *Literaturnaya Rossiya*, November 17, 1989; Eduard Volodin, "Pered vyborom," *Literaturnaya Rossiya*, December 8, 1989; P. Myagkov, "O denezhnoi reforme," *Literaturnaya Rossiya*, December 29, 1989; Aleksei Sergeev and A. Shulus, "Trudyashchiyasya i 'tenevaya' ekonomika: kto kogo?" *Literaturnaya Rossiya*, January 12, 1990; Aleksei Sergeev, "Eshche odna nadezhda?" *Moskovsky literator*, March 16, 1990.

33. In addition to the "Letter of the Soviet Government," the other source of the anti-Semitic plank in the platform of the United Council of Russia was an essay by Igor Shafarevich entitled "Russophobia." Originally written in 1980 as a part of the debate over Russian nationalism within the dissident community, "Russophobia" was widely circulated in samizdat and abroad. In 1989, the essay was reprinted first in the provincial journal *Kuban* (issues nos. 5–7), and, ultimately, in the June and November issues of *Nash sovremennik*. The treatise attempts to give anti-Semitism a respectable theoretical base. According to Shafarevich, in the history of every nation there are periods in which small elitist groups, whose cultural and ideological values differ fundamentally from the rest of the nation, attempt to impose their values on the nation as a whole. Shafarevich calls the elitist group a "small nation" (*maly narod*) and claims that in Russia the role of "small nation" is performed by the liberal-reformist Jewish intellectuals. These intellectuals are full of hatred for Russia, its history, and its national traditions. If in the Lenin and Stalin eras Jewish nationals attempted to destroy the Russian nation by playing active roles in the communist terror, in the present, Jewish liberal-reformist intellectuals were attempting to destroy the Russian nation by attacking Russian national ideology and promoting Western political and cultural values. Immediately with its 1989 publication, "Russophobia" became one of the main ideological documents of the Russian nationalist opposition to Gorbachev's reforms, and its ideas could be found in virtually every programmatic Russian nationalist document to appear between the fall of 1989 and the summer of

1991. For the definitive text of "Russophobia," see Igor Shafarevich, *Est li u Rossii buduyushchee?* (Moscow: Sovetsky pisatel, 1991), pp. 390–486.

34. In addition to the Association of Russian Artists, the United Workers' Front, and the Intermovements, the main organizations that participated in the formation of the United Council of Russia were the Union for the Spiritual Rebirth of the Fatherland; the Fatherland societies of Moscow, Leningrad, and Tyumen (all unrelated organizations with the same name); the Public Committee to Save the Volga; the Union of the Patriotic Organizations of the Urals and Siberia; the Union for the Struggle for the Nation's Sobriety; and the Russian Chapter of the International Foundation for Slavic Literatures and Cultures. Information about the founding conference of the United Council of Russia, as well as the full text of its program, was printed in "Sozdana Assotsiatsiya 'Obyedenneny Sovet Rossii,'" *Moskovsky literator,* September 22, 1989.

35. Litvinova's presentation in Tyumen was a reiteration of the arguments she presented in the June 1989 issue of *Nash sovremennik,* see Galina Litvinova, "Starshy ili ravny," *Nash sovremennik,* no. 6 (1989), pp. 10–20.

36. "Na printsypakh ravnopraviya," *Moskovsky literator,* November 17, 1989; "Eto vystradano zhizniyu," *Literaturnaya Rossiya,* December 1, 1989; "Obrash-chenie k narodnym deputatam SSSR," *Nash sovremennik,* no. 12 (1989), pp. 3–6; Yury Shatalov, "Osoznat i deistvovat," *Sovetskaya Rossiya,* November 21, 1989 (an interview with Sergei Vasiliev). For an account of the Tyumen meeting, see also Pavel Emelin, "Russky vopros," *Literaturnaya Rossiya,* November 17, 1989.

37. On the Russia Club, see "Deputatsky klub 'Rossiya,'" *Sovetskaya Rossiya,* October 25, 1989; "Sozdan klub 'Rossiya,'" *Literaturnaya Rossiya,* October 27, 1989.

38. On December 10, while the Second Congress was still in session, a meeting of over a hundred deputies affiliated with the Russia Club and a group of their Russian nationalist advisers took place in Moscow. According to a report of the meeting, the advisers thoroughly briefed the deputies on a range of issues. Of these briefings, only a paper about subsidies to other republics was published: V. Chepurenko, "Pora, nakonets, i Rossii vzyat slovo!" *Literaturnaya Rossiya,* December 15, 1989.

39. Although Yarin participated in the formation of Soyuz, he never became one of its leaders. The latter—Viktor Alksnis, Yury Blokhin, Anatoly Chekhoev, Georgy Komarov, and Nikolai Petrushenko—all came from non-Russian republics and viewed the preservation of the territorial integrity of the USSR as a much higher priority than addressing the Russia Club's concerns articulated in the Tyumen manifesto. On the Soyuz bloc, see *Slovar*

oppozitsii: Novye politicheskie partii i organizatsii Rossii (Moscow: Postfactum, April 1991), pp. 42–43.

40. Officially, twelve organizations participated in the Patriotic Bloc. Close scrutiny reveals, however, that it was simply a new name for the Russia Club; both the Russia Club and the United Council of Russia were listed as participating organizations; the remaining ten organizations were members of the United Council of Russia.

41. For Democratic Russia's electoral program, see *Ogonyok*, no. 6 (1990), pp. 17–18.

42. "Za politiku narodnogo soglasiya i rossiiskogo vozrozhdeniya," *Literaturnaya Rossiya*, December 29, 1989. This program was reprinted in the February 9, 1990, issue of *Literaturnaya Rossiya*, as well as in the February issue of *Rossiya*, the newsletter of the Russia Club, which also contained a list of the Patriotic Bloc candidates to RSFSR Supreme Soviet and Moscow city Soviet. See "Za narodnoe soglasie i rossiiskoe vozrozhdenie," *Rossiya*, no. 4 (1990).

43. It is not clear whether the Patriotic Bloc program, as it was published in *Literaturnaya Rossiya*, was accepted by Russian nationalist electoral alliances in other cities. Judging from the extended excerpts published in a local paper, the program of the Novosibirsk alliance of Russian nationalist organizations did differ from the Moscow program. Its primary focus was on environmental issues. The economic section of the program asserted that private enterprises were engaging in speculation and should be shut down. The section devoted to the mass media was similar to the program published in *Literaturnaya Rossiya*. It demanded a ban of all television programs that "propagate violence, cruelty, immoral forms of behavior, drinking, and smoking." See "Iz sotsialno-politicheskoi programmy obshchestvenno-patrioticheskikh dvizheny Novosibirska," *Sovetskaya Sibir*, March 3, 1990.

44. Among Russian nationalist thick journals, only *Nash sovremennik*, whose editor was a bloc candidate to the RSFSR Supreme Soviet, printed material related to the elections; see "Rossiya zhivet khuzhe chem rabotaet. RSFSR nakanune vyborov," *Nash sovremennik*, 2 (1990), pp. 3–14.

45. Aleksandr Prokhanov, "Tragediya tsentralizma," *Literaturnaya Rossiya*, January 5, 1990. Five months later, a greatly expanded version of this essay was published: Aleksandr Prokhanov, "Zametki konservatora," *Nash sovremennik*, no. 5 (1990), pp. 85–98.

46. For the publication of the campaign programs of the Patriotic Bloc candidates, see Dmitry Barabashev, "Rossiya pered vyborom," *Literaturnaya Rossiya*, January 19, 1990; Eduard Volodin, "Novaya Rossiya v menyayushchemsya mire," *Literaturnaya Rossiya*, January 26, 1990; Mikhail Lemeshev and Yury Yushkin, "Otvesti smertelnuyu ugrozu," *Literaturnaya Rossiya*, February 16, 1990; Anatoly Salutsky, "Bolshaya igra," *Literaturnaya Rossiya*, February

23, 1990; Maya Ganina, "Bol zemli," *Literaturnaya Rossiya*, February 23, 1990; Eduard Volodin, "Vam ne sniskat priznaniya Evropy," *Literaturnaya Rossiya*, February 23, 1990; Yury Vorobyevsky, "Dengi dlya bednykh: gde ikh vzyat, kto ikh dast?" *Literaturnaya Rossiya*, February 23, 1990; Feliks Kuznetsov, "Put sobiraniya," *Literaturnaya Rossiya*, February 23, 1990; Viktor Kalugin, "Inoe dano," *Literaturnaya Rossiya*, March 2, 1990; Yury Selishchev, "Tolko s pravdoi," *Literaturnaya Rossiya*, March 2, 1990; Nikolai Doroshenko, "Buduyushchee dolzhno byt prognoziruemym," *Literaturnaya Rossiya*, March 2, 1990. For the list of Patriotic Bloc candidates to the RSFSR Supreme Soviet and the Moscow City Soviet, see "Za politiku narodnogo soglasiya i rossiisk-ogo vozhrozhdeniya," *Literaturnaya Rossiya*, March 2, 1990.

47. For examples of *Sovetskaya Rossiya*'s promotion of Patriotic Bloc candidates, see Stanislav Kunyaev, "Veryu v Rossiyu," *Sovetskaya Rossiya*, February 23, 1990; Feliks Kuznetsov, "Rify ekstremizma," *Sovetskaya Rossiya*, March 1, 1990; Eduard Volodin, "Smerdyakovshchina," *Sovetskaya Rossiya*, March 4, 1990; A. Brazhnikov, A. Bugaev, N. Mikhailov, V. Sevastiyanov, and E. Safonov, "Ne poddatsya smute," *Sovetskaya Rossiya*, March 17, 1990.

48. Timothy J. Colton, "The Politics of Democratization: The Moscow Election of 1990," *Soviet Economy*, vol. 6, no. 4 (October–December 1990), p. 318.

49. Robert W. Orttung, *From Leningrad to St. Petersburg* (New York: St. Martin's Press, 1995), pp. 106–107, 117, 121. As in Moscow and Leningrad, the conservative party apparat in the provinces attempted to help the Russian nationalist electoral alliances defeat their democratic opponents. This support was very clear in Novosibirsk. On March 3, *Sovetskaya Sibir*, the daily paper of the regional party organization, printed the program of the local Russian nationalist alliance. On March 16, two days before the second round of the election, it published an essay by the alliance's candidate, Lidiya Shvets, who was opposing the liberal-reformist candidate, Aleksandr Granberg, for a seat in the RSFSR Supreme Soviet. The support of *Sovetskaya Sibir* did not help Shvets, who was defeated by her opponent; see "Iz sotsialno-politicheskoi programmy obshchestvenno-patrioticheskikh dvizheny g. Novosibirska," *Sovetskaya Sibir*, March 3, 1990; Lidiya Shvets, "Mne ne bezralichno," *Sovetskaya Sibir*, March 16, 1990.

50. Nikolai Doroshenko, "Vybory, rezultaty kotorykh v Moskve byli splani-rovany," *Moskovsky literator*, March 16, 1990; "Grimasy demokratii," *Literaturnaya Rossiya*, March 16, 23, 30, April 20, 1990.

51. At the March 1990 meeting of the Governing Board of the RSFSR Writers' Union, the sole supporter of Bondarenko was Vladimir Krupin; see "Sudby Rossii, chayaniya Rossiyan," *Literaturnaya Rossiya*, March 30, 1990.

52. Writing a month before the final collapse of the communist regime, a minor Russian nationalist writer clearly expressed the rationale for these actions: "I

support the [Communist] party because it is the only force capable of resist-
ing the disintegration . . . of the system which holds together the walls and the
roof of [our] statehood." Anatoly Builov, "Kak ya v gazetu statiyu pisal,"
Literaturnaya Rossiya, July 12, 1991.

53. "Pismo pisatelei Rossii," *Literaturnaya Rossiya,* March 2, 1990.

54. *Nash sovremennik,* no. 4 (1990), p. 145. An earlier version of these lines was
quoted by Tatiyana Glushkova, one of the drafters of the "Letter of Seventy-
four." It called for the protection of Russia from "politicians seeking to transform it into a "colonial state, an international market of cheap slave labor,
[and] a raw material supplier to the barbarously civilized states." See Tatiyana
Glushkova, "Posle 'Pisma pisatelei Rossii,'" *Moskovsky literator,* April 13, 1990.

55. The Russian nationalist attacks against Yakovlev intensified in December 1989
and became especially virulent in the spring of 1990. See Stanislav Zolotsev,
"O vole ili o 'svobodakh,'" *Moskovsky literator,* December 8, 1989; Stanislav
Zolotsev, "Chas muzhestva ili zhatva beznravstvennosti?" *Moskovsky literator,*
February 23, 1989; Vladimir Bushin, "Azbuka, arifmetika, i khimiya," *Mosk-
ovsky literator,* March 16, 1990

56. "Pismo pisatelei, deyatelei kulturu i nauki Rossii," *Nash sovremennik,* no. 4
(1990), pp. 136–145; "Pismo pisatelei Rossii," *Moskva,* no. 5 (1990), pp. 192–
199; "Pismo pisatelei Rossii," *Molodaya gvardiya,* no. 5 (1990), pp. 3–19;
"Pismo pisatelei Rossii," *Sibirskie ogni,* no. 4 (1990), pp. 3–11; "V podderzhku
'Pisma pisatelei Rossii,'" *Literaturnaya Rossiya,* March 9, 16, 23, 30, April 6, 13,
20, 27, May 5, 12, 1990; May 12, 18, 25, June 1, 1990.

57. *Rabochy put* (Smolensk), March 8, 1990; *Znamya* (Kaluga), April 14, 1990.
The "Letter" was also reprinted in the newsletter of the Liepaya chapter of the
Latvian Intermovement, *Tribuna,* April 20, 1990.

58. Eduard Volodin, "Vperedi progressa," *Literaturnaya Rossiya,* April 20, 1990.

59. Pavel Emelin, "Poka est nadezhda," *Literaturnaya Rossiya,* May 25, 1990; Mikhail Lobanov, "Moe delo—skazat," *Moskovsky literator,* May 25, 1990; Vasily
Belov, "Sirotstvo Rossii," *Literaturnaya Rossiya,* May 25, 1990.

60. "K narodu i deputatam Rossii!" *Literaturnaya Rossiya,* June 1, 1990.

61. "Za progressivnoe razvitie partii! Deklaratsiya Leningradskogo Initsiat-
sivnogo komiteta po podgotovke Uchreditelnogo siezda Rossiiskoi Komunis-
ticheskoi Partii (RKP) v sostave KPSS," *Literaturnaya Rossiya,* March 9, 1990;
"Za spravedlivost, progress i soglasie! Programma vozrozhdeniaya RKP," *Leningradskaya pravda,* March 20, 1990.

62. "K narodam Rossii. Obrashchenie uchastnikov VII plenuma pravleniya SP
RSFSR," *Literaturnaya Rossiya,* March 23, 1990. For examples of promotion
of the RCP idea in the Russian nationalist press, see "Vyyavit resursy sotsializma," *Literaturnaya Rossiya,* March 30, 1990; Yury Terentiev, "RKP: Ideii,
tseli, zadachi," *Literaturnaya Rossiya,* April 13, 1990; N. Voropaeva, "Opiratsya

na dukhovnye traditsii," *Moskovsky literator,* May 18, 1990; Anatoly Salutsky, "Naiskosok ot Smolnogo," *Literaturnaya Rossiya,* June 1, 1990; "Rossiiskoi kompartii—byt!" *Molodaya gvardiya,* no. 6 (1990), pp. 167–170.

63. In his memoirs, Gorbachev claims that he viewed the creation of the RCP as an unavoidable result of the transformation of the USSR into a true federation. However, he thought that the best time for the creation of RCP would be after the signing of the new Union Treaty which would officially transform USSR into a federal state. He also was not interested in the creation of a powerful institutional tool to be used by his political opponents. Gorbachev admits that initially the Politburo was deeply split on the issue, with Ligachev the leading supporter of the RCP, but ultimately they bowed to the pressure from below and agreed to the formation of the new party. As archival records, indeed, indicate on June 17, 1990, all seventeen attending members of the Politburo, including Gorbachev, Shevardnadze, and Yakovlev, voted for the creation of the RCP. See Gorbachev, *Memoirs* pp. 455–458; TsKhSD f. 89, op. 8, d. 72, pp. 1–5. Although Gorbachev officially withdrew his opposition to the idea of the RCP after this meeting of the Politburo, during the June conference he was accused by a conservative member of the organizing committee of obstructing its work in order to prevent the formation of the party. See *Materialy Uchreditelnogo siezda Kommunisticheskoi partii RSFSR* (Moscow: Politizdat, 1990), pp. 31–33.

64. Ivan Polozkov, "Bolshe dela," *Sovetskaya Rossiya,* July 1, 1990.

65. Between 1990 and 1991, the combined circulation of *Novy mir, Znamya, Yunost, Druzhba narodov,* and *Oktyabr* declined by 66 percent.

66. The Experimental Creative Center was created in mid-1989. Its first contribution to the Russian nationalist discourse was a long essay by Kurginyan published in three installments in *Literaturnaya Rossiya:* Sergei Kurginyan, "O mekhanizme soskalzovaniya," *Literaturnaya Rossiya,* June 30, July 7, 14, 1989.

67. S. Kurginyan, B. Autenshlus, P. Goncharov, Yu. Gromyko, I. Sundiev, and V. Ovchinsky, *Postperestroika* (Moscow: Izdatelstvo politicheskoi literatury, 1990).

68. Sergei Kurgiyan et al., "Sudba kommunisma. Ot dogmatzma i konformizma—k osmysleniyu i reformatsii," *Moskovskaya pravda,* July 26, 1991. For a sample of Kurginyan's writings during this period, which elaborated different aspects of his argument, see Sergei Kurginyan, Vladimir Ovchinsky, and Gennady Avrekh, "Finansovaya voina," *Nash sovremennik,* no. 5 (1991), pp. 160–171; Sergei Kurginyan, "Sedmoi stsenary," *Moskva,* no. 9 (1991), pp. 110–125.

69. John B. Dunlop, *The Rise of Russia and the Fall of the Soviet Empire* (Princeton, N.J.: Princeton University Press, 1993), p. 165.

70. Analysis of members of the Fatherland faction is based upon membership in

the faction in May 1991. The list of members is taken from *Politicheskie fraktsii i deputatskie gruppy Rosiiskogo parlamenta*, ed. Vladimir Pribylovsky (Moscow: Panorama, March 1993), pp. 57–58.

71. The documents of the Fatherland movement appeared in *Rossiya: Partii, Assotsiatsii, Soyuzy*, vol. 5, pp. 71–80.

72. *Literaturnaya Rossiya*, December 21, 1990.

73. "Za edinuyu Rus, za edinny Soyuz," *Sovetskaya Rossiya*, February 28, 1991.

74. The main documents of the Coordinating Council of the National-Patriotic Forces were published in *Rossiya: Partii, Assotsiatsii, Soyuzy*, vol. 5, pp. 3–6. Zyuganov would assume the chairmanship of this organization in 1992.

75. Eduard Volodin, "Vozrozhdenie realno," *Literaturnaya Rossiya*, May 6, 1991.

76. "Slovo k narodu," *Sovetskaya Rossiya*, July 23, 1991. In addition to Zyuganov and Prokhanov, the manifesto was signed by such prominent Russian nationalist intellectuals as Bondarev and Rasputin and such high-ranking conservative members of the military and political establishment as the commander of the USSR ground forces, General Valentin Varennikov; Deputy Interior Minister General Boris Gromov; the head of the Association of Military-Industrial Enterprises, Aleksandr Tizyakov; and the head of the Union of Collective and State Farms, Vasily Starodubtsev. In less than two months, Varennikov, Tizyakov, and Starodubtsev would become the ringleaders of the abortive coup attempt. For a claim that Zyuganov was one of the manifesto's initiators, see Velijko Vujacic, "Gennadiy Zyuganov and the 'Third Road,'" *Post-Soviet Affairs*, vol. 12, no. 2 (April–June 1996) , p. 135.

77. "Ot 'Slova'—k delu!" *Sovetskaya Rossiya*, August 16, 1991; Eduard Volodin, "Osenny predel," *Sovetskaya Rossiya*, August 3, 1991.

78. For the text of Zhirinovsky's 1991 electoral platform, see *Russkie nastsionalisticheskie i pravo-radikalnye organizatsii, 1989–1995*, pt. I (Moscow: Panorama, 1995), pp. 112–114.

Epilogue

1. For definitions of the liberal and antiliberal conceptions of nationalism in postcommunist countries, see Vladimir Tismaneaunu, "Fantasies of Salvation: Varieties of Nationalism in Postcommunist Eastern Europe," in *Envisioning Eastern Europe*, ed. Michael D. Kennedy (Ann Arbor: University of Michigan Press, 1994), pp. 114–119.

2. George Schöpflin, "Nationalism and Ethnicity in Europe," in *Nationalism and Nationalities in Europe*, ed. Charles A. Kupchan (Ithaca, N.Y.: Cornell University Press, 1995), p. 60.

3. George Kolankiewicz, "Elites in Search of a Political Formula," *Daedalus*, vol. 123, no. 3 (Summer 1994), p. 147.

4. Andrei Sakharov, "Konstitutsiya Soyuza Sovetskikh Respublik Evropy i Azii: Proekt," in Andrei Sakharov, *Gorky, Moskva, dalee vezde* (New York: Izdatelstvo imeni Chekhova, 1990), pp. 263–271. For a detailed discussion of Sakharov and Starovoitova's ideas, see John B. Dunlop, *The Rise of Russia and the Fall of the Soviet Empire* (Princeton, N.J.: Princeton University Press, 1993), pp. 90–91, 118–120.

5. For the implications for democracy of different conceptions of nationhood, see Liah Greenfeld, *Nationalism* (Cambridge, Mass.: Harvard University Press, 1992), pp. 10–11.

6. See, for example, Ruslan Khasbulatov, *Vybor sudby* (Moscow: Respublika, 1993), pp. 85–288; Ruslan Khasbulatov, "Ne shutite s gosudarstvom. I budte vsegda chestnymi s druziyami," *Den*, no. 35 (1993), pp. 1–2.

7. Stankevich provided a programmatic statement of this emerging consensus in his famous *Nezavisimaya gazeta* essay: "Derzhava v poiskakh sebya," *Nezavisimaya gazeta*, March 28, 1992.

8. Jerry F. Hough, Evelyn Davidheiser, and Susan Goodrich Lehmann, *The 1996 Russian Presidential Election* (Washington, D.C.: Brookings Institution Press, 1996), p. 44.

9. Ian S. Lustick, in *Unsettled States, Disputed Lands* (Ithaca, N.Y.: Cornell University Press, 1993), depicts the process of how elites of dominant ethnic groups become convinced that they have to rid themselves of territories commonly regarded as an intergal part of their state (Ireland in the case of England, Algeria in the case of France, and the West Bank in the case of Israel), and how to convince the general public that this is the necessary thing to be done. In Lustick's case, it is a one-way process. The Russian example, however, suggests that the elites can come to the conclusion that they must dismantle the empire, convince the general public that it is the only viable course of action, and then repeat the same process in reverse.

10. Polish sociologist Jerzy Szacki, in his discussion of economic reform in Poland, suggests that it is typical of current liberalism in Eastern Europe to preoccupy itself exclusively with the issue of the construction of capitalism. See Jerzy Szacki, *Liberalism after Communism* (Budapest: Central European University Press, 1994), esp. chap. 5.

Index

173. *See also* Agriculture; *Molodaya gvardiya;* Politburo; Village prose
Brubaker, Rogers, 5–6, 270n24
Bryusova, Vera, 246
Brzezinski, Zbigniew, 2
Bukharin, Nikolai, 201, 202, 207, 217, 218, 219
Bulgarin, Faddei, 112
Burlatsky, Fyodor, 287n8, 297n98
Bushin, Vladimir, 233
Bykov, Vasil, 291n38

Calvin, 189
Canada, 100, 101, 110, 125, 290n21, 297n97
Caucasus, 29, 41, 154, 220, 229, 234, 240
Censorship, 60, 65, 127, 132–136, 289nn3,5, 299n11, 302n47, 303nn52,58, 304n63. *See also* Glavlit; Romanov
Central Asia, 41, 147, 154, 172
Central Committee (CPSU), 33, 64, 99, 109, 141, 142, 226, 247; decrees, 58–59, 82, 95, 102, 120, 122, 124, 125–126, 143, 145, 284n70, 295n81; Propaganda Department, 61, 63, 90, 96, 98, 99, 100, 101, 107, 109, 113, 114, 122, 123, 137, 173, 197, 255, 279n16, 288n10, 289n16, 296n82, 298n7, 313n91; Cultural Department, 61, 63, 67, 91, 93, 96, 101,107, 109, 113, 114, 120, 122, 124, 125, 173, 197, 279n15, 298n7; Secretariat, 66, 90, 92, 93, 95, 108, 111, 117, 173, 287n96, 289n16; apparat, 86, 88, 89, 90, 91, 97, 98, 110, 114, 115, 125, 134, 173, 246, 286n93; Academy of Social Sciences, 95, 296n82; plenums, 100, 125–126, 138, 296n86, 316n18; Chemical Industry Department, 137; Science and Education Department, 173, 313n91; Ideological Department, 213, 214, 321n70. *See also* Andropov; Belyaev; Brezhnev; Inclusionary politics; Melentiev; Shauro; Stepakov; Suslov; Tyazhelnikov; Yakovlev, Aleksandr; Zimyanin
Chagall, Marc, 201
Chalmaev, Viktor, 66, 67, 73, 74, 82–83, 84, 85, 89, 95, 176, 287n5; the *Molodaya gvardiya* essays, 75–76
Chapchakhov, Fyodor, 82

Chebrikov, Viktor, 319n48
Chechnya, 260, 263, 265
Chekhoev, Anatoly, 329n39
Chelovek i zakon, 118
Chelyabinsk, 205
Chernenko, Konstantin, 125, 128, 129, 192; period of (1984–1985), 131, 196
Chernichenko, Yury, 229
Chernyaev, Anatoly, 101, 289n16, 290nn19,24
Chervonopissky, Sergei, 228–229
Chestyakov, Antonin, 143
Chiladze, Otar, 130
China, 60, 65, 116
Chivilikhin, Vladimir, 55–56, 70, 105, 123, 127, 136
Christian Patriotic Union, 223, 224, 324n92
Chubais, Anatoly, 264
Chuev, Feliks, 130
Chuprynin, Sergei, 130
Church of Christ the Savior, 71
Church of Simeon Stolpnik, 276n59
"Classics and We" (debate), 169–172
Cold War, 12
Colton, Timothy, J., 116, 140, 244
Command economy, 216, 217, 218, 219, 220, 243
Committee Neva-Ladoga-Onega, 223, 224
Commonwealth of Independent States, 8
Connor, Walker, 4
Connor, Walter D., 29
Conservative nationalism, 8–9, 10, 11–12, 17, 21, 22, 23, 25–26; and anti-Semitism, 9; and Gorbachev's reforms, 9, 12, 199–200; and Western values, 9, 11; and preservation of the USSR, 9, 19; and Stalin's legacy, 11. *See also* Astafiev; Belov; Bondarev; Rasputin, Valentin; Soloukhin; Village prose
Coordinating Council of the National-Patriotic Movements of Russia, 10, 255–256
Countryside, 119, 146; depopulation of, 18, 41, 55, 110, 132, 143–144, 146, 302n45, 303n53; Stalin's legacy, 24, 39, 52, 53, 77, 81, 86, 152, 161. *See also* Village prose
CPRF (Communist Party of the Russian Federation), 23, 27, 259